To Die in This Way

myth of mestizaje p3, $ p 9 $10, 139
author's politics p4
indigenous female voices p 6
language & identity p. 7 *
book's primary goal p10
hegemony p. 12
indian population p. 16
defensive role of
    comunidad p. 18
indians & church 1893 p 39
of S. Zelaya p. 38
Zelaya opposes of the comunidades p 40
informal debt peonage p 50
education p. 58
citizenship, the comunidad p. 77 see 69, 70, two
consequences of ladinoization p. 96-97 *
exception of Sutiaba p 103 -104
Pan de Arena p.106
journalistic attacks on the indians of Sutiaba p 122 *
annexation p. 102
134-135 - synchronony & diachrony
Carlos Fonseca, guilt by association, p. 211
ladino concepts p. 136

136 Sandino anti-imperialism

following several strands of thought - difficult to follow

*A book in the series*

*Latin America Otherwise:*

*Languages, Empires, Nations*

*Series editors*

Walter D. Mignolo, Duke University

Irene Silverblatt, Duke University

Sonia Saldívar-Hull,

University of California

at Los Angeles

# TO

# DIE

# IN

# THIS WAY

Nicaraguan Indians

and the

Myth of Mestizaje

1880–1965

Jeffrey L. Gould

Duke University Press   Durham & London   1998

© 1998 Duke University Press

All rights reserved

Printed in the United States of America on acid-free paper ∞

Typeset in Minion by Keystone Typesetting, Inc.

Library of Congress Cataloging-in-Publication Data

appear on the last page of this book.

A la memoria de Juan Suazo Martínez,

valiente luchador del pueblo chinandegano, 1914–1990

Al pueblo indígena de Nicaragua

A María Elidieth, Gabriela, Mónica y Carlos.

A mis padres

# Contents

# About the Series

*Latin America Otherwise: Languages, Empires, Nations* is a critical series. It aims to explore the emergence and consequences of concepts used to define "Latin America" while at the same time exploring the broad interplay of political, economic, and cultural practices that have shaped Latin American worlds. Latin America, at the crossroads of competing imperial designs and local responses, has been construed as a geocultural and geopolitical entity since the nineteenth century. This series provides a starting point to redefine Latin America as a configuration of political, linguistic, cultural, and economic intersections that demands a continuous reappraisal of the role of the Americas in history, and of the ongoing process of globalization and the relocation of people and cultures that have characterized Latin America's experience. *Latin America Otherwise: Languages, Empires, Nations* is a forum that confronts established geocultural constructions, that rethinks area studies and disciplinary boundaries, that assesses convictions of the academy and of public policy, and that, correspondingly, demands that the practices through which we produce knowledge and understanding about and from Latin America be subject to rigorous and critical scrutiny.

Since the turn of the century, nationalist ideologies in Nicaragua have been built on a powerful myth, one that claims that Nicaragua is a homogeneous country, its citizens the product of "mestizaje" between the original inhabitants and the Spaniards. In this telling, Nicaragua's native peoples no longer exist and Nicaragua's advance into the modern world of capitalism and nationhood depended on this disappearance.

*To Die in This Way* tears apart this myth. Rather than accepting a version of the past shared by both scholars and popular culture, Jeffrey Gould points to the complex, tangled history of relations between Nicaragua's native peoples—themselves divided into distinct Communidades—and the nation's governing elite. Through often brilliant excavations into Nicaragua's cultural history, Gould resurrects the category "Indian" as a hidden dimension of the struggles to secure the hegemony of nationalist ideologies. These protracted conflicts, Gould points out, were violent—rooted in the confiscation of land, physical intimidation, and ideological extortion. Contrary, then, to accepted wisdom, Nicaragua's Indians engaged Nicaraguan history over the long century when they were said to no longer exist. *To Die in This Way*, in the best of critical traditions, confronts the past and challenges us to rethink "history," how "discourse" shapes the making of national hegemonies, and the way power insinuates itself in the telling.

Walter D. Mignolo, Duke University
Irene Silverblatt, Duke University
Sonia Saldívar-Hull,
University of California at Los Angeles

# Acknowledgments

I would like to express my gratitude for the following postdoctoral research grants that made this project possible: the Fulbright Faculty Research Abroad program and the Fulbright-Hays Research/Lecturer program, the Social Science Research Council, and the Rockefeller Foundation Humanities Program. In addition, I have benefited from Summer Faculty fellowships from Indiana University. I would also like to thank the staff, fellows, and faculty of the Institute of Latin American Studies of the University of Texas, Austin, for their hospitality during my tenure as a postdoctoral fellow in 1991 to 1992. I profited greatly from the stimulating intellectual climate at the institute. Similarly I am extremely thankful to the Centro de Investigaciones Históricas de Centroamérica and to its director Victor Hugo Acuña for treating me so graciously during my semester there as a Fulbright fellow in 1995.

I would also like to thank John French and Daniel James, the organizers, and the participants of the Latin American Labor History conferences (1988 and 1991). The perspicacious commentaries of Emilia Viotti da Costa, Michael Jiménez, and Peter Winn were particularly useful to me.

I owe a profound debt of gratitude to Sra. Aurora Martínez, without whose generous help I never would have been able to accomplish this project. She kindly allowed me to consult the family archive in her home, permission she had not previously granted to anyone.

The leadership groups of the Comunidades Indígenas of Sutiaba, Jinotega, and Matagalpa (1990–1993) lent their cooperation to this project. I am thankful for their assistance and hope this research will be of some use in their struggles. I am also grateful to the following Central American institutions that aided this project: the Hermeoteca Nacional (especially Mundo), the Archivo Nacional de Nicaragua and its director, Alfredo González; the Instituto de Historia de Nicaragua and its energetic director, Margarita Vannini; the Instituto Histórico Centroamericano (Universidad Centroamericana); the Consejo Regional de Pueblos Indígenas (especially to mi compadre Oscar Rojas Flores); and the mayoral offices of Boaco and Camoapa (especially Jorge Duarte).

I would also like to thank Holger Cisneros for all of his help and friendship. Other people who helped me with crucial aspects of this project include Julia Cummings, Mónica Díaz, Victoria González, Mark Morris, Ethan Sharp, and Shirley Stephenson.

I am also profoundly grateful to all the informants mentioned in the text; without their collaboration this book would never have been written. In particular I'd like to thank Adelaida Aguilera, Esteban Bárcenas, Delfina Díaz, Eusebio García, Francisco González, Macaria Hernández, Carmela López, Mercedes López, Juan Andrés Ochoa, Patrocinio López, Hipólito López, Roger Montoya, Ernestina Roque, Juan Polanco, and Vidal Rivera.

Lowell Gudmundson and William Roseberry read the entire manuscript and offered me their usual brilliant commentary, analysis, and suggestions. Many other people have read and commented upon earlier versions of chapters and I thank them: in particular, I would like to single out Richard N. Adams, Eduardo Baumeister, Casey Blake, Mac Chapin, Aviva Chomsky, Elizabeth Dore, Michel Gobat, Peter Guardino, Padre Xabier Gorastiaga, Ted Gordon, Charles R. Hale, Galio Gurdián, Edmund Gordon, Miguel Angel Herrera, Alan Knight, Iván Molina, Steve Palmer, Mario Samper, Michael Schroeder, Carol A. Smith, Greg Urban, Knut Walter, Jeffrey Wassertrom, Alexis White, Robert G. Williams, Justin Wolfe, Volker Wünderich, and Judith Zeitlin.

My family—Ely, Gabriela, Mónica, and (to a lesser extent) Carlos—put up with a lot of disruption in their lives over the past eight years. Our four major moves took a toll on their lives, friendships, and work, and for that I am sorry. I only hope that in the long run the great diversity of their experiences will balance out the costs of this ordeal. I also hope that this work is worthy of their sacrifices.

# Chronology

| | |
|---|---|
| 1871–1881 | Jesuits active in Nicaragua. |
| 1872 | Electoral violence on the rise in Sutiaba, leading to the assassination of "Pan de Arena." |
| 1881 | Rebellion carried out by Indians of Matagalpa. Violent protests occur in Sutiaba, Telica, and Masaya against expulsion of Jesuits. |
| 1884 | Antigovernment conspiracy involving Matagalpino Indians broken up. |
| 1893 | Liberal revolution triumphs under General José Santos Zelaya. In Boaco, Indians provide main backing for ancien régime. Rigoberto Cabezas serves as local leader of ladinos. |
| 1895 | Revitilizaton movement among Matagalpan Indians repressed by government. |
| 1902 | Sutiaba annexed by León. |
| 1905 | Commissioner attempts to resolve land disputes in Boaco and Camoapa involving the relationship of municipal to Comunidad Indígena lands. |
| 1906 | Comunidades Indígenas abolished for third time in twenty-five years. |
| 1909–1910 | Zelaya and Liberals overthrown by U.S.-backed counterrevolution with much Indian support. |
| 1914 | Conservative government annuls the Zelaya-era abolition of the Comunidades Indígenas. |
| 1916 | Conservative primary elections cause much violence against pro-Chamorro Indians. |
| 1919 | Mass protest movements occur in Monimbó and Nindirí. |
| 1922–1923 | Protest movements occur in Sutiaba and Masaya. |
| 1923–1925 | Coalition governments under Bartolomé Martínez and Carlos Solórzano make political inroads among Chamorrista Indians in Central Highlands. Much electoral violence occurs between different coalition and Chamorrista forces. |

| | |
|---|---|
| 1926–1927 | Civil War between Liberals and Conservatives causes much internal strife among indigenous peoples. |
| 1927–1933 | Augusto C. Sandino leads resistance against U. S. Marine Corps presence. |
| 1941 | Signing of Pátzcuaro agreement leads to creation of Instituto Indigenista Nicaragüense. |
| 1942 | Guardia Nacional uproots cotton plants in Matagalpa, violently represses indigenous protesters in Ometepe. |
| 1954 | Hugo Cerna assassinated; massive anti-indigenous repression carried out in Camoapa; Sutiaban agrarian protest movement begins |
| 1963–1965 | Agrarian protest movements in Yúcul, Uluse, and Sutiaba; Ciriaco Salgado deposed after more than two decades in power in Matagalpa. |

To Die in This Way

Source: Adapted from Cathryn L. and John Lombardi, *Latin American History: A Teaching Atlas* (Madison: University of Wisconsin Press, 1983).

# Introduction

The Indian townships are better managed than those of the Spaniards and Mestizos; the plazas are kept freer from weeds, and the roads are in good order. Probably nowhere but in tropical America can it be said that the introduction of European civilization has caused a retrogression.

—Thomas Belt, *The Naturalist in Nicaragua,* 1874

In Nicaragua the separation of the Indians from the rest of society is far from so disastrous as in Guatemala or Mexico; but the fusion is not so intimate as in Salvador or Costa Rica. The Indians, [are] preferable to the mestizos, for the simple reason that the pure races are always superior physically and morally over the mixed races. . . . So that they come to enjoy effective civil equality rather than the *de jure* equality that they now enjoy, they must decide to break out of their isolation and from their customary lack of confidence towards outsiders.

—Pablo Levy, *Notas geográficas y económicas sobre la República de
    Nicaragua,* 1873

A few days after the Sandinista electoral defeat of 1990, I set out in search of a man named Victor Guillén whom I wanted to interview. I had been told that he was managing a small state farm near the village of Pancasán in the highlands of Matagalpa. That village was famous in Sandinista history as the site of a military defeat in 1967 that came to symbolize both a heroic alternative to reformism and the depth of peasant support for the guerrilla movement. Guillén had been one of the few survivors of that battle. However, I was interested in talking to him about his childhood and parents; they had been members of the Comunidad Indígena (communal indigenous organization) of Muy Muy.

Thick jungle underbrush crowded the road as it curved up a mountain and then leveled out along a ridge. As I came to a clearing, I peered down into a valley and saw what seemed to be a settlement dotted with corrugated tin shacks. Then I realized that many of the dwellings had collapsed and that it must have been a state farm destroyed by the contras.

The road ended at an old, overgrown coffee plantation. This state farm looked like an advertisement for neo-Liberalism (the ad, of course, wouldn't show the contra attacks that ensured the collapse of the project). These were anxious and depressing times for Guillén; he had no clue where anything was going: the farm, the revolutionary process that he had fought for more than twenty-five years, much less his own future. It did not surprise me that he wasn't particularly thrilled to have this interview. But as a good militant used to this sort of thing, he obliged politely.

Guillén's parents had belonged to the last generation of the Comunidad Indígena of Muy Muy (a nearby village). An American coffee planter's expropriation of part of the communal land (including the Guillén farm) had dealt a mortal blow to that Comunidad. I had found documents about the case in a closet in Matagalpa strewn in roughly equal proportion with rat feces and legal documents. The copy that I showed him piqued his interest somewhat, and he related his father's tale of how the president of the Comunidad Indígena had taken all of the community funds in order to travel to Managua to plead their case before the president of the Republic, Juan B. Sacasa. "He drank it all up in parties before he ever got to Managua," Guillén remarked. The Comunidad lost, the "yanqui" won and then proceeded to burn their family's home to the ground. "The Comunidad was worthless."

Compared to the remarkable courage and abnegation of Victor Guillén and his comrades on the front lines of the revolution, the former leaders of the Comunidad surely did not measure up as defenders of their people. Especially in those days following the Sandinista defeat, Guillén's lack of interest in the Comunidad was not difficult to fathom. As I headed back to Pancasán, I began to muddle through some troubling questions that gnawed at me during this research journey. If the children of the *indígenas* did not care about the history of the Comunidades, why should I bother attempting to reconstruct their history? Worse, wasn't I potentially attributing identities to them that derived from Western categories soaked in nostalgia? Who was I, then, to devise ethnic identities around the stories of people who rejected those identities as irrelevant?

These questions reemerged at other research sites and later around conference tables. In Yúcul, a *cañada* (a dispersed settlement of Indians) between

Pancasán and the city of Matagalpa, the grandchildren of a man who had lost a decisive land battle in 1916 did not realize that their grandfather had been an important leader of the Comunidad Indígena of Matagalpa. Similarly, in Salinas, a small, isolated village in the department of Boaco, an elderly man who did claim an indigenous identity lamented, "the youth do not care about our history" and that they were uninterested in the story of what he called *la casta indígena*.

The irrelevance of indigenous history for the youth was in part a generational stance. But I would suggest that this irrelevance is also a product of what I have called a myth of *mestizaje*. This myth has made the indigenous people of central and western Nicaragua largely invisible to intellectuals, politicians, and most city folk throughout the twentieth century. During the course of my doctoral research in the northwestern department of Chinandega, I first became aware of an ethnic dimension to modern Nicaraguan history that had been totally ignored. Scholars and public figures alike had posited the virtual extinction of all Indian groups since the turn of the century (except for the Miskitos and Sumos of the Atlantic Coast). I strongly doubted that view, in part because of my experiences among the people of Sutiaba, today a barrio of the city of León.

In Sutiaba during the mid-1980s I interviewed people who had spearheaded the 1950s agrarian protest movement in western Nicaragua. In speech and appearance, they closely resembled their counterparts in Chinandega. Yet the Sutiabas, unlike the Chinandeganos, shared a strong indigenous identity (my observation received some confirmation in a 1992 survey that showed 84 percent of residents of the barrio of Sutiaba as claiming an indigenous identity).[1] It became clear to me that Nicaraguan indigenous identity posed a complex problem for which traditional anthropological models would be of little use. The survival of indigenous ethnicity as well as its demise appeared to lie in the people's collective memory of specific forms of oppression and conflict rather than in language and material culture. At the same time, I realized that their memory was itself inextricably bound up with the myth of Nicaragua *mestiza*. The formation of that myth, its place in nationalist discourse, and its devastating effects on the surviving indigenous communities comprise the subject matter of this book.

Throughout this project I have carried several pieces of ideological-political baggage. Since the early 1980s I had both sympathized with the Nicaraguan revolution and (constructively and softly) criticized the politics of the Frente Sandinista de Liberación Nacional (FSLN). Indeed my first book could be read in part as a critique of the FSLN's failure to recognize the importance of local history and the relatively autonomous popular movements that helped to shape the revolutionary process. My belief that somehow critical scholarship could help to push the FSLN onto a more democratic path was surely one of the greatest conceits of that enterprise. This second project also had a degree of political impetus. From its inception I realized that if the Sandinistas before 1990 had been uninterested in the history of the Chinandegano popular movements, they had a veritable blind spot when it came to the contemporary history or reality of the Comunidades Indígenas. That blindness translated into concrete policies that failed to address the pressing needs of the Comunidades as organizations. Thus, to cite one example, the cooperatives and state farms that emerged on the former lands of the Comunidad Indígena did not pay the nominal rent the indigenous leaders requested nor did the government give priority to members of the Comunidad. In response to my query, one district leader of the FSLN told me that the Indians weren't "real Indians" and that the Comunidad was "a farce." At the time of his comment, the Sandinista leader had direct access to an extensive survey of thousands of people who lived in the villages associated with the Comunidad Indígena of Matagalpa in which people were asked if they identified themselves as indígenas. Over 80 percent had answered affirmatively.[2]

I believe that the FSLN paid at the polls in 1990 for their myopia, for their participation in the reproduction of the myth of mestizaje. In those precincts that I identified as belonging to the Comunidades Indígenas of Jinotega and Matagalpa, the FSLN lost to the opposition alliance by margins of 5 to 1 and 4 to 1, whereas nationwide they lost 54 percent to 41 percent. Of course, in no way did the opposition or the contras have any special sensitivity for the indigenous people either before or after the elections. Thus, communal demands unfulfilled by the revolution are even more pressing today—a pro-Indian agrarian reform; vast improvements in transportation, sanitation, and education; and a degree of political autonomy. I have been conscious from the beginning of this project that the Indians live in more precarious circumstances than most other Nicaraguans, that even recent generations have suffered very special forms of oppression and discrimination that have gone largely undetected, and that elementary forms of justice for them would have to begin with a recognition of the historic legitimacy of their Comunidades and their identities.

When I started out I did not foresee that in the early 1990s a revitalization of indigenous movements would take place. Throughout the 1980s there had been sporadic attempts by Sandinista indigenous leaders to forge a federation of all Comunidades (twelve outside of the Atlantic Coast), but the FSLN blocked their efforts, wary of repeating their bitter conflict with the Miskitos. Spurred on by the continental quincentenary campaign and the political opening of 1990, new mobilizations and efforts took place. In 1992, a group of indigenous leaders came together to found a Federación de Comunidades Indígenas. Their founding document is worth quoting at length:

> They made us believe that Indians were inferior beings and they incul-
> cated into the consciousness of our youth that it was shameful to be an
> Indian and that we represented the worst of the country. They asked us
> to renounce our rich cultural heritage and they hid it so that we would
> never know our true history.[3]

This movement has been ripped apart by factional disputes and thus has not borne much fruit for its subjects. Nevertheless, I have placed my own research (that I first published in Spanish) at its disposal. My most rewarding experience as a researcher was a presentation at the Bibilioteca Fray Bartolomé de las Casas (see chapter 3 for its peculiar origins) in Sutiaba. The audience was composed of members of two bitterly opposed factions and I was told it was the first time they had met (without government mediators present) under the same roof for several years. My talk summarized much of the material in chapter 3 and emphasized the role of internal divisions in the community's history. The ensuing discussion was lively, free-flowing, and respectful of the opposing side. I wish I could say that the meeting somehow began to salve the internal wounds in the community, but I seriously doubt that.

Throughout the course of my eighteen months of research in Nicaragua, I often found myself comparing my experiences with those during my two years of doctoral research in Chinandega. The one major advantage I have enjoyed with this project has been my success in locating far more documentation than I could in the mid-1980s. My fortune was due to several factors. On a national level, with the end of the war, the government could devote more effort to making documentation available to researchers. More significant for my purposes, many of the areas I worked in had not been affected by the insurrections of 1978 to 1979 that leveled the center of Chinandega or by the earthquakes of 1931 and 1972 that destroyed Managua.

Although I did not miss the heat of the Chinandegano plain, I did regret that in the highlands I could not match the level of intimacy I developed with my informants during the mid-1980s. Again, several factors came into play. First, from its inception I realized that this project would have to have a comparative dimension. The distance and difficulties of communication between the research sites—Matagalpa, Jinotega, Camoapa, Monimbó, Ometepe, and Sutiaba—ruled out extended stays in any one of them. Second, although I attempted to keep them in an open life-history format, the interviews nonetheless touched on themes that were often painful, difficult, and embarrassing for people. The Guillén interview would be one of many examples. Moreover, in addition to the painfulness of the subject matter, most of the folks I dealt with, particularly those who identified themselves as indígenas, were far more reticent than the Chinandegano peasants. As the narratives will show, that extreme reticence with outsiders has been well founded. Finally, despite my attempts to compensate for the lack of subaltern female voices in my previous book, I found myself constantly frustrated by prevailing rigid patriarchal norms in the remote areas of the highlands. Typically, when I arrived at an indigenous hut, women would literally hide from sight and I was only allowed to interview the male elder. Repeated visits did not alter this behavior. Thus my frustration at my failure to recover the "indigenous voices" is compounded by the failure to recover specifically female ones. I can only hope that future historians or anthropologists who locate themselves in one site will have an opportunity to do a better job. At the very least, I have provided something of a road map that points to the submerged existence of those voices.

Since the 1880s, when official discourse trumpeted the victory of ladino "civilization" over Indian "barbarism," elite liberal and popular ideologies have denied the validity of indigenous identity. This denial has been so powerful and convincing that many Indians, out of fear or shame, shed the markers of their indigenous identities: their distinctive dress and their language. To cite one example, in 1908, Walter Lehmann, a German linguist, initiated fieldwork in Sutiaba as part of his research on the Indian languages of Central America. For days he wandered through the village, searching unsuccessfully for a native speaker of the Sutiaban language. He eventually met an elderly lady, Victoria Carrillo, who offered to help him record a vocabulary. Carrillo informed Lehmann that the other elderly Indians had feigned ignorance because they were "ashamed of their language."[4]

This experience of linguistic shame was not unique to Sutiaba. As early as 1850, Fermín Ferrer, a government minister, reported that education had spread so widely throughout Nicaragua that literate people inhabited every town. "Under this benign influence almost all of the aboriginal dialects have disappeared except those of the Indians of the Masaya and Managua," he observed.[5] In neighboring Honduras similar processes were at work, especially among the Lenca in the mountainous west. By the late 1880s in the department of La Paz the younger generation of Indians could not understand their elders when they spoke Lenca.[6] An indigenous woman, interviewed in 1983 in Guajiquiro, La Paz, recalled that her mother scolded her when she listened in on conversations in Lenca among her elders, warning her that if she repeated the indigenous words she would be treated as an "india."[7]

The demise of the indigenous languages in Mesoamerica and Central America has had a devastating impact on indigenous cultures. Indeed, as several authors have shown, monolingual language policy in Latin America has been a very effective vehicle of cultural domination. And even where indigenous languages survived they were radically deformed through Iberian domination. Richard Adams writes, "the loss of language signals not only the loss of basic tools of self expression, but also much of the cognitive framework that depends on the persistence of those forms."[8]

Notwithstanding such a fundamental cultural transformation, this book (along with other studies) argues that it is erroneous to equate language with identity and that the elimination of the former does not extinguish the latter.[9]

Two decades ago, Jaime Wheelock offered an explanation for the demise of the indigenous population that has been widely accepted. The pioneering social scientist underscored the loss of land and consequent proletarianization as the principal cause of ladinoization. For Wheelock, the decisive moment in this process came in 1881, following the repression of the Matagalpino Indian rebellion, when "the oligarchic avalanche swallowed up morsels of thousands of hectares apiece. The rupture of the communities produced the separation of the Indian from his communal parcel and threw him onto the labor market . . . converting him into a rural worker."[10] Similarly, the authors of the otherwise excellent agrarian history *Por eso defendemos la frontera* support this perspective, stating that "the indigenous communities near Jinotega and Matagalpa were destroyed . . . before the turn of the century."[11]

Three of Nicaragua's leading writers describe the mestizaje process through potent metaphors of the triumph of *mestizo* culture in Nicaragua and the merging of the Indian into the national population. José Coronel Urtecho writes of the harmonious merging of Indians and Spaniards in the *tiangüe*, the marketplace, "where the Indians of Nicaragua became Nicaraguan and where they Nicaraguanized the creoles and mestizos."[12] Similarly, Jorge Eduardo Arellano and Pablo Antonio Cuadra situated the origins of Nicaraguan mestizo culture in "el Güegüense," a picaresque native drama that mocked colonial authorities in a Hispano Nahuatl dialect. The scholars underscored both the emergence of the social figure of the mestizo traveling merchant and the hybrid dialect as evidence of advanced cultural mestizaje during the late colonial period. Reflecting on the broad sweep of colonial history, Cuadra noted, "The Indian contribution is not eliminated but remains at the center of our identity as a challenge to be untangled."[13] Similarly Arellano described the Güegüense/mestizo "as the prototype of the Nicaraguan mode of being."[14] Finally, these analyses are substantiated by the research of the historian Germán Romero Vargas, which shows the dramatic rise of the mestizos in late colonial society.[15]

Although Arellano, Coronel, and Cuadra have provided vivid descriptions of Nicaraguan popular culture, they used primordialist assumptions about Indian identity that led them to believe that once the pre-Columbian cultural essence disappeared—especially language and racial "purity"—Indians turned into mestizos. In the words of Coronel, "The truly indigenous comes to be mestizo, that in Nicaragua is the Nicaraguan."[16] But already during the last century, such ethnic markers as language, religion, and racial appearance were not crucial to at least external characterizations of indigenous ethnicity. Indeed throughout the nineteenth century, travelers, linguists, and government officials easily distinguished Indians from ladinos, even when the former were monolingual Spanish speakers. Nineteenth-century outsiders could identify Indians by their dress, religious customs, housing, and artisanal production.[17]

Two quite typical examples of the European view of indigenous difference will suffice. Frederick Boyle, describing the Indians of Masaya during the 1860s, wrote that they

> all bore that stealthy look which long centuries of oppression have stamped into their eyes. The costumes are simple, and with better figures, would be elegant. The men wear short trousers half way to the knee, and the women twist a long strip of blue-checked cotton round their waists. When out of doors they cover the breasts with a squared handkerchief, which is held in place by passing the upper corners under the straps of the load they carry on their shoulders.[18]

Carl Scherzer, an Austrian physician who traveled through Nicaragua during the 1850s, searched assiduously for native speakers of indigenous languages with no success. Nevertheless he made constant reference to differences between Indians and ladinos, such as those contained in discussions such as the following:

> The pure Indians form the most industrious, useful, and respectable portion of the population. . . . These Indians all exhibit in their features the well-known type of the South American races, except that they are of a somewhat lighter complexion. Unfortunately, though they are peaceful and well disposed, they are very timid, apparently incapable of intellectual progress, and chiefly animated by two passions, namely hatred to the Ladinos, and love for brandy.[19]

These travel accounts are not particularly congruent with either perspective on the demise of the indigenous peoples; they emphasize both the numerical preponderance of Indians and their strongly distinct cultural characteristics despite their loss of indigenous language. Both the social scientific and the literary critics' perspective reflect different aspects of the myth of a Nicaragua mestiza, a collective belief that Nicaragua has been an ethnically homogenous society since the late nineteenth century.[20] This myth, a cornerstone of Nicaraguan nationalism, has been so believable precisely because it has both fostered and reflected the disintegration of many Indian communities through migrations and the loss of communal land. Biological mestizaje has often accompanied such communal disintegration, providing physical evidence to support the myth. In the latter part of the nineteenth century ladinoization gathered force as many Indians (often, like the Sutiabas, living in close geographic proximity to mestizos) were shamed into shedding their dress and language.

The primary goal of this book is to describe the tensions and ambiguities that characterized the relationship between the highlands indigenous communities and the forces of assimilation throughout the late nineteenth and early twentieth centuries. Rather than an epiphenomenon of proletarianization (or nation-state formation), ladinoization during this period was a multidimensional process, propelled by an array of friendly and antagonistic interventions in the indigenous communities by the church, the state, political parties, local intellectuals, and landed elites. That process combined real violence—land expropriation and coerced labor—and the symbolic violence that discredited indigenous identity, exacerbated cultural alienation, and enhanced the elites' claim to rule the nation.[21] Both forms of violence were mutually supportive, for the rejection of an indigenous and the acceptance of a mestizo Nicaraguan identity usually involved the withdrawal of claims to communal land and a loss of community-level political and cultural autonomy. However, this was not a one-way road to assimilation with the Indian at the beginning and the ladino citizen at the destination. On the contrary, many paths branched off the road leading to interstitial communities and cultures.

This study, then, attempts to historicize the process of mestizaje in Nicaragua. My use of mestizaje emerges both from this research and from an interchange with Charles R. Hale and Carol A. Smith. Here I would like to quote from our work:

> The notion of "mestizaje" is the analytical centerpiece of this study. It refers both to the outcome of an individual or collective shift away from strong self-identification with indigenous culture, and to the myth of cultural homogeneity which elites imposed from above as a standard part of their repertoire of nation building. Mestizaje is also useful in theoretical terms because it emphasizes the openness, fluidity, and multiplicity of the identities that we seek to understand. Most simply, mestizo is a "mixed race" identity category, and mestizaje refers to the process through which that category is created. But the culturally elaborated content and meaning of the identity that results varies widely—from the complete suppression of Indianness such that it remains only a distant memory; to the superficial acceptance of the dominant society as facade,

behind which a deep adherence to Indian culture persists; to a simultaneous affinity with multiple cultural traditions not completely compatible with one another.[22]

Thus, a central contribution of this particular study is its examination of the interconnectedness of these dimensions of the mestizaje process. That interconnectedness will be revealed in part by an examination of the distinct nature of the attacks against different indigenous communities that occurred at various moments during the late nineteenth century and the twentieth century.

Although this book begins in the 1870s, the starting point was somewhat arbitrary; it represented a convenient moment from which to gauge the origins of the Matagalpino Indian rebellion of 1881, a major event in indigenous history. But it was not representative of some golden age of the Comunidades Indígenas or of Indian identity. Indeed, the very notion of an officially recognized Comunidad would have been strange and unfamiliar to many of the indigenous groups during the mid nineteenth century. Many of the groups under assault in the early twentieth century may have looked back at the mid-nineteenth century as a time of unity and harmony, but the fragmentary evidence from that period suggests otherwise. It would have been wonderful to have been able to consult Indian community studies for either the late colonial period or the nineteenth century; I would then have had some kind of benchmark with which to work. I suspect that the researcher who does undertake such a fascinating project as the study of early nineteenth-century Indian communities will run into some difficulties.[23] Scherzer was also frustrated in his efforts to uncover something of the contemporary history of the Indian population. He remarked:

> I left the vicar of Mosonte accordingly, not much wiser concerning the state of the people than I had been when I went to him. Even of the Indians, amongst whom he had lived for twenty years, of their manners, customs, and traditions he could tell me little more than that the brown children of the mountains had lived in peaceful intercourse with the Spanish races till they had nearly forgotten their native tongue without having acquired any other. The good priest was the spiritual and temporal advisor of his flock, their consoler and their helper in all seasons of distress; but he had never made their intellectual and moral condition

the objects of any special study, nor dreamed of searching out the causes of their present wretched condition with a view to guiding them towards a better path for the future.[24]

Although I cannot but think that Nicaraguan ladinos had a peculiar aversion to writing about contemporary Indians, none of the stories that I have managed to reconstruct are particularly unique in the annals of state-Indian relations in Latin America.[25] What is far less documented, however, is the process through which those attacks have been written out of history and excised from common sense. Nor has there been much inquiry about how that erasure affected the balance of power in the local class and ethnic conflicts.

In uncovering this ethnic dimension of Nicaraguan history, we attempt to follow the injunction of Michel-Rolph Trouillot: "Effective silencing does not require a conspiracy, not even a political consensus. Its roots are structural . . . the exercise of power is much more important than the alleged conservative or liberal adherence of the historians involved."[26] Our examination of the relationship of discourse formation on the national level and its active relation to local culture and conflict thus forms part of a growing literature on hegemony. Two important approaches to hegemony have emerged recently: as naturalized, invisible ideology and as shared discursive field of contestation. Jean and John Comaroff's definition of hegemony resembles Bourdieu's "doxa" in that they both emphasize that part of a worldview that is "naturalized," that no longer appears to represent the ideology of a particular group.[27] William Roseberry, on the other hand, writes:

> I propose that we use the concept *not* to understand consent but to understand struggle, the ways in which the words, images, symbols, forms, organizations, institutions, and movements used by subordinate populations to talk about, understand, confront, accommodate themselves to, or resist their domination are shaped by the process of domination itself. What hegemony constructs, then, is not a shared ideology but a common material and meaningful framework for living through, talking about, and acting upon social orders characterized by domination.[28]

These statements of hegemony's operation are closely related. My own work touches upon both by probing the historical moment in which mestizaje as an ideology becomes a hegemonic worldview, a doxic practice, common sense. At the same time, following Roseberry we examine how the particular discourse of mestizaje shaped the field in which questions of indigenous rights and identity were played out. In both problematics, as in this study, the role of local and national intellectuals is fundamental.

Elite discourse on the highland "Indian problem" was created through the communication of provincial "experts" with the national elite. To participate in national-level discourse that tended to suppress all expressions of cultural difference, the provincial intellectuals communicated their perception of local reality in a way that both established their expertise on the Indians and effectively silenced their indigenous neighbors. They succeeded only after a violent process involving assaults on Indian land and labor.

Elites projected images of Indians as marginal primitives who blocked progress because of their ignorance and wasteful practices on their communal property. These images at once rationalized and reflected policies that led to the expropriation of the Indians' land and the crude exploitation of their labor. The images of abject misery or of a bound Indian being dragged to labor both justified "civilizing" practices and reflected the Indians' changing social reality of land loss, forced labor, and military recruitment. Indigenous resistance merely confirmed the ladino discourse; evading debt obligations demonstrated the Indians' deviousness and childish irresponsibility. Similarly, indigenous protests reiterated the need to educate the primitives and to abolish the Comunidades.

This study shows that the Nicaraguan Indians played such a vital economic and political role from 1880 to 1925 that their absence from the standard historical portrait leaves a seriously distorted image of Nicaragua's social and political development. Without understanding this prolonged, multifront assault against the Comunidades Indígenas it would be impossible to recognize a submerged cornerstone of elite hegemony. Such recognition is important because many interpretations of modern Nicaraguan history have hinged on the putative incapacity of its bourgeoisie to construct hegemonic forms of domination. My first book, *To Lead as Equals*, questioned that view through a study of labor and peasant movements; this book extends that challenge by examining one of the elite's most enduring hegemonic achievements, the commonsense notion that Nicaragua is an ethnically homogenous society.

In recent years some social scientists have begun to strip all primordial references from their concept of ethnicity, choosing to analyze the phenomenon instead as a historically specific and contingent mode of consciousness and social interaction. For these scholars, ethnic consciousness is not a given transmitted from the distant past but rather a constructed identity mediated by contact with nation-states and with other ethnic groups. This perspective has been best summarized by Kay Warren, in discussing ethnic relations in Guatemala:

> The constructionist approach notes that the Guatemalan categories *indígena, natural,* or *maya,* may be contrasted with *ladino.* But in practice both the significance of the contrast and the labels used to mark "self" and "other" are tremendously variable over events, lifetimes, and recent history. From this viewpoint, there is no Mayan or Ladino except as these identities are constructed, contested, negotiated, imposed, imputed, resisted and redefined in action.[29]

Indeed, as alluded to earlier, traditional anthropological models of indigenous ethnicity would not have guided this study successfully. My project should contribute, instead, to the theoretical enterprise that Warren announced by providing a historical perspective on the interpenetration of suppressed indigenous and dominant ladino cultures in Central America.

Despite the broad contours of my agreement with the "constructionist" approach, I disagree about the rejection *tout court* of the notion of "cultural loss." In arguing against those "cultural survivalists" who see ethnicity and ethnic identity contained within a bundle of distinct traits, beliefs, and practices, Warren and others state that the transformation of those traits negates neither ethnic identity nor culture. Therefore, "culture," understood as "continually reworked understandings of the world . . . is not 'lost' but transformed."[30]

The contemporary history of Nicaraguan indigenous communities suggests, on the contrary, that there has been significant cultural loss. But that loss has far less to do with essentialist representations of ethnicity crucial to cultural survivalism and far more to do with the destruction of communities, communal organizations, and identities. We will examine two cases in which the assault on the land, labor, religion, and political autonomy of the Comunidades Indígenas, the organizational matrix of the indigenous communities of central and Pacific Nicaragua, was crowned with success: those Comunidades ceased to function decades ago.

On one level, the destruction of the Comunidades entailed the destruction of a crucially important organization, roughly the equivalent of the destruction of a trade union, a powerful local government–cum–political party, and a church rolled into one. The progressive weakening of those organizations then left their members virtually defenseless against tyrannical forces in society. Landlords backed by the state compelled those inhabitants of confederations of small villages with a choice: either flee to the jungle wilderness or become *colonos* (resident laborers). The former choice involved carving out an inconceivably difficult marginal and atomized existence. The latter often enough involved the lowest forms of degradation, arbitrary whippings, jailings, and rape.

The strength of the Comunidades resided in their material and cultural defenses. As an organization, the Comunidad could engage in legal and extralegal forms of defense. As with other organizations its ability to do so hinged upon the ideological commitment of its members. Given the crucial role of the Comunidad in people's lives, the people's militancy also expressed a powerful form of identity. That identity as an indígena in turn was crucial for the defense of the community. The prolonged, agonizing death of these communities had to do with the indigenous peoples' increased difficulty in defending themselves from the advances of the state and agrarian capitalism. Moreover, it was a question of cultural loss: the disarticulation of those local discourses and identities that had allowed for a modicum of self-respect, humanity, and well-being in daily existence.

In this sense, rather than the transformation of culture and identity in many cases we see dispersal, terror, atomization, and anomie. At the same time, because collective identity was bound up more with an institution, the Comunidad Indígena became particularly vulnerable to a charge that resounded from the discourse of mestizaje: the Indians were unauthentic and therefore unworthy of recognition. Moreover, the link of identity and institution created the conditions for a particularly nasty kind of factional power struggle that persists today. Those who, for example, did not support the leaders of the Comunidad were banished as non-Indians.

Finally, this study can be placed within the growing field of postcolonial studies. It is useful to think of mestizaje in Nicaragua as part of a postcolonial discourse particularly because so much of the nationalist discourse, in particular the revolutionary nationalism of Augusto César Sandino and the contemporary Sandinistas, was framed in terms of colonialism.[31] The FSLN consistently attacked Somocismo as a neocolonial system and cast the dictators as colonial-style tyrants beholden to the United States. As with other forms of nationalism, revolutionary nationalism contained its own forms of erasure and amnesia, in particular with regard to the lived history of the indigenous communities.[32] Here, Wheelock's vision of the demise of the indigenous communities can be seen as reflective and conditioning of specific historical processes such as the expropriations of Yúcul and the lands of the Comunidad of Muy Muy. In this sense, the death of the communities is both a precondition and rallying cry of vengeance for revolutionary nationalism. This postcolonial perspective helps us grapple with the question of why the Sandinistas had such an abysmal record with those who continued to define themselves in relationship to Comunidades Indígenas and yet registered stunning political successes with those people who had rejected the indigenous identity of their parents' generation.[33]

The number of Indians in Nicaragua has long been a subject of dispute. In 1881, the presence of census takers in Matagalpa helped provoke the rebellion. In 1907, a Nicaraguan official lamented "the customary failure of the indigenous race to provide reliable statistical information."[34]

Even during the colonial era, when the authorities were systematic about recording such information, the record is not at all clear. Among the difficulties for colonial statisticians were the thousands of Indians in the Central Highlands outside of Spanish control and probably an equal number who passed in and out between the categories of *bravos* and *civilizados*. Moreover, different censuses recorded wildly conflicting figures. Not surprisingly, modern scholars also differ. Germán Romero Vargas argues that Indians accounted for less than 50 percent of the population during the early nineteenth century. Linda Newson calculates that 82,000 Indians represented between 50 and 78 percent of the total population during the late eighteenth century.[35] Although I have no argument with the view that up to 50 percent of the population was non-Indian in 1820, in this book I do question the supposition that the decline in the Indian population continued unabated throughout the nineteenth century.

With Independence, census taking became at best chaotic. On the basis of an 1846 census, the diplomat/ethnographer E. G. Squier calculated that the Indian population was 80,000, representing 32 percent of the total population. Pablo Levy, the French geographer, after dismissing the accuracy of previous censuses, offered the estimate of the Indian population as 55 percent in 1870. The next census in 1890 noted 198,000 Indians out of a total population of 360,000, or exactly 55 percent. Most likely, some bureaucrat, after arriving at a very rough estimate, simplified his work by rigorously applying Levy's 55 percent estimate from seventeen years earlier to the country's total population (also a wild estimate no doubt).[36] Government statistics from later in the decade show that Indians accounted for 30.7 percent of recorded births and 35 percent of deaths during the 1890s. If we add to that figure 30,000 or 40,000 "indios bravos" of eastern Chontales and Matagalpa we can estimate the indigenous population of western and central Nicaragua at around 40 percent in 1900.[37]

Census reports have played an important role in justifying the view that the Indians disappeared around the turn of the century. The 1920 Nicaraguan census, for example, showed that the indigenous population had dropped precipitously from 30–40 percent to under 4 percent between 1906 and 1920.[38] These statistics are profoundly misleading, however, for the census recorded no Indians (listed as *cobrizos,* or "copper-colored") in the semiurban communities of Sutiaba and Masaya, which had highly visible indigenous populations. The miscount did not stop there: not a single cobrizo is listed in eleven out of the remaining thirteen Comunidades Indígenas. Finally, by omission, the census assumed that some 30,000 to 40,000 indios bravos had become ladinoized overnight.[39]

It is not at all clear what the census designers expected to demonstrate with their categories. Nevertheless, those scholars and statesmen who wished to point to the success of mestizaje could use the census as justification. Although the census phenotypical category "cobrizo" included most people defined as indígenas, biological mestizaje did not automatically affect ethnic definition. A review of birth records in Boaco at the turn of the century, for example, shows that people listed as indígenas were often described as *trigüeno* (wheat colored).

If color did not define the indigenous, what did? By 1920, no Indians beyond the Atlantic Coast region spoke a native language anymore (although many spoke distinct dialects of Spanish) and few wore native dress. To analyze this problem it is useful to begin with Richard N. Adams's definition of an ethnic group: "a self-reproducing collectivity identified by myths of a common provenance and by identifying markers . . . The sociological salience of an ethnic group emerges most importantly when it is both self-identified and externally identified."[40] This study assumes that the internal and external definitions of an Indian involved primarily a sense of belonging to a Comunidad Indígena, an institution that has been an important site of cultural, political, and economic battles throughout this century. In effect, the Comunidad evolved into the last ethnic "marker" for many Indians. Membership in a Nicaraguan Comunidad during the early decades of this century entailed notions of group endogamy, common origins, land rights, religious and political autonomy, and a bitter history of conflict with ladino neighbors.[41]

The Comunidad has played a defensive role similar to that of the *municipio* (municipality) and the *cofradías* (lay fraternities) in the other Central American republics. In El Salvador, in 1881, the government effectively abolished the Comunidades Indígenas and their communal land. In Nicaragua, by contrast, the threats and actions of indigenous resistance in the context of a deeply divided political elite thwarted eight governmental attempts to abolish the Comunidades between 1877 and 1923.[42]

Although we can make no great claims of accuracy, we can estimate the size of the indigenous population in 1920 by examining the same census (and election returns) for the settlements and cañadas that belonged to the Comunidades. This yields an estimate of the membership at between 90,000 and 125,000, or between 15 and 20 percent of Nicaragua's population.[43] Moreover, Indians surely made up the majority or a substantial minority of specific areas in the country such as Boaco and Matagalpa.

The construction of a myth of an ethnically homogenous society has involved the appropriation of racial categories that scholars have come to take for granted. Before the 1930s, all sectors of society employed the term "ladino" to refer to non-Indians or to "whites." During the same period the term "mestizo" meant the offspring of unions between Indians and whites (broadly defined). By 1950, however, "mestizo" not only had supplanted "ladino" but had become a self-description for the whole of society. This linguistic transformation symbolized the triumph of the myth of Nicaragua mestiza. Although it reflected a growing trend toward biological mestizaje, the myth also rendered spurious all claims to indigenous identity and rights.

The first three chapters of this book deal with different stories of primitive accumulation: the separation of indigenous communities from their land and from control over their own labor. The period commences and ends with war: the Matagalpino Indian rebellion of 1881 and the civil war of 1926 to 1927 that effectively ended fifteen years of Conservative party rule that depended as much upon Indian support as it did upon its alliance with the United States. The first chapter focuses on the Comunidades Indígenas of Matagalpa and Jinotega and emphasizes their response to the frontal assault on their land and labor resources. In that chapter we also introduce a discussion of the relation of local intellectuals to the formation of national discourse. The second chapter moves south to Boaco and Camoapa, where ladino politicians supplanted indigenous-controlled municipalities. The ensuing battle over communal land involved intense discussions over the nature of citizenship and community. The chapter attempts to come to grips with a notion of "cultural loss" and the impact of nonrecognition on indigenous identity. The third chapter narrates the history of Sutiaba, where the annexation of the indigenous municipality to León accelerated the process of communal land privatization and dealt a serious blow to the cohesiveness of the community. Yet within a little more than a decade, Sutiaba witnessed a dramatic mobilization that reaffirmed the people's rights to land and political autonomy.

The fourth chapter concentrates on gender and politics in the development of the discourse of mestizaje. It starts with a discussion of the search for an anti-imperial national symbol that would supplant the opposition between ladinos and Indians. Next, we delve into the gendered language of factional politics among the Indians of Matagalpa, followed by a shift into a discussion of anti-interventionist struggles spearheaded by the people of Monimbó, a semiurban barrio of the city of Masaya. Those struggles helped prepare the political and ideological terrain for "Indo Hispanism." Then, we move to analyzing the significance of Sandino's discourse of mestizaje and its silence with respect to the indigenous communities in the context of the discourse of Indo Hispanism. Picking up again our analysis of the language of factional politics, we study gender and mestizaje, moving from a discussion of discourse to the memory of sexual coercion and "perversion." Finally, we touch on the political legacy of Sandino.

The fifth and sixth chapters focus on ladino assaults and indigenous resistance, mainly but not exclusively in the highlands, during the 1930s and 1940s. These chapters develop an analysis of the role local and national intellectuals played in the creation of national ideology and practice toward Indians. In particular, we examine the growing gulf between the national discourse of ethnic homogeneity and grassroots ethnic conflict and repression.

The final chapter attempts to reconstruct the role of collective memory in the peasant movements of the 1950s and 1960s. We discuss two interrelated aspects of those memories. First, we analyze instances of memories of mestizaje, that is memories of the symbolic or real destruction of indigenous communities and identities. Those memories of indigenous roots were, in turn, connected to memories of accumulation, often the loss of land. The analysis of memory then opens up into a wider discussion of revolutionary nationalist discourse, local memory, and ethnicity.

This book is an endeavor that may have salient political and social consequences; the suppression of indigenous communal identity throughout the twentieth century has played a major role in the creation of a culture of repression whose long-term effects became visible to the world in the region's violent conflicts of the 1970s and 1980s. As Benedict Anderson remarked, "All profound changes in consciousness, by their very nature, bring with them characteristic amnesias."[44] In Nicaragua, and throughout much of the region, the birth of national consciousness has coincided with a pervasive form of amnesia: the forgetting of the existence of hundreds of thousands of Indians. This book will have accomplished much of its mission if it helps recover at least fragments of that collective memory, a restoration that might alleviate some of the spiritual pain left by traumatic events that have shaped modern Central America's history.

## Notes

Unless otherwise noted, all translations of quotations are my own.

1 Marcos Membreño Idiaquez, *La estructura de las comunidades étnicas* (Managua: Editorial Envío, 1994), 308. According to a survey carried out by NITLAPAN of the Universidad Centroamericana, 84.3 percent of the Sutiaban population identified themselves as indígenas; in Monimbó the figure was 86.1 percent.

2  The Censo de la Comunidad Indígena de Matagalpa was carried out in 1987. The raw census data was lodged in the president of the Comunidad's office. The 80-percent-plus figure was based on two independent tallying procedures carried out by me and by Victoria González.

3  "Documento constitutivo de la Federación de Comunidades Indígenas," Monimbó Nicaragua, March 27, 1992.

4  Walter Lehmann, *Zentral America*, 2 vols. (Berlin: D. Reimer, 1920), 2:907.

5  "Noticias sobre la jeografía y estadística del departamento oriental," *El Correo del Istmo*, no. 48 (August 19, 1850): 45–49.

6  In 1870, for example, a priest prohibited the use of the Lenca language in his parish. Antonio Vallejo (chief statistician), *Censo de la República de Honduras levantado el 15 de junio de 1887* (Tegucigalpa: Tipografía del Gobierno), description of La Paz department. I have not encountered reports of such extreme measures in Nicaragua.

7  Atanasio Herranz, *Estado, sociedad y lenguaje: la política lingüística en Honduras* (Tegucigalpa: Editorial Guaymuras, 1996), 199.

8  Richard N. Adams, "Strategies of Ethnic Survival in Central America," in *Nation-States and Indians in Latin America*, eds. Greg Urban and Joel Sherzer (Austin: University of Texas Press, 1991), 191. Similarly, according to William Hanks, in the Yucatán, where a bilingual policy was pursued, the creation of a written language through the translation of the Bible involved a suppression of alternative meanings that eventually resulted in a decisive shift of the conceptual terrain through which the Maya operated. William Hanks, "From Doctrine to Discourse in Colonial Yucatán," paper presented at Indiana University, October 28, 1996.

9  As the anthropologist Greg Urban has shown, "Over time strategic manipulations of linguistic relationships can pull language and culture apart." Greg Urban, "The Semiotics of State-Indian Relationships: Peru, Paraguay and Brazil," in Urban and Sherzer, eds., *Nation-States and Indians in Latin America*, 327. Urban's argument is far more nuanced than this brief quotation. He argues against the major tendency to "put language and culture together, that is to interpret the linguistic code as an index of one culture and of one people."

10  Jaime Wheelock, *Raices indígenas de las luchas anticolonialistas* (Managua: Editorial Nueva Nicaragua, 1981), 117.

11  CIERA-MIDINRA, por eso defendemos la frontera: historia agraria de las Segovias Occidentales (Managua: MIDINRA, 1984), 107.

12  José Coronel Urtecho, *Reflexiones sobre la historia de Nicaragua*, 3 vols. (León: Editorial Hospicio, 1962), 1:125.

13  Pablo Antonio Cuadra, *La aventura literaria del mestizaje* (San José: Editorial Libro Libre, Costa Rica, 1988), 38.

14  Jorge Eduardo Arellano, *El güegüence o macho ratón* (Managua, 1984), 36.

15  See Germán Romero Vargas, *Las estructuras sociales de Nicaragua en el siglo XVIII* (Managua: Editorial Vanguardia, 1988). Basing his observations more on the indis-

putable rise of the mestizos and the proportional decline of the indigenous population during the colonial period, Romero has lent his considerable (and well-
earned) prestige to pushing the notion that by the end of the nineteenth century,
indigenous communities had ceased to function or have any significance. See
*Apuntes sobre la historia de Nicaragua* (Managua, 1980).

16  Coronel Urtecho, *Reflexiones,* 126. On primordialist assumptions about ethnicity,
see John Comaroff, "Of Totemism and Ethnicity: Consciousness, Practice, and the
Signs of Inequality," *Ethnos* 52, nos. 3–4 (1987): 301–323. More research is needed on
the development of the Hispano Nahuatl dialect.

17  See, for example, E. G. Squier, *Nicaragua: Its People, Scenery and Movements* (New
York, 1860), 261–279; Carl Scherzer, *Travels in the Free States of Central America:
Nicaragua, Honduras and El Salvador,* 2 vols. (London: Longman, 1857), vol. 1;
George Byam, *Wildlife in the Interior of Central America* (London, 1849); and
Bedford Pim, *Dottings on the Roadside in Panama, Nicaragua, and Mosquito* (Lon-
don, 1869). Richard N. Adams, in his *Cultural Surveys of Panama, Nicaragua,
Guatemala, El Salvador, and Honduras* (Washington, 1957), 250, makes a similar
point.

18  Frederick Boyle, *A Ride Across a Continent: A Personal Narrative of Wanderings
through Nicaragua and Costa Rica* (London: Bentley, 1868), 9.

19  Scherzer, *Travels,* 1:60–61.

20  On myths in history see Emilia Viotti da Costa, *The Brazilian Empire: Myths and
Histories* (Chicago: University of Chicago Press, 1985).

21  My own use of symbolic and real violence is inspired by the work of Pierre
Bourdieu. He defines "symbolic violence" as "the violence which is exercised upon
a social agent with his or her complicity." Pierre Bourdieu and Loic J. D. Wacquant,
*An Invitation to Reflexive Sociology* (Chicago: University of Chicago Press, 1992),
167. Rather than incorporate his overall theoretical perspective into this book, I am
more interested in studying how physical violence creates the conditions for the
long-term exercise of symbolic forms.

22  Jeffrey Gould, Charles R. Hale, and Carol A. Smith, "Memories of Mestizaje:
Cultural Politics in Central America since 1920," unpublished manuscript, 1994.

23  See the late E. B. Burns' study, *Patriarch and Folk: The Emergence of Nicaragua,
1795–1858* (Cambridge: Harvard University Press, 1991). Though not a community
study, the book sheds valuable light on Indian-ladino relations.

24  Carl Scherzer, *Travels,* 1:217.

25  Indeed the linguist Walter Lehmann strongly resented the dominant ladino notion that his work amongst the Indians was meaningless. "If I had relied on so-
called educated people I would not have succeeded with language research. . . .
Only with pure Indians did I find cooperation and understanding without being
bothered by stupid questions like: 'Digame una cosa, porque quiere ud. saber todo
esto?' " He found the ladino Nicaraguans particularly symptomatic of the "total

unjust arrogance of the Central Americans toward the Indians." Lehmann, *Zentral Amerika*, 968.

26  Michel-Rolph Trouillot, *Silencing the Past: Power and the Production of History* (Boston: Beacon, 1995), 106.

27  "Hegemony . . . exists in reciprocal interdependence with ideology; it is that part of a dominant world-view which has been naturalized and, having hidden itself in orthodoxy, no more appears as ideology at all." Jean and John Comaroff, *Of Revelation and Revolution: Christianity, Colonialism, and Consciousness in South Africa* (Chicago: University of Chicago Press, 1991), 25. Bourdieu uses "doxa" in various ways but all related to "an uncontested acceptance of the daily lifeworld." Bourdieu and Wacquant, *An Invitation to Reflexive Sociology*, 73.

28  William Roseberry, "The Language of Contention," in Gilbert Joseph and Daniel Nugent, eds., *Everyday Forms of State Formation: Revolution and the Negotiation of Rule in Modern Mexico* (Durham, N.C.: Duke University Press, 1994), 360–361.

29  Kay Warren, "Transforming Memories and Histories: The Meanings of Ethnic Resurgence for Mayan Indians," in Alfred Stepan, ed., *Americas: New Interpretive Essays* (New York: Oxford University Press, 1992), 205.

30  Ibid.

31  Jorge Klor de Alva has pointed out the difficulty in situating the Latin American mestizo experience as postcolonial. Indeed, we share his analysis of mestizaje as an integral part of nationalist discourse that promotes national amnesia. On subalternity and neocolonialism see Fernando Coronil, "Listening to the Subaltern: The Poetics of Neocolonial States," *Poetics Today* 15, no. 4 (Winter 1994): 643–658 (special issue edited by Walter Mignolo). Also see Partha Chatterjee, *The Nation and Its Fragments: Colonial and Postcolonial Histories* (Princeton: Princeton University Press, 1993). I would like to thank Peter Guardino for pointing out the discursive uses of colonialism by the Sandinistas.

32  On the erasure of community in nationalist discourse, see Chatterjee, *The Nation and Its Fragments*.

33  One of the methodological limitations of this study is a failure to engage in contemporary theories of race and racism. In part, this limitation is due to my refusal to accept the scientific legitimacy of the concept of "race." I thus failed to recognize the necessity of grounding racism in a discussion of "race" as a social construct whose cultural dominance is too important not to historicize. Since writing the text, I have become aware of three studies that would have enriched my discussion by pointing the way toward a theoretical engagement with race that does not accept the scientific validity of its premises: Peter Wade, *Blackness and Race Mixture: The Dynamics of Racial Identity in Colombia* (Baltimore: Johns Hopkins Press, 1993); Charles R. Hale, "El discurso del racismo al revés en Guatemala," in C. Arenas, C. Hale, and G. Palma, eds., *Racismo e identidades en Guatemala* (Guatemala City: Avancso, 1997); and Michel Wieviorka, *The Arena of Racism* (London: Sage, 1995).

Without granting scientific status to "race" these scholars nonetheless demonstrate how crucial it is to study how race is used by social groups as an organizing principle. In this sense, the subjective dimension of "mestizaje," on the one hand, and the Indian's self-descriptive *raza,* on the other, need much further study and contextualization.

34  *Boletín de Estadística de la República de Nicaragua* (Managua), June 1907.

35  Romero Vargas, *Las estructuras sociales de Nicaragua,* 300; Linda Newson, *Indian Survival in Colonial Nicaragua* (Norman, Oklahoma, 1987), 323.

36  Squier, *Nicaragua,* 33; Pablo Levy, *Notas geográficas y económicas sobre la República de Nicaragua* (Paris, 1873), 240; "Handbook of Nicaragua," Bulletin 51, *Bulletin of the American Republics* (Washington, D.C., 1892), 8. It is extremely unlikely that a census figure would replicate exactly an earlier population estimate.

37  Gustavo Niederlin, *The State of Nicaragua in the Greater Republic of Central America* (Philadelphia: Philadelphia Commercial Museum, 1898), 45. Neiderlin copied his statistics directly from reports of vital statistics compiled by the Ministerio de Gobernación. I have studied the births and deaths recorded in Boaco and Camoapa for those years and if anything, Neiderlin and Gobernación underestimate the indigenous population.

38  The U.S. State Department, in 1911, estimated on the basis of the 1906 census that there were 170,000 Nicaraguan Indians out of a total population of 520,000 (27 percent—both figures include 20,000 indios bravos). Wands to secretary of state, May 3, 1911, U.S. National Archives, RG 59, 817.51/31, p. 52; See Niederlein, *The State of Nicaragua,* 45. Using vital statistics from the mid-1890s, he cited Indian births as slightly over 30 percent and Indian deaths as 35 percent of the total (not including Atlantic coast and indios bravos). The 1920 census, Oficina Central del Censo, *Censo general de la República* (Managua: Tipografía y Encuadernación Nacional, 1920), reports under 4 percent *cobrizos* ("copper colored") in the country and 2 percent excluding the Atlantic Coast.

39  On the number of indios bravos, see Wands to secretary of state and W. H. Koebel, *Central America: Guatemala, Nicaragua, Costa Rica, Honduras, Panama and Salvador* (London: T. F. Unwin, 1917).

40  See Richard N. Adams, "Ethnic Images and Strategies in 1944," in Carol Smith, ed., *Guatemalan Indians and the State* (Austin: University of Texas Press, 1990), 152.

41  Fourteen communities were still functioning in 1942. See report by Leonardo Argüello, ministro de gobernación, in *Memorias del Ministerio de Gobernación, 1942* (Managua, 1943), 90.

42  The government decreed the abolition of the Comunidades in 1877, 1881, 1895, 1906, and 1918. See *Nicaragua Indígena* 1, nos. 4–6 (April–December 1947), 3–20. In 1919 and 1923 abolition legislation was blocked.

43  Similarly, the "cobrizos" in the departments of Chontales and Matagalpa accounted for only 15 instead of 60 percent of the population. If we include the Atlantic Coast, and the unrecorded estimates of "indios bravos" in the Central

Highlands, the indigenous proportion of the total Nicaraguan population was between 20 and 25 percent. For a more detailed explanation of my estimates for 1920 and 1950, see the appendices of my *El mito de Nicaragua mestiza y la resistencia indígena* (San José: Editorial de la Universidad de Costa Rica, 1997).

44 Benedict Anderson, *Imagined Communities: Reflections on the Origin and Spread of Nationalism* (London: Verso, 1994), 204.

# 1

## "¡Vana Ilusión!": The Highlands Indians
## and the Myth of Nicaragua Mestiza, 1880–1925

An Indian girl of 18 years old came to tell us all about the suffering her people
[the Guatusos of Río San Juan] endured and that many people treated them
badly, they treated them like monkeys, like wild animals; more than half of
her people had died from these treatments. . . . The Indian girl came with a
child, crying, and she told the Bishop how she had been sold to a woman for
forty pesos.
—Bishop Bernardo Thiel (Costa Rica), reporting on his observations of the
slavery of Guatuso Indians in San Carlos, Nicaragua, 1882

In order to help the indigenous caste emerge from the state it is immersed
in . . . it is vital to provide this race with some kind of industry to whom they
could provide 20,000 to 30,000 workers and learn to love to labor and to live
in settlements.
—Gregorio Cuadra, *jefe político* (departmental governor), Matagalpa, 1880

It is notable that around here there are a multitude of people who live
dispersed and isolated and mostly without work, without any known means
of subsistence, without hope and without a future. It is thus very necessary
to apply the law so that they must move to settlements.
—William Reuling, jefe político, Matagalpa, 1897

In the disgraced Matagalpa that hosted organized fanaticism [there oc-
curred] a caste rebellion against civilization; thirsty for blood they attempted to exterminate civilized people.—Editorial in *El Ferrocarril,* 1882

I'm 70 years old and I'm going to live another 50 years so I can go on making
revolutions.—Toribio Mendoza, Indian rebel leader, 1884

Following Mass on August 4, 1881, most of the congregation walked over
to attend the inaugural ceremonies of the new telegraph office. The telegraph

26

would connect Matagalpa, a mountain settlement of 3,000, with Managua, 140 kilometers to the southwest. After several speeches lauding the government, town, and progress, the two telegraph operators tapped out their message and awaited the response. None came. One of the operators, Alejandro Miranda, shook off his shame and disappointment and set off on horseback to the valley town of Metapa to see where the problem lay. Because Metapa still had communication with Managua, Miranda rode back up to Matagalpa following the line. After riding for seven hours he found the problem—six posts had been torn down and the lines cut. As he stared at the damage an old man approached and informed him that the Indians, as they had on March 30, once again were laying siege to Matagalpa. The old man told him: "It's that piece-of-shit telegraph, they screw those poor folks and make them work for nothing, and what's more, they ran off the Jesuits and prohibit them from making *chicha*" [a corn- and sugar-based alcoholic drink].[1]

Miranda was worried, but not entirely surprised. A few days earlier a band of 200 Indians had attacked the village of Esquipulas, thirty kilometers south of Matagalpa, and a week earlier an Indian band had defeated a military patrol in the cañada of Yúcul. Many families had left Matagalpa in fear of an invasion, but others thought that they would be safe in town.[2] As he arrived at the outskirts of the city, Miranda could hear the shouts of the Indians in praise of their chief and in condemnation of the government: "¡Viva Lorenzo Pérez, Muera la Gobierna!"[3]

On the afternoon of August 8, the townsfolk looked up to the mountains and could make out the Indian positions. The women and children were rushed to the *cabildo* (town hall) and to the priest's house and a few people snuck out of town to try to reach Metapa to wire for reinforcements.

At seven-thirty the next morning the skies darkened with *tafistes* (spearlike arrows) as two groups of several hundred Indians each came down from the hills and occupied positions in the city's abandoned south side. From their base in the Laborío church, throughout the day, some 3,000 to 7,000 Indians advanced through the town. The 170 soldiers and volunteers defending the town counted only a good defensive position and rifles (repeating and single-loading) in their favor, but they enjoyed the superiority in weapons (the Indians had hunting rifles and shotguns with the women carrying the gunpowder) for only a brief two hours. The garrison's commander, Captain Villalta, ordered firing to cease when ammunition ran low.

All night long, the ladinos peered out to see the glow of *ocote* (a type of pine) torches throughout the rest of the town. From across enemy lines, the Indians howled (like hungry wolves in the words of a government soldier) threats against the ladinos: "Tomorrow we will see those ladinos, we will see what happens to them."[4] Captain Villalta began to lose hope. Embittered he exclaimed: "By tomorrow we will all be dead because of that son-of-a-bitch telegraph."[5]

The next morning the Indians attacked again. Shortly after noon, as the rebels prepared another attack and the townsfolk were about to use up the last of their ammunition, reinforcements miraculously appeared on the horizon. "We saw the troops from Managua approaching from the Laborío side of town. We were overcome with relief and everyone shouted 'Viva el Gobierno!' and the shooting began with renewed vigor."[6] The eighty troops from Managua led by Captain Inocente Moreira, armed with a canon and repeating rifles, battled for three hours, claiming the city street by street. The Indian forces were not only taken by surprise; they were tricked by Captain Moreira into believing that the troops came from León to support them. In a letter captured by government forces, the Indian leader Lorenzo Pérez explained to an ally,

> The sad part was the betrayal when 200 Managuas loaded with ammunition and a cannon came in and passed our outpost by the León entrance. So our troops started firing and then one of their officers told our leaders that we shouldn't shoot at them because they had come to fight on the side of the nation and that they believed them because they saw that half of them had white emblems on their clothes, and that's the way that they let them advance. It was that military plan of betrayal that allowed them to give us that terrible blow, so that in one hour they killed one hundred and fifty of our soldiers.[7]

The cannon ripped apart the Indian positions. Of thirty Indians holed up in one house, cannon balls killed twenty-two. By nightfall, the Indian forces retreated into the mountains leaving behind 400 to 500 dead. Fewer than thirty ladinos died in the fighting. Within days 500 well-armed government troops arrived in Matagalpa and fanned out into the mountains in search of the rebels.

President Zavala participated in strategy planning and followed the troop movements closely. In a letter to the commander of military operations, he scolded him for not carrying out his orders to destroy all homes and crops:

> In the report that you gave me regarding the expedition in Yúcul, I did not see that you had destroyed huts or cultivated lands. It is necessary that you look after this matter because only in this way will we be able to obligate the Indians to surrender unconditionally.[8]

Government troops killed hundreds of Indians during the several months of this scorched-earth campaign. By February of 1882 the troops had caught most of the Indian leaders and had executed many. Some thirty years later the memory of the insurrection was still fresh in the minds of the Indian survivors. A German Nicaraguan son of a coffee planter recounted how plantation workers who had fought in the rebellion enjoyed reminiscing:

> We had encircled them in Matagalpa, and not even an armadillo could get through there, and we were advancing toward the center of the town . . . but when the ladinos got there with the cannon, they wiped us out. Yeah, that cannon was awful, it killed us off like flies.[9]

Thus, the last major Indian uprising in western Nicaragua ended in disaster and defeat. Matagalpino intellectual Carlos Arroyo Buitrago, reflecting in 1954 on the event, was moved to write, "The truth is that the uprising of the Matagalpino indios in 1881 was the death sentence for this race."[10]

This chapter will examine some of the causes of the rebellion and of the tenaciousness of indigenous resistance; we will concentrate on how ladino elites came to view and act upon "the Indian problem" following the uprising. Moreover, we will attempt to reconstruct how those views and policies, in short the emerging discourse of Nicaragua mestiza, affected the lives of the Matagalpino Indians. If the defeat was indeed "the death sentence for the race," under what conditions was it carried out and how did the condemned endure the constant stays of execution?

## The Formation of the Matagalpino Indians

Migrations and ethnic fusions over the previous 100 years created the Matagalpino Indians—estimated at between 25,000 and 60,000—who rebelled

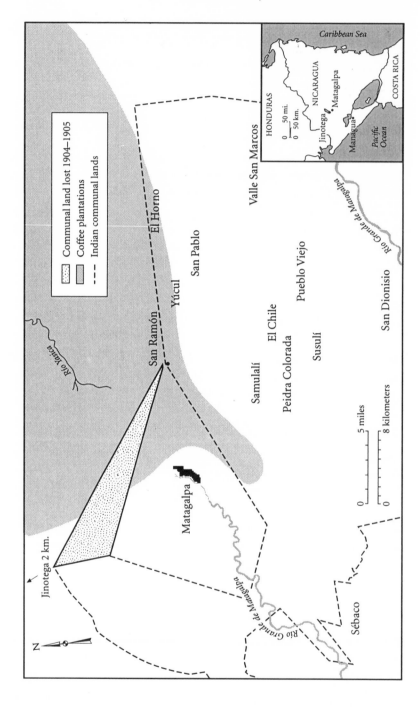

in 1881.[11] During the early eighteenth century three *parcialidades* (lineage groups, also called "barrios"), residents of the pueblos of Matagalpa, Molagüina, and Solingalpa, united for the purposes of purchasing a large tract of communal land. Between 1750 and 1820 these lineage-based, dispersed settlements apparently disbanded and the people moved into nearby mountains.[12] Excessive colonial tribute demands and ladino migration contributed to this slow disintegration of the settlements. In the mountains, the three parcialidades formed cañadas or joined preexisting ones.

During the eighteenth century the Matagalpino Indians also experienced the birth of a new parcialidad, Laborío, composed of converted and resettled "Caribe" (a branch of the Sumo) Indians. These Caribes had been hostile to Spanish rule and had often raided the "pacified" Indians of the highlands. By 1816, Laborío, augmented by a flow of "reduced" Caribes, formed the largest parcialidad among the Matagalpino Indians.[13] Moreover, it continued to grow at a faster rate than the other groups over the next decades; by 1841, Laborío accounted for 43 percent of all Indian births.[14] The rapid growth of Laborío suggests a continuous process of integration of "Caribes" and a quite fluid boundary between the "civilized" and the "wild" Indians. Their acceptance of escaped "civilized" Indians into their ranks prompted one Spanish official to explain the rebellious character of the highlands peoples by the "facility with which they pass over into the *Bárbaros*."[15]

Throughout the nineteenth century the four parcialidades continued to maintain a vital existence, although their members no longer inhabited specific geographical areas. Two neighbors of the cañada of Samulalí, for example, might belong to different parcialidades, but they would all cooperate within the same local political structure led by a *capitán de cañada* (the low-level official in charge of the cañada). The military structure of the Matagalpinos, shared by the Indians of Boaco and Jinotega, was a legacy of the colonial period in which the Spanish relied on them to fight against the English allies: the Miskitos, Zambos, and Sumos. At the same time, the neighbors would belong to different civil-religious hierarchies led by *alcaldes de vara* corresponding to their respective parcialidades. The religious function of lineage groups united parcialidad members in different cañadas and thus perpetuated a basic unit of ethnic identity despite the scattering of the original populations. The elders of each lineage group appointed helpers, *regidores, priostes,* and *mayordomos* for each of the seven saints. The four *alcaldes de vara* also comprised the political directorate of the entire Comunidad.

The slow growth of the ladino population in the city of Matagalpa—ladinos made up 20 percent of the department's population in 1880—had a significant impact on the economy of the highlands Indians well before the introduction of coffee. One writer, recalling a visit in the mid-1850s, offered a description of the Indians' economy, commenting that they used the many rivers and streams to power "the simple machines . . . that milled the large quantities of wheat to make flour, grown in abundance [and to bake bread]. The agriculture of Matagalpa was impressive: sugarcane, rice, beans, potatoes, garlic, onions."[16]

Market relations between the Indians and ladinos were not harmonious, however. During the 1860s townsfolk would travel several miles to meet Indian traders, indicative of the strained ethnic relations. At one point, the Indians, in effect, went "on strike," refusing to sell any produce to the ladinos, "being dissatisfied with the shabby way in which the townspeople had behaved."[17] A reinforced military garrison eventually persuaded the Matagalpinos to resume trade.

The missionary work of the Jesuits from 1871 to 1881 also played an important role in stimulating the ethnic pride and unity of those Indians who rebelled in 1881. The Jesuits' willingness to go out and minister to the Indians in their cañadas contrasted notably with other ladino political and ecclesiastical authorities.[18] Moreover, the Jesuits' aura of grace and mystery appealed directly to the Indians' religiosity; they did not attack the beliefs of these people whose only previous exposure to Christianity was at baptism. In 1877, one missionary wrote about 696 people who confessed for the first time in one village:

> And the most marvelous part of it was that as soon as I spoke to them and repeated [the gospel], they lost their fear, and they became adept at repeating it . . . then they brought the rest of their families and ended up becoming extremely affectionate. . . . From Samulalí only three people did not take part in confession.[19]

Moreover, the Jesuits' antidemocratic convictions—a disdain for the progressive Conservative government and for parliamentary democracy—in no way impeded their evangelical efforts among society's most marginalized groups. Whatever their intentions, the Jesuits contributed to the ethnic unity of the Matagalpinos.

Evidence demonstrates the overwhelming success of the Jesuits among the country's indigenous population. First, the Matagalpino Indians provided voluntary labor (all accounts agree on this) throughout the 1870s for the construction of the cathedral. Second, upon the expulsion of the Jesuits, the Indians of Sutiaba and Monimbó rioted in protest. Finally, indigenous prisoners in 1881 cited the defense of religion as the principal cause for the August uprising.[20] As indicated by Bishop Thiel's remarks at the beginning of this chapter, Indian slavery was still practiced, albeit in a limited and informal way, in Nicaragua. The Jesuits offered an antidote to such a venomous level of racism.

### The Roots of Rebellion in Matagalpa

On the morning of March 30, 1881, some 1,000 Indians attacked the town of Matagalpa; their principal military objective was to storm the barracks. For two and a half hours they shot arrows, hurled stones, and fired some shotguns. Then they retreated, leaving behind twenty-five dead and five prisoners. Three soldiers died in the fighting.[21] The rebellion was not, as Jaime Wheelock and others have argued, directly related to coffee cultivation. In 1880, there were only 18,000 coffee trees in production.[22] Although there had been some complaints and petitions about land over the previous decade, agrarian capitalism contributed to the rebellion chiefly in the form of a rumor that circulated through the Indian villages: "the government wanted to sell their children to the yanquis and take 500 women to Managua to make them pick coffee for nothing."[23]

However, the drive to modernize infrastructure did contribute to indigenous discontent. The Jesuits' account, supported by the rebels' letters and by other observers, cited compulsory and underpaid labor for building the telegraph from Managua, roads, and the cabildos as the major cause of the armed protest. In addition to protesting conscripted labor, the Indians had other grievances: census taking for tax and military purposes and a prohibition against making chicha.[24] A letter to the Jesuit priest Cáceres underscored the Indians' resentment against the labor drafts:

We rose up because we couldn't stand that nasty whip any longer. . . .
We're not going to let any more of our people go work for nothing. . . .
Since these señores see that we are indios, they want to have a yoke
around our neck, but we just can't stand it anymore. . . . Today there is no
division between the captains, it's all the people of the casta indígena that
are resolved to take part. Today we say as the casta indígena that the
Señor Perfecto should moderate his orders because we aren't thieves to
be carried off with our hands tied behind our back.[25]

Following the attack on March 30, the rebels withdrew into the mountains,
but did not disarm. Throughout April they avoided military engagement
while negotiating by letter with the Jesuits and then directly with President
Zavala. Their principal demands were for a general pardon for the March 30
action and a promise that unpaid, forced labor would be eliminated. From the
beginning, Zavala was convinced that the Indians were manipulated by outsiders, in particular a political-personalistic group opposed to the prefect
(governor) and loosely aligned with the *iglesieros*, a pro-Jesuit, traditionalist
faction of the Conservative party. He thus offered the Indians a general pardon and promised "that they would never again be forced to work for no
wages" (implying that forced work, however, was still acceptable).[26]

Yet President Zavala was not prepared to grant a pardon either to the
*cabecillas* (leaders) or to the yet-to-be-identified outside agitators. The failure
to grant an amnesty for the leaders and Zavala's failure to impede legal proceedings against ninety Indians in Matagalpa were reasons enough for rebel
groups to stay mobilized in the countryside.

From the first news of the outbreak, Zavala decided on a strategy that
would prevent further problems. On April 14 he wrote to his minister of war:

This opportunity can be used to induce those poor peoples, by way of
their Capitanes, to establish towns, offering them in this case the help
of the government, giving to each family lands and providing them a
church with a priest, schools, and officials elected among themselves, if
they wish.[27]

Shortly before the rebellion Zavala had been presented with a report by the
prefect of Matagalpa in which he expressly called on the government to push
the Indians into towns and provide them with "an industry that teaches them

to love work."[28] Following the revolt, the prefect's proposal seemed clair-
voyant; the *reducción* policy for all the Matagalpino Indians (not just the
rebels) became an obsession with Zavala. Part of the urgency for Zavala had to
do with breaking up the Indians' military-political structure, which he believed was predicated upon dispersed settlement (the term "capitán de cañada" certainly lent credence to that belief). But whether the Indians really
lived a nomadic or even seminomadic existence is another matter. Regardless
of how much time the Indians spent hunting they had time to grow and mill
wheat and supply the city with its basic foodstuffs. Whatever the limits of
Zavala's access to local knowledge, the notion of "la reducción of the Indians into towns" was inseparable from his desire that "the military organization that they have disappear along with the danger embedded in it of new
uprisings."[29]

Zavala and others were also convinced that the Jesuits had a role in the
uprising. Although he could never find any evidence of direct involvement,
Zavala probably agreed with one of his friends who believed that the Jesuits'
"were making Matagalpa into a little Paraguay."[30] When the minister of war
discovered on his expedition that the Jesuits had established a convent, thus
contravening a Nicaraguan law of 1830, Zavala seized on the opportunity. In
late May, the government decreed the expulsion of the order, and in so doing
alleviated long-time pressures from Guatemala and from Zavala's domestic
Liberal allies.[31] The expulsion set off a wave of spontaneous riots primarily
among the Indians of Sutiaba (León) and Monimbó (Masaya) but also among
poor ladinos in those cities. The Matagalpino Indians, under heavy pressure
from the minister of war's military presence, apparently feigned acceptance of
the president's pardon and made no statement regarding the expulsion.[32]

The exile of the Jesuits did provoke deep resentment among the Indians of
Matagalpa and of the rest of the country. Moreover, members of the Iglesiero
faction of the Conservative party apparently began to organize the disparate
indigenous groups (and others) in an alliance that would lead to the overthrow of Zavala's government or at least force the return of the Jesuits. One
captured Matagalpino Indian explained that he fought because "Our chiefs
told us that we were defending our religion."[33]

The Matagalpino Indian leaders believed that they formed part of an alternative, religiously infused "nation." When the minister of war's expedition
returned to Managua, the indigenous movement began to reorganize. During

this new phase, the rebels began to broaden their language of protest to include notions of ethnic solidarity and an Indian "nation." Thus, one leader wrote to a sympathizer: "we consider and feel you to be at the side of your Indian Nation."[34] An Indian captain used the same term to describe the indigenous forces, in a note ordering a rancher to sell steers to his troops: "so that the nation can wage war against the enemy."[35] Their employment of the term *nación* was probably not a linguistic survival from the colonial-era nomenclature for tribes or groups. Rather their usage was placed in a contemporary context. For example, they authorized military mobilization through an act of the "Congreso de la Nación." At the same time, "nación" was not merely a synonym for the Indians of Matagalpa, because the usual term was, in fact, the colonial one: "casta indígena." As Lorenzo Pérez's letter quoted earlier suggested, the "nation" had very close real or imagined allies, if not members outside the ethnic boundaries of Matagalpa: "they came to fight on the side of the nation." In addition to the expected support from Sutiaban Indians and others from León, the Matagalpa counted among allies or members of this nation other Indian groups, including Caribes (Sumos), groups to the south near Boaco, and those of Masaya. At the same time, the "nation" had a nonethnic meaning, including the Jesuits and all of their supporters.

However the Indians came upon and came to use "nation," during June and July of 1881, their practice suggested a desire to invert the established order. Consider the report that fifty Indians under the command of capitán de la cañada de Matasano, Manuel Pérez: "They are becoming more audacious and their depredations against the ladinos of the nearby cañadas are getting worse, demanding contributions of money and personal services . . . [Not complying, the ladinos were . . .] 'pursued and punished.' "[36] Similarly, the Indians tied the ladino *juez del campo* (justice of the peace) of Jumaiquí to a tree and beat him one hundred times with a stick after he informed the Matagalpino authorities of their organizing efforts. He had to pay a fine of six pesos to obtain his liberty.[37] The beating and fining of the juez reflected their experiences at the hands of ladino authorities. More strikingly, the "tribute" and "personal services" demanded of ladino neighbors underlined the Indians' intention to invert the order and to create a new one, a new nation where the ladino would be the Indian's *mozo arreado* (bound and dragged peon) who must "purchase" his liberty.

Even as the Indian rebels demonstrated to the ladinos their repudiation of racist treatment and their desire for a new order, they also solidified and disciplined their own ranks. The methods were not at all democratic, ranging from fining people for selling goods in the city to assassinating two capitanes who refused to collaborate with the rebels.[38]

The wave of ethnic reaffirmation (or perhaps protonationalism) that swept the highlands communities gathered tremendous force following the expulsion of the Jesuits. Whatever disunity existed in March had disappeared in August. But the Matagalpino movement remained isolated from the national movement organized by the iglesieros, which never extended beyond the armed revolts in Sutiaba and Telica (in León). In October, the government's scorched-earth policy began to pay dividends, and by the end of the year hundreds of Indians had been killed in battle or executed and many more had fled to the east.

The defeat of the insurrection brought death, destruction, and dissension to the Indians. Indeed, the rebel movement ended in a spectacle of disunity. The military defeat exacerbated old divisions and created new ones. According to a government report, toward the end of the rebellion many Indians turned on their leaders. Similarly, some capitanes de cañada with their followers joined the government troops.[39] A government report graphically illustrated this point: "[in Managua] an escort of Indians loyal to the government, armed with arrows, [brought] into custody prisoners of their caste."[40]

Nevertheless, it would be a mistake to interpret the rebellion as the last battle cry of a dying way of life. On the contrary, the movement's protonationalistic rhetoric expressed a strong, if implicit, demand for autonomy. Military defeat did not eradicate those feelings nor those demands. In 1884 Indian rebels joined an antigovernment conspiracy in alliance with iglesieros and radical Liberals. The two factions had diametrically opposed political agendas and shared only a hatred for the moderate Conservative regime. The movement collapsed due, in part, to internal dissensions. But, in Matagalpa, the conspiracy underscored a fact that the local ladinos knew quite well: many Indians had not accepted their defeat as final.[41]

Successive regimes strove to carry out modern reducción policies without notable success.[42] What was more successful was the government's discursive casting of their repression as "a struggle of civilization against barbarism, of darkness against light, of idleness against labor."[43] This military victory over the Indians, construed as a triumph of civilization, gave birth to the myth of Nicaragua mestiza.[44]

### The Highlands Indians under the Zelaya Regime, 1893–1909

Nicaraguan historiography portrays the regime of José Santos Zelaya (1893–1909) as one that modernized the country, effectively mobilizing resources for the agro-export sector. Scholars disagree about whether such economic growth was "capitalistic" or not, given the extensive use of extraeconomic labor coercion.[45] Clearly, however, the regime did foster the expropriation of land and the coercion of Indian labor, although in this regard Zelaya did little more than intensify the policies of his Conservative predecessors.

What the historiography has overlooked is the regime's flexibility in confronting diverse forms of indigenous resistance. The Indian rebellion of 1881 compelled the state to devise methods to contain the Indians' military potential. It also delayed the development of the coffee industry by a decade.[46] In 1890, however, the government sold Americans, Germans, and Nicaraguans more than 13,000 acres of land, which the buyers soon planted with more than 1.2 million coffee bushes. The *cafetaleros* attempted to create a permanent labor force of Indian colonos to clear, plant, tend, and harvest their plantations. The Indians, however, were fairly successful in resisting the imposition of this new labor regime through escape and occasional violence. In 1895, for example, of 196 workers obliged to pay off debts or finish contracts with nine planters, 92 had escaped.[47]

The Matagalpino Indians also directly resisted church efforts to transform their religious practices during this period. In 1891, for example, the Indian alcaldes wrote to the church authorities asking them to replace the local priest. They claimed that the priest had hidden two of their sacred images and had told them "the Virgin is a mask of an old face." Underscoring the cultural difference between the Indian and church authorities, they declared that the priest was "very tyrannical with our way of being."[48] The ecclesiastical authorities responded favorably to the alcaldes' petition and removed the priest from Matagalpa.

Toward the end of the nineteenth century, however, church policy shifted away from its tolerance of indigenous control over sacred images; in the 1890s, the church launched an attack on Indian religious practices.[49] Several factors influenced this change from a protective role to a global effort to undermine ethnic culture. Faced with economic retrenchment under Zelaya, the church needed to collect the fees it charged for the masses and processions associated with the sacred images. Moreover, triumphant Liberalism probably provoked the church into tightening its ideological control over its flock; the clergy needed to mobilize its forces for the struggle against the Zelaya regime.

In 1893, immediately following the triumph of the Liberal revolution, the new priest, Alfonso Martínez, ordered a Matagalpino cofradía to deliver four steers to finance the anti-Zelayista "Unión Católica." The Indians refused and despite the priest's threats, remained intransigent. The priest lamented, "they still think they run the cofradías. You know how the Indians are incapable of deliberating on anything but small matters."[50] Indigenous cultural resistance evidently wore some holes in the church's traditional habit of paternalism.

The Indians' rupture with the church reached dramatic proportions on August 1, 1895, when the government newspaper reported the following: "A few days ago the Indians who live in the cañadas . . . created a movement due to the most absurd spells cast by a few fanatics; recently they have risen in rebellion in several places near the departmental capital."[51] The following day, after announcing the end of the movement, the paper published the Indians' letter to the church, written before the brief rebellion. The letter recounted twelve apparitions they claimed to have seen since April of that year, declaring that these were figures of the Twelve Apostles. The Indians asserted that the church authorities did not understand these miracles and were

> threatening to burn us because they say that we have become witches. . . . [The apostles appeared] because we had abandoned the Devotions to the Sacred Heart. God has wished to use his forgiveness by having the apostles come down to this earth to give us the Examples and show us that if we do not mend our ways we will be punished with Divine justice. . . . [The authorities] are trying to intimidate us. . . . They locked up the Indian Alcaldes.[52]

The letter also included a request that the church send a priest whom the Indians knew and trusted and "any Jesuit" to aid them.

The letter states that the apostles appeared in the villages to purify the

Indians. This belief and the accompanying movement should be understood in the context of five years of violent changes: thousands of lost acres of communal land, forced labor, internal economic and political divisions, and a conflict with the church over ownership of their cofradías and possession of sacred images including representations of the apostles. The movement both responded to and fomented ethnic strife: the apostles "appeared" so that the Indians would rectify their own ways. But the ladino authorities were aborting this purification process, violently disobeying the apostles' message.

The Indians' re-creation of the religious symbols—especially the inclusion of women among the Twelve Apostles—also suggests a relatively autonomous and complex belief system. The ladino authorities did not, of course, view the apparitions with much ethnographic curiosity. For the regime, the movement revealed "a social sore that it is necessary to heal as soon as possible . . . an evil to be eradicated at its roots."[53]

Although the Zelaya regime made some attempts to heal the social "sore" through education, its principal cure involved strong doses of repression.[54] General William Reuling, the jefe político of Matagalpa from 1897 to 1898, not only used ample coercion to compel Indians to labor on plantations but also collected tribute in the form of "food contributions."[55] To carry out these policies, Reuling relied on the army and on the capitanes de cañada. A treaty (perhaps informal) between the victorious government and the Indian leaders who survived the rebellion of 1881 aided Reuling's efforts to manipulate the capitanes. A key proviso established that although the capitanes would be elected by the Indians and would be responsible for defending Indian communities, the state reserved the power to ratify their election and to exert authority over them.[56] More prosaically, Reuling jailed capitanes who disobeyed his commands, often burning their huts for emphasis.

Reuling had the support of the military, but the extent to which Zelaya approved of his activities is not clear. For example, the regime did not respond to Reuling's call for the resettlement of the Indians near the coffee plantations (echoing Zavala's 1881 proposal).[57] The central government, however, was surely aware of Reuling's colonial-style policies and his military pressure on the villagers. Indeed, it was the threat of another Indian rebellion in March 1898 that forced Zelaya to remove Reuling from his post.

The Matagalpino Indians resisted Reuling even though they had to confront their own capitanes. *El Comercio* reported in March 1898 that the jefe político "had given such scandalous orders to the capitanes that every day a murder took place in the cañadas."[58] Several days later the same paper reported that the townsfolk feared for their lives: "The Indians conspire and are planning to attack the city." The attack never materialized, but the Indians achieved their objective: the replacement of Reuling as jefe político and the end of "the forced contributions of goods."[59]

Reuling left his stamp on the political culture of the highlands. He wreaked havoc in the cañadas, sowing bitter divisions between those who obeyed and those who resisted his brutal reign. Moreover, despite the key role played by indigenous resistance in toppling Reuling, the Matagalpinos' reliance on Zelaya legitimated the regime's power over the comunidades.[60] The regime formalized its control in 1904, when it approved the statutes of the Comunidad Indígena of Matagalpa. It was surely no coincidence that Zelaya chose to legitimate the Comunidad the same year he sanctioned a survey of communal lands, which the Indians had demanded. When the alcaldes bitterly protested the surveyor's methods, the official response was to approve the settlements that eliminated the alcaldes' temporal authority.[61] Before 1904 the four alcaldes, elected by La Reforma (the Council of Elders), had formed the political directorate of the Comunidad Indígena. The statutes, however, mandated the election of a directorate that had no connection either to the communal religious structure or to the parcialidades. Although the alcaldes continued to exercise a religious role as well as informal political authority, their removal from the state-sanctioned political leadership eventually led to the secularization of communal authority.

Although the Zelaya era was a trying one for the Matagalpino Indians, at times the Liberal government responded favorably to indigenous pressure, as it had in the Reuling case. For instance, the government chose to loosen its repressive grip on rural labor. In 1903, part of the indigenous population of Chontales backed an abortive Conservative rebellion. During the uprising, the government sought to appease the Indians by abolishing forced labor in that area. The same year, at least partially in response to petitions from highlands Indians, the Congress voted 26 to 1 to abolish the *boleta de ocupación*, a work pass that all adults with a capital of less than 500 pesos had to carry. The boleta system in effect obliged the majority of rural inhabitants, including small landholders, to work for an employer.[62] The legislators defied Zelaya by overriding his veto, thus revealing serious cracks in the Liberal party. Many congressmen seemed to have tired of seeing their region's workers shipped off to work for the Managua cafetaleros, and others probably chafed at seeing artisans treated like peons. Their formal opposition to the boleta, however, was based on the principles of the Liberal revolution of 1893. As one congressman stated, "the system kept the worker tied to the boss's hitching post."[63]

In 1904, compromise legislation once again encouraged coercive labor relations by outlawing vagrancy, requiring a passbook, and sentencing workers to fifteen days of public works for breaking a contract. Nevertheless, the new labor code was less coercive than earlier ones and it prohibited *mandamiento* (labor draft) style practices. Similarly, the 1905 Constitution outlawed imprisonment for debt. This loosening of the system, it seems, stimulated high levels of labor disobedience, despite a police presence on the haciendas and in the cañadas.[64] In 1908, the Matagalpino coffee planters' organization complained to Zelaya that the 1904 legislation had "led to immorality and disorder . . . today the workers, whether they owe or not, do not want to go to work, not even those who have debts."[65]

The government also responded positively to Indian demands when it halted land evictions in Boaco and Jinotega. As we will see in the next chapter, in 1893 the Indians of Boaco had played an important role in the revolutionary events and had seized upon the political conflict to militarily confront the local ladino population.[66] In 1904, following political unrest, the government sent a commissioner to resolve land conflicts between the Indians and the ladino-controlled municipal government. The commissioner urged the regime to block evictions caused by the municipal government's rental of formerly indigenous lands.[67]

In 1906, after two years of relative political tranquility, the Zelaya regime fulfilled a decade-old promise by decreeing the abolition of the Comunidades Indígenas. Following a venerable Latin American Liberal formula, the law called for the distribution of one-half of the communal land to individual Indian families and the sale of the remainder to ladinos, using the profit for indigenous education. Despite indigenous resistance, the surveyors began their work in 1908, and as a consequence most of the highlands Indians lost additional land to ladinos.[68]

The abolition of the Comunidades was the culmination of the prolonged attack on the highlands Indians that followed the defeat of the rebellion of

1881 and gathered strength with the development of the coffee industry in the 1890s. This said, it must be added that the common assumption that coffee growers expropriated most of the communal lands in the highlands is simply not borne out by an examination of available data. Coffee growers did appropriate some 50,000 acres of Indian territory in Matagalpa from 1890 to 1910.[69] Indeed, some of the area's leading coffee plantations sit on former communal plots sold as *terreno nacional* (national land) during the Zelaya era. Yet when Zelaya fell in 1909, the Comunidad of Matagalpa was still functioning with 5,000 to 7,000 families possessing more than 135,000 acres of land.[70]

The coffee industry eventually stratified Indian society more than proletarianized it. The Matagalpino Indians controlled a large proportion of coffee land at least until the 1930s. Since the dawn of the industry, kin groups had planted coffee as a cash crop on their communal land. Although the elites insisted that they needed to privatize the Comunidades to develop export agriculture, often they expropriated not subsistence farmers but small coffee producers. It should also be stressed that some of the expropriators were themselves Indians. The coffee industry and the Liberal revolution did not destroy the Comunidad Indígena, but they did weaken its economic base and divide indigenous society in ways that could not be reversed. In the end, the Comunidades of Matagalpa and Boaco wreaked revenge on the regime; they joined en masse the anti-Zelayista counterrevolution.[71]

## The Indian-Conservative Alliance, 1911–1924

Zelaya's policies toward the Indians aimed to put into practice what his Conservative predecessors had already codified in laws. From 1880 to 1910, bipartisan elite policy had favored the formula holding that privatization of communal lands plus education equals civilization. The post-Zelaya Conservative regime substantially modified that program. The most important change came in 1914, when the Congress reversed Zelaya's abolition of the Comunidades Indígenas. Legalization of the communal lands and organizations proved vital to the survival of many Indian groups.[72]

The policy shift probably had less to do with ideological differences between Liberal and Conservative elites than with a pragmatic recognition by the new, U.S.-supported regime that it needed indigenous support. The anti-Zelayista revolution had already manifested the importance of that support.

Similarly, the Conservative caudillo Emiliano Chamorro—and in this he sharply delineated himself from the Liberals and indeed most Conservatives— had cultivated long-standing political and family ties with the Matagalpino and Boaqueño Indians. Chamorro's political skills and the legalization of the Comunidades solidified indigenous support for his party. Finally, the Conservatives used the legislation as a political entrée into Comunidades in historically Liberal areas such as León and Jinotega.

The change produced immediate consequences in Matagalpa. Although the alcaldes had lost their legal status under Zelaya, they had continued to play an important political role. Nevertheless, their undefined status had become a source of internal conflict and outside political manipulation. In March 1912, La Reforma withdrew recognition from the alcaldes and staged new elections, arguing "without carrying out a legal election these people appear as alcaldes since the Jefe Político installed them in office without knowing by whose authority."[73] The elders suggested that the jefe político, through ignorance or design, had intervened in Comunidad affairs, arbitrarily naming three of the four alcaldes. Moreover, they said, he had refused to recognize the authority of the capitanes de cañada. Whatever the jefe político's motives, and Conservative factionalism was surely one, the problem was exacerbated when the three ousted alcaldes refused to recognize the winners of the new elections, thereby throwing the Comunidad into turmoil.

In May 1912, as the Liberals unleashed a revolutionary insurrection in León, the government sent a commissioner, J. Bárcenas Meneses, to resolve the problems of the Comunidad. Prompted by Bartolomé Martínez, a local Chamorrista leader who was convinced that the alcaldes were Liberals, Bárcenas wrote a report urging the government to call new elections, which he was sure would result in a Conservative victory.[74] More significant, he argued for a reformulation of the Comunidad statutes that would legitimate the alcaldes, the capitán-general (the chief indigenous official in charge of the department), and other traditional authorities. He stated: "[they] play such an important role that I believe it to be extremely useful, indeed, indispensable, to include them in the statutes."[75]

The capitanes, perhaps for military reasons, did receive government recognition, but the alcaldes never did regain the political and cultural prominence that the position had commanded before 1904.[76] As a direct consequence, the barrio began to lose its importance. Over the next forty years, as the alcaldes were reduced to ceremonial roles, the parcialidades lost their function as endogamous kinship units and as the principal site of religious practice.

Bárcenas, who shared with Emiliano Chamorro an understanding of the Indians' importance to the Conservative party, sought to protect not only the alcaldes' role but also the Comunidad's land. He attacked the usurpers, pointing an angry finger at one Antonio Belli, whose "atrocious survey" in 1904 had purposefully left out the communal lands to the north of Matagalpa. From Bárcenas's report and the land title, it appears that Belli's survey had converted perhaps 29,000 of 170,000 acres of communal land into national land that was sold to coffee growers. To counteract these effects Bárcenas urged measures that would impede ladino settlement on communal lands.[77] The commissioner's recommendations were never fully enacted, revealing the limits of the government's Indian policy.

In 1917, President Chamorro explained his support for the Matagalpino Indians' land claims in the following terms: "Knowing your feelings . . . the Comunidades Indígenas that were victims of outrages in past administrations and moreover have been the most loyal . . . when they were called upon to sacrifice for the prestige of the party [deserve retribution]."[78]

Chamorro's position yielded political dividends. Although migration from Conservative Granada had somewhat changed the political complexion of the Matagalpino elite, Chamorro could still play on the highlands Indians' tendency to identify ladinos with Liberalism. Both Chamorro and the local caudillo, Bartolomé Martínez, continued to court Indian support through patronage and favorable responses to Indian petitions. To cite a crucial example, in 1924 Martínez, as president of the Republic, distributed 3,600 manzanas (1 manzana is equal to 1.7 acres) of land to the Comunidad Indígena.[79]

The Indians not only supplied crucial political support for the Conservatives but also created a space, however reduced, in which they defended their Comunidades and defined their identity in a hostile ladino world. In 1919, the Matagalpinos spurred the land distribution process through occupations. In turn, indigenous mobilizations in Boaco, Jinotega, and Sutiaba received Conservative backing.[80]

The case of Jinotega illustrates that continued support. Since 1895, some 2,000 Indian families who inhabited small villages near the town of Jinotega had struggled to defend their 35,000 manzanas of communal land against encroaching ladino ranchers and coffee growers. On May 29, 1915, the conflict entered a violent phase. That morning, capitán-general Macedonio Aguilar led 100 Indians in cutting down the barbed wire fences that enclosed the cattle ranch López Guerra had built on communal land. Several months later the police captured twenty of the Indians, including Aguilar and his sons. Two rebels, Benigno Granados and Abraham González, escaped the roundup, but sometime later the authorities killed González.[81]

With the tacit backing of the Chamorristas, the Indians continued to practice direct action in defense of their land. In 1918, *El Correo* reported that they had "repeatedly engaged in destroying all the ladinos' properties on these lands, thus deepening caste hatred."[82] In early 1919, when the court in Matagalpa sentenced twelve Indians to eight months in jail, Jinotegano rebels cut the barbed wire on many ladino properties. The local Chamorrista police chief voiced sympathy for them.

> Our strength has been with the Comunidad and now its chiefs are on trial for destruction of property. The Liberals have done this to prevent the leaders from helping us; those that are being tried were the true friends of General Chamorro, and they will continue to be so if they are set free.[83]

Chamorrista support of the Jinotegano Indians led to the release of the prisoners and a halt in ladino encroachment on their lands. Moreover, the Chamorristas' pro-Indian policy created a firm base of support where none had existed before 1914. In Jinotega, the ladinos' Liberal allegiance created such a clear polarization that by the 1920s, to favor Chamorrismo often was to express indigenous identity. Thus, for example, a U.S. Marine Corps officer stationed in Jinotega wrote: "We have found that the Indians around here, those who are Conservative, worship only one GOD, and that one is Chamorro. Some of them have letters that they treasure as one would an earned medal of honor."[84]

The political identification, of course, was neither as immutable nor as irrational as observers suggested. Less than two decades earlier it had been nonexistent, and within a year a large number of those same Chamorrista Indians would become Sandinistas. What remained constant in the politics of the Jinotegano Indians was the Liberalism of their ladino opponents and their own understanding that cross-ethnic alliances were necessary to the defense of their lands and community.

### Varieties of Ladino Discourse

Although they showed decisive support and sympathy for the highlands Indians, neither Bartolomé Martínez nor Emiliano Chamorro ever mounted an ideological challenge to the dominant discourse of ladinoization. At the same time, although they took abolition arguments seriously, neither of the two presidents ever pushed to eliminate the Comunidades Indígenas.[85] Both demonstrated ambivalence toward the Comunidades. In part, this reflected the need to maintain their legitimacy among the national elites. They also shared the positivistic view that Indians must become ladinoized or perish as obstacles to progress.

Ambivalence notwithstanding, Chamorro and Martínez stood alone among Nicaragua's political elite as Indian sympathizers. Their pro-Indian position, traceable partly to individual psychology, had a specifically regional focus and was heavily biased in favor of the indigenous elite. The biography of Martínez bears this out: the illegitimate son of a planter and a Jinotegano Indian woman, he was nicknamed "El Indio." Late in life (and following the birth of several children) he married the daughter of a mozo on his coffee plantation in the indigenous area of Muy Muy. Later, perhaps not surprisingly, as jefe político in Matagalpa he developed an easy rapport with the highlands Indians.

Despite his unusual background, Martínez worked with his clients like any other politician. To cite a typical example, he bought an accordion as a birthday present for the son of the capitán-general of the Comunidad of Jinotega. His relationship with the capitán-general of Matagalpa, Ceferino Aguilar, however, stands out because of its duration and because it often resembled a friendship between equals. Aguilar received numerous favors from Martínez ranging from scholarships for his children to his release from prison for political and less noble offenses. Aguilar, for his part, offered Martínez incisive political analysis from the grass roots and consistent efforts that aided Martínez politically and economically. Aguilar promoted his friend's programs, particularly in education. The friendship was strong and fruitful enough to give Martínez a constant awareness of how policies would take shape among the highlands Indians. Although Martínez never embraced an Indian communitarian political perspective, his friendship with Aguilar allowed him to appreciate the political value of Indian leadership, a value that would erode with the abolition or the disintegration of the Comunidad.[86]

Martínez juggled his political needs, sympathies, and search for a method to "civilize" his indigenous friends, workers, and neighbors. During his presidential term of thirteen months, in addition to returning the land to the Comunidad of Matagalpa he founded a teacher training school for Indians.[87] Among the national elite, however, such a project was contradictory, for to be educated was indeed to cease to be Indian. Although "El Indio" understood that the relatively educated Aguilar was an Indian, most ladinos relegated the Indian category to distant "primitives." Consider the view of the León municipal government regarding the neighboring Sutiabas, who were fighting for official recognition as a Comunidad Indígena with territorial rights:

> The castes live in complete separation and never mix in the Matagalpino cañadas; they live in ignorance of the laws of the state. The Sutiabas are quite advanced intellectually and cannot be confused with the Indian castes who live in areas inhabited by uncivilized Indians.[88]

Congruent with the discourse of Nicaragua mestiza, the Indian here is defined as noncivilized, as barbarous. Thus the Sutiabas, culturally more advanced and more urbanized than the Matagalpinos, no longer qualified as Indians. True Indians were pitiful, static, locked in the past, and incapable of progressing on their own. Education, then, would wrench the Indians out of the past and would convert them into civilized ladinos, with the same rights as other citizens; but with the abolition of the Comunidades they would hold no special rights to the land. Elite discourse thereby portrayed the Comunidad Indígena of Sutiaba as a farcical ruse to hold onto territory better suited to elite needs.

The question raised by the Leonés elite is worth pondering. What distinguished the Indian from the ladino, at a time when pressures were brought to bear on the former to change ethnic identities? Few if any Indians west of the Atlantic region still spoke a native language in 1920. Whether in urban Sutiaba or rural Matagalpa, the Indians' lives had changed dramatically compared with the language, dress, religion, labor relations, and communal organization of their parents' generation. Nevertheless, indigenous ethnicity had become tightly interwoven with the Comunidad Indígena and with those political alliances necessary for its defense.

The highlands ladinos helped shape national opinion against the Comunidades. Modesto Armijo, a progressive Liberal lawyer who for ten years had engineered land grabs in Matagalpa, in 1919 headed a national commission to study "the Indian problem." Another highlands ladino involved in a land conflict claimed that the Comunidades perpetuated the Indians' "stubborn way of life, refractory to all progress."[89] A Managua newspaper supported a petition from the Jinotegano ladinos in similar terms: "We judge that the Comunidades retard national progress. . . . [The Indians] live hermetically. . . . Certainly they conserve their racial tradition and the stamp of primitive sovereignty but at the center everything stagnates and petrifies."[90]

Although partisan Liberals (out of power) draped themselves in the same banner of progress, they blamed the Indian problem on Conservative "slave-drivers" who manipulated the Indian vote. In 1920, Juan Mendoza, a Liberal, added an important twist: "For them [the Conservative oligarchs] the ladino was the quintessence of perfection."[91] Mendoza's view of ethnic relations is significant because he articulates the mestizo component of the myth of ethnic homogeneity (later to be radicalized by Augusto César Sandino and then appropriated by Anastacio Somoza). In so doing, he underscored the limits of Conservative *indigenismo*, particularly the deep-seated racism of its "white" leadership (curiously both Chamorro and Martínez were mestizo exceptions). But at the same time, Mendoza's construction of an ideal mestizaje that would guide Nicaragua to capitalistic progress depended upon a dehumanized vision of the Indian: "Thus we see the Indian move in herds, like beasts, half-naked, like a primitive. . . . And the patrón looks at him with disdain; . . . the governments indifferently, with eternal neglect."[92]

The Indian as an autonomous subject simply did not exist in ladino discourse during this era. When Indians achieved education but still desired an indigenous identity, lands, and organization, they were dubbed ersatz, artificial creations, as in Sutiaba. When they rebelled as they did in Sutiaba or Jinotega, landowners and editorial writers depicted them as primitive savages and stooges of unscrupulous politicians. Moreover, the class position (as cafetaleros) of even a Chamorro or a Martínez blinded them from seeing any alternative to a ladino road of progress. By 1950, after the ladino state had crippled the institutions that defined indigenous ethnicity, it took but a short leap of faith to declare the Indians dead upon the arrival of the twentieth century.

Nevertheless, in 1919 the ladino imagery was still blurry—Indians slothfully vegetated in the past were primitive and petrified yet incorrigible enough to block progress and stir up ethnic hatred by cutting the barbed wire of ladino ranchers. The ladinos viewed Indians as objects of pity, a degraded race moving in "herds" but redeemable through education. These conflicting images of passivity-violence and bestiality-goodness related, it seems, to conflicting ladino needs and to the bitterness of ethnic relations in the highlands. The highlands elite wished to convert Indians into laborers and Indian land into plantations; but at the same time, they needed to justify coerced labor in ethnic terms. The violence that surrounded labor relations merely confirmed ladino notions about Indians as a degraded race.

## Labor, Authority, and Violence

The Matagalpino cafetaleros therefore had difficulty envisioning this inherently slothful "degraded race" as a free labor force on their plantations. Despite the abolition of forced labor in the 1905 and 1911 constitutions, an informal debt peonage system remained a key feature of the coffee industry in the Central Highlands until the 1930s. As Dana Munro, the scholar-diplomat, explained in 1918, "the cafetaleros, incapable of enforcing their contracts with the Indians, often have difficulty with their harvest. The fact is that the local authorities, in many cases, illegally have enforced the old laws."[93] Moreover, the cafetaleros unsuccessfully lobbied Congress to pass debt enforcement legislation in the 1910 to 1911 session but won approval in 1919. Finally, the Matagalpino cafetaleros lobbied alone in 1923 against a law that once again abolished all forms of debt bondage and forced labor.[94]

The highlands cafetaleros obtained significant benefits from the system. They used its credit advances not only to attract local labor but also to maintain subsistence-level wages despite rapidly rising productivity. Between 1919 and 1925, for example, coffee production in Matagalpa doubled without any corresponding increase in wages or in the labor supply.[95] Thus the cafetaleros' argument that they needed to pay subsistence-level wages because of the high cost of transportation seems weak. Also unconvincing is the argument that Indians would not have responded to wage incentives because of the conflicting demands of their own family economy. On the contrary, as will be demonstrated, workers did respond to wage incentives and often moved from hacienda to hacienda in search of advances rather than return to their milpas.

A more adequate understanding of highlands labor relations might be obtained by situating them within Alan Knight's innovative typology of debt labor. Knight distinguishes where debt was "an inducement" in the creation of a voluntary labor force (type 1), where debts were a "customary" part of the negotiation between the landlord and resident labor (type 2), and where debts were a central feature of a coercive system of recruitment and retention of labor (type 3).[96]

Matagalpino labor relations, however, seem to spill into all three categories. Although the Indians themselves demanded advances (type 2) they did not resemble a resident labor force (or use hacienda land, as did the Peruvian sheepherders). Unlike as occurred in the Guatemalan case (type 3), the Matagalpino planters did not face an absolute shortage of pickers in the coffee region. Harold Playter, the United States consul in 1925, wrote: "Labor is more plentiful in the Matagalpa region, hence cheaper, but the Indian of that section, 60 percent of the population, although a good worker cannot be counted on to report when needed."[97] Finally, despite a degree of labor mobility, highlands labor relations did not resemble those of coastal Peru or Soconusco, Mexico (type 1), because coercion was used to retain laborers well after their initial recruitment.

Although the Matagalpino case seems anomalous, the array of forces that shaped it were not unique. The highlands laboring class came into existence as the state and the cafetaleros expropriated nearly 30 percent of the indigenous land. The loss of land may have contributed to the availability of indigenous labor, but the nature of that expropriation—by the very cafetaleros who sought their labor—decisively influenced the quality of social relations of production. Moreover, as noted earlier, ladino authorities often treated the Matagalpinos as a conquered people. Thus the question of whether labor was free can be grasped only in the context of a highly unequal ethnic power struggle. Laborers were at the same time an ethnic group working for another ethnic group that had imposed on them its own domination.

If these interconnections of land, power, and ethnicity are not taken into account, highlands labor relations appear to a large degree voluntary, for Indians and planters did share a mutual dependency on the *adelanto* system.

Demanding advances worth several weeks' wages at the start of the harvest, the indigenous workers seem to fit the revisionist view of Arnold Bauer and others who argue for a predominantly noncoercive role of debt in rural labor relations.[98] But the planters did use force against those who, like their contemporaries in Guatemala and El Salvador, treated their cash advances as earned wages and sought work on other plantations. According to the cafetalero Alberto Vogl Baldizón,

> With time all the Indians became legally obligated to work with the finqueros. Then they would leave to go work in Managua or Jinotega where they worked as *ganadores* [nondebtors] and not as *desquita-dores* [debtors]. The Indian authorities did not carry out the orders because it would be like capturing their own fathers or brothers. . . . In reality it bled the cafetaleros dry and provided an easy source of income for the Indians.[99]

This recollection coincides with documentary sources in one important respect: the Matagalpino Indians usually did not desert the plantation to return to their milpas but rather to work on other coffee plantations. Indeed, they played one cafetalero off against another. For example, in 1913 Bartolomé Martínez, then jefe político and owner of a coffee plantation, received a telegram from his foreman: "There are mozos registered to you working in the hacienda of Federico Fley."[100] That this indigenous labor resistance involved moving from cafetal to cafetal suggests that the planters' problem with the "reliability" of labor had little to do with the Indians' degree of commitment to seasonal wage labor. Female workers in particular responded to piecework incentives, often earning enough to pay off their debts.[101]

The perpetuation of this system into the 1920s, therefore, seems to derive from the conflict between the cafetaleros' desire to maintain subsistence-level wages and the Indians' defense of "customary" rights to a cash advance that reflected their own concept of a just wage. Vogl's idyllic vision of the advances as a form of welfare notwithstanding, the cafetaleros' reaction to labor resistance brought out the brutality of the adelanto system and corroded the bonds of the Comunidad Indígena.[102] The elite's unwillingness to accept a voluntary labor system also derived in large part from its racist view of indigenous labor.[103]

The system legitimized a repressive apparatus that turned foremen and indigenous authorities into police agents. Indeed, this police presence on the plantation makes the problem of free labor even more complex. When foremen jailed laborers for failing to show up for work they put severe limitations on the workers' freedom, even when the laborer might have arrived at the plantation voluntarily. Moreover, the ladinos' racist conception of Indians permeated those relations of production just as did indigenous resentment of the cafetaleros' land expropriations. The ladinos could not see the Indians as worth the higher wages that might end their desire for advances; nor could they conceive of the Indians working in a system that did not depend ultimately on coercion. The labor system, itself, generated evidence for this picture of the Indian as a creature submerged in a world of violence.

Despite Vogl's recollection, local indigenous authorities often *did* capture fellow Indians. Servando Ochoa, for example, complained to the jefe político that a capitán had jailed his sons for not possessing a work pass. Similarly, in 1921 an American cafetalero complained to then vice-president Martínez, that "the capitán de cañada was capturing people . . . who owe no money to anybody."[104] The gradual conversion of Indian village officials into government authorities provided the labor system with its political underpinning. Once the indigenous authorities ceased to derive their legitimacy from the Comunidad, the incidence of violent abuses increased dramatically. In 1910, Jorge Pérez, a capitán de cañada, received an order to take Ciriaco Obregón prisoner and deliver him to a coffee plantation as a "labor deserter." After Pérez had delivered Obregón to the plantation and cut his hands loose, Obregón turned to Pérez and said, "sooner or later you're going to pay for this." Two years later Obregón, by then an Indian village authority himself, captured Pérez and nearly killed him.[105] This case and others previously mentioned suggest that in the highlands the terms "free labor" or "servile labor" have meaning only in the context of the surrounding web of contradictory social relations mediated by ladino authority and power.

Authoritarian violence also erupted over land disputes. Ladino efforts to expropriate property turned indigenous authorities against their own people. Thus, in 1913 Ceferino Aguilar protested to Martínez about the complicity of Indian leaders in the loss of communal territory. Aguilar accused the Comunidad president of forcibly evicting Indians in order to rent lands to ladinos:

On March 17 in Matazano, Bacilio Figueroa, accompanied by 20 people arrived to look over some land that a non-comunero wanted to fence. Since the land belonged to us comuneros we decided to fence it off. When we finished the president came back and had six [Indians] tied up.[106]

Although his tactics were brutal, Figueroa, the president of the Comunidad, believed he was acting on behalf of his people. As noted earlier, between 1904 and 1913 the Matagalpinos had lost thousands of acres of land to "defense" lawyers and surveyors who charged exorbitant rates to the community, thereby forcing land sales as payment. President Figueroa wished to rent this land to head off yet another forced sale.

The growing commodification of the products and structures of the communal land—the crops, fences, buildings, and corrals—also gnawed away at indigenous ties. By the second decade of the century, dozens of Indian kinship groups were planting coffee for the commercial market. Their *mejoras* (improvements such as coffee bushes, fruit trees, fences, and dwellings) could be legally seized for nonpayment of debts. Although the land itself could not be expropriated (after the 1914 law), Indians could lose their mejoras to other Indians or to ladinos. Indeed most of the land conflicts during the period of 1916 to 1924 pitted Indians against other Indians allied with ladinos.

The ladino elite's manipulation of Indian authorities and the divisions it created among the Matagalpinos over labor recruitment and land impeded the kind of unified resistance that formed to the north in Jinotega. Although Chamorrista politics often aided the indigenous communities, politics in general weakened communal solidarity. During the election campaign of 1916, for example, the government and Chamorrista factions of the Conservative party competed for Indian votes. The government's method of "campaigning" consisted of the forcible recruitment of Chamorrista Indians into the military; the jefe político replaced forty of the forty-five captains with anti-Chamorristas.[107] Ceferino Aguilar recounted to Martínez the actions of one Indian authority:

The captain, Félix Pérez recruited a great many people; many were tied up. Those citizens sadly await with the hope that he will be removed from that post. Pérez caused much disorder. The prisoners are bound, dying of hunger, *why should we Indians have to die in this way?*[108]

Thus the Indian authorities, following ladino orders, unleashed a campaign to terrorize the Chamorristas into submission. They provided yet another glimpse of the epoch's defining image of indigenous life: the *amarrados* (the bound ones), a long file of Indians with their hands tied behind their backs, led by their ethnic brethren on horseback toward an army encampment or to the peons' quarters of the plantation.

The Matagalpino Indians clearly did not wish "to die in this way." In their own defense, they pursued three different strategies to cope with the reign of violence that afflicted their communities. Migration was the response that probably had the greatest long-term consequences for the Comunidades. For the coercive quality of politics and labor drove many Indians east into the sparsely inhabited mountains. Thus, one capitán complained to Vice-President Bartolomé Martínez in 1921: "The Indians have been much exploited and have come to these mountains fleeing from the communities."[109]

Although it is as yet impossible to quantify the emigration from the Indian villages, oral testimony suggests that many villages lost more than one-half of their inhabitants to *la montaña* (the mountain jungle) during this period. Of Matagalpa's turn-of-the-century Indian population of approximately 30,000 to 35,000, perhaps 25 percent fled the area between 1910 and 1950.[110] Moreover, those who established small farms in the mountains lost contact with the rest of the Indian population. Emilio Sobalvarro commented on a similar migratory process fifty miles to the south that took place during the 1940s.

As the ladinos acquired more and more lands, the Indian withdrew far away. The law always went against them. . . . The immigration was constant and by the hundreds. Towards the east where the millenarian trees had never been touched by a hatchet. To these mountains they fled.[111]

Others attempted to withdraw from ladino society while remaining in their villages. The withdrawal was as much psychological as physical, symbolized by the epithet *ladinazo*. One elderly Indian summarized the perspective of those who remained in their villages:

When we saw the Indians tied up and dragged off to a hacienda . . . we learned that we had to stay out of debt to the ladinazos. And the only way to do that was to have nothing to do with them. For a long time you never saw a ladinazo around here. We'd go to Matagalpa to sell our coffee and oranges, but we'd stay in the Común [the Indian center] and never mix with anybody.[112]

## Los Mozos de Vita: Land Expropriation and Ladinoization

The third and least typical strategic response began with direct resistance but eventually gave way to relative submission to ladino power. The most significant example was a case of simple acquisition. In 1881, the cañada of Yúcul had been the bastion of the rebellion, but between 1911 and 1916 José Vita, the second largest cafetalero in Matagalpa, conquered the village and its lands. Vita accomplished what most of his elite compañeros had only dreamed about: the abolition of communal land and the conversion of Indians into peons.

In 1910 Vita paid U.S. $1,000 for 1,000 manzanas of Yúcul land at an auction. The Comunidad had to sell the land because it owed money to Eudoro Baca, a lawyer who had purchased the debt from Antonio Belli, director of the infamous 1904 survey. Vita manipulated the title to include an extra 1,500 manzanas bordering La Laguna, his coffee plantation. Claiming Yúcul as his own, Vita ordered thirty-five extended families who cultivated cash crops and basic grains on some 2,000 manzanas either to leave or to work on his plantation.

By 1913, Vita had persuaded ten extended families who cultivated some 500 manzanas to accept his deal: "those who have cultivated lots can keep them if they agree to clean one cafetal (3,000 cafetos [coffee bushes] three times a year); the owner will pay them what the labor is worth, and those who do not fulfill their obligation will have to leave."[113] This brief accord reveals primitive accumulation at work; in Yúcul, as elsewhere, the process was not peaceful.

Bibiano Díaz, a leader of the Comunidad of Matagalpa, argued that Vita had "used his superiority and influence to do what he wishes with the Indians of Yúcul. . . . He founded his *vinculación* through terror."[114] Díaz inverted the sense of the word "vinculación" (entailment), which the elite had been using to question the legality of the Comunidades. At the same time, he deftly attacked Vita in ways that would appeal to the ladino elite: he called Vita "un extranjero pernicioso" (a pernicious foreigner) and accused him of reestablishing "slavery in the twentieth century."[115] No ladinos, however, were listening.

Díaz organized more than verbal resistance against Vita. For three years, most of the Indian families remained on their land while refusing to fulfill their labor obligation to Vita. But the Italian cafetalero was not easily intimidated. During 1913 he managed to evict four families. According to one account, "because they could no longer endure Vita's hostilities against the Indians [16 families] . . . abandoned their fincas."[116] By the end of 1913 only five families continued to resist.

Despite Bibiano Díaz's prominence in the Comunidad, his group fought alone. The Comunidad's internal divisions ran deep. Díaz suspected that its president had aided Vita. Nor was Martínez available in this battle; he had a long-standing friendship with Vita, his next-door neighbor in Matagalpa.

While Díaz argued in the courtroom, Vita ordered his mozos to tear down Díaz's fences and destroy his crops. Moreover, as Díaz testified: "Many times he has slandered me and even whipped me for no motive, only because he has grown accustomed to doing that to the servants and hired help that he has established." Díaz's travails in court taught him bitter lessons about power and justice: "At the beginning of the trial, out of love for the land I innocently believed in the equality of rights. ¡Vana ilusión!"[117] Vita's henchmen terrorized the Indian witnesses, and the presiding judge sent them to jail before they could testify. Díaz and the other four families held out until 1916. Finally, rather than become part of Vita's *servidumbre* Díaz left behind his fifty-manzana farm and went to live on a relative's land in another village.

The other four extended families joined the servidumbre. Soon the victorious Vita confiscated their fincas, leaving them with but one manzana per male adult. In return for that parcel, all family members were obliged to pick his coffee and weed 8,000 coffee trees a year, at far less than the going wage. From 1916 to 1963 if a Yuculeño did not show up to work Vita (and later his son) sent his own "civilian police" to drag the recalcitrant worker off to the plantation jail.[118]

## Conclusion

The defeat of the Yuculeños and the high level of Indian emigration provide evidence for the view that the highlands communities were, if not dead, at least severely wounded early in this century. One reading of this chapter might reasonably point out, then, that it essentially involves a scholarly dispute about chronology with Wheelock and other social scientists. But our differences are more substantial. Wheelock, for example, posits the demise of the

Nicaraguan Indians (except for those of the Atlantic Coast) before 1900, whereas my research suggests that many indigenous groups survived as ethnic communities well into this century—indeed, many of their descendants today consider themselves to be "indígenas."[119]

Why the ethnic conflicts that plagued the highlands during the first decades of the century have slipped into the crevasses of history is explained by the formative process of the ladino discourse on the "Indian problem." From 1880 to 1920 ladino elites projected images of Indians as marginal primitives who blocked progress through ignorance and wasteful practices on their communal property. These images at once rationalized and reflected policies that led to the expropriation of that land and the exploitation of Indian labor. Similarly, the religious-based protests of 1895 in Matagalpa or the agrarian battles in Jinotega from 1915 to 1920 reiterated the need to educate the primitives and to abolish the Comunidades.

During this epoch, then, ladino discourse exhibited a remarkable, totalizing capacity as it parried, then assimilated, every indigenous effort at autonomous expression. But the question remains as to how and when this discourse was transformed from an ideological weapon into a form of hegemony. As Jean and John Comaroff suggest, "Hegemony . . . exists in reciprocal interdependence with ideology; it is that part of a dominant world-view which has been naturalized and, having hidden itself in orthodoxy, no more appears as ideology at all."[120]

In the Nicaraguan highlands, the transformation was symbolized by the actions of the putative experts and defenders of the Indians. The lawyer-poet Samuel Meza appropriated 1,500 hectares of communal lands from the Indians of Sébaco, while writing articles in his capacity as Indian expert and benefactor. Meza argued, for example, that the abolition of the Comunidades would be "an extremely noble, great act that would save this *raza desgraciada* from the clutches of ignorance and superstition."[121] Modesto Armijo, though perhaps less enriched in the process, aided in the expropriation of Matagalpino lands and then in 1919 headed a national commission that studied the Indian question. Eudoro Baca, the lawyer who in 1910 delivered Yúcul to José Vita, became in 1923 the defense attorney of the Comunidad Indígena of Matagalpa. And Alberto Vogl, the kindly cafetalero, declared that the Indians bled his class dry. Not one ironic smile shines through this historical record.

These ladinos apparently believed in their own expertise and goodwill; what's more, the bureaucrats and intellectuals in Managua believed their testimony.

These individual triumphs suggest the intimate connection between "real" and "symbolic" violence. For the discourse of the ladino experts became meaningful only in the context of the real violence waged against the communities. Moreover the very creation of these "experts" involved what Pierre Bourdieu calls their "complicity."[122] They were compelled to remain silent about the radical distortions of recent history that those careers signified. Perhaps the Indians' desperate circumstances led them to passively accept these "defenders," who offered "solutions"—usually a kinder version of the venerable formula "privatization plus education equals civilization"—at precisely the moment when the disintegrating Comunidad was under attack from all sides. Compared to some of the thugs dragging people through the mountains, Armijo, Baca, and Meza might have seemed friendly faces indeed. Whatever the cause, these lawyers, poets, and cafetaleros could take advantage of the indigenous silence and invent a version of social history that notwithstanding a blatant disregard for local facts rapidly became a canon: despite the noble efforts of their enlightened defenders, a primitive race tragically died off, victims of its inability to modernize and of unscrupulous outsiders who took advantage of its simplicity.

The ladinos' creation of a mythical history that suppressed the existence of Indians in the twentieth century has produced devastating effects on those highlands communities that have managed to survive the epoch of violence. Since 1950, the indigenous groups have distinguished themselves from the ladino rural poor through a collective sense of history. Yet as they lost land, dress, religious symbols, and institutions that allowed them to understand their identity, there remained little that made indigenous history vital to the new generations.

This chapter has shown how the indigenous peoples resisted on many fronts: from the 1870s until the 1940s they blocked church efforts to control their religious practices, they waged an often successful struggle against service labor relations, and they thwarted elite efforts to abolish their Comunidades Indígenas. Indeed, a century after their scheduled disappearance thousands of highlands folk still identify with their Comunidades that survive in the shadows of official history.

## Notes

1 Enrique Miranda Casij, "La guerra olvidada," *Revista Conservadora de Pensamiento Centroaméricano* no. 142:78. The narrative of Miranda's experience comes from a diary that Miranda Casij relied upon for his article.

2 *El Centroamericano,* August 6, 1881.

3 Miranda Casij, "La guerra olvidada," 78. "Muera la Gobierna" (in contrast to "el Gobierno") was repeated in many accounts. The Indians clearly had difficulty with Spanish and evidently spoke a dialect of that language well into the twentieth century. Several accounts mention that some ladinos fought with the Indians. The government condemned two ladinos for selling weapons to the Indians, but involvement of ladinos on their side in the actual fighting is intriguing, though hard to substantiate.

4 *El Centroamericano,* August 27, 1881.

5 Miranda Casij, "La guerra olvidada," 81.

6 Carlos Téllez to his father General Carlos Téllez, reprinted in *El Centroamericano* (Granada), August 27, 1881.

7 Teniente Coronel José Lorenzo Pérez to a ladino ally, Pedro Garquín, August 20, 1881, published in *El Porvenir,* September 24, 1881. "Lo triste fue le los dentro de trasion de retra guarda la cantidad de dosientos managuas con dos cargas de parque y un cañon pues habiendo tenido nosotros un reten por la entrado de lion [León] y al tiempo de topar la fuerza con el reen el reten le hiso fuego al comensaar el fuego el oficial ue veia encabezando la tropa ce presento al reten diciendoles que no isieron fuego por que ellos benillan a peliar a favor de la nasion y ellos se crelleyeron por haber bisto la mitad de la ropa ue benilla adelante benillan de devisa blanca y fue como degaron abasnar y no abia sido mas que un plano militar de trasion fue por lo que la dio el terrible golpe que entre una ora los mataron siento sincuenta soldados por que los cañabas del sientro y de aguera asi fue como nos abrasaron" (original dialect and spelling preserved).

8 Joaquín Zavala to Colonel Enrique Solórzano, September 5, 1881, Zavala Correspondence, Tulane University Library, box 57, folder 8. Thanks go to Edmund Konrad for alerting me about these documents.

9 Alberto Vogl Baldizón, *Nicaragua: con amor y humor* (Managua: Editorial Garco, 1977), 131.

10 Carlos Arroyo Buitrago, prologue to J. R. Gutiérrez Castro, *En el 73 aniversario de la guerra de los indios,* pamphlet (Matagalpa, 1954).

11 Because census taking was itself one of the causes of the rebellion, numbers are extremely unreliable and moreover the exact area under consideration is not clear. The Jesuits estimated 25,000, and Minister of War Elizondo estimated 60,000 though he was surely including some of the Caribes to the east in his calculation. *La Gaceta,* June 6, 1881. A census published in *Memorias del Ministerio de Gobernación y negocios eclesiásticos, 1881* (Managua, 1882), lists the department's population at

39,401, and our own study of the 1860s baptismal certificates in the Casa Cural of Matagalpa shows that Indian births accounted for over 80 percent of the total.

12 See "Relación geográfica del partido de Chontales y Sébaco," written by the *corregidor* (royal official with administrative and judicial authority at a regional level) Francisco de Posada in 1740 and reproduced in *Revista Conservadora del Pensamiento Centroamericano* 98 (November 1968). Posada suggested that most lived in dispersed settlements. However, Bishop Morel, who visited in 1751, averred that many Indians lived in settlements that corresponded to the parcialidades. See "Visita apostólica del Obispo Fray Augustín de Morel," *Revista Conservadora del Pensamiento Centroamericano* 82 (July 1967).

13 See Julián N. Guerrero, *Monografía de Matagalpa* (Managua, 1967), 67. Citing a "Tabla de tributaciones," he lists Laborío with 447 tribute payers; Pueblo Grande (formerly Matagalpa), 379; Molagüina, 343; Solingalpa, 323.

14 Based on a study of baptismal records in the Casa Cural of Matagalpa for the years 1817, 1841, and 1865. For the latter date, births were no longer recorded by parcialidad, but rather divided into indígena or ladino.

15 Quotation by *ingeniero* (engineer) Luis Díez Navarro in 1743, cited in Guerrero, *Monografía de Matagalpa*, 21. Bishop Morel in his *relación* of 1752 commented that many Indians had fled to the mountains to escape tribute payments. See Morel, "Visita apostólica," 9.

16 Francisco Ortega Arancibia, *Cuarenta años de historia de Nicaragua, 1838–1878* (Managua: Banco de América, 1975), 108–109.

17 Bedford Pim, *Dottings on the Roadside in Panama, Nicaragua, and Mosquito* (London: Chapman and Hall, 1869), 78.

18 Rafael Pérez, S.J., *La Compañía de Jesús en Colombia y Centroamérica*, 4 vols. (Valladolid: Imprenta Castellana, 1898), 3:432–433.

19 Pérez, *La Compañía de Jesús*, 3:432–433.

20 Melchor López, a prisoner, explained: "nuestros jefes nos dijeron que íbamos a defender la religión porque nosotros hemos trabajado con mucho gusto en la Iglesia de los Padres." Cited in *El Porvenir* (Managua), September 17, 1881.

21 *La Gaceta*, April 2, 4, and 7, 1881; *El Porvenir*, April 9, 1881. According to the latter account, the retreating rebels encountered some 500 rebels who apparently were arriving late; they chose not to attack again.

22 *La Gaceta* (Managua), May 5, 1881. A total of 500,000 coffee trees in roughly 500 acres had been planted before the rebellion. The only coffee grower of any importance, a German, repaired the muskets of the Indian rebels. See G. Von Houwold, *Los alemanes en Nicaragua* (Managua: Banco de América, 1975), 270. It is unclear whether the German performed this service out of fear for his life or out of sympathy for the rebels.

23 Padre P. M. Valenzuela, S.J., quoted in a pamphlet by Padre F. M. Crispolti, S.J., "El mensaje del 24 de febrero y el dictamen del 21 de febrero en el Congreso de Nicaragua en 1882" (New York, 1882), 64.

24  Pérez, *La Compañía de Jesús*, 491–492. The Jesuit Cáceres also alluded to the effects of a decree that aimed to abolish the Comunidad Indígena and sell its land (approved March 1881). It is certainly possible that the Indians heard of the decree issued the same month as the rebellion, but it is extremely doubtful that the decree was put into effect.

25  Letter to Alejandro Cáceres, S.J., dated April 6, 1881, signed, "todos en jeneral la gente," reproduced in Pérez, *La Compañía de Jesús*, 500–501.

26  Zavala to the capitanes de cañada, April 14, 1881, Correspondencia Joaquín Zavala (cjz), Tulane University Library, box III-357.

27  Zavala to Joaquín Elizondo, April 14, 1881, cjz, III-403.

28  "Informe del Prefecto de Matagalpa," December 22, 1880, in *Memorias del Ministerio de Gobernación y negocios eclesiásticos, 1880* (Managua, 1881).

29  Zavala to Elizondo, April 16, 1881, cjz, III-409.

30  Gustavo Guzmán to Zavala, July 31, 1881, cjz, folder 3, no. 4.

31  On the government view of Jesuit involvement, see *El Porvenir* (Managua), June 11, 1881. For a more thorough treatment see Franco Cerutti, *Los jesuitas en Nicaragua en el siglo XIX* (San José: Libro Libre, 1984). On the insurrections see Julián Guerrero and Lola Soriano, *Caciques heróicos de Centroamérica, rebelión indígena en 1881 y expulsión de los jesuitas* (Managua, 1982) and Miranda Casij, "La guerra olvidada," 75–82.

32  See letter from a large group of Matagalpino *vecinos* (residents) to the president, published in *El Centroamericano*, July 2, 1881.

33  Cited in *El Porvenir*, September 17, 1881.

34  Teniente Coronel José Lorenzo Pérez to a ladino ally, Pedro Garquín, August 20, 1881, published in *El Porvenir*, September 24, 1881.

35  Letter from Máximo Moreno to Sr. Don Isaac Sobalbarro, August 14, 1881, published in *El Porvenir*, September 24, 1881.

36  *El Centroamericano*, July 2, 1881.

37  Ibid. Escobar survived this experience and fourteen years later he became a coffee grower, appropriating indigenous land. It is also possible that the treatment of Escobar was an effort to forcibly integrate him into the "Indian nation."

38  *El Centroamericano*, August 6, 1881.

39  *La Gaceta*, October 29, 1881. One official report of a battle at Yúcul on September 24 listed ten Indian rebels dead and two dead and two wounded on the government side, "tres de estos individuos de la casta indígena y recién aliados a las fuerzas nacionales."

40  *La Gaceta*, October 29, 1881.

41  On the conspiracy of 1884, see "Informe del Prefecto de Matagalpa," November 30, 1884, in *Memorias del Ministerio de Gobernación, 1884* (Managua, 1885), and *La Gaceta*, November 11, 1884. As late as 1910, former rebels fondly reminisced about the insurrection. See Vogl Baldizón, *Nicaragua con amor y humor*, 131.

42 By 1897, nothing had been accomplished (see report from the *jefe político*, July 15, 1897, in *Memorias del Ministerio de Gobernación, 1897* (Managua, 1898)). In 1907, under the Zelaya regime there did exist a *ley de poblado* that authorities attempted to use to keep people more or less in the same area. See *El Diario de Granada*, August 6, 1907. One of the striking characteristics of the indigenous villages today is that they lack the plaza structure of other places and that indeed most people still live "dispersed" relative to ladino villagers.

43 *La Gaceta*, September 20, 1881.

44 For an excellent discussion of foreign views of the Indian as a progressive figure during the middle of the nineteenth century, see E. Bradford Burns, *Patriarch and Folk: The Emergence of Nicaragua, 1798–1858* (Cambridge: Harvard University Press, 1991), 143–145. In this sense, the defeat of the rebellion marked a downgrading of the Indians' status to that of "semisavage."

45 On the debate, see Oscar-René Vargas, *La revolución que inició el progreso: Nicaragua, 1893–1909* (Managua: Ecotextura, 1991), 25–37, and Amaru Barahona, "El gobierno de José Santos Zelaya," *Revista de Historia* 1 (January–June 1990): 90–91. Also see Charles Stansifer, "José Santos Zelaya: A New Look at Nicaragua's Liberal Dictator," *Revista Interamericana* 7 (1977). Benjamin Teplitz, in "Political Foundations of Modernization in Nicaragua, the Administration of José Santos Zelaya, 1893–1909" (Ph.D. diss., Howard University, 1974), points out that Zelaya tried to persuade Sioux Indians to migrate to Nicaragua as farmers, suggesting a nonracist dimension to his indigenous policies.

46 The 1881 movement had coincided with other Indian-led rebellions in León and Masaya, raising the specter of a caste war. See, for example, *El Porvenir*, June 11, 1881, August 27, 1881, and September 24, 1881.

47 See W. C. Newell, *The Handbook of Nicaragua* (Washington: Bureau of the American Republics, 1892), 31. The data on land is confirmed by the *Indice del Archivo Nacional*, Sección de Tierras (Managua, 1916). On resistance, see *Diario Oficial*, June 8, 1895. The leading German planter, Wilhelm Jericho, was assassinated in 1893. Von Houwold, *Los alemanes*, 271.

48 Indian alcaldes to vicario general, Matagalpa, April 20, 1891, Archivo de la Diócesis de León (ADL), León, sección de correspondencia, box 389/1.

49 Letters to vicario general in ADL, sección de correspondencia, sent from Rivas, November 26, 1893, box 386/1; sent from El Viejo, September 7, 1896, box 220/3; sent from Sutiaba, September 24, 1894, box 220/3.

50 Letters from Alfonso Martínez to secretary of Bishop, Matagalpa, August 25, 1893, and September 25, 1893, ADL, sección de correspondencia, box 389/1.

51 *El Diario de Nicaragua* (Managua), August 1, 1895.

52 *El Diario de Nicaragua*, August 2, 1895.

53 Ibid.

54 *El Diario de Nicaragua*, September 17, 1895. The Zelaya government proposed the

establishment of an "Indian Normal School." Although the idea never got off the drawing board, the government did found at least a dozen schools in Indian villages.

55   The labor system in the early 1900s functioned better in Matagalpa (where only 18 percent of the workers deserted in 1900) than elsewhere. Teplitz, in "Political Foundations of Modernization," suggests that Indian passivity—their compliance with labor laws—derived from their loss of land in the 1890s; their loss of access to land gave them little alternative to wage labor.

56   For examples of naming capitanes de cañada in Matagalpa, see *Diario Oficial,* March 12, March 15, and September 9, 1898. For references to the treaty and to the role of the capitanes see Beaulac to the secretary of state, March 18, 1932, U.S. National Archives, U.S. State Department, RG 57, 817.00/7373, and J. A. Willey to Allen Dawson, October 18, 1934, 817.00/8160.

57   On the relocation decree, whose efficacy is unknown, see "Informe del jefe político de Matagalpa al ministro de gobernación," July 15, 1897, Matagalpa, in *Memorias del Ministerio de Gobernación, 1897* (Managua, 1898).

58   *El Comercio,* March 11, 1898.

59   *El Comercio* (Managua), March 11 and April 15, 1898.

60   In 1899, the regime exercised that authority with little apparent resistance, as the Indians' nightmare of 1881 became a reality when they were forced to pick coffee in the Sierras. See Emiliano Chamorro, *El último caudillo, autobiografía* (Managua: Editorial Unión, 1983), 28, 145.

61   On the numerous protests of the alcaldes, see the testimony included in the land title of the Comunidad reprinted in *Nicaragua Indígena* 2, nos. 7–10 (January–December 1948): 98–246.

62   On the vote, see *Diario Oficial,* October 25, 1903. On January 10, 1901, for example, the Indian-led municipal government of Boaco sent a protest letter to Zelaya asking him to rescind the orders that sent local laborers to the Sierra coffee plantations; he responded positively to the petition. *Libro de actas y acuerdos de la Acaldía de Boaco de 1901,* January 10, 1901.

63   *Diario Oficial,* January 11, 1903.

64   See, for example, the Matagalpino weekly, *El Noticiero,* January 12, 1908: "Eight roving police agents will visit the coffee plantation so that there will be no difficulties during the coffee harvest." The same paper suggested on November 7, 1907, that all workers without a passbook would be imprisoned or sent to the plantations "so that the harvest does not suffer." This seems to be an example of coffee region exceptionalism insofar as the labor law was concerned.

65   *Diario de Granada* (Granada), September 20, 1908. The Matagalpino demand for the reimplantation of forced labor should be taken as evidence for the relative success of the abolition of the 1901 labor legislation.

66   On Jinotega, see testimony in land title of Comunidad Indígena de Jinotega pub-

lished in *Nicaragua Indígena* 1, nos. 4–6 (April–December 1947): 13–14 and 60–81. On the 1893 conflict, see Julián Guerrero, *Boaco* (Managua: Tipografía Alemana, 1957), 195–198.

67 See "Informe del comisionado del gobierno" sent to resolve the dispute between the Comunidad Indígena of Boaco and the municipality of Boaco in *Memorias del Ministerio de Gobernación, 1904–1905* (Managua: Compañía Tipográfica Internacional, 1905).

68 On the decree, see *Nicaragua Indígena* 1, nos. 4–6 (1947): 81; *Memorias del Ministro de Gobernación, 1905* (Managua: Compañía Tipográfica Internacional, 1906). On resistance, see *Nicaragua Indígena* 1, nos. 4–6 (1947): 38.

69 For an extensive discussion of the loss of land during this period, see Jeffrey Gould, "El café, el trabajo y la Comunidad Indígena de Matagalpa, 1880–1925," in Héctor Pérez-Brignoli and Mario Samper, eds., *Tierra, café y Sociedad* (San José, Costa Rica: FLACSO, 1994), 279–363. Also see the title of the Comunidad Indígena of Matagalpa, surveyed in 1904 and published in *Nicaragua Indígena* 1, nos. 4–6 (1948), and in *Memorias del Ministerio de Gobernación, 1911–12* (Managua: Tipografía y Encuadernación Nacional, 1913).

70 Harold Playter, in 1925, noted that the Indians comprised 60 percent of Matagalpa's population (or 46,800), U.S. National Archives, U.S. State Department, RG 59, 817.61333/1, p. 34. It is probable that such an estimate reflects the Comunidad population of Matagalpa, Muy Muy, and Sébaco.

71 *La Regeneración*, September 30, 1910.

72 *Nicaragua Indígena* 45 (1947).

73 *Libro de actas de la Comunidad Indígena de Matagalpa* (1911–1913 fragments) in private archives of Aurora Martínez (daughter of Bartolomé Martínez), Matagalpa, hereafter cited as PAAM.

74 Bartolomé Martínez to Emiliano Chamorro, May 23, 1912, in *Correspondencia privada escrita y recebida por el Gral. Emiliano Chamorro, 1904–1929*, Biblioteca del Banco Central, Managua, unpublished letters.

75 "Informe al Ministerio de Gobernación, J. Bárcenas June 4, 1912," in *Memorias del Ministerio de Gobernación, 1911–1912* (Managua: Tipografía y Encuadernación Nacional, 1913), 199–200.

76 Ibid. Martínez did not necessarily want to eliminate the institution but merely the Liberal alcaldes. Eight years later the alcaldes still played roles of political importance.

77 *Memorias del Ministerio de Gobernación, 1911–1912* (Managua, Tipografía y Encuadernación Nacional, 1913), 204. He also noted that fifteen properties within their territory had also been sold to ladinos. Belli, an Italian architect by profession, was the brother-in-law of Emiliano Chamorro.

78 Speech printed in *Memorias del Ministerio de Gobernación, 1917* (Managua: Tipografía y Encuadernación Nacional, 1918), 302.

79  *La Gaceta,* May 14, 1924. The 3,600 manzanas represented the fifteen properties inside the revised Comunidad boundaries cited in Bárcenas's report and not the lost 17,000 manzanas (100 square kilometers). On Martínez's relations with the Indians, see Gould, "El café, el trabajo, y la comunidad," 335–340.

80  On the land occupation, see letter from Luis Arrieta (jefe político) to Bartolomé Martínez, Matagalpa, June 8, 1919, PAAM. On Camoapa, see *Libro de actas y acuerdos, 1920–1923,* in the Municipality of Camoapa. On Sutiaba, see Jeffrey Gould, "La Raza Rebelde," *Revista de Historia* 21 (1990): 85–98.

81  Based on an examination of court documents without titles in the Juzgado Civil of Matagalpa, March 1–25, 1919, and on letter from M. Borgen to Bartolomé Martínez, July 18, 1918, PAAM.

82  *El Correo* (Granada), March 22, 1918. See also, *Memorias del Ministerio de Gobernación y Anexos, 1918* (Managua: Tipografía Nacional, 1919), 342.

83  Lisandro Moreira to Bartolomé Martínez, Jinotega, March 6, 1919. PAAM. An internal party report underscored the recent origin of that base: "The Conservative party barely had five members before the campaign [of 1916]." M. Borgen to Bartolomé Martínez, Granada, July 22, 1918, PAAM.

84  Julian Frisbie to Major H. Schmidt, Jinotega, July 13, 1928, U.S. National Archives, U.S. Marine Corps section, RA 127, E220, box 11. Copy kindly facilitated by Michael Schroeder, University of Michigan.

85  In 1919, the Chamorro administration called for a public discussion on the (re)abolition of the Comunidades. *La Tribuna* (Managua), March 11, 1919. New Conservative abolition legislation was introduced in 1923 but shelved by Martínez in 1924, notwithstanding his public appeal for abolition in 1918. See *Memorias del Ministerio de Gobernación, 1918,* 312.

86  This paragraph is based on ten letters from Aguilar to Martínez between 1911 and 1925, PAAM.

87  On the normal school, see Josefa T. de Aguerri, *Puntos críticos sobre la enseñanza nicargüense* (Managua: Imprenta Nacional, 1933), 327–329. On the contradictions of government education policy, see *Memorias del Ministerio de Instrucción Pública, 1919* (Managua: Tipografía y Encuadernación Nacional, 1920), 156–157.

88  *El Cronista* (León), July 18, 1919.

89  *El Correo,* March 22, 1918. See *La Evolución* (Managua), February 20, 1919.

90  *El Comercio* (Managua), February 18, 1919.

91  Juan Mendoza, *Historia de Diriamba* (Guatemala City: Staebler, 1920), 78–81.

92  Mendoza, *Diriamba,* 4.

93  Dana Munro, *The Five Republics of Central America: Their Political Development and Their Relations with the United States* (New York: Russell and Russell, 1967), 94.

94  See report by Admiral Kimball, March 12, 1910, U.S. National Archives, U.S. State Department, RG 59 no. 6369/811. On Matagalpino opposition to abolition, see *La Gaceta,* May 11, 1923. The Managua cafetaleros favored the abolition because they realized that forced labor hurt productivity and that many workers were fleeing to

Costa Rica. For a discussion of this issue see Gould, "El café, el trabajo, y la Comunidad."

95  Harold Playter, "Report on Coffee," National Archives, U.S. State Department, RG 59, 817.00/6133/1.

96  Alan Knight, "Debt Bondage in Latin America," in *Slavery and Other Forms of Unfree Labor,* Leonie Archer, ed. (London: Routledge, 1988), 106–107.

97  Ibid.

98  See, especially, Arnold Bauer, "Rural Workers in Spanish America: Problems of Peonage and Oppression," *Hispanic American Historical Review* 59, no. 1 (1979): 34–63, and Peter Blanchard, *The Origins of the Peruvian Labor Movement* (Pittsburgh: University of Pittsburgh, 1982). For a critical review of the literature, see Tom Brass, "The Latin American Enganche System: Some Revisionist Interpretations Revisited," *Slavery and Abolition* 11, no. 1 (May 1990): 74–101. Knight's "Debt Bondage in Latin America," 116, does point out in a footnote the existence of "additional factors" within a mode of exploitation that induce workers to yield a surplus. He would undoubtedly recognize land expropriation by employers as one of those factors.

99  Vogl Baldizón, *Nicaragua: con amor y humor,* 129.

100  Telegram from J. L. Fernández to Bartolomé Martínez, Muy Muy, Matagalpa, January 13, 1913, PAAM. In another case located in the Matagalpa Juzgado Civil, March 24, 1913, *Jacinta Hernández v. Florentino Pérez,* a worker deserted three different local cafetaleros in two years running up debts for the equivalent of seventy-five dollars, which yet another cafetalero paid off.

101  Based on data from the *corte* log books from Bartolomé Martínez's coffee plantation "El Bosque." In 1918 when he paid less than ten cents a *medio* (40 medios of picked berries produced 100 pounds of beans), women averaged 24.3 medios a week while men averaged 15.8.

102  Despite Vogl's lament, on the average coffee planters earned annual profits of 35 percent on the sales price and 10 to 15 percent on the investment after five to ten years. See Harold Playter, *Nicaragua: A Commercial and Economic Survey* (Washington: U.S. Government Printing Office, 1927), 30.

103  For a benign example, consider Samuel Meza, poet, lawyer, landowner, and reputed defender of Indians. In his opinion, "this disgraced race will never emerge from its abject misery without schooling." *El Noticiero* (Matagalpa), March 2, 1919.

104  Servando Ochoa to Bartolomé Martínez, San Dionisio, Matagalpa, January 14, 1913; Eric Smith to Martínez, El Gorrión, Matagalpa, November 28, 1921, PAAM. Even Ceferino Aguilar probably used his authority to recruit mozos for Martínez. In 1919, when his hacienda was short of labor, Martínez received the following telegram from the jefe político, L. Arrieta: "Capitán-general, Ceferino Aguilar, tiene gente lista para trabajar en su hacienda." October 24, 1919, PAAM.

105  "Jorge Pérez demanda a Ciriaco Obregón, por lesiones," May 9, 1912, document located in Juzgado Civil, Matagalpa.

106  Ceferino Aguilar to Bartolomé Martínez, Susulí, Matagalpa, June 10, 1913, PAAM.

107  Report sent to Bartolomé Martínez, August 1916, PAAM.

108  Ceferino Aguilar to Bartolomé Martínez, Susulí, September 8, 1916, PAAM. Four letters from other Indians asked Martínez for protection from the indigenous authorities, Bibiano Herrera and Félix Pérez.

109  Letter from capitán de cañada to Bartolomé Martínez, Guasaca, Matagalpa, December 21, 1921, PAAM.

110  Census returns make it impossible to quantify intramunicipal migration. Given the vast eastern regions of the Indian municipalities, migration estimates are also impossible. However, the census does show that the Indian cañada population did not grow at the same rate as did the national population. See the appendix of Jeffrey L. Gould, *El mito de Nicaragua mestiza y la resistencia indígena* (San José: Editorial de la Universidad de Costa Rica, 1997). My estimate is based on interviews with members of the council of elders of the Comunidad, including Gregorio Aráuz, Francisco Arceda, Pablo García, Patrocinio López, Valerio Mercado, and Santos Pérez. Matagalpa, January 1992.

111  *La Flecha,* June 17, 1950.

112  Interview with Patricinio López, El Chile, Matagalpa, April 1990.

113  The data on Yúcul derives from a series of court cases found in the Juzgado of Matagalpa. Vita's takeover of the Yúcul land is revealed in "Ejecutoria a favor de Eudoro Baca contra los indígenas de esta ciudad, 1909–1910." The citation comes from "Recurso de apelación de Bibiano Díaz et al.," July 21, 1913, Juzgado de Matagalpa.

114  "Recurso de Apelación de Bibiano Díaz et al.," September 2, 1913, Juzgado of Matagalpa.

115  Ibid.

116  "Recurso de Apelación de Bibiano Díaz et al.," September 2, 1913. In "Recurso de Apelación," July 21, 1913, one witness on Díaz's behalf claimed that Vita "shot an Indian for shouting near the casa hacienda."

117  "Recurso de Apelación de Bibiano Díaz et al.," September 2, 1913.

118  Interviews with Delfina Díaz (1990), Blas García (January 1992), Macaria Hernández (1990–1992), Juan Polanco (1990), Urbano Pérez (1990), and Eusebio Urbina (1990, 1992), each conducted in Yúcul, Matagalpa.

119  On indigenous organizing, see *La Prensa* (Managua), January 27, 1992.

120  Jean and John Comaroff, *Of Revelation and Revolution: Christianity, Colonialism, and Consciousness in South Africa* (Chicago: University of Chicago Press, 1991), 25.

121  *El Noticiero,* March 2, 1919. Later, as we will see, he served as rector of the national university and as minister of education.

122  Pierre Bourdieu and Loïc J. D. Wacquant, *An Invitation to Reflexive Sociology* (Chicago: Chicago University Press), 167.

# 2

# "Not Even a Handful of Dirt": The Dawn of Citizenship and the Suppression of Community in Boaco, 1890–1930

The predisposition that the Indian class has against the ladino one is a powerful motive that should lead to a law that will suppress municipal governments in several towns [in Chontales].
—Ponciano Corral, prefect, Granada, February 17, 1846

The same economic factors that caused local mestizos to covet indigenous lands propelled Indians to approve almost overwhelmingly the extinction of their Resguardos [communal indigenous lands]. Comuneros were persuaded by the government that their holdings would be more secure under deeds than under usufruct documents; bureaucrats argued that the cabildo was a source of disputes within the community, due to its unethical ways of distributing land. In some cases, such arguments were channeled through deindianized comuneros or local mestizos whose own Indian identity had only recently been lost. . . .

. . . Colombian Indians reformulate their image of themselves in a struggle to maintain their ethnic distinctiveness in late twentieth-century Colombia, their historical role as forgers of their own destiny is denied them by the very dominant society that obliged them to follow the path of cultural invention in the first place.—Joanne Rappaport, *Cumbé Reborn*

In contemporary ethnographic theory, indigenous ethnicity is increasingly viewed as a social construct with no reference to any primordial essence. The attack on "essentialism," a view that characterized indigenous groups as possessing certain inherent cultural traits that lay at the core of their identities, has been aptly summarized by Thomas Abercrombie's analytical injunction: "indigenous ethnic groups and indigenous cosmologies are unintelligible apart from their struggle with the state."[1] By focusing on the nation-state–indigenous relation Abercrombie and other "constructionists" have greatly enhanced our understanding of local and national histories and identities.

There is, however, one aspect of the new ethnographic paradigm that I will question in this chapter: the view that "cultural loss" is a concept that depends upon a primordialist conception of ethnic identity.[2] Placing this concept in contemporary political perspective, Les Field argues against the "cultural survival school" in the following terms:

> This mode of analysis locks indigenous cultures and identities into a dualism of survival versus extinction in which social scientists inevitably play the role of experts. . . . Such a dualism is not useful in analyzing many, if not most historical indigenous groups, whose existence should be seen more as an ensemble of possibilities for transformation.[3]

Although he offers a strong and coherent argument against paternalistic strands of cultural survivalism, I would suggest that it is possible to approach the problem of cultural loss without slipping back into an essentialist paradigm and without arrogating to the scholar the role of arbiter-expert.

In this chapter, I want to probe the question of cultural loss among the indigenous communities of Boaco and Camoapa. We will see how the Camoapans and Boaqueños not only lost power struggles, but simultaneously lost discursive struggles for control over meanings and memories. Between the turn of the century and 1960, the indigenous peoples of the present-day department of Boaco lost their land, their homes, and their communal civil and religious organizations.[4] In other words, they lost on the battlefield and in the courtroom that which had previously formed central aspects of their identity and culture. Thus, that discursive and political "loss" contributed to the destruction, dispersal, and disarticulation of native communal identities and cultures. It is indeed, quite hard to reflect on this history and read it as the creation of new opportunities, rather than as a series of devastating state-inflicted political and repressive defeats accompanied by divisions and migrations, interrupted by only occasional moments of reprieve.

This process has left us with but few fragments of documentary and oral testimony. Principally for that reason, I will not attempt a thick reconstruction of the impact of this defeat on indigenous consciousness and identity. Rather, I will attempt to show how the local and national victors contributed to and assimilated the indigenous "loss" into their evolving political and historical discourses.

The nationalist intellectuals' incorporation of the indigenous defeat into their own reworking of local and national history can be situated within a broader discussion recently opened up by Partha Chatterjee. The theorist argues that the "narrative of capital" of progress, freedom, and individual rights "seeks to suppress that other narrative of community . . . based on affective bonds of real and imaginary kinship." He continues,

> Community is not easily appropriated within the narrative of capital. Community, from the latter's standpoint belongs to the domain of the natural, the primordial. . . . It is not so much the state/civil opposition but rather the capital/community opposition that seems to me to be the great unsurpassed contradiction in Western social philosophy. . . . Community, which ideally should have been banished from the kingdom of capital, continues to lead a subterranean, potentially subversive life within it because it refuses to go away.[5]

Chatterjee suggests that a fundamental critique of modernity would emerge from an investigation of that contradiction within the idea of the nation. He points to the anticolonialist movements as fertile terrain for such an investigation, pointing out how they adopted communitarian ideologies to combat colonialism. But when the movements achieved state power, they began to suppress the narrative of community that had nurtured them:

> The modern state, embedded as it is within the universal narrative of capital, cannot recognize within its jurisdiction any form of community except the single, determinate, demographically ennumberable form of the nation. It must therefore subjugate, if necessary by the use of state violence, all such aspirations of community identity.[6]

Chatterjee then argues that for these communities to escape suppression by achieving some form of historical legitimation they must develop alternative nationalisms that, in turn, will march in step with the narrative of capital.

In this chapter, we will probe more deeply into another dimension of the myth of Nicaragua mestiza. Here, we are particularly interested in how the emergence of a discourse of citizenship rights involved the material and cultural suppression of a discourse of community.

## A National Hero in a Local Conflict

In 1892, the Liberal leader Rigoberto Cabezas moved from Masaya to the Boaco region, hoping to find political tranquility and a modicum of economic well-being. Cabezas, who would become a heroic figure in Nicaraguan history for his military leadership in the Reincorporation of the Mosquitia in 1894, had struggled against the Conservative regime over the preceding eight years, suffering exile and penury as a result. When a wealthy friend offered to invest in a joint ranching enterprise if Cabezas promised to forego politics, he immediately accepted. The recent predominantly Liberal migration to the Boaco region probably influenced Cabezas's choice of location for his new venture.

Despite the migration, during the 1890s the casta indígena still formed the decisive majority of the region's population. In 1897, for example, some 80 percent of the births in the municipality of Boaco (whose population was 14,000) were identified as indigenous; in the newly formed municipality of Camoapa (whose total population was 5,000) 70 percent of the births were to indigenous parents. However, over the previous decade, the ladino migrants had become an important political and economic presence in the zone, founding haciendas and contesting indigenous control over the municipality. Camoapa and Boaco, still remote villages in the 1890s, were just beginning to experience economic growth: their combined urban properties were valued at only 40,000 pesos and their rural properties at 140,000 pesos.[7]

The municipality of Boaco rented Cabezas 500 acres of uncultivated land just north of an indigenous-inhabited cofradía ranch. Under the guidance of a Conservative hacendado, Cabezas immediately made efforts to learn about "the ways of the Indians and the manner of treating them so as to gain their friendship."[8] But gaining their friendship was a complex task in 1892, for the cultural differences between Indians and ladinos in the Boaco region were profound and palpable.

Dress and language (a very distinct dialect of Spanish), and the Indians' civil-religious organization were obvious indicators of difference. Indian religious practices were particularly bizarre to ladino sensibilities. One writer, who lived on a cattle hacienda in the region at the turn of the century, wrote in reference to their religious practices: "Deep within the collection of aboriginal rarities exist vestiges of ancient rites that the centuries have been slowly dissipating, with that slowness with which water wears away stone."[9] In a similar vein he wrote: "The boaqueño aborigines have customs that drive ladinos to distraction."[10] Although Indians were integrated into the local and national markets through the sale of their goods and labor, their economic activities differed significantly from those of ladinos of all classes. Indigenous families combined slash-and-burn agriculture, hunting, the manufacture of sombreros, wage labor, and cattle raising on open, natural pasture. Most distinctively, 200 indigenous women earned themselves a national reputation for their *sombreros de pita* (a type of palm leaf). To local ladino eyes, equally unique was the collective and festive nature of the cattle drive, known as *el rodeo*. The communal cattle drive depended on unfenced pastures and thus would be a constant source of friction with ladino ranchers. One elderly man of indigenous origin, recalling the 1910 to 1930 period, noted that "when I was a kid, the land had no owner. . . . Back then, each person would graze their cattle wherever. All the animals would move together and everyone recognized their own cattle."[11]

It was in the realm of ethnic naming and stereotyping that the high level of tension between both groups can be discerned. Emilio Sobalvarro, a Boaqueño intellectual and functionary, commented on the Indians he knew during his youth in the 1920s and 1930s: "The Indian at his core is timid."[12] The ladino imagination's dominant image of Indians was as fearful and submissive creatures, with a "horror of authorities." Indeed, as we shall see, whatever fears of authority they may have had were well grounded. Well into the 1920s, Indians supposedly would hide when any unknown ladino or known functionary would appear near their homes.

The sheer quantity of colloquial expressions for "Indian" also pointed to both the social distance between the groups and the elevated degree of anxiety that such distance provoked among the ladino minority. During the early 1900s, Boaqueño ladinos in polite conversation referred to the region's Indians by the terms "indígena," "natural," and "indio." But they had an ample supply of other terms as well: *indigesto, indino, jincho* (*jinchería* for a large quantity of them), *napiro, natucho* (*natuchada*). Although the etymological origins of "natucho" and "napiro" are obscure, the other derogatory expressions have a distinctly physical quality to them. "Indigesto" referred to indigestion. "Jincho" either derived from "hinchar," to swell up, commonly used in relation to the body, or "hincha" meaning hatred or aversion. Although the region's indigenous population apparently did not reciprocate with such a plethora of names for their "other," the term "ladino" was often employed as a synonym for *lépero* or *sinvergüenza* (scoundrels). Finally, the Indians of Boaco referred to any official authority as a *chingo,* a colloquial expression for "naked"; it also meant a special breed of tailless dog.[13]

In Boaco, these cultural differences were exacerbated by a political conflict over control of the municipal government related, in turn, to the Indians' defense of their communal holdings. Sharp ethnic conflict dated back at least to the 1840s, as the chapter's epigraph indicates. During the 1870s, a Jesuit reported that "hatred of the races consumed the other people. . . . Hostile confrontations happened between Indians and ladinos . . . thefts, wounded men, dead men."[14]

In 1889, to cite another crucial example of political conflict, the ladino-controlled municipal government sold 1,200 manzanas of indigenous cofradía land to Rafael Caldera, a prominent Liberal hacendado. Over the next few months, Indians organized to retake the municipality and in so doing thwart the sale of land. The political battle threatened to explode in "caste warfare." In December 1889, the government had to conscript soldiers throughout the country to put down a feared "uprising of the Indians against the ladinos."[15] The official report on the near uprising underlined the explosive mixture of politics and ethnicity as the cause of the strife:

> Entirely local issues had divided the neighborhood of Boaco into two groups that had been disputing political power for a long time, and to attain it, they squared off annually in a heated conflict disputing the outcome of elections for municipal officials. The division had a rational basis, but went to dangerous extremes developing almost into caste warfare.[16]

The moderate Conservative Sacasa government intervened in the conflict by sending the Liberal politician and historian José Dolores Gámez to mediate. Although the details of the negotiations are murky, Gámez apparently engineered a compromise satisfactory to both parties.[17] The land sale to Caldera was stalled, and as a result the Sacasa government emerged from the conflict with the strong support of the casta indígena.

When Cabezas arrived in Boaco, the Indians were still intensely politicized;

they maintained an alliance with the Sacasa government despite growing opposition from Liberals and dissident Conservatives (the iglesiero faction).

As part of a national revolutionary movement, Cabezas led a successful attack on the military command in Boaco on April 29, 1893. Salvador Barquero, a member of the ladino elite and Cabezas's comrade-in-arms, described the political-military situation in the following terms:

> During this epoch, local politics was divided between Indians and Ladinos, but the true Indians were led by Ladinos who exploited them. These Ladino leaders inculcated in the Indians [the notion] that they should defend the Sacasa government, attacking the revolutionary forces led by General Cabezas. Thus the Indians rose up, poorly counseled and even worse led by their caudillos.[18]

Barquero's account, written in 1939, then jumps back in time to May 4, 1893, when Cabezas led a victorious assault on the Indian positions on the outskirts of Boaco. The next day Cabezas attacked again, and his forces killed "numerous Indians." On May 7, a Conservative general, allied with the anti-Sacasa movement, marched into Boaco, "accompanied by some 500 Indians, whose aggressiveness he had managed to calm by offering them all kinds of guarantees."[19] Cabezas's military exploits against the Indians of Boaco positioned him for a key role in the next stage of the Liberal revolutionary movement that triumphed on July 11, 1893, and gave rise to José Santos Zelaya's sixteen-year presidency.

Barquero's narrative captured a key element of Nicaraguan Liberal discourse as it evolved from the 1880s until the 1920s. He stated that "ladinos" politically dominated and exploited the "verdaderos [true] indios." Yet his account generalizes too much. Although the indigenous elite did negotiate alliances with local ladinos, Cabezas's writings mention that the Indians had organized themselves into a "Partido Indigenista." Barquero's perception, I would argue, reflected his immersion in the formative stages of a Liberal discourse that portrayed "authentic" Indians as incapable of self-directed political activity.

For Barquero and other Liberals, literate, urban indigenous leaders could not be Indians precisely because of those social-economic characteristics that differentiated them from the rank and file of their communities. Here we can glimpse how such Liberal ideas and beliefs began to place limits around indigenous culture and identity. Indigenous authenticity, the only kind of indigenous identity worthy of sympathy (if not respect) depended on indigenous submission to ladinos (usually non-Liberals). The most effective way to aid Indians was to break through the ignorance that fueled outside domination. Yet upon receiving an education the Indians, in the eyes of ladinos, ceased to be Indians, for they lost their defining characteristics of ignorance and dependence.

These discursive limits on indigenous identity were a logical extension of the civilization-barbarism opposition at the core of nineteenth-century Latin American Liberalism: to educate an Indian is to render him or her an autonomous actor, therefore a nonsavage, a non-Indian. In Barquero's document, we witness the emergence of this discursive tension between an external definition of indigenous leaders as inauthentic non-Indians and the simultaneous creation of the primordial, savage "other."

Such a definition might have had a certain resonance among the Boaqueño Indians, both elite and rank and file, precisely because their own origins in the seventeenth century were due to their voluntary pacification and separation from Sumo groups who refused to accept Spanish rule. Throughout the eighteenth century they had been the victims of constant attacks by "Caribes" (Sumos) and by the Zambo-Miskitos from the Atlantic Coast. Those attacks and their own valiant defense both reinforced their own sense of "civilized" difference and their loyalty and usefulness to the Crown.[20] Such historically conditioned notions of "civilization" propagated by their economically successful and literate elite were also connected to the ideal of citizenship and progress: it was an indigenous municipal government that funded the installation of a large clock in the town square.

Indigenous political participation in municipal government throughout the nineteenth century shaped both their political and cultural identities. A notion of local and national citizenship was an integral part of indigenous political discourse. Thus, Cabezas reported, "These Indians do not look askance at me for the Directorate of the Partido Indígena made me a *ciudadano* [citizen]."[21] In heavily indigenous areas of Nicaragua such as Boaco, Camoapa, and Sutiaba—as in Guatemala and parts of Mexico—the municipality was coterminous with the indigenous community. Citizenship then both linked the local indigenous leadership with the nation and served as a guarantee of political autonomy and defense of communal lands.[22]

With the triumph of the Liberal revolution, Liberal ladinos gained control of the municipal governments of Boaco and Camoapa. Their first years in power coincided with many *denuncias* (claims) of indigenous land and the forced recruitment of indigenous labor. However, the numerical strength and the organizational solidarity of the casta indígena, on the one hand, and a degree of temporary political democracy ushered in by the revolution of 1893 on the other, continually posed a threat to ladino rule. As we saw in the preceding chapter, the Liberal Zelaya regime, despite its commitment to the abolition of the Comunidades Indígenas, at times sought to gain the political support of indigenous groups.[23] It was probably such a play for local popular support that allowed members of the casta indígena to regain control of the municipal government in 1898.[24]

For the indigenous leadership, citizenship was first and foremost defined within the Comunidad, conceived primarily but not exclusively as the indigenous community. Given the importance of a 1765 Crown grant to the indigenous people, it is highly probable that the term "comunidad" directly referred to the land grantees: "Naturales del Común de Indios de Santiago de Boaco."[25] The "común de Indios," then, was synonymous with a municipality that was no longer exclusively indigenous as it was during the 1700s.

This linguistic and political confusion among the terms "citizen," "municipality," and "indigenous community" became particularly salient in the interethnic conflicts of the 1890s and early 1900s. In 1898, the indigenous-led government battled against those ladinos within and on the edges of the municipality of Boaco who sought to expropriate communal lands. The indigenous leaders typically phrased such a problem as "the land problem caused by Don Pedro Mena against this Comunidad."[26] Similarly, the council minutes referred to "Don Pedro López, elected by the people to conserve the land title of this comunidad."[27] Here "Comunidad" seems to have signified both the indigenous community and the community of Boaco that also included ladinos. The use of "Comunidad" in reference to the land similarly blurred the distinction between the lands of the Comunidad and those that belonged to the municipality, traditionally controlled by indígenas.

Like the awarding of "citizenship" to Cabezas, the Indians' uses of "community" to defend members of the "indigenous caste" suggests an effort to rethink the interconnections between citizenship, community, and indigenous political and economic institutions. But this attempt to redefine citizenship and community from an indigenous perspective had a difficult time prospering in a hostile political environment. Despite tactical concessions, the Liberal Zelaya regime was opposed to all communal forms of land. Moreover, prominent members of the Boaqueño ladino elite, closely allied to the regime, were intent on privatizing indigenous lands and converting them into cattle ranches and coffee plantations.

In 1899, the ladinos received a boost when the Zelaya government expropriated cofradía lands throughout the country and turned the land over to the municipalities for distribution. In 1900, the new ladino-dominated municipal administration immediately defined its control over the 1,400 *caballerías* (152,320 acres) of land. By May 1901, they had persuaded the departmental jefe político to order the casta indígena to pay for a surveyor who would decide if the "lands were ejidal [municipal] or belonged to the Comunidad."[28]

The ladino elite's move to gain unrestricted access to the communal lands pushed the term "comunidad" toward a fixed meaning as the collective organization of the indigenous people. Yet the emergence of this discursive equivalence—"indigenous caste equals community equals indigenous community"—probably did not strengthen a collective sense of indigenous identity. On the contrary, the external determination of this shift proved to be culturally and politically disorienting. Not only did the newly christened Comunidad Indígena find itself playing for high stakes, but it lacked the institutional legitimacy of its forerunners: the indigenous-run municipal government and the village-based organization of the casta indígena. The new Comunidad Indígena could not simply inherit the legitimacy of the casta indígena, because the source of the latter's authority resided in its control over the municipal government.

The new ladino takeover of the municipal government transformed the organization of the casta indígena. Previously the Boaqueño organization had characteristics similar to the Matagalpino's and to those Mexican cases Florencia Mallon has described as "democratic patriarchies."[29] Several thousand adult members in Camoapa and Boaco were organized in small cañadas under the male leadership of democratically elected capitanes and of subordinate lieutenants, sergeants, and corporals who collectively elected a capitán-general. The military structure of indigenous organization was a legacy of the colonial period, when the highlands Indians had to defend themselves and the Spanish Crown against the indios bravos, such as the Sumo and the Zambo-Miskitos. But rather than take on a strictly defensive, military role, the captains also served as village representatives to the indigenous municipal government.

Under ladino municipal administration, the captains' defensive and representative roles became transformed. Throughout the nineteenth century municipal-national citizenship and communal membership had been nonantagonistic. But during the early decades of the twentieth century, in part due to growing ladino migration, participation in municipal politics obliged any indigenous leader to represent two increasingly antagonistic constituencies: the casta indígena and the municipality.

During the period of 1900 to 1904, the alliance between the national, departmental, and municipal governments seemed to assure that the more than 150,000 acres of communal holdings would be awarded to the municipality to then be distributed to individual families. Indeed, most indigenous petitions to the municipal government between 1901 and 1904 were phrased in a way that recognized the claim of the municipality. For example, nine indigenous people, in protesting against a ladino's privatization of two water holes, argued in the following terms to the mayor: "Under no circumstances do we stand opposed to lands being distributed in the way that the authority determines, especially since these processes promote agriculture, the source of wealth for our country."[30]

Although such phrasing might have weakened a sense of indigenous solidarity, following James Scott we might recognize such exaggerated deference as a form of resistance.[31] Yet another petition from one Aureliano Bello is harder to interpret as resistance and instead pointed to the potentially negative effect of municipal control of the land on indigenous identity and solidarity. Bello claimed that "even though he belonged to the indigenous caste he would renounce any rights that the community might have so that he might rent land from the municipality."[32]

Politics as well as group identities was in ferment: a Conservative-led revolutionary movement broke out in the department of Chontales in May 1903, shifting the local balance of forces. The revolutionary army led by the famous caudillo Emiliano Chamorro, a native of Comalapa (near Camoapa), captured Juigalpa, the departmental capital of Chontales and imprisoned the jefe político. Chamorro's forces moved out of Chontales within a week, and the national army defeated them within a couple of months. But the ease with which Chamorro organized his movement in Chontales underscored the threat of subversion in that heavily indigenous region. Several years later, a U.S. Marine observer would comment on Chamorro's regional support: "Chamorro comes from Chontales and the Indian population which constitutes the majority of the inhabitants are his enthusiastic supporters."[33]

Given the regime's perception of a serious political threat coming from the indigenous people, the Boaqueño and Camoapan communities suddenly found themselves in a position to press their defensive claims. In 1903, citing the peril of subversion, the National Assembly passed a law abrogating the anti-indigenous land and labor laws in the department of Chontales. Similarly, in 1905, the Zelaya regime sent José León Sandino, a Liberal lawyer-judge from Granada, to Boaco to study and attempt to resolve the land conflict.

J. L. Sandino's report supported the municipality's claim to the land as "the legitimate representative" of the people, thus adumbrating a dimension of political discourse with crucial consequences for the indigenous population.[34] However, Sandino also underscored the subversive threat by warning that if his recommendations were not carried out, "our enemies would find a favorable conjuncture to lead the masses of Indians in rebellion."[35]

The report's pragmatic politics articulated the real space of indigenous politics. For J. L. Sandino, there was no doubt that the regime had to respond positively to the numerous protests of indígenas against land evictions in both Camoapa and Boaco. The commissioner recommended an immediate halt to all forms of ladino encroachment onto indigenous land and that "it be distributed equitably and freely among the Indian families . . . in order to end this outmoded system of communities and the natural negligence of our primitive race, these being the most formidable hindrances to progress."[36]

The commissioner's report blended racism and the liberal vision of privatization with a significant compassion for the indigenous families, support for their collective rights, and a trust in their version of events. Consider his phrasing:

Considering the Indians' inveterate idea [that they need] to be comuneros on their land, not without some truth to it . . . it is a fact that many ladinos have been doing what the indígenas are saying they do . . . through a bad interpretation of this court decision, many lands have been taken over.[37]

This respect for indigenous voices and rights (if not initially for their communal rights) framed within a racist discourse would be a constant in J. L. Sandino's unique career.

We can assume that Sandino was not surprised when in February 1906, for the third time in twenty-five years, the state decreed the abolition of the Comunidades Indígenas and all forms of communal land. However, the commissioner's seemingly objective synthesis of the demands and militancy of the Boaqueño and Camoapan Indians probably had a positive effect on the regime's policy in the region. Although the 1906 decree announced the abolition of all Comunidades, it called for several preliminary measures including the surveying of the communal land. Ironically, in the very actions the regime took toward the abolition of all Comunidades, it implicitly sided with the indígenas of Boaco in its dispute with the municipality; for the regime ordered that the 152,000 acres of the land belonging to the Comunidad Indígena of Boaco (and not to the municipality) be the first to be surveyed and divided.[38] Indeed, two decrees in 1907 specified in an unusual, if not obsessive, manner how the Comunidad Indígena de Boaco should receive preferential treatment (out of the thirteen recognized Comunidades in the country). From the regime's perspective, there was ample reason to soften the bitter medicine of privatization with what they assumed would be but a Pyrrhic victory for the Indians. Thus, in their attempt to abolish all Comunidades, the regime legitimated the recently named Comunidad Indígena and its land claim.

That official recognition would become all the more significant when, in 1914, the Conservative government rescinded the 1906 decree and the Comunidades were once again legalized. Notwithstanding these measures, the ladino push against indigenous land continued unabated. During the first two decades of the century, scores of Indians were evicted from the land as the courts listened to new ladino voices and arguments that constantly attacked the indigenous defense, now dependent upon the regime's invention: the Comunidades Indígenas of Boaco and Camoapa.

Let us turn to the most important case. In May 1906, six indigenous families filed suit against the hacendado Leopoldo Ramírez Mairena and the Sociedad

Sánchez y Montenegro over the cofradía land, in conflict since Rafael Caldera had attempted to purchase it in 1889. The municipal government finalized the sale of the cofradía in 1904, when Caldera became the departmental jefe político. The Indian families claimed that, "in community" with the rest of the "casta indígena," they owned one-half of the land in question. Their claim to the 1,000 acres was specifically based on the February 1906 decree that called for the distribution of one-half the communal lands to indigenous families. They accompanied their claim with a copy of the original land title of the Común de Indios of 1765.

The hacendados' lawyers, closely allied to the municipal government, attacked the identity of the plaintiffs: "the lack of legal standing of the plaintiffs as members of the Casta Indígena." Here, it seems that the hacendados' local lawyers were playing on the discrepancy between the "Casta Indígena," which legally no longer existed, and the recently created "Comunidad Indígena."

By suggesting a new reading of the land title, the attorneys attacked the core of the indigenous position. Although they recognized that King Charles had given the land to the Indians, they denied that it was exclusively for the casta indígena. Rather, they argued that the land had been awarded to the municipality because " 'comunidad' is synonymous with Municipalidad, Ayuntamiento, etc." The district judges not only agreed with the reasoning of the hacendados' lawyers, but they strove to develop the argument. The judges' ruling stated that although King Charles had given the land to the "pueblo de indios," "[the term] that he used and continued to be used in the Iberian Peninsula to refer to all the inhabitants of the lands discovered by Christopher Columbus." He went on to say,

> It's commonly known that since time immemorial the Municipalidades have been those who have run the administrative machinery of the communities whose destiny they rule, and it doesn't seem right that the indigenous people of Boaco have been governed by two Municipalidades, one that represents the ladinos' interests and another that represents the indios' interests; but in the course of time, immigration and other social and political circumstances that contributed to the growth of the towns had promoted to the better local positions those who stood out for their skills and knowledge, without excluding the indígenas from the administration.[39]

This ruling merits a serious reading, as it melded elements of local and national history and ideology into a discourse of rights and representation that would suppress indigenous communities as a legitimate historical subject. First, the legal text makes several ahistorical claims about the equivalence of colonial and modern forms of municipal government, such as the following: "the current Municipalidad of Boaco is the same institution that existed in the era when the Spanish Monarch granted the title." The municipal government was the same government that received the land title, and the fact that the former was composed of "indios" had no relevance to the argument of institutional equivalence. This claim was backed by a benign evolutionary vision of "immigration and other political and social circumstances" that allowed for highly intelligent and efficient administrators to take over the municipal reigns of power, ruling fairly over everyone including "indígenas."

As the emerging Liberal elites sought to define a coherent vision of existing society, they had to confront the problem of how "communities" could fit within Liberal juridical order. As Chatterjee argued, the narrative of capital (or liberalism) suppressed the narrative of communities. I would suggest that this court decision revealed a key moment in the process of suppression, signaled by a degree of elite tension and confusion about the question of "community." Although representing the same class interests, the judges implicitly contradicted the attorneys' assertion that "comunidad" was synonymous with "ayuntamiento," or "municipal" government. The court stated, on the contrary, that since "time immemorial" the municipalities had subordinated the (ethnic) communities: "[they] have run the administrative machinery of the communities whose destiny they control." This contradiction in an otherwise seamless transition from the attorneys' to the judges' argument suggests that both were groping their way along new conceptual terrain. Although the ladino elite (the judges and the attorneys) knew who would win this particular battle and who would win the cultural war (those "outstanding" citizens who would rule the nation-state), the method for dealing with the real, existing indigenous communities had not yet been established.

Because the communities had always been subordinated to municipal rule and indigenous identity was implicitly defined in terms of its dependence on ladino power, it followed that the "pueblo indígena" (a community) of Boaco should not be subjected to two ethnically distinct municipal authorities. The judges surely knew that during the colonial era many of the pueblos indígenas were in fact ruled by two such authorities (even in the latter part of the nineteenth century in Jinotega and elsewhere, there were alcaldes ladinos and alcaldes indígenas). Given that the linchpin of the judges' argument was the stated equivalence of the colonial municipality with the modern municipality, this omission of common historical knowledge about the colonial era and recent political institutions is significant. The omission again points not only to bad faith, but moreover to an underlying anxiety the judges experienced as they wrote a decision of immense political importance.

The discursive and material suppression of communities involved the suppression of the identities of the people who formed them. Thus the allusion to Columbus conjured up the arbitrary quality to the naming of "indios," a point amply supported by modern social historians and ethnographers. Yet there is a peculiar resonance at once archaic, imprecise, and exclusionary to the phrase "llamó y llamaban a todos los habitantes." Why did they employ the past and the imperfect tenses but not the present tense? The exclusion of the present as a time when "indios" no longer exist was echoed by the ethnically neutral "outstanding" citizens who emerged to control the new, democratic municipal government.

The judges joined the defense attorneys in impugning the authenticity of the indigenous peasants and their organization: "they called themselves [se hicieron llamar] members of the comunidad indígena and the lack of juridical personality of the 'casta' at the time of the sale has been much argued." The phrase "se hicieron llamar" reflected the artificiality of indigenous identity and in that sense was consistent with the earlier text. The court argued that in the specific case of the cofradía, even though the deed was made in the name of the "casta indígena," that organization did not possess *personalidad jurídica* (legal standing) and by the time it acquired such a dubious (given the abolition of the Comunidades) legal status, the land had already been sold to the hacendados.[40] This particular argument not only carried the day (1909) but also withstood appeals to the court of appeals in Granada (1913) and the Supreme Court (1917).

This series of court decisions was of decisive importance for the six extended families who had lived and worked in Santiago de Brito, for the indigenous peoples of Boaco and Camoapa, and for the emergence of a nationalist political discourse that would efface the history and lived experience of those communities of Nicaraguans who identified themselves as "indios" or "indígenas."

This process can be captured in two examples of the local ladino memory of the court decision and the era of conflict between the municipality and the casta indígena. First, consider the graphic representation that can be seen in a beautiful engraving on a wooden door in the house of the mayor of Boaco (1990–1996), a descendant of the ladino elite of the 1890s. The engraving reproduces the words of the original deed that refer to what the "común de indios" paid for the land: "cien botijas de miel, cien arrobas de cera, cien arrobas de pita, una águila de oro, y medio almud de plata" (100 jugs of honey, 100 arrobas of wax, 100 arrobas of pita [fiber from which hats and baskets are made], a golden eagle, and a half almud of silver). The mayor's explanation, rooted in local lore, was that the engraving represented the deed to the municipality's ejidos.

The second example concerns Emilio Sobalvarro, the principal local historian of Boaco, whose writings evince great pride in the indigenous forebearers of the *autóctonos* of Boaco (as opposed to outsiders) and indeed express much sympathy for the casta indígena. Sobalvarro wrote about the court case:

> One day [during the 1910s], when it was least expected, the sentence appeared. . . . It confirmed that the democratically elected Municipios are the Community representatives and also the owners of the ejidal lands. . . . Despite the unfavorable sentence, the Casta indígena continued to elect its leadership. . . . If memory serves us, we can assure that the last president of the Boaco Indios was Don Rosendo Pérez.[41]

Sobalvarro erred on a fundamental point: the verdict only had affected the twenty caballerías of cofradía land, not the other 1,400 caballerías of land the casta indígena and the municipality disputed. Moreover, the use of the phrase "sudden decision" suppressed the agency of the ladino elite in the judicial process. Sobalvarro's writings reproduced collective misunderstandings embedded in the local ladino memory. Since 1909 Boaqueño ladinos publicly and privately acted as if the court decision was also about the *ejidos* (municipal land). Nevertheless, the battle over the lands continued into the late 1930s.

Sobalvarro was correct in pointing out that the casta indígena continued to elect its authorities following the decision, and it is probable that Rosendo Pérez was one of its last presidents. He also stated that for several years after the decision, "the Indians paid rent to the municipality and the Comuni-dad."[42] Although it is possible that at times Indians had paid two land rents, Sobalvarro's statement more likely referred to the decades-long, smoldering protest of the indigenous groups of Boaco and Camoapa, who continued to contest the municipality through nonpayment of land rent. Finally, we should note the local historian's transcription of an undated, typical land rental contract issued by the casta indígena. Following the transcription, Sobalvarro concluded: "We have tried to imbue these notes with something of the tradi-tion and a lot of what is written here is for those boaqueños or not, who read us to relish in these references the history of our land [or town]."[43]

My point here is not to criticize a sensitive local historian who loves his hometown and its people. Rather, it is to suggest, first, that the collective memory of Boaco, as recorded by Sobalvarro, does not so much suppress the class-ethnic conflicts as displace them chronologically and transform the meanings of such critical moments as the court decision and subsequent indigenous efforts to fight for the land. Such a narrative leads to a harmonious portrait of the contemporary history of a beloved land. Moreover, the ladino interpretation of the court decisions both fortified the denial of indigenous claims and provided a powerful political basis for further ladino encroach-ments on indigenous land. It also contributed to the creation of a historical memory of the slow, nostalgic, inevitable march of civilization.

This memory, I would argue, emerged as part of a legal and political discourse that compulsively questioned the authenticity of indigenous orga-nization and identity. The local elite did not doubt that the casta indígena inhabited a radically distinct social-cultural world from ladinos of all social classes. Yet, to accept the validity of indigenous claims to citizenship and communal rights would be to delegitimize and destabilize local ladino identi-ties and power.

It is impossible to ascertain how the official and extraofficial impugning of the authenticity of indigenous organization and their members' potential for autonomous action affected the development of indigenous identities. How-ever, the writings of Charles Taylor offer us a clue to its importance. Following a discussion of the dialogic basis of modern identity, he writes,

> Of course, the point is not that this dependence on others arose with the
> age of authenticity. A form of dependence was always there. The socially

derived identity was by its very nature dependent on society. But in the earlier age recognition never arose as a problem. General recognition was built into the socially derived identity by virtue of the very fact that it was based on social categories that everyone took for granted. Yet inwardly derived, personal, original identity doesn't enjoy this recognition *a priori*. It has to win it through exchange and the attempt can fail. What has come about with the modern age is not the need for recognition but the conditions in which the attempt to be recognized can fail. That is why the need is acknowledged for the first time.[44]

Taylor's discussion of recognition is closely tied to his argument that certain forms of liberalism are inhospitable to cultural "difference" because they cannot support goals of cultural survival. I would suggest that the failure to recognize the authenticity of indigenous organization in Boaco and Camoapa strongly conditioned the effacement of indigenous community and the identities that sustained and were nurtured by it.

Joanne Rappaport's study of Colombian Indians uncovers a remarkably similar process at work during the 1930s, when many indigenous people lost their land, their communal organization, and their identity. She depicts local indigenous identities under a siege not unlike that which afflicted the Boaqueños:

> What constitutes identity within the community was precisely that which identifies *comuneros* as non-Indians on the outside. Neighboring mestizos proffer these same cultural attributes, including Spanish monolingualism and articulation with the market economy, as examples of the Cumbales' loss of indigenous lifeways in the hopes of persuading the government authorities to extinguish the *resguardo* [communal land] and free its lands for privatization.[45]

Regardless of the accuracy of Taylor's general argument about the "age of authenticity" and its teleological assumptions, his observation does help us grasp a particular moment in Boaco. The lack of recognition there occurred precisely at a critical moment of transition when for the first time identities based on social categories could no longer be assumed. Thus at the moment when the ladino expansion forced a redefinition of indigenous communities and identities, their calculated lack of recognition of the organizational matrix of those identities and their physical displacement of so many villagers gravely compromised the indigenous capacity for renewing their ethnic identities.

## The Language of Ethnic Conflict

Although local ladino historical memory associates the disappearance of the casta indígena with their defeat in the courtroom, the victory of the Conservative counterrevolution of 1909 to 1910 ushered in a new era of intense militancy for the region's Indians. Thus, for example, in 1911 two indígenas wrote a letter to a Managua newspaper, emphasizing how their collectivity expected the Conservative regime installed in 1910 to respect their rights and to

> sink the ambitions of all those who by the power of their money have wrenched our lands from us all our lives, taking us from our homes without consideration. They will be convinced that in this new regime justice can't be bought. . . . Sirs this business is over. . . . We the *indios* have to look after our own interests.[46]

In this brief declaration, we can sense the degree to which the overthrow of Zelaya stimulated indigenous defense against the ladino encroachment on their land. Although the complete declaration employs the formal term "Comunidad Indígena," the key expression of identity in the text is "nosotros los indios (we the indios)." That choice of words was significant given other available options, especially "indígena," but moreover because "indio" as elsewhere in Latin America had heavily negative connotations of ignorance and barbarism. I would suggest that the use of "indio" instead of "indígena" was at least in part a response to the intensity of ethnic and class strife in the region. Moreover, in the context of ladino efforts to delegitimize the authenticity of indigenous organization and identities the choice of the term "indio" was perhaps an expression of pride, a now familiar practice of inverting a denigrating label.

The Conservative regime in Managua acted as if it understood this indigenous message; it took important steps to solidify an alliance with the leaders of the casta indígena of Boaco and Camoapa. In 1914 Ildefonso Cerda, an indigenous leader who had served as mayor and regidor during the 1890s, won election as president of the casta indígena. He assumed office one month after the Conservative government restored legality to the indigenous communities that the Zelaya regime had abolished in 1906.[47] Most important, the government-approved statutes of the indigenous organization allowed the Boaqueño Indians to reclaim their authority over the disputed lands. Indeed the government edict ordered all fenced-in savanna land to be opened up within three months. Moreover, as if to symbolically reaffirm the previous unity between community and municipality, in 1915, Ildefonso Cerda became the mayor of Boaco.[48]

The Conservative regime consistently supported the region's indigenous population in their conflicts with the local ladino elites. The Conservative commitment to the Indians, however, had limits; they refused to back the Comunidad's judicial appeals in the cofradía land case. Regime support came less out of an ideological predisposition to indigenous organization and culture or to colonial-style paternalism than from astutely pragmatic politics. The urban ladino population of the core cities in the highlands—such as Jinotega, Matagalpa, Boaco, and Camoapa—was overwhelmingly Liberal. Their political domination over the indigenous population and, in particular, their growing control over Indian land and labor had antagonized what could be a major base of available military or electoral support for the Conservatives. As late as 1932, after four years of Liberal national and local rule, the indigenous districts of Boaco still voted Conservative by a margin of 3 to 1.[49]

Regardless of party affiliation, however, the question of indigenous authenticity became vital in attempting to gain national allies in the local conflict. Consider, for example, the 1922 response of the mayor of Camoapa, Virgilio Falla, to the departmental jefe político and the *ministro de gobernación* (minister of government) concerning indigenous protests about "violent abuses" connected to the assessment of land taxes:

> I have not answered before because I wanted to have truthful information and base myself on justice and law . . . [about the] unfair and illegal claims of the directive and people of the "casta indígena." . . . There are three kinds of lands here, national, ejidal and private. . . . There are no lands of the comunidad indígena. . . . They always protest when they measure the national land for purchase, but the surveyor has not taken them into consideration because they don't present any document to give proof of their ownership of even a handful of dirt.[50]

The Camoapan mayor's defense of the municipality's right to tax the Indians framed the entire issue in terms of the indigenous organization's illegitimacy. First, his phrase "no existen terrenos de la comunidad indígena" referred back to the artificial naming of the Comunidades in Boaco and Camoapa. No indigenous documents during this period—not even the Statutes of the Comunidad Indígena of Boaco—refer to themselves as the Comunidad Indígena, but rather as the casta indígena. The Mayor's declaration, at once bitter and uncompromising, questioned the legitimacy of the indigenous organization because its raison d'être was the communal possession of land, of which they owned "not even a handful of dirt." The mayor went on to point out that many individual indígenas had little farms and garden plots but that they had to pay municipal tax on the land.

Mayor Falla's superiors were not easily convinced. Over the next ten months, the conflict between the municipal government and the casta indígena intensified as the latter pressed for the intervention of the departmental and national authorities. In July 1922, the indigenous leaders convinced the jefe político to abrogate the land tax. Falla responded in outrage against that action and against the Indians' suggestion to the jefe político that Falla was a closet Liberal:

> The charge was made with the sole objective of punishing this municipio by saying that we are enemies of the government, a crazy idea, because we are all conservatives and supporters of the sacred principles . . . of the great Conservative Party.[51]

Backed by local judges, Falla continued to punish the casta indígena. His harsh verbal treatment of his superiors must have reflected the sharpness and perhaps desperation of the local struggle and Falla's view that outsiders who simply did not understand the Indians were exacerbating a difficult situation. In a communication from the mayor to the jefe político, Falla complained:

> Even the jefe político doesn't tell the truth in assuring that the casta indígena does preserve their title, while the municipio hasn't been able to present any documentation. . . . The title that exists and that this municipio preserves refers to the municipalidad and not to the casta indígena. . . . About the abuses and the immoral actions committed against the casta indígena, we don't know what they are. If the municipal treasurer has fined people in the local court . . . if it's immoral to collect a local tax.[52]

At this point, there was no patch of common ground, much less a bridge across the ethnic divide in Camoapa or Boaco. Falla was willing to risk his political career by calling the jefe político a liar, so as to convey the local ladino view of reality: the Indians have no claim to the land; they have no land title; it is all a lie. What to Indians were abuses and immoral acts, to the ladinos were merely their law-abiding efforts on behalf of progress. Falla's outburst also suggested an equally large gulf between those ladinos locked in conflict with the casta indígena and those on the outside who, at best, were interested in votes.

The local indigenous groups, empowered by the Conservative regime, similarly had no space for local compromise in their language. The following court testimony in 1918 by fifty-year-old indígena Esteban Martínez presents again a view of reality that would have seemed inverted to the local ladinos:

> I do not grow anything nor sow in the land that you affirm is yours. I cultivate and sow in lands that my parents possessed as one of the members of the *naturales Indios* of this city whose ownership was never threatened. In the same way that I have never been disturbed during the thirty years in my possession. Thus I find it incredibly strange that you claim to make it yours, Mr. Montenegro . . . 2,000 palos of coffee, 51 cacao trees, "chaguites de palma" to make hats. Thus . . . we the naturales Indios own these lands.[53]

Martínez ironically phrased his defense as a misunderstanding: he did not cultivate Montenegro's land, and it was therefore baffling that the hacendado should make such an accusation. Martínez only cultivated the land that his family had always possessed along with the other "naturales Indios" who collectively owned the land. He reaffirmed the legitimacy of the family's land possession with the use of the term "naturales Indios" of Boaco, a direct reference to the original land title. Once again, the failure to use the official term recognized by the Conservative regime, "Comunidad Indígena," reflects not only a degree of stubbornness among the indigenous folk, but moreover the regional inflection of illegitimacy associated with that name. In general, however, Indians could question local ladino pretensions and authority precisely because of the relationship with the national regime that the Indian leaders were careful to cultivate. Thus, for example, the capitán-general of the casta indígena of Camoapa sent a letter congratulating Bartolomé Martínez, upon his inauguration as vice-president in 1921: "The casta indígena is pleased because of the felicitous success obtained by the great conservative party . . . and of your honorable inauguration because the nation so willed it."[54]

The Conservative-Indian alliance was able to slow the mass expulsion of the casta indígena from their lands. But the constant skirmishes fought by the hacendados and their employees against individual indigenous families in courtrooms and on the savannas took their toll. In 1923, a Leonés newspaper reported that land concentration in Boaco was driving large numbers of Indians to migrate toward the Atlantic Coast.[55] Between 1897 and 1920, the population of the indigenous villages declined from some 14,000 to approximately 10,000. Between 1920 and 1940 that rate of population decline would continue as the total municipal population dropped by one-third, with the large bulk of the decline among the indigenous population. For example, the population of the indigenous village of San Buenaventura that had 1,695 inhabitants at the turn of the century dropped to 425 by 1950. Similarly, the cañadas of Sácal had 526 inhabitants in 1897 and only 225 in 1950.[56] Oral testimony, newspaper reports, and the myriad of lost land cases strongly suggest that the population decline reflected the migration of Indians following land evictions or as a result of political conflict.[57]

## Politics and the Disintegration of the Casta Indígena

The partisan conflicts and warfare of the 1920s played themselves out with a special brutality among the indigenous population of the Central Highlands. The Liberal-Conservative coalition governments of Bartolomé Martínez (1923–1924) and Carlos Solórzano (1925) made a serious, if not successful, effort to penetrate the Chamorrista Conservative base among the indigenous population. The failure to sway the casta indígena away from Chamorro, the one national political figure who had consistently supported their cause, led the coalition government to practice the same form of politics their predecessors had mastered: violence and intimidation.[58] Typically, the coalition government forces imprisoned or recruited Indians into the army so that they would be ineligible to vote in the elections. Chamorrista Indian resistance led to violence and perhaps scores of deaths.

Chamorro staged a successful coup in 1925 that by early 1926 had provoked a civil war. In Camoapa, the casta indígena took advantage of the shift in power, as the local ladinos had aligned themselves with the coalition government. Francisco Pérez Picado—a scribe, rural schoolteacher, and former capitán-general and president of the casta indígena—became mayor of Camoapa.[59] Oral tradition recalls this period as one of indigenous unity and hope. Yet Picado's ascendance to local power was but a brief interlude, brought to a sharp halt by the civil war (1926–1927) and the 1928 inauguration of a long line of Liberal national governments.

From 1923 to 1925, the coalition government had managed to gain a degree of support among the highlands Indians (support that subsequently was transferred to the Liberal party). But they advanced at the cost of much violence. Chamorrista Conservatives reported the following electoral incidents:

> In Camoapa election day was horrifying: it is a very conservative town. They wanted to get votes by force, to jail all the conservative leaders and conscript all the indígenas. In Masigüe [indigenous village near Camoapa] they killed another one of ours . . . to avoid responsibilities they spread alarming news of revolt. . . . Camoapa was the scene of the persecutions, jailings and killings.[60]

In the indigenous villages near Camoapa and Boaco, the elections were brutal farces. Yet, Chamorro won the elections in those indigenous villages where the government did not blatantly coerce the electoral result.[61] When the Conservatives returned to power, they began to engage in the same game of intimidation and coercion against dissident Indians. According to the reports of the occupying marine force, in 1927 Conservative-instilled fear played an important political role among the casta indígena of Boaco. According to marine officer L. E. Fagan, the capitán-general, Rosendo Pérez, a Liberal, failed to appear at a scheduled meeting because he expected the Conservative-run police to arrest him and his fellow capitanes de cañada. Fagan understood that when the capitanes were arrested they would be barred automatically from voting in the next election. When the marine officer could finally arrange a meeting, Pérez presented him with a petition that Fagan summarized as follows:

> The politicians have taken the Indian lands. They are oppressed. . . . Attempts have been made to break up the Casta Indígena and at the last elections the Indians in general Liberals were prevented from voting by Conservative soldiers armed with rifles.[62]

Rosendo Pérez's complaint about "attempts to break up the Casta Indígena" referred to concrete actions by each party to suppress the indigenous leadership aligned with their adversaries. Thus, the Liberal-Conservative coalition government installed a Liberal casta indígena leadership in 1925 that remained locked in conflict with the Conservatives who had served in the Junta Directiva (Board of Directors) since 1914. The conflict between the two groups in the context of the civil war of 1926 to 1927 had devastating consequences for the Boaqueño Indians.

The marine officers generally concurred with the dominant ladino image of the Indians as docile, fearful creatures. In 1928, the commanding officer of the marines at Boaco reported

> The Indians are largely Liberal and their vote is essential in this town for the coming election. These Indians are very superstitious and religious and can be easily swayed by either party. The priest here is a strong Conservative and mixes politics with religion and in so doing succeeds to a certain degree in frightening the Indians into becoming Conservatives. The Indians are very ignorant and led by a chief named Pérez and represented in politics by Don Juan Morales who acts for them and is a Liberal. They naturally bend towards him, but could easily be made to bend toward the opposite party through the medium of fear.[63]

Despite their sympathy for the Indians, these marines were not soldier-ethnographers: they assimilated the dominant ladino stereotypes about Indians without much local knowledge to question them. This report was misleading about the church; over the previous decade it had cracked down hard on all manner of indigenous religious expression, if anything diminishing its political influence.[64] The marine also erred about politics: Chamorrista Conservatism had deep support among the Boaqueño and Camoapan Indians as evidenced by the voting patterns in 1924 (and post facto in 1928 and 1932).

In addition to assimilating the dominant stereotypes about the cowed, fearful political behavior of the Indians, the 1928 report did reveal something important about the crisis that confronted the divided organization. The marine report stated that Juan B. Morales was the Liberal "representative" of the casta. Morales was one of the principal latifundistas of the region, a man who had already expropriated thousands of acres of indigenous land, particularly in the Camoapa area. Thus, in Camoapa, the triumph of Liberalism meant not only losing an indigenous mayor but converting a latifundista into the key leader of an indigenous faction of the dominant party. The effects of the political reversal became apparent within a few years. In the early 1930s a wealthy cattle rancher, Eduardo Duarte Mena, bailed out the financially strapped municipal government, loaning it $12,000 (from 1912 to 1940, one dollar equaled one peso) for a land survey, the repair of the electrical plant, and the repair of the slaughterhouse. In return, the municipality offered Duarte 1,600 hectares of municipal-indigenous lands.[65]

Meanwhile, Juan B. Morales's star was rising: he became in 1935 the first jefe político of the department of Boaco. But his position as patron of a faction of the region's Indians was indicative of the deep divisions within the community and deeper ones between Boaco and Camoapa. Morales's power evidenced the increasingly subordinate role played by indigenous leaders in any political alliance. As Gerald Sider points out in his discussion of Native Americans,

> None of the available strategies for coping with domination can possibly be very effective, or effective for very long. Isolation, confrontation, accommodation, opposition: all have their partial successes and their costs, their adherents and their opponents. . . . One of the pressures on native peoples that often engenders splits is the *changing* ways that ethnic otherness is integrated into, used, and also marginalized and made useless by the large society and the changing opportunities and costs this creates for native people.[66]

Sider's analysis of native divisions is in part relevant to Boaco; by the 1920s and 1930s Boaqueño ethnic otherness was integrated and marginalized largely through its political identifications. The Indians' placing of Juan B. Morales in a role as representative was a type of accommodationist strategy, but one with a greater cost than most. For Morales to assume the representation of indigenous reality—even if just in the eyes of the marines and national authorities—both effectively camouflaged his role as a great land grabber and legitimized his status as "Indian expert." By the late 1930s when Somoza's nascent dictatorship at once made partisan affiliation a less important matter and enshrined Juan B. Morales as the undisputed political boss of the department of Boaco (including Camoapa), the full-scale marginalization and disintegration of the community could become a reality.

## Conclusion

Over the first few decades of the century, the failure to recognize the legit-imacy of indigenous organization and culture had multiple effects on its members. The most important consequences surely were similar to those of any colonized people: the internalization of the dominant cultural view of the Indian and its accompanying self-hatred. More immediately, however, the ladino denial of the validity and authenticity of indigenous organization con-ditioned the fragmentation of indigenous identity and resistance. In the con-text of a wave of ladino encroachments on their land and violent changes in the national political landscape, that fragmentation of communal resistance had by the 1930s contributed to the disintegration of the remaining threads of communal organization.

Florencia Mallon, in her recent *Peasant and Nation,* argues:

> Concrete historical actors struggle over power, but they articulate the meaning of their struggles through discourses about citizenship, legit-imacy, justice and community. Discourses are not political or historical actors but the products of alliance and confrontation among human beings as they attempt to construct and own the meanings of their actions.[67]

We have examined the power struggle between local elites and indigenous leadership groups, both searching for alliances with the state. As Mallon's perspective implies, the indigenous groups of Boaco not only lost their power struggles but they simultaneously lost discursive struggles for control over meanings and memories. That discursive and political "loss" contributed to the destruction, dispersal, and disarticulation of native communal identities and cultures. Moreover, the silencing of indigenous voices set the stage for the devastating anti-indigenous repression that crippled the highlands commu-nities during the 1940s and 1950s.

This local history of Boaco allows us to see how Chatterjee's "suppression of the narrative of community" relates to the question of "cultural loss." For the loss occurred in that area of discursive suppression of communities, a sup-pression that embedded itself in the consciousness of its members. The sup-pression was so powerful because it worked on two interrelated levels: the denial of communal identities as valid constituents of the nation and the appropriation of communal resources that that refusal motivated and justi-fied. Combined, they make the universal narrative of liberalism and capital appear as the destiny of humanity, and the narrative of communal history seem like a quaint foxhunt in a forest of primordial essences.

## Notes

1  "To Be Indian, to Be Bolivian: Ethnic and National Discourses of Identity," in Joel Sherzer and Greg Urban, eds. *Nation-States and Indians in Latin America* (Austin: University of Texas Press), p. 111.

2  Kay Warren writes: "culture is not 'lost' but transformed," in Kay Warren, "Trans-forming Memories and Histories: The Meanings of Ethnic Resurgence for Mayan Indians," in Alfred Stepan, ed., *Americas: New Interpretive Essays* (New York: Oxford University Press, 1992), 205.

3  Les Field, "Who Are the Indians? Reconceptualizing Indigenous Identity, Re-sistance, and the Role of Social Science in Latin America," *Latin American Research Review* 29, no. 3 (1994): 240–241. Field, of course, recognizes that states have destroyed indigenous groups. Warren, in her fascinating essay "Transforming Memories" underscores the fact that the indigenous movements indeed fully ac-cept essentialist models of loss and survival.

4  The town of Camoapa lies twelve miles to the southeast of the town of Boaco. Both towns formed part of the department of Chontales, save for several years during the first decade of the twentieth century when they combined to form Jerez. Since 1935 they have both belonged to the department of Boaco.

5  Partha Chatterjee, *The Nation and Its Fragments: Colonial and Postcolonial Histories* (Princeton: Princeton University Press, 1993), 236.

6  Chatterjee, *The Nation and Its Fragments*, 238.

7  Gustavo Niederlin, *The State of Nicaragua* (Philadelphia: Philadelphia Commercial Museum, 1898), 62–63. The combined wealth of Camoapa and Boaco represented less than one-half of 1 percent of national property values.

8  Francisco Acuña Escobar, *Biografía de General Rigoberto Cabezas* (Masaya: Tipo-grafía El Espectador, 1940), p. 69.

9  Fernando Buitrago Morales, *Lo que he visto al pasar* (León: Editorial Hospicio, 1961), 24.

10  Buitrago Morales, *Lo que he visto*, 155.

11  Testimony cited in Mina Namdar Irani and Laurent Levard, *Estudio de sistema agrario en la zona de Camoapa, departamento de Boaco* (Managua 1984), p. 70.

12  *La Flecha* (Managua), June 17, 1950.

13  Buitrago Morales, *Lo que he visto*, 160–161.

14  Rafael Pérez, S.J., *La Compañía de Jesús en Colombia y Centroamérica*, 4 vols. (Valladolid: Imprenta Castellana, 1898), 3:326.

15  *Gaceta Oficial,* December 21, 1890.

16  *Gaceta Oficial,* January 5, 1890.

17  Ibid. Also see Manuel Castrillo Gámez, *Reseña histórica de Nicaragua, 1887–1895* (Managua: Talleres Nacionales, 1963).

18  Coronel Salvador Barquero to Francisco Acuña Escobar, November 7, 1939; cited in Acuña Escobar, *Biografía de General Rigoberto Cabezas,* 74.

19  Ibid., 75.

20  "Certificación del título de la tierra de Boaco," September 2, 1905, in *Nicaragua Indígena* 1, nos. 4–6 (April–December 1947): 16–25. This title has a description of the formation of Boaco. Indeed the Crown awarded the Boaqueños and the Camoapans generous land grants precisely because of their military valor against the nomadic and hostile indigenous groups to the east. Similarly, they were exempted from tribute precisely because they had not been conquered by the Spanish. Also see Francisco de Posada, "Relación geográfica del partido de Chontales y Sébaco" in *Revista Conservadora del Pensamiento Centroamericano* 98 (November 1968): 24–27.

21  Cited in Acuña Escobar, *Biografía de General Rigoberto Cabezas,* 71. It is, of course, possible that the Indians used a term they had used before: "vecino." For example, Julián Guerrero, *Boaco* (Managua: Tipografía Alemán, 1957), cites a municipal document from 1883 that awarded the status of "vecino" to one Elio Huete, which conferred on him the right to cultivate land and graze cattle. However, Cabezas claimed that they had made him a "ciudadano."

22  The use of the term "ciudadano" suggests that the indigenous elite envisioned their own organization as something of a parallel indigenous-controlled municipality. Moreover, citizenship officially was reserved for males with 100 pesos of wealth, far beyond the reach of the overwhelming majority of Nicaraguans. At the same time, the indigenous conferral of "citizenship" on Cabezas perhaps suggests that his access to land depended on his acceptance of indigenous political hegemony.

23  See Jeffrey Gould, "Vana Ilusión: The Highlands Indians and the Myth of Nicaragua Mestiza," *Hispanic American Historical Review* 73, no. 3 (August 1993): 403–408.

24  *Libro de actas de la Alcaldía de Boaco, 1895–1898,* municipality of Boaco. In 1898, the mayor and a majority of the regidores (municipal council) were indigenous. I identified the indigenous members with the help of Emilio Sobalvarro Suárez's pamphlet entitled "Retazos de Boaco: tierra de encantadores" (Boaco, 1971). Many of the identifications have been confirmed in other documents that refer specifically to the Comunidad or casta indígena.

25  "*Leopoldo Mairena v. Alejandro Suazo et al.,* Expediente judicial de la Corte Suprema de Justicia, 1908–1917." Located in the Juzgado Civil of Boaco, p. 11, folio 89615.

26  *Libro de actas de la Alcaldía de Boaco, 1895–1898,* November 2, 1898.

27  Ibid. Specifically the council named two indigenous people to fill the role as *fiadores* (guarantors) of the elected guardian of the land title.

28  *Libro de actas de la Alcaldía de Boaco, 1895–1898,* May 15, 1901. It is worth stressing that this new multiethnic council controlled by ladinos also issued a strong and effective protest to the regime against the forced recruitment of indigenous labor for the coffee plantations near Managua. This concern for the rural poor did not translate into a commitment to the indigenous organization, much less to its land claims.

29  Florencia Mallon, *Peasant and Nation: The Making of Postcolonial Mexico and Peru* (Berkeley: University of California Press, 1995), 63–88.

30  *Libro de actas de la Alcaldía de Boaco, alcaldía* (mayor's office) of Boaco, January 5, 1905.

31  James Scott, *The Hidden Transcripts: Domination and the Arts of Resistance* (New Haven: Yale University Press, 1990), 23–36.

32  *Libro de actas de la Alcaldía de Boaco,* August 5, 1905.

33  "Election Report of Major Jesse Miller," November 11, 1920, U.S. National Archives, U.S. State Department, RG 57, no. 2760. Chamorro was president from 1917 to 1921, a period in which he solidified preexisting indigenous support.

34  Sandino wrote, "Juzgo que la municipalidad de Boaco tiene perfecto derecho sobre la administración de los terrenos porque a ella le fueron concedidos como lo expresa el mismo título." *Memorias del Ministerio de Gobernación y anexos, 1905* (Managua, 1906).

35  "Informe del comisionado del gobierno para el arreglo de las dificultades surgidas contra los bienes de la casta indígena de Boaco," September 1, 1905, in *Memorias del Ministerio de Gobernación, 1905,* appendix A.

36  *Memorias del Ministerio de Gobernación, 1905* (Managua, 1906), appendix A.

37  Ibid.

38  "Decreto de 7 de mayo 1907" and "Decreto de 21 de julio 1907," *Memorias del Ministerio de Gobernación y Sus Anexos, 1906–1907* (Managua: Compañía Tipografía Internacional, 1907), 32–34. The ministro de gobernación chose Miguel Arana to be the surveyor. Arana had accompanied Sandino on the mission to Boaco in 1905 and served as his assistant.

39  "*Expediente Alejandro Suazo, Pedro Rodríguez et al. v. Dr. Ramírez Mairena,* Corte Suprema de Justicia," February 25, 1917, Juzgado Civil of Boaco folio 89618. The document includes the different stages of the case starting in 1906. The court of appeals first ruled on the case in 1909. The judges also cited the complex precedent of the former indigenous municipality of Sutiaba, which was annexed to León in 1902, thereby losing its political autonomy and its ejidos. The citing of the Sutiaban precedent is complicated, for in that case, unlike in Boaco, two geographically distinct municipalities were merged with no other goal than to undermine indigenous political and economic autonomy. The judges cited the case, however, to show that there were indeed two municipal governments.

40  In Boaco, the founding of the Comunidad Indígena was a state-imposed turn-of-the-century phenomenon. Sandino reports that in neighboring Camoapa, where a

very similar conflict occurred, the Indians' claim was invalidated precisely because their "Comunidad Indígena" still lacked *personería jurídica* (legal recognition).

41  Sobalvarro Suárez, *Retazos de Boaco,* 41.

42  Interview with Emilio Sobalvarro Suárez, Boaco, January 1992.

43  Sobalvarro Suárez, *Retazos de Boaco,* 42. The land was rented at two centavos per manzana, a figure that suggests a date after 1914.

44  Charles Taylor, *An Essay on Multiculturalism and the Politics of Recognition* (Princeton: Princeton University Press, 1992), 34–35.

45  Joanne Rappaport, *Cumbé Reborn: An Andean Ethnography of History* (Chicago: University of Chicago Press, 1994), 36–37.

46  *El Correo de Managua,* September 14, 1911.

47  *Nicaragua Indígena* 1, no. 1 (July–December 1946), 58.

48  *Libro de acuerdos,* Boaco, June 1915. Unfortunately there remains no relevant information contained in the 1915 book that might shed light on Cerda's administration. No books exist for the following two years.

49  See, for example, Consejo Nacional de Elecciones, "Informe sobre las elecciones de 1924 and 1928" (Managua: Tipografía Nacional, 1929). After four years of Liberal government, in the 1932 elections, the Conservatives won in the indigenous cañada of Sácal, for example, by a margin of 284 to 124 and in Saguatepe by 209 to 263.

50  Entry for March 30, 1922, in *Libro de notas y telegramas,* Alcaldía de Camoapa, 1922–1923.

51  Entry for July 24, 1922, in ibid.

52  Entry for January 2, 1923, in ibid.

53  "*Esteban Martínez v. Andrés Montenegro,* Juzgado Civil de Boaco," May 7, 1918.

54  Francisco Picado López to Bartolomé Martínez, January 4, 1921, Private archives of Aurora Martínez (PAAM).

55  *El Cronista* (León), June 22, 1923.

56  Population data for 1897 comes from Niederlin, *The State of Nicaragua.* Data for 1950 comes from Dirección General de Estadísticas y Censos, *Censo general de la República de Nicaragua, 1950* (Managua: Talleres Nacionales, 1952).

57  For a sensitive, if nostalgic and impressionistic, portrait of indigenous migration from the Boaqueño cañadas to the mountainous jungles to the east, see Emilio Sobalvarro Suárez's article "La Montaña" in *La Flecha* (Managua), June 17, 1950.

58  *La coalición ante el Congreso: recurso de nulidad contra las elecciones de autoridades supremas de 1920* (Managua: Tipografía Alemán, 1920), 48–49. The Conservatives played a very similar game with the casta indígena out of local habit or national political desperation or both. In the 1920 elections, Liberals reported that the ruling Conservative party recruited Liberal activists among the highlands Indians into the military, tied their hands behind their back, and marched them to the Honduran frontier. Similarly, on election day, capitanes de cañada marched masses of Indians into town and led them to the voting booths under military discipline. One observer in Matagalpa saw the Indians as "a flock of tame sheep."

59 I have found no documentary evidence that Picado became mayor. Juan Hernández López, a schoolteacher, in the four-page document "Datos históricos y
monográficos de la Comunidad de Salinas y Mombacho del Municipio de Camoapa," written in 1991, states that Picado was mayor. In conversation he cited
community elders as his source. On the other hand, the *Libro de actas de la
municipalidad de Camoapa, 1926* does list Rosendo Ortiz as *alcalde suplente* (substitute mayor). Ortiz was a leader of the Comunidad Indígena.

60 See "Informe del Consejo Nacional de Elecciones," November 22, 1924, in U.S.
National Archives, U.S. State Department, RG 57, 817.00/3278.

61 Ibid. In Masigüe, mentioned in the preceding quote, the Liberals triumphed 217 to
0 and they racked up similar tallies in Tesorero (118 to 0) and Gigantepe (95 to 0).
The Conservatives, however, won in the Camoapa area by 1009 to 992 and in the
Boaco district by 1761 to 995.

62 "Report of Captain L. E. Fagan, May 29, 1927, Boaco, Nicaragua," U.S. National
Archives, RG 127, entry 43-A, file 5th Regiment, 43 and 49 Co., box 24.

63 "Report of F. W. Harlon," Boaco, July 15, 1928, U.S. National Archives, RG 127, entry
220, box 801 (2).

64 Under the guidance of a Father Niebrowski, who arrived in Boaco in 1916, the
church cracked down on indigenous religious festivals. For example, Guerrero,
*Boaco*, 105, and interview with Emilio Sobalvarro, Boaco, January 1992.

65 *Libro de actas de la municipalidad de Camoapa*, May 26, 1933, October 2, 1933, and
December 15, 1933. The Ministerio de Gobernación did not give immediate approval for this sale of ejidal land.

66 Gerald M. Sider, *Lumbee Indian Histories: Race, Ethnicity, and Indian Identity in the
Southern United States* (New York: Cambridge University Press, 1994), 280–281.

67 Mallon, *Peasant and Nation*, 312.

# 3

## "The Rebel Race": The Struggles of the
## Indigenous Community of Sutiaba, 1900–1960

Sutiaba existed before the arrival of the Spanish and it was a free people who cultivated the land. The Conquest was a curse and not a benediction. Instead of helping the Indian they came to rob, to assassinate, and to take away the best we had.—Dr. Feliciano Pacheco Antón, *Barricada*, October 12, 1990

It was sometime around 1810 when Fray Nicolás García Jerez [maximum leader of the church], a truly superior man, but perhaps influenced by his high-class Spanish background, only called Padre Ruiz, his secretary, "Padre Indio." One day, Thursday of Corpus, a day of great pomp, Fray Nicolás was followed by a large procession of dignitaries and happened upon Padre Ruiz [of Sutiaba] who, under an unrelenting sun, was moving bones from the cemetery to the Pantheon. Fray Nicolás was so surprised to see him doing such difficult manual labor that he asked him with great concern, "What are you doing there Padre Indio?" Padre Ruiz responded, "Your lordship, I am trying to figure out the difference between the bones of an Indian and a Spaniard."—Nicolás Buitrago Matus, *León: la sombra de Pedrarias*

Soy indio de Sutiaba
vengo desde la gleva que sufre los zarpazos del despojo
Comunidad Indígena
saqueada y dividida por arteras maniobras demagogas

Yo quiero preguntarle con un grito
para que el grito vaya por la selva
y se haga fortaleza en la montaña.

¿Dónde está la libertad del indio,
el derecho que tuvo sobre el río
que fue de sus manglares y sus llanos
por donde galopaba su esperanza al son de su tambor
y de su canto?

Virge rural,

muchacha campesina,

dejaste de cantar cuando la guerra te

arrebató el pregón de tu marisco.

—Enrique Concepción de la Fonseca, "Grito Indio," Sutiaba, 1988

In Sutiaba there is a large tree known as El Tamarindón (the Great Tamarind). According to the Indians, in 1610 the Spanish hanged Adiact, their last cacique, from El Tamarindón. The hanging of Adiact, who was betrayed by a jealous suitor of his daughter, Flor de Caña, provoked a massacre of many Indians. For the Sutiabas, El Tamarindón commemorates the tragedy of the conquest and at the same time symbolizes their threatened ethnic solidarity. This communal solidarity was evident during the 1950s, when the Sutiabas launched militant activities in which up to 1,000 people participated, without a single word of the preparations being discovered by the authorities (something inconceivable in any other part of Nicaragua). One Sutiaba, when questioned about this admirable capacity to maintain internal security, responded, "Isn't El Tamarindón there for traitors?"

In the preceding chapters we have looked at indigenous communities who struggled for land and institutional autonomy and whose ethnic markers—in particular dress, dialect, and religious practices—were sharply defined at least until the 1930s and 1940s. This chapter will attempt to explain how Sutiaba, a community with significantly less-defined ethnic markers, was able to resist the advances of mestizaje and of agrarian capitalism and thus survive as an indigenous community. Indeed, the reproduction of indigenous ethnicity in Sutiaba has little to do with the cultural survival, in the traditional anthropological sense, of language, clothing, and customs. Rather, constantly changing internal divisions were crucial not only to the defeats but also to the victories of the Sutiaban community. Internal divisions, as described by Sider in the previous chapter, allowed the Sutiabas to march in step with progressive artisans and workers and at the same time re-create an ethnic discourse rooted in the countryside.

Since the end of the last century, the social structure of Sutiaba has included artisans, *agricultores* (rural small landholders, who did not work for wages), and *jornaleros* (fieldworkers). These social divisions of labor had a contradictory impact on communal identity and organization. At key moments, such as in 1902, when León annexed Sutiaba, and in the 1920s, during the height of the indigenous movement, these divisions provoked decisive defeats for the community. Yet, it is also true that these internal class fissures assisted the survival of the Sutiabas as an ethnic group. The artisan-worker sector of the population became tied first to the *obrerista* (whose approximate meaning is "labor") movement and then to the labor movement of León. Such ties, in the long run, allowed Sutiaban obreristas to attain civil and economic rights and also to overcome the racist ideology prevalent in many sectors of the Leonés population. At the same time, the fact that the working-class sector of the community became increasingly "ladinoized," as much in their dress as in their level of education, obliged the Indian leadership to broaden the concept of "indigenous." As such, they were better able to confront the myth of Nicaragua mestiza, a discourse that equated the Indian with the uncivilized. The existence of educated indigenous people in Sutiaba tended to question this discourse. With the broadening of the notion of "indigenous," then, the community movement in certain conjunctures was able to unite workers, artisans, agricultural laborers, and small landholders. Such multiclass unity permitted the Sutiabas, in spite of their internal tensions, to survive in a hostile climate of racism and capitalist expansion.

### Pan de Arena and the Indigenous Municipality

In 1900, the Sutiabas resembled other Pacific Coast indigenous groups on the brink of extinction in that they possessed few cultural traits that could symbolize their ethnicity. In fact, only the oldest Sutiabas spoke their native language fluently. Nevertheless, the Sutiabas were distinguished from other groups primarily because they had defended successfully their political and economic autonomy throughout the nineteenth century. Their ethnic identity was tied intimately to their political status as a self-governing municipality.

Their high degree of political autonomy was unique among the coastal indigenous communities. The Sutiabas attained municipal status primarily because they had been the seat of a colonial *corregimiento* (a provincial-sized administrative unit) and because during the 1820s their 4,000 members were ethnically homogenous and lived in a geographically well-defined area. Throughout the nineteenth century, the municipal government maintained control over education, the police, the market, public works, and some 40,000 manzanas of communal lands. The municipality assigned to each head of family the land that he needed (the usual assignment appearing to be from twenty to fifty manzanas). At least until the 1880s, land rights were passed on to eldest sons and the community assigned new lands to new heads of families.[1]

In spite of the devastation and the killings during the civil wars of the 1840s, the population of Sutiaba grew to 8,500 by 1890.[2] Moreover, the community's relative political and economic self-sufficiency provoked the Leonés elite, who constantly sought to undermine Sutiaba's autonomy. The story of Pan de Arena, which still has a vague resonance in Sutiaban memory, is about one such effort.

In order to understand the story of Pan de Arena we must place it in the broader political and social scene. The late 1860s through the early 1870s was a period of political flux: the old partisan loyalties and ideologies had lost their meanings without having clear replacements. "Moderate Conservatives," also called "Liberal Conservatives," were the main partners in the alliance that buttressed the government of Vicente Cuadra at the time of the National Assembly elections of 1872. Although the Liberal Conservatives wished to restrict the exercise of power to the elite, they nonetheless sought to widen their base of support beyond the Granadan oligarchy. This Conservative faction, which would hold the reins of power until the 1890s, thus worked out an alliance with the traditional Liberals, whose revolutionary uprising they had defeated in 1869. Beyond tactical considerations, the two partners shared a broad ideological affinity centered on the traditional nineteenth-century liberal program: a commitment to progress and nation building. In particular, the Conservative regime devoted the resources it could command to the building of infrastructure and the creation of labor and land markets necessary to foment agro-export development. Their commitment to an agro-export program that hinged on coercion and their alliance with anticlerical Liberals often put them at loggerheads with indigenous groups.

The opposition alliance was more eclectic, including more traditional, proclerical conservatives based in Granada and their allies in León (known as Olanchanos) as well as the followers of former President Martínez (including defeated Liberal revolutionaries of 1869). The conflict between Liberal-Conservative government and Conservative (and at times Liberal) opposition played itself out differently among the different popular sectors of society. One of the few consistencies on the political scene was the general opposition of the country's indigenous groups to the government.

On Sunday October 6, 1872, José María Solís, alias "Pan de Arena," together with five national policemen under his command, marched into the cabildo of Sutiaba. Local officials were counting the ballots from the legislative elections. Shortly after Solís entered the building, Francisco Zapata, a Sutiaban ally of the government party, grabbed some of the ballots. Solís later claimed that he returned the ballots and then arrested Zapata. At the moment, however, the municipal officials were doubtful about corporal Solís's motives because the previous day he had released Zapata from the Sutiaban jail. As Solís and his group started off on horseback, someone from the crowd knocked Solís off his horse with a rifle butt. The alcalde of Sutiaba then ordered the arrest of Solís and Zapata for obstructing the electoral process, and the crowd dragged the two off to jail. In the ensuing scuffle, one of the government soldiers apparently struck and wounded the alcalde. The five policemen, heavily outnumbered, fled toward León, where they immediately informed the departmental authorities of the arrest of their commanding officer. Several hours later, following street fighting between Sutiabas and the military, Solís and Zapata were murdered in jail.

We have the testimonies of two key participants, the departmental *gobernador militar* and *gobernador de policía*, about the murders of Solís and Zapata. Upon hearing the news from Sutiaba, General Manuel Rivas, the gobernador militar, went to the indigenous town to "calm" the "exalted spirits." Rivas, a landowner in Sutiaban territory and reportedly a personal friend of the Indian alcalde, seemed to be well situated to accomplish this task. Nevertheless, according to his testimony he was not able to calm down the increasingly "inebriated" Sutiabas, who, he recognized, seemed capable of threatening the lives of the prisoners. Returning to León, he crossed paths with the gobernador de policía, Juan Ramón Salgado, who was on a mission to free the prisoners in Sutiaba. Rivas managed to persuade Salgado that it would be prudent to hold off until further efforts at negotiation proved fruitless. Rivas then proceeded to the office of the prefect (the maximum authority in the department). After listening to his report, the prefect asked

Rivas to return to Sutiaba in an unofficial capacity and deliver a note to the alcalde asking for the release of the prisoners. The conciliatory note emphasized that Rivas was on a mission not as a government official but "as a citizen and friend of yours." The prefect was allowing Rivas to seek a peaceful settlement, despite the departmental government's obligation to intervene militarily to bring back Solís. Moreover, the prefect promised to support whatever agreement was reached by Rivas and the alcalde, understanding that armed force would not be employed against the Sutiabas.

Rivas then returned to the cabildo in Sutiaba and delivered the prefect's note to his friend, the alcalde, Pedro Sánchez. According to Rivas, "he received [the note] with such coldness that he did not deign to open it. . . . He said that he would look at it and that he would not hand over the prisoners until after the elections."[3] Rivas asked to see the prisoners and after a brief interview met once more with the alcalde. Rivas asked if Sánchez could guarantee their lives. The alcalde replied that "the prisoners were secure . . . and were not running any risk." Rivas returned to the departmental prefect full of trepidation. He stated that the prisoners "were in immediate danger due to the exaltation of the masses." Rivas then decided to make a third attempt to persuade the Sutiaban authorities to release Solís and Zapata. Late in the afternoon, accompanied by a few friends, he set off to Sutiaba. While Rivas looked for the house of Florencio Roque (the *vicealcalde*), nearby gunfire startled him. He saw that the shooting "was produced by a patrol," commanded by Juan Ramón Salgado, the gobernador de policía, who

> was delivering a paper to the *rondín*, who led a numerous *ronda* [community patrol], armed with all types of weapons. . . . Seeing that the ronda charged the patrol again, I started to go back to the barracks, but then Dolores Mendoza [a Sutiaba] implored me: "General don't go back! You're the only person who can calm these people." Profoundly moved by these words I went over . . . and raising my voice I managed to get the attention of those who were fighting. But then other groups came from all directions some even armed with guns, charged with an extraordinary furor. . . . The patrol had to display tremendous courage to organize their retreat.[4]

In the fighting three Sutiabas died, and four soldiers and twelve Sutiabas were wounded. As Rivas headed back to León, he ran into more Sutiaban rondines, whom he implored not to attack the government soldiers. But Rivas's pleas for peace were in vain; a large number of Sutiabas rushed the jail, where they hacked to death Solís and Zapata with machetes.

Rivas and the departmental prefect asked the city's religious leaders to intervene in order to calm the Sutiabas and avoid further bloodshed. But the prelate who attempted to negotiate returned to León at 11 P.M. with the news that 600 armed Sutiabas were prepared to attack the León military barracks at dawn. General Rivas heard rumors that many people in the poor barrios were ready to join "the insurrection." In response, he issued a call for volunteers and some 400 "patriots of all classes: proletarians, artisans, merchants, and agricultores" showed up at the barracks ready to defend the city. Nevertheless, Rivas made one more effort to enlist the support of the church. The bishop and three Jesuit priests (recently arrived in León) journeyed to Sutiaba but found the streets empty and silent. They saw the corpses in the cabildo, recited prayers, and then searched for the indigenous authorities with no success: "It seemed like the Indians, who knew about everything that had happened but did not want to implicate anyone, had gone to hide."[5] Despite their inability to negotiate, upon their return to León the bishop and the Jesuits were able to allay the fears of the citizenry, and "tranquility was restored."

Rivas's testimony implied that politics was a key cause of the disturbance and that the gobernador de policía had committed a grave error by sending his troops to Sutiaba during an otherwise calm election: "with such order it was judged unnecessary to send the police."[6] Similarly, his description of the street fight was ambiguous in that he first claimed that Salgado's group fired the first shots but then suggested that he was delivering a paper when the fighting broke out. Rivas was playing a dangerous game, and he would continue to do so for the next two decades.[7] On the one hand, he portrayed himself as the only person capable of bridging the gap between the Indians of Sutiaba and official, legitimate society—in the words of the Indian bystander the "only person who could calm these people." At the same time, he positioned himself at some distance from the government. First, he insinuated that Salgado, in particular, was guilty of misconduct. Rivas also implicitly criticized the lack of governmental legitimacy, noting that large numbers of people from the poor barrios of San Felipe and Guadalupe openly sympathized with the indigenous rebels.

The gobernador de policía, Juan Ramón Salgado, accused directly by the opposition (and indirectly by Rivas) of precipitating the bloodshed, voluntarily rendered testimony before a judge in order to clear his name. In his testimony, Salgado positioned himself as the only dependable person in high office, the only one to uphold law and order:

> As Gobernador de Policía my job is to avoid the commission of crimes; although I am not the only one with this duty I am not afraid to say that I am the only one who carries out his duty.[8]

Salgado made it clear that the "events of Subtiava" were political in origin: caused by the "eternal instigators of the masses . . . hateful of all Governments that are not instruments of their detestable passions."[9] Upon hearing of the arrest of Solís, Salgado headed off to Sutiaba: "No one will deny that my duty not only as a functionary but as a friend was to find out what really was happening to Solís."[10]

Salgado highlighted his own prudence in turning back at the "division street between the two towns" upon being informed by Rivas about the degree of agitation among the Indians. But he then scored the prefect for practicing a degree of moderation that amounted to humiliation: "The terms of the note were almost humiliating. The Prefect appeared to be treating the Alcalde as an equal . . . prudence reached the limits of excess."[11] This was indeed a bold accusation of a superior, particularly when examined in the context of the decorous, indirect language that characterized elite political discourse. Salgado implied not only the incorrectness of the prefect's treatment of an inferior as an equal, but in particular these inferiors, the troublesome Indian alcaldes of Sutiaba.

Salgado, unlike Rivas, employed only hostile and mocking language about the Sutiabas:

> It is not believable that I would have ordered to shoot at that tumult that they want to baptize with the name *ronda*. . . . Presenting the note [from the prefect] to the head of the *turba* [mob] . . . our patrol is attacked by the mob. . . . The mob wounded three soldiers, I received some blows. . . . Could you scarcely expect the soldiers to let themselves get killed? It was only natural to defend ourselves.[12]

By employing the phrase "baptizing them with the name *ronda*," he delegitimized the municipal government of Sutiaba. According to Salgado, the

Sutiabas were bent on violence against a government that was undermined by the weakness and moderation of its leaders.

Although the Sutiabas' testimony has not been recovered (indeed it was eliminated from the official record), opposition statements probably reflected something of the perspective of the indigenous authorities. The antigovernment opposition offered a sharply different version of events. The Jesuits, recent arrivals in León, directly attacked the government. The Jesuit historian, Rafael Pérez, claimed that the elections were going smoothly in Sutiaba and that the opposition was headed for victory when the "Liberal" government intervened: "they were trying to disturb the balloting when they were surprised by the local authorities and put in prison."[13] According to Pérez, the Indians came very close to attacking León.

We have a more elaborate account of the events, published in an opposition newspaper, *Los Anales.* N. Almendares, the opposition writer, argued that the events of Sutiaba were the result of a government attempt at electoral fraud. The writer brought out one key point unmentioned in the other two narratives: Solís had recently been jailed (presumably in Sutiaba) "for an assault on the house of Doña Leona Fonseca."[14] The gobernador de policía was able to obtain Solís's immediate release and reincorporated him into the police. Similarly, Zapata was in jail for attacking a woman: "These were thus the men chosen by the government to oppress and harass the people of Sutiaba,"[15] the report stated. According to the opposition account, Solís and Zapata stormed into the cabildo together; the former pounded on the table and shouted: "I'm the one in charge here!"[16] Zapata then took several of the ballots. Almendares places exclusive blame for violence on Solís and his troops.

Almendares thus created a coherent narrative that stressed the government's intention to obstruct the election by employing two men who had violated Sutiaban women. In so doing, he introduced powerful reasons for Sutiaban hatred of Solís and Zapata, where only their irrationality served as an explanation in the two other narratives. Almendares's mordant aside that the government immediately lost any interest in Zapata's fate added to his critique of government ideology and practice. His description of the subsequent violence differed markedly from those of Salgado and Rivas.

The Gobernador de Policía (with fifty troops) goes into Sutiaba and encounters a ronda of 15 *paisanos* [local militia], armed only with sticks and machetes and without the slightest provocation he starts firing at them, killing, wounding, and spilling the blood of a multitude of innocent victims.[17]

Despite the radically different interpretations of Rivas, Salgado, and Almendares, they contain only one significant factual discrepancy: the number of Sutiabas and troops involved in the confrontation. Indeed, the number of combatants is at the center of each narrative's structure of proof. Almendares's numbers, for example, suggest overwhelming military force against poorly armed Indians. Salgado had stated that fifty Sutiabas met his seventeen troops, thus creating the image of a heroic defense against an unprovoked attack. The prefect's own justification of his actions to the president of the republic also hinges on his use of numbers: "Salgado was met by 300 Indians who with machetes, clubs, rocks and a few shotguns attacked the patrol."[18] Rivas, on the other hand, did not estimate a number of Indians in the ronda and carefully mentioned that the number of government troops "was reported as seventeen," the only statement in his report that was not based on his direct observation.[19]

It is difficult to ascertain the true number of combatants or to reconstruct who attacked first on the Calle Real of Sutiaba that afternoon. Beyond their accuracy, the various narratives offer insight into the Leonés elite's attitude toward the political autonomy of their indigenous neighbors. There is little doubt that the government's effort to commit electoral fraud in Sutiaba created the conditions for violence. Simply put, there was no way of executing that fraud without provoking violence given the degree of municipal autonomy and the high level of interethnic tension.

Similar occurrences in indigenous communities throughout the country suggest some provisional conclusions. Violence erupted during the 1870s in elections in Ometepe, Masatepe, Masaya, Boaco, and San Jorge. Invariably, the indigenous groups supported antigovernment candidates. Indian communities, then, in the late nineteenth century formed a bulwark of political opposition to the reigning Liberal-Conservative alliance. The conversion of Indians from dissidents and rebels to *gobiernistas*—"progovernment" (recall the remarks of the marine and Sobalvarro in the last chapter)—was a process, as we saw, that involved major doses of repression and state centralization.

Religion also spurred Indians to vigorous action against the government. In

1881, as we saw, not only did the Matagalpinos rise up in insurrection, but the Sutiabas and the Monimboseños rioted in opposition to the government expulsion of the Jesuits. Indeed the Sutiabas participated in an abortive insurrectionary movement in support of the Matagalpino rebellion. But, their religious fervor had nothing to do with blind subservience to the church, as charged their Liberal critics. On the contrary, during the 1890s, they resisted church efforts to take over their cofradía. The Sutiaba alcalde, for example, protested before the general *vicario* (curate) in the following energetic terms: "Sutiaba is ready—prepared to make a thousand sacrifices—to defend this *cofradía,* because it was formed by our ancestors."[20]

Throughout the country, indigenous economic, cultural, and political autonomy was a constant source of frustration to local ladino elites. In León, the memory of 1872 was summarized by the martyrdom of Pan de Arena, and vengeance could only be consummated with the complete suppression of the indigenous municipality.[21] In 1877, a León deputy proposed legislation that would annex Sutiaba to the city of León. In 1881, the newspaper *El Municipio* once more brought up the necessity of eradicating the municipality through its annexation to León. According to the editorial, indigenous sovereignty over and attachment to indigenous lands were the fundamental reasons for eliminating the "indigenous municipality." There was a subsidiary racist discourse that provided additional justification for that goal. Evidence for supposed racial inferiority, beyond the memory of Pan de Arena, included the fact that the Sutiaban cabildo was "in ruins" and that the municipal government was unable to pay the minimum departmental tax, in spite of enjoying good financial earnings.[22]

The primary source of friction with the Leonés elite, however, was the Sutiabas' extensive landholdings, a total of sixty-three *caballerías medida antigua* (some 42,000 manzanas). To cite one example, the León newspaper complained about a Sutiaban protest over the boundaries of their lands: "Sutiaba still is not satisfied with possessing all of the lands that are to the west of town. . . . In a few years we will be little more than the feudal serfs of the Indians of Sutiaba."[23]

The threat of an expansionist indigenous "feudalism" is intriguing because it seems so irrational, given that there was no evidence whatsoever that the Indians sought to expand their domain. Rather, feudalism as a synonym of colonialism was always a convenient charge to conjure up about the "origins" of Indians. We might also interpret the heavy dose of irony as a response to the split between reality and the dream of converting Indians to their rightful place as peons and ladinos to theirs as hacienda owners.

According to *El Municipio*, the Indians only rented their land "to a very few people," and they refused to sell it in spite of the laws of 1877 and 1881 compelling the division and sale of the lands of the Comunidades Indígenas. The Indians, the article asserts, "believe that, as absolute owners, no one can force them to separate themselves from the beloved fields that they consider inherent to their race."[24] For the Leonés elite, the essence of the problem of indigenous autonomy was their distinctive relationship to the land. An 1895 land-use concession to a Sutiaba, Ramón Mairena, reveals something of this relationship between the indigenous people and their land: "As a son of this people you may use it and cultivate it without payment of any rights and may it not be sold to any outsider, only to a son or daughter of this people."[25]

According to judicial sources, the municipality of Sutiaba also had a "prohibition against" selling to ladinos.[26] Such a relationship between the indigenous community and their lands raised a problem for the Leonés elite as it slowed the growth of agricultural enterprises in a vast zone of more than 40,000 manzanas, the largest tract of land in the area. Notwithstanding the reticence to sell land to ladinos, the number of haciendas grew from three to twenty between 1885 and 1900 (a few of those were Indian owned). Most of the communal land, however, remained under Indian control; the Sutiabas were always prepared to turn to the courts to defend them. In 1888, for example, a group of Leonés hacendados brought a suit against the municipality of Sutiaba over the site of Abangasco. Twelve years later, the hacendados were still awaiting the resolution of the case.[27]

### "Our Division Was Exploited": The Annexation of Sutiaba

Despite the successful resistance of the indigenous municipality before 1902, it would be incorrect to assume that the entire community joined the defense or that the Sutiabas themselves enjoyed equal access to the land. On the contrary, by the end of the last century Sutiaba was far from a cooperative, homogeneous community. Rather, it found itself strongly divided economically and socially, and the León elite took advantage of these divisions to eliminate the municipality of Sutiaba in 1902.

With its promotion of agro-export development, the Zelayista revolution exerted pressure on the Sutiaban social fabric. Sutiaban entrepreneurs, often in alliance with Leonés hacendados, began to exploit the ejidos for cotton and sugarcane production. At least a decade before the annexation, such entrepreneurs began to develop interests opposed to those of the rest of the indigenous community. A census from one of the Sutiaban neighborhoods in 1915 helps us to understand these social divisions.[28] Data from that census clashes dramatically with the image of an agricultural village dedicated to its lands, immersed in a rural economy with strong communal features. First, the census classifies 34.4 percent of the economically active male population as *artesanos* (artisans)/ *obreros* (workers). The construction trades accounted for most of these workers; masons, alone, made up 13 percent of the labor force. Those who worked in the fields were equally differentiated: 33.1 percent of the labor force were jornaleros and 28 percent were agricultores.[29] Although the annexation of 1902 might have accelerated the proletarianization of the labor force, partial evidence from before 1902 suggests that the Sutiaban social division of labor was already quite pronounced.[30]

Before 1902, some of the agricultores favored the conversion of communal land into private real estate. Some farmers—akin to a nascent indigenous bourgeoisie—who had possession of communal land, wanted to either obtain more or to sell the land. The process of commercialization of the "improvements" among Sutiabas was already under way, leading to the growth of that nascent rural middle class. For example, by 1900 Nicolás Berríos, an Indian, possessed several plots of communal land totaling several hundred manzanas. Another Sutiaba, Leandro Rojas, had by 1902 accumulated a quarry, a saw mill, a ranch, a "small farm," and two *solares* (plots) of two manzanas each in the urban area. Similarly, Leandro Amaya held contiguously a solar, an orchard, and a "patch" of land in the urban center and its surroundings. Ramón Mairena, mentioned earlier as a "son of Sutiaba," managed to take possession of a chunk of land valued at $440. For these indigenous cultivators, the annexation of Sutiaba meant the conversion of their land possession to legal, private ownership. At the moment of annexation, Sutiaban and Leonés large-scale farms possessed less than 15 percent of the communal land, with 30 percent of that apt for cattle raising and agriculture.

Nevertheless, not all of the economically powerful Sutiabas favored the privatization of communal land. In particular, the Roque, Vásquez, and Bárcenas families held important pieces of land, but for reasons of family tradition zealously defended the integrity of the indigenous community.[31] The Roque family, for example, had been *principales* during the colonial period and continued to play a leadership role in the nineteenth century. Simón Roque's signature appears on the 1828 Sutiaba village land title. Also, Simón Roque, either the very same or possibly his son, was a community leader at midcentury. Salvador Vásquez, also from a rural landholding family, was the alcalde who confronted the church in defense of the village's cofradías. Vásquez continued as a municipal functionary until the annexation.

The traditional leaders belonged to the same parcialidad (lineage group), called Jiquilapa. The two parcialidades of Sutiaba (Pueblo Grande and Jiquilapa) formed endogamous kinship structures. Belonging to a parcialidad involved a shared perception of the importance of indigenous lineage, exemplified clearly in the neighborhood work activities known as fajinas, which involved the cleaning and maintenance of the cemeteries. Similarly, the barrio promoted certain collective labor methods and celebrations related to the harvest and the shelling of the harvested corn. At least until 1930, parcialidad identity was as important as Sutiaban identity.[32] Well into the twentieth century, a male from one of the neighborhoods would risk his life crossing Calle Real at night to go into the other. The hostility, symbolic and real, between Jiquilapa and Pueblo Grande was at the same time a mechanism for the preservation of the endogamy of the district. The oral testimony of several Sutiabas who grew up in the 1920s grants equal symbolic worth to the two borders, one between Sutiaba and León, and the other between the parcialidades.

The existence of strong parcialidades was a mixed blessing for Sutiaba as a whole. On the one hand, they might have contributed to its survival, for in the majority of the indigenous communities that disappeared before 1920 the community membership was coterminous with the parcialidad.[33] Given strong parcialidad identity, people might have been able to better resist an attack on the political and cultural institutions of the entire community. On the other hand, there are strong indications that the regime was so easily able to annex Sutiaba because of the parcialidad divisions.

December 27, 1902, the Nicaraguan Congress abolished the community of Sutiaba and decreed its annexation to León. The annexation was both a response to the political pressure of the León elite and to Zelaya's national program for the ladinoization of the indigenous population and the privatization of their communal lands.[34] Nevertheless, the annexation encountered resistance not only from many Sutiabas but also from a congressional deputy. During the debate, in the words of the newspaper *Diario Oficial,* "the vecinos of Sutiaba brought a treatise before the Chamber of Deputies in which they declared their rejection of their incorporation into the city of León."[35] The Sutiabas then obtained the support of a Liberal deputy, General (retired) Asisco Ramírez, a carpenter and obrerista leader in León. After the approval of the annexation, Ramírez (who also headed the congressional opposition to forced labor) presented a motion to reconsider the decree in light of the Sutiaba opposition. His motion failed by 20 to 3.[36]

Oral tradition suggests that repression followed the annexation and that the police used torture and perhaps even murder to locate the titles to the ejidos.[37] Despite the annexation and repression, Sutiaban political pressure perhaps had some positive effect: the decree mandated the authorization of property titles to "the natives of the village of Sutiaba" (and not to the ladinos) who possessed lands within the ejidos. What is more, all indigenous peoples who had no land now had the right to request land "at no cost." The decree mentions no rights for the seven ladino hacendados who occupied ejidal land.

Notwithstanding the positive side effects, the annexation debilitated the community. Indeed, the traditional rivalry between the two parcialidades and the recent formation of an incipient agrarian bourgeoisie facilitated the abolition of the municipality and seriously weakened indigenous resistance. Barely two weeks after the annexation, the government designated authorities to serve the new barrio of Sutiaba. No members of the traditional leadership group—the Vásquez, Roque, or the Bárcenas families—were among the fourteen governmental appointments. Of the six functionaries named for Jiquilapa, four were linked to the Pueblo Grande district and another was from the Berríos family, which had monopolized much communal land. Less than three weeks after the Sutiaban petition against the annexation, Pueblo Grande families were willing to collaborate with the new Leonés authorities.

The annexation's first impact, then, was to strengthen the Sutiaban small and medium peasants, as most were able to obtain title to their possessions.[38] Notwithstanding its somewhat benign effect on the small indigenous landholders, the annexation also meant the legalization of some large ladino haciendas and the creation of others on the boundaries of the communal lands. Years later these haciendas would become nationally famous as the object of Sutiaban protest: the Sacasa family's "La Gallina," originally measuring 150 manzanas (mz.); the Lacayo family's "Las Canales" (800 mz.); and "San Silvestre," previously a cofradía (1,000 mz.), appropriated by the Mayorga family (and later passed on to the Marín family). In addition, Bishop Pereira y Castellón purchased lands on the Sutiaba ejido for 4,000 pesos (more than 500 mz.). A dozen smaller properties also passed from indigenous to ladino hands.[39]

The privatization of ejidal lands, whether in indigenous or ladino hands, dealt a strong blow to indigenous jornaleros and to future Sutiaban generations, who would have fewer and fewer opportunities to obtain land. In this sense, the annexation hastened the proletarianization of the indigenous population and the division between landholders and wage workers.

In spite of the attack on its political autonomy and the privatization of its lands, the indigenous community did not disintegrate after the annexation. Despite their political divisions (to some extent related to the parcialidades), the Sutiabas did organize collective forms of resistance. During the years immediately following the annexation, any ladino obstruction of a public thoroughfare provoked a rapid indigenous response. In January 1905, twenty-nine Sutiaban rural landholders (almost all of them from Jiquilapa) protested to the mayor of León when a hacendado, Alonso Saravia, blocked access to a public path. The mayor supported the Sutiabas' petition and ordered the hacendado to open the path.[40] Similarly, in August 1906 a group of Sutiabas, accompanied by the *juez de mesta* (rural policeman), threatened to arrest the Leonés hacienda administrator Arturo Baca if he did not remove the wire blocking another public thoroughfare.[41] These defensive actions on behalf of the Sutiabas relied on the support of the authorities. Such support, at least from the mayor, most likely did not derive from a sense of solidarity with the indigenous population but rather from political calculations that considered the Sutiabas' capacity for violence or for opposition to the Zelaya regime.

Another example of the influence the Sutiabas exerted on the local government involved a petition by Elías Gurdián for 200 manzanas of land from the formerly Sutiaban ejidos. In September 1907, the municipality of León approved the petition of Gurdián, a member of a wealthy Leonés family. At the same time, however, three Sutiabas applied for the same ejidal land. In spite of the legality of his claim and his strong initial opposition, Gurdián withdrew his petition in October 1907, and the municipality granted the land to the three Sutiabas.[42]

The annexation did not resolve the problem of the Sutiaban land for the Leonés elite, despite their appropriation of perhaps 20 percent of the ejidos. Consequently, they appealed once again to the national government. In January 1908, the municipality of León sent a statement to Congress asking for the "transfer or division of the land of the indigenous community of Sutiaba." One month later, when the petition had gone to the legislative committee, a law was introduced to authorize the sale of half of the ejidos. But Congress did not act before the Zelaya regime fell in 1909, and thus the "Sutiaban or ejidal land" remained in an ambiguous state: ladinos or Indians were given titles to 30 to 40 percent of the land, while the remaining 25,000 manzanas continued to be disputed. The Leonés elite demanded its distribution, whereas for the Sutiabas it was "the land of their ancestors."[43]

### Politics and the Comunidad Indígena of Sutiaba, 1915–1920

While the struggles for political, economic, and cultural autonomy during the late nineteenth and early twentieth centuries shaped Sutiaban resistance, the United States intervention in Nicaragua indirectly provided an opportunity to regain, to some extent, such autonomy. The Sutiabas in particular took advantage of the 1914 law that annulled the Zelaya-imposed abolition of the Comunidades.[44] At least some Sutiabas avenged the Leonés elite by fighting on the side of the Conservatives in the 1912 Liberal revolution, which had overwhelming support in León.[45] In 1915, shortly after the Leonés elite made yet another attempt to appropriate Sutiaba's ejidos, the communal leaders petitioned the government for the legal recognition of Sutiaba and of its sixty-three caballerías of ancestral lands.[46] In addition, the Sutiabas proposed in their statutes substantial community control over all natural resources, public works, education, and rural public order.[47]

From 1915 to 1918, the León municipal government actively opposed the legal recognition of the Comunidad. Several local officials offered the specious argument that the Comunidad Indígena could not exist because its members did not have title to their own communal land. More prosaically, they feared that upon receiving legal recognition the Sutiabas would block the construction of a highway to Poneloya beach, a project long desired by the Leonés elite for economic and recreational reasons. Notwithstanding the opposition, the national government approved the statutes of the Comunidad Indígena in 1918.[48] As we saw in previous chapters, government recognition of the Sutiaban claim was perfectly compatible with Emiliano Chamorro's politics in Matagalpa, Boaco, and Jinotega, where he actively supported the Comunidades whether out of ideological conviction or tactical necessity. Moreover, local factors compelled Chamorro to create a political base in León. The 1916 election, in which the Liberal candidate Julián Irías was banned from participation by U.S. fiat, convinced many Liberals that insurrection was their only political recourse.[49] It follows that the Conservative regime had sufficient motive to strike an agreement with the Sutiabas as a step toward establishing a base deep in Liberal territory.

The Conservative alliance did not alone account for the revival of the indigenous movement in Sutiaba. A leadership group with much experience in government was a key factor in the rebirth. It is symptomatic that Sotero Téllez, the last of the municipality's *síndicos* (syndics), was one of the founders of the new Comunidad Indígena of Sutiaba in 1915. Likewise, Salvador Vásquez, municipal alcalde during the 1890s and juez during the annexation, became the central figure in the indigenous movement. Although at its birth, the Comunidad drew leaders from both parcialidades, after a few years the traditional leaders from Jiquilapa again became dominant.[50]

In February 1919 the fears of the Leonés elite were realized, as the newly legalized Comunidad Indígena lodged a protest against the building of a road through their territory. What most aggravated the Sutiabas was that the company had proceeded "without giving notice to the directorate of the Comunidad Indígena."[51] The Indians demanded respect for the community and control of their own territory. The jefe político of León, the Conservative Augusto Terán, supported the Indians' protest and the hacendados were unable to continue their project.[52]

In March 1919 the Sutiabas reaped another fruit from their alliance, at the convention of the Conservative party held in Granada. At the convention, two Sutiaban delegates made a motion to nullify the annexation to León and to reestablish the municipality of Sutiaba.[53] The convention carried the motion in spite of the vehement protests from the Leonés press, which argued against Sutiaban autonomy, citing "motives of public utility and of our civilization."[54]

Despite the failure of this resolution to become law, the Sutiaban leaders were able to add this moral victory to other concrete benefits, most important the legalization of the Comunidad Indígena and its lands. One minor victory of economic and symbolic import took place during the same year. Against the strong objections of the Liberal-dominated municipal government, the Comunidad Indígena established its right to tax vehicles and *ramadas* (palm leaf shelters) at Poneloya beach.

The rapid successes of the Comunidad Indígena ironically failed to unify the community. Most significant, their alliance with the Conservatives alienated the indigenous militants from their political base. Many Sutiaban activists saw this alliance as problematic. Referring to a public health program, one Sutiaba complained in 1920 that

> the policy of the jefe político (a conservative) of building latrines is dividing us. It would be better for the government to save this money and then we would not be obliged to vote for Diego Manuel Chamorro. We do not want these tricks. We, the Indians, are many, but they never want to take us seriously.[55]

Against the will of the combative leaders of the Comunidad Indígena, in 1920 the Sutiabas voted 740 to 110 in favor of the Liberal presidential candidate.[56]

The Sutiaban artisans were the bulwark of the Liberal party. The artisans and workers (more than a third of the labor force of Pueblo Grande) were tied to their militant, Liberal Leonés counterparts through an incipient trade union movement. By 1920 three Sutiabas—Leopoldo Amaya, Salvador Osejo, and José Hernández—had become local leaders of the Federación Obrera Nicaragüense (Nicaraguan Labor Federation; FON). Although it is likely that the FON supported some of the Comunidad Indígena's initiatives, it opposed others for ideological reasons.[57] Although *obrerismo* espoused democratic goals, it shared the dominant ideology of progress and concomitant necessity to ladinoize Indians through educational programs.

In the postwar period, then, the radical movement gaining force in Sutiaba had two currents that were to a certain extent antagonistic. The radical-Liberal current had its base in the urban center (most of all in Pueblo Grande). Tied to the FON the obreristas sought equal rights for the Sutiabas, especially as workers and as citizens; the Indians' struggle for their old municipality did not much concern them. Their deep commitment to education, however, did not lead the *obreristas* to deny their indigenous roots and identity. The second traditionalist current, equally radical and antielitist, had its base of support in the countryside (among the families of Jiquilapa). It fomented the tactical alliance with the Conservative party and also sought the support of the church.[58] This group's fundamental goal was the recovery of municipal autonomy and complete control over communal lands. Their struggles awakened (and to a certain degree depended on the resurgence of) an indigenista consciousness. At moments, both factions could work together and extend their bases of support and alliances. But their division was complicated not just by partisan attachments but by fundamentally different mentalities.

Nevertheless, both groups were proud to be from Sutiaba and that was remarkable in itself, the consequence of a "re-creation" of indigenous identity. We can speak of a re-creation because those Sutiaban identities that in the nineteenth century revolved around municipal politics and government, communal land, and distinctive religious, cultural, and linguistic practices (including a separate language) had come to an end. For at least a decade the demise of those identities, which coincided roughly with the annexation, made it, to quote one Sutiaba, a community "without life, without character, and without a future."[59]

The Comunidad's political offensive was accompanied by a resurgence of ethnic identity. If in 1910 the Sutiabas hid their ability to speak their native language, in 1918 a writer passing through Sutiaba found a different climate. He met "one of the many men who preserve a love of their race." The Sutiabas showed him large holes in the backyards that had served as places of refuge for entire families since colonial times. The Indian told him that

> the holes that you see there served as dwelling and tomb for our old Indians; they went there to hide and to cry their misfortune when they managed to save themselves from the clutches of the Spanish . . . that is why I say that the most offensive thing one could say to me is that I am a descendant of the Spanish.[60]

## "The Inferior Races" and "The Carriage of Progress": The Ladino Response

The Leonés elite immediately began a legal, political, and ideological counteroffensive. In June 1919, after the ministro de gobernación backed the Sutiaban claims to Poneloya and especially their right to collect rents for the ejidal land, the municipal government challenged the constitutionality of those measures in the Supreme Court. Most significant, the municipality argued that the ejidos belonged to León since the 1902 annexation. The municipality of León simultaneously challenged the constitutionality of the 1914 law of the Comunidades Indígenas, arguing that they were created with exclusively political ends.[61]

Beyond its legal arguments, the Municipal Corporation, as was cited earlier, launched an attack on the Sutiaban Comunidad Indígena that stressed its level of education in comparison with the castas indígenas of Matagalpa. It also underscored that "Sutiaba was always an indigenous *pueblo,* but not a Comunidad Indígena."[62] In 1922, a journalist continued the argument that Sutiaba "was not a Comunidad Indígena like that of the cañadas of Matagalpa, but was a pueblo with its temple, its municipal council."[63] These declarations formed the cornerstone of ideological attack on the authenticity of the indigenous identity of the Sutiabas. Here the similarity to the attack on the casta indígena of Boaco is striking. In both cases, municipalities in battle against indigenous groups over land questioned the authenticity of indigenous identity through challenging the indigenous communal organizations' real, historical past as legitimate, municipal governments.

This evolving discourse of mestizaje framed the Sutiaban population as nonindigenous. Defining "indigenous" as a synonym for uncivilized and barbarous, it converted an educated Indian into an oxymoron. Evidently the Sutiabas, like the Boaqueño indigenous leaders with more intellectual progress and with experience in municipal government and urban life, did not fit within this definition. Their Comunidad Indígena was somehow false, simply a political trick, and thus nullified their claims to the land. Within the elite intellectual framework, Indians were fixed in time, incapable of evolving in their own, autonomous manner. Once under the influence of "civilization" they simply ceased to be real Indians.

Many Sutiabas accepted, to varying degrees, the discourse of mestizaje. Especially among artisans and those who had attended one of the barrio's five schools, the notion that they were Nicaraguans, distinct from the semisavage Indians in the mountains, had some appeal. But that appeal did not necessarily clash with their identity as Sutiabas or as Jiquilapeños of Pueblo Grandinos. But the elite discourse not only reflected but also conditioned a reality of ethnic change (recall the discussion on Mallon at the end of chapter 2). That discourse was incapable of framing an image of Sutiabas literate in the Spanish language but also proud of belonging to "the rebel race," rooted in their ancestral lands but prepared to use all the modern political tools necessary to defend themselves.

When the Sutiabas strongly opposed Leonés interests, elite discourse revealed another dimension: racism. This facet held that when the Indians went beyond "civilized" channels, it was because of a genetic problem typical of inferior beings. The struggle over the highway to Poneloya beach, in particular, provoked the racism latent in the dominant discourse. From 1918 to 1922, those with haciendas in Sutiaban lands and other members of the Leonés elite pushed for that highway, which would join various haciendas with the city and allow people to drive their automobiles to the beach. The Comunidad Indígena argued that the highway would have to pass through their territory and that it would only serve automobile owners. One Liberal editorialist responded as follows: "This Comunidad Indígena is and has been an obstacle to progress. . . . The politicians are taking advantage of a negative legacy of colonial Spanish legislation."[64] Under strong bipartisan elite pressure, the Conservative government passed over the objections of their indigenous allies and financed the construction of the highway.

However, the government was sending mixed messages. In November 1922, the government encouraged the Comunidad Indígena with the approval of a "Plan de Arbitrios" (a municipal tax code) that included the right to charge rent on their ejidos. But on November 17 one of León's prominent citizens, perhaps emboldened by the real and symbolic progress of the highway, proposed the prohibition of oxcart traffic on the road.[65] On December 1, Salvador Vásquez and the Roque brothers, together with a force of more than 100 Sutiabas, occupied portions of the highway, "breaking fences and *acantarillados* [culverts], and chiseling the shoulder of the road."[66] In the ensuing skirmish, the highway construction foreman was wounded. The chief of the military police and the jefe político of León immediately granted the Indian demands, promising that the government would guarantee all the property of the Sutiabas and the right to free transit.[67] In response to elite petitions to jail the Indians, the chief of police responded that the use of force would "lead to a revolt, and there would not be a way to stop these people from attacking León."[68]

The public justification that one Sutiaba offered for their actions suggests an effort to transform their vertical alliance with the Conservatives into a class-based antioligarchic movement:

> The state's money, which belongs to all, is spent on this project. However, the right to use the highway belongs to a privileged few. . . . The American imperialists call abuses of force "progress." The highway crosses lands that legally belong to the Sutiabas, but there are few Indians who still maintain even a miserable piece of what was once a vast dominion. The people of León shall never join forces with those authorities who commit such injustice against the Sutiabas, whom they consider an inferior race.[69]

Because of its ideological content, it is clear that this declaration came from the obrerista sector of the community and that it was primarily directed to León's artisans and workers, who made up the bulk of the urban population. With the suggestion that elite injustice against the Indians was also abuse against the workers, the Sutiaba located the problem of racism within elite culture. Such analysis, cast in the rhetoric of anti-American obrerismo, may have found a receptive audience among many of the anti-imperialist mestizo artisans, who themselves suffered from racial prejudice.[70]

Although they were able to reach a negotiated solution to the conflict, Leonés Liberals launched a campaign against the Comunidad Indígena, with a rhetoric drenched in the discourse of "civilization" versus "barbarism." One journalist, for example, advised the jefe político:

> But it is good to make the Indians of Sutiaba know that the era of Pan de Arena has passed [in reference to the 1872 struggle] and that the day that any difficulty with the city of León emerges, they will be the ones that will suffer. . . . The priest of Sutiaba will know how to show them the path of obligation, combating that propensity to oppose the carriage of progress that the inferior races have.[71]

As if to answer that declaration, on January 17, 1923, Salvador Vásquez, the Roque brothers, and a group of followers knocked down the door of a school library that had just been founded by Father Evenor Urcuyo. The Indians warned the priest, a Leonés Conservative, that he was invading community property and that he would have to leave. Later they threatened "to flatten the old cabildo," which had been turned into a women's prison.[72] This demonstration in symbolic defense of the community's property and cultural autonomy marked a broadening of the goals of the community's struggle.

The seizure of the Fray Bartolomé de las Casas library did not attract as many followers as the highway mobilization. Although the action reaffirmed cultural autonomy, it also alienated many urban artisans and workers who wanted to attend night school. Without doubt, some Sutiabas resented the fact that the educated Roque and Vásquez families blocked their own access to education. Moreover, internal class divisions fused with those based on politics and on the parcialidades (the assault on the library was led by Jiquilapeños).[73]

Recognizing the relative weakness of the movement, Leonés Liberals issued a strong call for the repression of the leaders of the Comunidad Indígena. One journalist appealed to the racial and class prejudices of the local authorities:

> We know the attitude of this *raza rebelde*. Without doubt, General Argüello (the jefe político) does not know about the events of 1871 [*sic*] when the city was brutally surprised . . . when Pan de Arena's corpse was brought to the cabildo. . . . The leaders of this communist movement are Salvador Vásquez and Julián Roque Bamba.[74]

The appeal to anticommunism (if not necessarily to history) apparently worked with the Conservative regime in Managua. The government offered protection to Urcuyo and attempted to manipulate the election of new, moderate leaders of the Comunidad Indígena. But Vásquez and the Roque brothers resisted these efforts and continued to organize communal protests during the next three years. Indeed, relying on peaceful tactics, the leaders of the Comunidad Indígena successfully installed an anti-Urcuyo directorate in the library.[75]

Despite the weak turnout for the library takeover, Urcuyo's defeat and Vásquez's survival suggested that the majority of Sutiabas supported communal unity, despite the persistent tensions of class, politics, and parcialidad. Notwithstanding their occasional failures, Vásquez and the Roques' ability to call upon a multiclass alliance with a discourse of ethnic unity was the key both to the immediate success and the long-term survival of Sutiaba. Soon after the library conflict, for example, Vásquez led all sectors of the community in another battle for their cultural autonomy, this time against the church. Perhaps in retaliation for the library affair, the church officially disbanded the Sociedad de la Santísima, the cofradía in charge of the Holy Week religious festival. The priests argued that the money collected for the Sociedad should be managed directly by the church. Vásquez wrote to the bishop of León and underscored the community's desire to maintain "harmony with the ecclesiastical authorities," but he added:

> when Sutiaba administrated your lands [cofradías], we devoted the product we obtained to the religious organization; but it has been many years since all of this has been suspended. . . . Now the faithful directly sustain the organizations with their offerings. Sutiaba always has been the cradle of our Catholic beliefs in the *Occidente* [of Nicaragua—refers to the region of León and Chinandega].[76]

The bishop of León, like his predecessor in the 1890s, reconsidered his position when confronted with the Sutiabas' protest. But the church attacked on another front. In July 1924, the bishop ordered that the church appropriate the Sutiabas' "Señor del Santo Sepulcro," which played a central role in the community's Holy Week celebrations. As a response to the church's decision to place the image in the León cathedral, the cofradía members removed the sacred image from the temple. Father Urcuyo denounced the action as an "unfathomable abuse" that not only threatened the church but also the very foundation of the Catholic faith. Despite Urcuyo's anger, the church decided not to exacerbate the conflict with the Sutiabas, who thus maintained control over the principal symbol of their ethnicity. That same year Father Urcuyo abandoned Sutiaba a defeated and bitter man.[77]

## Conclusion: The End of an Era

León's annexation of Sutiaba left an open wound in the community. We should note, though, that it only accelerated the process of privatization of communal lands, a process in which many indigenous farmers were active accomplices. Likewise, the growing socioeconomic divisions at the end of the last century complicated Sutiaban resistance before and after the 1902 annexation.

Vásquez and the Roque brothers led vital struggles that involved a decisive reaffirmation of Sutiaban ethnicity. Between 1918 and 1924, the radical leaders won a series of important victories: the legalization of the community and its territorial claims, crucial access to the new highway, and the preservation of community control over cultural and religious institutions. Each victory was an act of resistance against elite attacks on the community. Elite racism most likely angered the Sutiabas instead of demoralizing them. Nevertheless, the discourse of mestizaje probably contributed to the widening of social divisions in the community because many village artisans intensified their relationship with their *compañeros* in the Leonés union movement.

Moreover, the radical traditionalists exacerbated those divisions through their alliance with the Conservatives, whose national policies were consistently pro-Indian (but whose local practices left much to be desired).[78] Although such an alliance brought the first significant triumphs, it was impossible to sustain precisely because of the Liberal affiliation of the majority of the community. This political identity intensified with the growth of the union movement in León and Sutiaba.[79]

By the 1929 elections, the obreristas had become a major political force in León and Sutiaba. The mayoral candidate of the Labor party (supported by the FON) defeated the officialist Liberal party candidate by the narrow margin of 2,904 to 2,806 in the city, while the obrerista candidate won in Sutiaba by 352 to 193.[80] At the moment of this great obrerista triumph in Sutiaba and León, the influence of the Roque family and Vásquez had all but disappeared, wiped out by the partisan warfare of 1926 to 1927.

The Liberal revolution of 1926 marked the end of a decade of community resistance and ethnic solidarity. The great majority of Sutiabas repudiated the occupation of their barrio by Conservative government troops.[81] During the revolutionary conflict, the Sutiaban members of the Liberal party expelled the "Conservatives" Vásquez and Roque from the community leadership. These leaders were unable to understand in time the flexibility of the Liberal ideology, or its very deep roots in Sutiaba. For at least seventy years, the Sutiaban ethnic identity had coexisted with the feeling of citizenship in the Republic of Nicaragua, and it was Liberalism itself that molded this sense of citizenship. Finally, for some Sutiabas antioligarchic obrerismo reinforced, instead of rejecting, the community's struggles against the elite.[82]

Ironically, Vásquez and the Roque family shared the same anti-imperialist perspective of many Liberal obreristas, but their goal of restoring Sutiaban autonomy brought them into an alliance with the Conservatives. Perhaps it was their own status as members of the elite within the Sutiaban community that impeded even the glimpse of a more plebeian alternative to that vertical alliance. Nevertheless, they left the community an important legacy: the memory of valiant warriors prepared to sacrifice their lives for Sutiaba, the legal status as a Comunidad Indígena, and various aged titles to sixty-three caballerías of land.[83]

## Notes

1 E. G. Squier, *Nicaragua: Its Scenery, People and Monuments* (New York, 1860), 274. Squier argues that during the mid nineteenth century the municipality of Sutiaba rented communal lands to families for the modest sum of between fifty cents and two dollars. Nevertheless, the land concessions made to the Indians in the 1880s and 1890s that I have consulted exempted natives of the community from payment, while requiring others to pay.

2 Gustavo Niederlin, *The State of Nicaragua in the Greater Republic of Nicaragua* (Philadelphia: Philadelphia Commercial Museum, 1898), 32. Niederlin reports data from the 1892 census.

3 *La Gaceta de Nicaragua,* October 19, 1872.

4 *La Gaceta de Nicaragua,* October 19, 1872.

5 Rafael Pérez, S.J., *La Compañía de Jesús en Colombia y Centroamérica* (Valladolid: Imprenta Castellana, 1898), 320.

6 Ibid.

7 See *La Semanal Nicaragüense,* December 27, 1873. A year later he was relieved of his command in León for failing to carry out his orders to put down a rebellion in Chinandega and for failing to discipline the indigenous population in general. An editorial in the same paper on January 15, 1874, graphically denounced Rivas's lack of action: "apareciese un indio García acaudillando quinientos o mil curarenes que no han faltado en Leon i en sus cercanías en estos últimos tiempos, cual sería la suerte de ese vecindario?" (original spelling and punctuation preserved). The reference to *curarenes* was to a recent indigenous rebellion in Honduras.

8 Ibid., 3. Salgado admitted that he should have rendered testimony to the prefect, but he adduced that his "bitter censorship" would not make him an impartial judge. Similarly, he could not testify before the alcaldes of Sutiaba, because they were potentially guilty of complicity in the murders.

9 "Memoria de los acontecimientos ocurridos en el pueblo de Subtiava el 6 del corriente mes en cuanto se relacionan con la conducta observada por el Gobernador de Policía del departamento Don Juan Ramón Salgado" (León: Imprenta del Istmo, 1872), 3.

10 Ibid., 4.

11 Ibid., 4.

12 Ibid., 5.

13 Pérez, *La Compañía de Jesús,* 319.

14 *Los Anales* (Masaya), November 1, 1872.

15 Ibid.

16 Ibid.

17 Ibid.

18 *La Gaceta Oficial,* October 12, 1872.

19 His refusal to use numbers to buttress his argument was nonetheless important in creating an aura of truth about his narrative. For the gobernador militar wished to portray his efforts as the work of the only potential mediator between two antag-onistic groups who were in different ways equally to blame.

20 Amaya to vicario, September 24, 1894, Archivos de la Diócesis de León (ADL) 220/3.

21 *Semanal Nicaragüense,* October 10, 1872.

22 Aside from coveting Sutiaban land (elite hacendados occupied a small fraction of indigenous territory), the elite found the Indians' amassing of cattle to be a con-stant source of irritation. To cite another example, those who wished to vacation at the beach at Poneloya had to pay indigenous authorities a transit tax and another tax to build cottages in Sutiaban territory. Archivo Municipal, June 23, 1883, ADL, box 419/4.

23 *El Municipio,* June 28, 1881.

24 *El Municipio,* June 28, 1881.

25 Título supletorio (Supplementary title) to Ramón Mairena, in the Archivo Munici-pal of León, box 91.

26 Título supletorio to Mariano Barreto, September 25, 1906, Archivo Municipal/ León-UNAN (AMLU) box 96.

27 It is also significant that during this same period, the federal government had to name a special attorney to mediate in the matter of the limits between the Sutiaban and Leonés ejidos.

28 It seems unlikely that the occupational structure of the community would have changed radically in thirteen years, so the figures ought to indicate the general tendencies of social development at the end of the last century.

29 Agricultores constituted 55 percent and jornaleros made up 45 percent of those who lived in the *comarcas* (villages) within the boundaries of Sutiaba.

30 The census of the neighborhood of Pueblo Grande is located in the AMLU, box 104; it is the only occupational census I found for Sutiaba. Its electoral figures show a total of 154 adult males in the neighborhood and 119 in three Sutiaban subdivisions. The total population of Sutiaba at that time was between 6,000 and 9,000. If we analyze the familial patterns of the two groups potentially descended from those who would have lost land between 1902 and 1915, we find that the groups of obreros/artisans were quite distinct from those of the jornaleros. Thus, for exam-

ple, among the six Flores brothers (aged twenty-two to thirty-two years) there were four masons, a tailor, and a barber, while of the four Hernández brothers (aged twenty-nine to seventy-eight), all were jornaleros. Such a pattern is reproduced by neighborhood. We assume, therefore, that if the social structure were a direct result of the loss of access to land such divisions between the families of artisans and jornaleros would not exist, as the former occupied a higher social and economic category. Although we lack sufficient data, an analysis of property registers and judicial archives for the period of 1902 to 1904 reveals the percentages of artisans and jornaleros to be similar to those documented in the 1915 census.

31  Juan Roque, for example, had two *propiedades agrícolas* (agricultural properties), with an extension of about thirty manzanas, a solar, and a house in the *casco urbano* (urban center); the total value of these holdings reached $450. Petition for a título supletorio, November 18, 1904, AMLU, box 93.

32  Anthropologist Carol Smith places much importance on the role the parcialidades have played in Guatemalan history and, despite certain obvious differences, her analysis seems to be pertinent to the Nicaraguan case. Carol Smith, "Local History in a Global Context: Social and Economic Transitions in Western Guatemala," *Comparative Studies in Society and History* 26 (1984): 199–200.

33  Citing cases of surviving indigenous communities we might mention the Matagalpas of the central highlands, which held four parcialidades, and Monimbó (barrio of Masaya) with two. Chinandega, Rivas, and San Jorge are examples of indigenous communities with one parcialidad, each of which upon losing its lands lost its organic structure and indigenous identity.

34  We must also remember that at this same time the municipality of León was involved in litigation with Sutiaba concerning the boundaries of the communal lands. The seven hacendado families of León had much to gain from the privatization of Sutiaban lands, as their tenancy on the land would become private property ownership.

35  *Diario Oficial,* January 9, 1903. Their sparse participation in the *cantonales* (district) elections of 1901 is perhaps symptomatic of the political distancing of the Sutiabas with respect to the Leoneses. Although the Sutiaba population comprised 10 percent of the departmental population, only 244 Indians voted, while 5,828 of the department's citizens voted. In the neighborhood of San Felipe de León, the same size as Sutiaba or smaller, 1,010 citizens voted. AMLU, box 87.

36  Although there are no more details, it is obvious that the Liberal party in León found itself divided between the elite, who had supported the anti-Zelaya revolution, and the artisanal sectors represented by A. Ramírez and by Francisco Ramírez, another deputy who also supported Sutiaba's petition. The Leonese elite, perhaps, named the annexation of Sutiaba and its lands as the price of their support for the Zelaya government and for tolerating the political role of the radicals, the Ramírez family in the party. On the other hand, General Ramírez,

though a carpenter, was not poor. In February 1902, Ramírez offered 4,500 pesos (more than $1,500) for the position in charge of the cock fights. Municipal document, January 16, 1902, AMLU, box 89.

37 In October 1902, the regime commenced its offensive against the Sutiabas. Due to a law of forced labor, more than 200 Sutiabas were obliged to work on neighboring sugar plantations. *Diario Oficial,* October 1, 1902.

Although the Roque family (descendants of the colonial principales) successfully hid the property titles, the Sutiabas lost collective control of the land. *Impacto,* May 3, 1960. Interviews with Julián Bárcenas and Ernestina Roque, Sutiaba, March 1988.

38 For more details, see Jeffrey L. Gould, "La raza rebelde: las luchas de la comunidad indígena de Subtiava," *Revista de Historia* (Costa Rica), 21–22 (January–December 1990): 69–117. In particular, the annexation favored those Indians who had the largest possessions because it increased the value of their land. In addition, with the annexation they were able not only to buy more property, but also to sell it.

39 *Registro de propiedades,* León, 1903–1904.

40 Petition to Alcalde Marín de Juan Jesús Bravo et al., January 13, 1905, AMLU, box 93.

41 August 13, 1905, AMLU, box 96.

42 Petition of Elías Gurdián, January 4, 1906, September 20, 1907, and October 28, 1907, AMLU, box 97. Similarly, at least twenty other Sutiabas successfully petitioned for land on their former ejidos during that same year.

43 In 1911, for example, Sutiaba's regidor succeeded in passing a municipal resolution that referred to the lands as "Sutiavan or ejidal." ADL, Archivo Municipal, box 362/2.

44 *Nicaragua indígena* 6, nos. 4–6 (1948).

45 In a talk in 1920, Alfonso Valle suggested that the Conservatives recruited Sutiabas to combat the 1912 Liberal insurrection, indicating that the Conservative-Sutiaba alliance already existed, or at least that the Sutiabas were prepared to vent their resentment of the Leoneses in a violent manner. *El Cronista,* June 1, 1920.

46 In 1913, twelve hacendados from León solicited the purchase, not the rental, of a total of 800 hectares of Sutiaba land. October 20, 1913, AMLU, box 104.

47 Ibid. Also consulted was written correspondence between 1915 and 1918 (maintained by the Sutiabas) among the leaders of the Comunidad Indígena, the jefe político of León, and the ministro de gobernación. During 1909, Sutiaba regidores in the municipality of León, all communal leaders since before the annexation, fought to obtain funds for improvements to their community, including health, road repairs, and maintenance of cemeteries (an important communal function even today).

48 A fundamental tenet of the original statutes emphasized the Indians' responsibility to support the government in case of insurrection. Chamorro Conservatives also offered the Sutiabas concrete improvements in exchange for indigenous support.

49  *El 93* (León), August 13, 1916. Some 3,000 Sutiabas reportedly attended a Liberal rally. The Sutiabas had been reliably Liberal since the 1820s; the opposition of León Liberals to the hated Zelaya regime apparently kept many Sutiabas in the party.

50  An exception was Camilo Díaz Argenal, a doctor and conservative leader of Pueblo Grande, who was secretary of the Indigenous Community.

51  *El Independiente,* February 26, 1919.

52  *El Cronista,* March 6, 1919. This Liberal newspaper argued that Terán, a landowner, supported the Comunidad Indígena against the León elite, exclusively because he sought indigenous votes for his party.

53  *El Heraldo,* March 6, 1919.

54  *El Cronista,* March 6, 1919.

55  *El Cronista,* June 24, 1920.

56  *El Cronista,* October 8, 1920.

57  It is crucial to note that the FON delegate to the conference of the Federación de Trabajo Panamericana (Pan-American Labor Federation) in Washington was Rubén Valladares, a Liberal leader from a family with agrarian interests in Sutiaba and, above all, one of the builders of a highway leading into Poneloya, which was opposed by the Comunidad Indígena.

58  In 1920, the Comunidad sent five of its members on a mission to the nuncio in Costa Rica. *El Cronista,* February 20, 1920.

59  *El Heraldo,* March 21, 1918.

60  *La Reforma,* May 30, 1918.

61  *El Eco Nacional,* June 9, 1919, and *El Cronista,* June 29, 1919. In January 1923 the Supreme Court blocked Sutiaba's "Plan de Arbitrios" (municipal tax code) pending its ruling. We have been unable to find a final ruling on either the Sutiaba case in particular or the 1914 law. It seems highly unlikely that the latter was ruled unconstitutional, and the Sutiaban Comunidad could not be legally challenged well without overturning that law. See *Memorias del Ministerio de Gobernación, 1922–1923* (Managua: Tipografía y Encuadernación Nacional, 1924), 107–113.

62  *El Cronista,* July 18, 1919.

63  *El Eco Nacional,* December 3, 1922.

64  *El Cronista,* February 26, 1919.

65  *El Centroamericano,* November 17, 1922.

66  *El Eco Nacional,* December 3, 1922. This newspaper cites 50 Indians in the movement, although others cite 100.

67  On the negotiated arrangement, see *Memorias del Ministerio de Fomento, 1922* (Managua: Tipografía y Encuadernación Nacional, 1923).

68  *El Cronista,* December 3–12, 1922.

69  *El Cronista,* December 5, 1922.

70  On obrerismo, see Jeffrey L. Gould, "Estábamos Principiando: Un estudio sobre el movimiento obrero en Chinandega, Nicaragua, 1920–1949," *Revista de Historia* no. 18 (July–December 1988).

71　*El Centroamericano,* December 3, 1922.

72　*El Eco Nacional,* January 16, 1923.

73　*El Cronista,* January 18, 1923. A petition signed by more than fifty residents of Sutiaba condemned the attack on the library. The petition was published in *El Centroamericano,* January 1922.

74　*El Cronista,* January 19, 1923. The newspaper repeated its attacks on the "communist" leadership of the Comunidad Indígena.

75　See *Actas de la Biblioteca Bartolomé de las Casas,* 1924, Biblioteca Fray Bartolomé de las Casas, Sutiaba, León, and *El Cronista,* April 7, 1924.

76　September 30, 1923, ADL 361/1.

77　July 27, 1924, ADL 361/1. On the sad departure of Urcuyo from the city of León in spite of "all . . . [his] sacrifices," see *El Cronista,* April 4, 1924.

78　For example, Camilo Díaz Argenal, president of the Conservative Club of Sutiaba, and at the same time member of the directorate of the Comunidad Indígena, announced the separation of his group from the Conservative party of León "because besides the small appreciation with which Sutiava is seen, because of their lands, without a doubt they are wasting a village which has more . . . conservatives than León." *El Cronista,* May 7, 1920.

79　Notwithstanding, as a reflection of the influence of Vásquez and the Roque brothers in the 1923 elections, the Conservatives only lost by a margin of 1 to 2 in Sutiaba, while in the city of León they lost 1 to 3.

80　On the 1923 elections, see *El Eco Nacional,* November 6, 1923. For 1929, see same, November 5, 1929. The results of these elections were nullified by the Moncada government.

81　According to an article in *El Eco Nacional,* November 16, 1929, in 1926, "the year of [conservative] terror," the conservative troops of General Pasos Díaz occupied the Bartolomé de las Casas library itself. The troops removed the books and exchanged them for fruit.

82　In the late 1920s to early 1930s, the Sutiaban obreristas founded the Sociedad el Progreso (Progress Society), which was affiliated with the FON; participated in the activities of the library; and became followers of the leftist Partido Laborista (Labor Party). See *Actas de la Biblioteca Bartolomé de las Casas,* 1927–1928, Biblioteca Fray Bartolomé de las Casas, Sutiaba, León.

83　Interviews with Julián Roque Bárcenas, Esteban Bárcenas, Ernestina Roque, Sutiaba, León, 1988–1992. *La Hora,* March 25, 1958, was responsible for reminding its readers that Julián Roque Bamba "trounced liberals" during the 1926 Conservative occupation.

# 4

## Gender, Politics, and the Triumph of Mestizaje, 1920–1940

Our boiling blood, our fiery temperament, our indomitable haughtiness of
the American and Gothic races of which our imagination is the legitimate
heir . . . our experience has pushed us off the road of republican life onto the
life of Diriangén and Diriamba and Xaltels, famous caciques in the 16th
century who constantly warred against each other.
—José Dolores Gámez, *Promesa cumplida*, 1899

What promises is General Chamorro going to offer the Indians now? School
for the Indians? Land for the Indians? Justice for the Indians? Mockery and
Contempt. Exploitation and Deceit.—Leaflet signed "El Autonomista," 1928

I used to look with resentment on the colonizing work of Spain, but today I
have profound admiration for it. . . . Spain gave us its language, its civilization, and its blood. We consider ourselves to be the Spanish Indians of
America.—Augusto César Sandino, 1933

The myth of Nicaragua mestiza, the commonsense notion that Nicaragua had long been an ethnically homogeneous society, is one of the elite's
most enduring hegemonic achievements.[1] This chapter aims to deepen our
understanding of that process. As argued in preceding chapters, the creation
of this nationalistic discourse in Nicaragua depended on the increasing disarticulation of the Comunidades Indígenas, wrought by ladino pressures on
labor and land.[2] Simultaneously, the incessant questioning of indigenous authenticity contributed both to the consolidation of ladino power and to the
erosion of indigenous communal identity. That delegitimization of indigenous authenticity, in turn, was related to the development of a democratic
discourse of equal rights and citizenship that effectively suppressed specific
indigenous rights to communal land and political autonomy.

This chapter expands the inquiry into the discourse of mestizaje both
synchronically and diachronically. Those axes are linked through an analysis

of the creation of the symbol of the *raza indohispana* and of the gendered dimensions of indigenous ethnicity. Mestizaje constituted an important part of the early twentieth-century discourse of anti-imperialism. Sandino, in particular, forged a revolutionary variant of the "raza indohispana." Yet both the moderate and revolutionary nationalist versions of mestizaje involved the discursive suppression of contemporary Indian males and the female transmission of heroic pre-Columbian blood into the virile Indo Hispanic race.

Overall, the chapter continues to question the trend in contemporary ethnography and political discourse that at times uncritically celebrates cultural hybridity, while assuming that the notion of cultural loss is but a vestige of colonialist anthropology.[3] Just as the notion of "Indian" has to be historicized and stripped of essentialism, so too should we deconstruct the notion of mestizaje or hybridity. This chapter portrays the intimate relationship between the construction of mestizaje in Nicaragua and the nationally unacknowledged assault on its indigenous communities. Klor de Alva has expressed this point well:

> Mestizaje . . . is the nation-building myth that has helped link dark to light-skinned hybrids and Euro-Americans, often in opposition to both foreigners and the indigenous "others" in their midst. And it has been effectively used to promote national amnesia about or to salve the national conscience in what concerns the dismal past and still colonized condition of most indigenous peoples of Latin America.[4]

## The Search for an Anti-imperial Symbol

The triumph of the Liberal revolutions in Central America, along with the growing impact of U.S. cultural, political, and economic imperialism, both exacerbated and displaced ethnic divisions. Foreign intervention, in particular, created a need for national symbols that would respond to imperial arrogance, essentialized as the Anglo Saxon race. Although ladino as a category has survived in local pockets throughout El Salvador, Honduras, and Nicaragua (the middle isthmus) and remains a fundamental ethnic category in Guatemala, it could not serve as an effective symbolic vehicle for nationalism in the era of U.S. intervention.[5] The greatest stumbling block toward the emergence of an anti-imperial symbol was the existence of a substantial and embattled minority of Indians, often located within the coffee-based areas of the middle isthmus. Despite the Indians' demographic weight—they represented between 20 percent and 35 percent at the turn of the century—elites situated them in the words of Lomnitz-Adler, as "standing on the margins of progress, on the margins of nationality and outside history."[6]

By the end of the colonial period we can discern at least three meanings for the term "ladino" that continued to circulate throughout the region. In the Americas, Spaniards first employed "ladino" to describe native peoples who had adopted Spanish dress and customs in addition to language, as in "es un indio muy ladino" or "es un indio ladino" (meaning 1). By the mid eighteenth century, however, "ladino" no longer referred exclusively to "Hispanicized" Indians but rather was used to refer to castas, all intermediate strata between Spaniard and Indian, including mestizos and mulattoes, as well as to "former" Indians (meaning 2). The mixed-race category "ladino" served remarkably well as a symbol that facilitated the smoothing over of colonial racial categories and therefore impeded a conflation of class and race that might have proved devastating to the Central American elites.[7] Finally, in regions of overwhelmingly indigenous population, such as Matagalpa, the term "ladino" was used on baptismal certificates as synonymous with all non-Indians. The emergence of ladino in a binary opposition with Indians in lieu of other available racial categories (mestizo, mulatto, or white) further extended the repertoire of its meanings, as it could now include "white" (meaning 3).[8]

By the end of the nineteenth century, under the stratifying impact of coffee and Liberalism, the meaning of ladino as Hispanicized Indian (1) had ceased to circulate. At a national level, people continued to employ the mixed-race meaning (2) of ladino.[9] But in the coffee zones of the middle isthmus, "ladino"'s dominant meaning emerged as the binary opposite of Indian (3). Indeed the locally salient meaning of ladino implicitly referred to the existence of a "ladino race." Thus, for example, the civil and ecclesiastical birth records in the Central Highlands of Nicaragua at the turn of the century list members of the "casta indígena" and the "casta ladina." Moreover, the birth records treated "ladino" as a racial category (roughly equivalent to white) when they employed the word "mestizo" to describe the offspring of an indígena and a ladino.[10]

Thus by the early twentieth century the multivocality of ladino, with meanings ranging from "white" to "nonwhite," reflected and conditioned the incapacity of both elites and opposition intellectuals to produce anything resembling hegemonic forms and categories that would include the active consent by the majority of the population to their rule. Anti-imperialists could not use "ladino" as a national symbol, because one of its powerful racial resonances communicated an unacceptable, blatant exclusion of Indians. Although their imagined nation promised to extend citizenship and rights (to males), it was impossible to envision an alliance with Indians while operating within the discursive field of the ladino (thinking with and through that symbol), because in each of its contemporary meanings ladino implied superiority over Indians.

The contradictory meanings of ladino in middle-isthmian anti-imperial discourse can be glimpsed in the writings of Salvador Mendieta and Juan Mendoza. In 1919, both men wrote studies that diagnosed the ills of Central America and proposed similar solutions that involved overcoming existing political and economic hierarchies; they both shared a vision of mestizaje at the core of Central American nationalism. Indeed, both were militants of the Central American Unity Party (Mendieta was the founder and leader). Moreover, they were natives of the same town—Diriamba, Nicaragua—and of the same generation and similar class background (provincial petit bourgeois). We would assume that they shared a common language. Mendieta wrote the following definition of ladino:

> Ladino in Central America refers to the type that emerges from the mixture of our three mother races and does not present the distinctive characteristics of any one of them: he is not white like the Spaniard; nor copper-colored like the Indian, nor black like the African.[11]

Yet Mendieta's compañero Juan Mendoza, used the term to mean, in effect, "white":

> All of the talent, riches, and honors belonged within the patrimony of the ladino. For the ladino, miscegenation with Indians was unacceptable. ["El cruzamiento con indígena era inaceptable."][12]

Thus in 1919 two intellectuals with nearly identical backgrounds and politics would have fundamentally misunderstood each other's usage of a common and important category. A national symbol could not be made of such radically contradictory meanings. "Ladino" failed as an intelligible term within the debate on the new nation because its range of meanings allowed for no consensus on the racial basis of national sovereignty.

I do not mean that the multivocality of the term "ladino" led to its demise. Rather, I think that those incompatible meanings revealed a society that was extraordinarily fractured. In part, the coffee plantations helped to produce the sharp bifurcation between ladino and Indian throughout the middle isthmus (and in Guatemala). Moreover, the importance of the coffee cultures, where the meaning of non-Indian (3) circulated, would have made it extraordinarily difficult for the alternative mixed-race meaning of ladino (2) to include the indigenous population. Because the two dominant meanings excluded Indians, "ladino" was indeed a doubtful vehicle for anti-imperialist unity. But no substitute national symbol for the people emerged—only "Honduran," "Nicaraguan," or the even more vague "nuestra raza."

As early as 1898, the "Guía ilustrada de Nicaragua" gave voice to the idea of that country as a heroic product of mestizaje in opposition to the cold, technical Anglo Saxon race: "From the fusion of the ancient American race with Spanish blood emerged this characteristic type in which are found the energies of a soldier, the tenacity of the farmer, and the dreams of a poet."[13] Modesto Armijo, who by the 1930s had become one of Nicaragua's leading intellectuals, in 1908 penned the following denunciation of annexationism:

> Understanding then the antagonism that exists between the two races that populate the American continent, understanding that the domination of one race necessarily occasions the disappearance of the other, we can only explain the pro-annexation sentiment within the context of a corrupt state, where the brutal satisfaction of appetites takes precedence over national dignity.[14]

In these declarations the writers discovered a method of challenging nascent U.S. imperialism by creating a fictitious racial opposition. Although the racial definition of the United States as Anglo Saxon was easy enough to conceptualize at the time, the imagined racial unity of Central and South America could only be based on some kind of hybrid, mestizo race.

By the late 1910s and early 1920s, intellectuals began to present an increasingly positive valorization of the hybrid nature of "nuestra raza." Thus, for example, Juan M. Mendoza looked to the mestizo as the new harbinger of progress and national cohesion: "The ladinos failed to understand what has been resolved by the most advanced sociologists . . . and confirmed by those elements, the product of miscegenation, who today forge ahead with the dynamic force of capital united with expert . . . and progressive leadership."[15] Mendoza invented a scientific underpinning for mestizaje as he counterposed a technologically progressive, mixed-race class to backward, seigneurial, racially pure, white "ladino" domination.[16]

Although in Mendoza's version of mestizaje the indigenous element was still subordinate, by the early 1920s, under the influence (we can assume) of the Mexican revolution, intellectuals increasingly valued the Indian blood within the "race." Thus, by 1923, Manuel Quintana, a Catholic intellectual, found the Spanish contribution, "la raza híbrida de nuestros conquistadores" (the hybrid race of our conquistadores), far less impressive than the indigenous. He wrote: "Our race is then the intersection of these two great currents. . . . We hope that from this conjunction of strength and light, of romanticism and heroism, surges a brilliant force that will protect us against the new invader!"[17]

Here Quintana drew out the logical consequences of the growth of the developing anti-imperial symbol of "nuestra raza," strongly emphasizing the heroic (pre-Columbian) indigenous component. As we will see later in the chapter, Augusto C. Sandino would grasp hold of that symbol, develop it, and give "nuestra raza" a name that was previously lacking: "la raza indohispana." In the next section we will examine one precondition of that creation: the role of politics in the feminization and the exclusion of contemporary indigenous males.

### The Corporeal Language of Indigenous Politics

Politics was an important avenue for indigenous resistance during the 1910s and 1920s. Most significant within this realm was the Comunidades Indígenas' obtainment of legal status in 1914 thanks to their alliance with the Conservative party. The Comunidades of the Central Highlands, in turn, represented the party's most important social base in the country. To this effect, a 1932 U.S. State Department report commented that "A large majority of the Indians who vote are located in the Departments of Chontales and Matagalpa, which have been controlled in the past by Emiliano Chamorro."[18] Additional evidence also suggests that in the contested elections from 1920 to 1934, the Indians formed the single most influential block of voters.[19]

The political conflicts discussed in the earlier chapters, which, by the 1930s, led to the eclipse of the Conservative party, seriously weakened the indigenous communities and contributed to the rise of mestizaje. In particular, the extreme identification of Indians with the Conservative leader Emiliano Chamorro produced a kind of disenfranchisement with his loss of power and influence. The decline of Chamorrismo meant more than the loss of a powerful ally; it also signified the transformation of this particular style of indigenous authority. For his caudillismo among the Indians was so powerful he could, as it were, anoint subalterns, bestowing upon them his aura of authority. Consider the following indigenous letter in support of the Matagalpino capitán-general of the cañadas:

> Ceferino Aguilar is a big man, carajo. . . . He has risked his neck for his nation [and] not just one time. Emiliano supports him as a guarantee, and for us, he is a recognized chief in the same way that colonel Bartolomé Martínez is our soul in Matagalpa.[20]

Chamorro legitimated Aguilar's virile leadership, as Aguilar's service to *la patria*. These images of Indian virility and heroic, patriotic Chamorrismo formed a pole in indigenous discourse opposed to that of servile, effeminate, dominated Indians.

We can sense the early stages of identification with Chamorro in another letter, from the president of the Comunidad Indígena of Jinotega to Bartolomé Martínez. The Comunidad was then engaged in an often violent land conflict with the predominately Liberal ladino elite. In 1916, the Conservative government, in search of political support against the Chamorrista faction of the party, jailed the president and many of his followers. The words of the indigenous leader reiterate the point made in chapter 2 that the Chamorrista-Indian alliance helped the Comunidades survive as institutions and often tipped the balance of power in favor of Indians in disputes with ladinos over land:

> The Comunidad leadership is being terrorized by the Sr. Director de Policia . . . eliminating authorities and stealing properties. . . . Then I and

the Indian people congratulate the Genuine Conservative Party so that
Sr. General Chamorro will give us protection and guarantees. ¡Viva Emi-
liano Chamorro! ¡Viva los indios de la Comunidad Jinotega y la Patria
Libre![21]

This metonymic relationship Chamorro: Indians: Patria Libre, hinged on
the representation of the Conservative caudillo as an emancipator, an image
fed by Chamorrista propaganda. A speech delivered to a crowd of Matagalpino Indians at a Conservative rally in 1920 illustrates the ideal portrayed:

> For the indígenas of this region, General Chamorro is the man who
> through long and bloody battles set us free from tyranny, liberating the
> slaves and transforming them into free gazelles that today roam in the
> land of their ancestors, their mountains . . . without fear of being ar-
> reados, hands bound together, creating fortunes for others, as in ancient
> times. . . . Chamorro for the Matagalpino indio is that same invincible
> warrior of yesterday, who one day pitched his tent in the hills . . . of his
> beloved land . . . and who like Aníbal shook the country to its foundation
> in order to bring down tyranny.[22]

In the speech sharply discernible are the metaphoric poles of freedom—
gazelles in their ancestral homeland today, and slavery—the *arreado* of the
Zelaya era. Another Chamorrista declaration directed at the indigenous population revolved around the same poles of servitude and emancipation: "The
Liberals that treated you like beasts . . . carried off your wives and your
daughters to take them to the haciendas in the sierra of Managua."[23] In this
declaration the opposition between servitude and Chamorrista emancipation
revealed a gendered dimension. The Indian "beasts" were emasculated by
their servitude but moreover by their inability to prevent their women's capture and (temporary) enslavement by ladino male authorities. Within this
framework, Chamorro and his Indian allies emancipated the women from
degradation and thus allowed Indian males to reassume masculine identities.

At the end of Emiliano Chamorro's first presidency, as we saw in chapter 1,
he reinstituted a legal form of extraeconomic coercion. Although that act
revealed his need for cafetalero support, the action did not dislodge the
fundamental identity of Emiliano as associated with indigenous emancipation. But the indigenous alliance with the Conservatives had other implica-

tions on a discursive level, strongly influencing ladino perceptions of Indians that, in turn, affected indigenous identity.

Consider the anti-Chamorrista gloss on the 1924 campaign and electoral violence as it revealed the place of the Indian in ladino political logic:

> The strength of Chamorrismo rests here in the indigenous and illiterate masses that become fearful with little provocation. . . . Nevertheless, with this type of support, Chamorrismo won the election in Matagalpa, which clearly proves that there was no government imposition in the election in Matagalpa.[24]

Because Indians were deemed to be fearful by nature, and because they voted overwhelmingly for Chamorro, the government, according to this line of reasoning, could not have used force to swing the Indian vote. The highlands Indians were caught at the heart of this vicious logical construction. Ladinos possessed an essentialized view of the Indians as "naturally timid of authority" (the ladinos harped on the effeminate characteristics of contemporary as opposed to pre-Columbian Indians). Even Bartolomé Martínez, one of the few politicians who had close relations with the Matagalpino Indians, commented in a letter in 1912 to Emiliano Chamorro: "everyone knows that this caste is very pusillanimous."[25] The intensified violent subjection of the Indians during the 1910s and 1920s—land evictions, military recruitment, and forced labor on the coffee plantations—had solidified that image.

Also relevant is a report by a Liberal observer during the 1920 presidential election: "Ceferino Aguilar [capitán-general of the Comunidad Indígena of Matagalpa], in his military uniform, armed and with a whip in his hand arrived and cast his ballot as he led his people like a flock of tame sheep."[26] Whatever its basis in historical reality, this report perpetuated the image of barbarous Indian leaders and weak, effeminate male followers. A sympathetic Matagalpino ladino observer in 1916 suggested a similar argument: "The individuals . . . of the casta indígena have the custom since time immemorial of nearly blindly, but voluntarily obeying their leaders."[27] These gendered images of the capitanes de cañada cajoling their flock to the voting booth fed Liberal views of Indians as major impediments to effective electoral democracy. Although Indians often inverted the imagery, the ladino political discourse framed indigenous understandings of their own role in politics.

Fragmentary extant texts affirm that Indians, to a degree, accepted the dominant view that they as a people were subservient to authority and that their leaders could, and even should, coerce the vote of the rank and file. Yet, this affirmation of ladino views of indigenous leadership emanated from a profound crisis of leadership. In particular, the involvement of Indian officials in violently disciplining Indian laborers shook the structures of patriarchal rule (see chapter 1).

A bitter rift between two of the principal indigenous leaders between 1910 and 1925 symbolized that crisis: Alvino and Ceferino Aguilar, father and son, represented different Conservative factions and hated each other venomously. The crisis of local authority derived from the pressures against communal resources and increasing class differentiation. These pressures and opportunities made it difficult for leaders to operate within the moral economic boundaries that had guided the previous generations, shaping the moves of the rebel chieftains of 1881 or Salvador Vásquez and Julián Roque Bamba in Sutiaba.

The following discussion examines letters written in the early 1920s by local Matagalpino indigenous leaders to capitán-general of the Comunidad Indígena, Ceferino Aguilar, and to his close friend and ally Bartolomé Martínez, the vice-president of Nicaragua. The context of the letters was a bitter intra-party fight (jockeying for the next presidential nomination) that pitted Vice-President Bartolomé Martínez against Martín Benard, a leading member of the Granadan oligarchy. In Matagalpa, Domingo Portillo was in charge of wooing the indigenous vote away from Martínez, still allied with Emiliano Chamorro. Portillo's job then was to politically destroy Ceferino Aguilar, the principal Chamorrista chieftain. The politician was aided in that task by Aguilar's father, Alvino Aguilar, a former president of the Comunidad. Portillo also gained the allegiance of other key allies, including former Comunidad president Miguel Martínez Sancho and four alcaldes de vara. The following letter informed Ceferino Aguilar of Portillo's tactics in response to a petition drive in the cañadas against Benard's presidential candidacy.

Sr. Capitan General, so as to make you aware, we state clearly and publicly the actions of Domingo Portillo and his compatriots Albino Aguilar and Miguel Sancho Martínez that have deeply disturbed the true *indios emilianistas*. . . . Every day Portillo gives them a shot of guaro and a piece of meat. Aguilar makes up for this service putting down the Indians. See

Sebastián, Bartolo Martínez [the vice-president] is crazy, don't listen to him. Ceferino is out of his mind, he can't give orders, he's finished, and anyone who sees him around the cañadas trying to win over people and asking for signatures must let Colonel Portillo know immediately, [Colonel Portillo's] the one in charge and anyone who signs will be punished, fined, and jailed. It's true this jerk is through, the Indians, ha, ha, ha.[28]

Within this text, an opposition emerges between "the true Indian Emilianistas," committed to freedom, and the false leaders, who implicitly lost their indigenous identity through their scorn for the "true" Indians and by virtue of their status as Portillo's dependents, beholden to his liquor and to his meat. The two Indian leaders were banished from the Comunidad because of their dependence on an enemy of the Indians (one opposed to Bartolomé Martínez), but also because of their depraved and abject behavior—all characteristics that were incompatible with virile indigenous leadership.

Albino Aguilar and Miguel Sancho's most grievous sin was their complicity with the "buying and selling" of Indians. Although the buying and selling implicitly referred to votes, there is an important slippage in the text that referred back to the arreado, the slavery trope. Indeed, we can detect what was a pervasive fear of "slavery," whether as a form of labor, jail, or military conscription. The following letter excerpt from local indigenous leaders to Martínez protests Portillo's "selling of Indians":

[He was] offering to Don Diego [President Chamorro] all the indios of Matagalpa. That he was the caudillo. . . . Don Diego made an agreement with Martín Bernard to accept the deal of the catracho [Honduran]. The deal would give him . . . fifteen hundred pesos and a thousand liters of guaro in exchange for Portillo's sale of indios. . . . Immediately they went and Cerna resold the same indios for eight hundred pesos.[29]

Those indigenous leaders who trafficked with the ladino politicians (President Diego Chamorro, Benard, Congressman Cerna) in the "sale" of Indians, then, were violating an implicit social contract with the rank and file. This image of buying and selling Indians is even more compelling if read in relation to the strong antislavery subtext: Emiliano, the emancipator converting the slaves into gazelles in the hills.

Finally, the language of slander is worth pondering; it was a peculiar political dialect in which notions of authenticity and legitimacy were worked out through references to the indigenous body. The more typical forms of slander referred to alcoholism, cowardice, sexual deviancy, and betrayal of Indians into chains. An indigenous ally of Martínez, to cite one graphic example, referred to Portillo in the following terms: "Dirty *cochón* [passive homosexual], there he has Marcelino Aguilar and several other indios in jail . . . shameless man . . . vulgar cochón, pot-bellied, weak."[30]

The ferocious and vulgar tone of this attack is unusual for its Indian authorship and ladino target. Focusing on Portillo's putative physical and sexual qualities, the writer portrayed him as a dirty, crude, fat, deformed, and (passive) homosexual. The attack on Portillo's sexuality—"un cochón"—would be strong language in any context, and indeed as a public insult such words would lead to violence. Moreover, as Roger Lancaster has shown conclusively the term refers to the dominated, the dependent, the receptacle of virility.[31] Portillo appeared as the embodiment of weakness and filth, whose very being violated the indigenous community and contaminated all he touched. Given the leadership model whereby ladino superiors passed on their attributes and authority to their indigenous subordinates, those remarks reflected upon Portillo's allies. In fact, a letter of protest signed by dozens of indigenous villagers casts similar aspersions on Miguel Martínez, former president of the Comunidad:

> Miguel Sancho Martínez the lifelong friend of Portillo . . . because he is a well-known fake, deceitful, treacherous, he doesn't remember that they [General Chamorro] were going to shoot him for being a bandit before the attack on Hato Grande. . . . We know him to be the most prosperous imbecile, he sells people, dirty son of a whore.[32]

As with the slander of Portillo, the attack on the Indian leader Martínez Sancho mixed a sense of contamination, physical revulsion, cowardice, and political betrayal.

It is hard to grasp the meaning of these personal slanders. Should we think of our own electoral campaigns, in which negative campaigning has increasingly replaced substantive political disagreements? The shades of political difference between the Conservative factions cannot explain such hatred. Nonetheless, the stakes were very high. The Indian leaders could live decently if their ladino friends were in power. Moreover, the loss of a position could mean imprisonment or worse. For the ordinary comunero, aligning oneself with the losing side could spell the worst kinds of disaster: loss of land, whippings, chains.

The corporeal language of insult can be seen as part of a struggle for power in the highlands that revolved around physical control over indigenous bodies. Portillo and Sancho were charged with the arrest and forcible military recruitment of Indians in order to serve their narrow political interests. In a world already dominated by coercive labor and land relations, Portillo and his indigenous allies became the locus of contamination and were therefore expelled in revulsion from the imagined indigenous community.

We can explain some of the meaning of physical revulsion when we place it in the context of its opposite—an expression of political praise. For example, the adjectives that described Chamorro camped out in the mountains of Matagalpa and those describing Ceferino Aguilar as "muy hombre carajo" stand in direct opposition to the physical characteristics of Portillo and Sancho.

Although Portillo was the concrete object of scorn in all of the cited letters, they also denounced how electoral politics cheapened, humiliated, and coerced the members of the Comunidad. Although Chamorro's and Bartolomé Martínez's indigenous allies contested those practices, both the protests and the practices resonated with the dominant liberal views of the Indian as ignorant, easily frightened, and, in general, unfit for democracy.

Political identification did not depend only on notions of contamination versus valor and loyalty, for as we saw, there was an ethnic-communal dimension signaled by the term "indios emilianistas." Indians bent national alliances to meet local political needs. But concomitantly, the indigenous political expressions and alliances reflected somewhat, and thereby justified, the dominant view of indigenous politics, summarized by one Boaqueño ladino intellectual: "The Indians were always gobiernistas." That notion would have been absurd forty years earlier.[33]

As the letters against Portillo indicated, a key criterion for indigenous leadership was the support of relevant ladino leaders. The dependence on outside power made the internal struggle for power all the more destructive and arbitrary. Thus, dependent factionalism led to the weakening of the indigenous communities as each group banished the other. At the same time, progressive intellectuals used such evidence from indigenous politics to support their contention that Comunidades Indígenas and democracy were incompatible. Moreover, those intellectuals who supported Indians as workers or peasants refused to recognize the historical legitimacy of the Comunidades Indígenas, which they viewed as hierarchical, dependent organizations (to control the capitanes de cañada appeared to control the indigenous vote), inimical to effective electoral democracy.[34] Finally, they misapprehended the dominant opposition in indigenous discourse between emancipation and slavery. Rather they fused images from dependent and authoritarian indigenous politics into their emerging portrait of a virile, democratic, and mestizo Nicaragua.

### Monimbó: Cradle of Anti-imperialism and Difference

If in the highlands, the Indians formed a bulwark of Conservative support, in the urbanized coastal area they played the role of vanguard in the anti-interventionist movement. Indeed, the unfurling of the banner of the hybrid "nuestra raza" on a national level coincided with the outbreak of several popular, nationalistic struggles. The most important of these urban-based struggles—virtually the only popular social movement in the country since 1912—involved the Indians of Monimbó, Sutiaba, and Nindirí. In 1919, the Indian villagers of Nindirí (five miles from Monimbó) rioted against the rate hikes of the oligarchic-owned water company.[35] As discussed in chapter 3, in 1922 and 1923 the Indians of Sutiaba led a similar struggle framed within an anti-imperialist discourse.[36]

This section concentrates on the movement spearheaded by the Monimboseños. On January 23, 1919, a train ran off the tracks on the outskirts of the city of Masaya. Four passengers died, including a child from the indigenous barrio of Monimbó; there were sixteen injured. The railroad, once the pride of urban Nicaragua, was owned and operated by a U.S. company and thus had become a target for growing dissatisfaction with the Conservative regime and the U.S. military presence that supported it.

That night the cacique Vital Noriongue led some 500 Monimboseños in a march out of their barrio located on the outskirts of Masaya. They headed toward the center of the small city shouting "Viva el Pueblo Soberano," "Viva

Nicaragua Libre," and "Muera O'Connell" (the manager). When they reached the center they were joined by citizens "of all social classes and political affiliation." The government sent fifty soldiers to protect the railroad station. A reporter wrote about what happened next: "they tried to take the station looking for Mr. Gaylord and the other [North American] employees. The enraged people, finding the doors of the station closed, tore down the high fence . . . and broke in."[37] The soldiers' shots in the air persuaded the demonstrators to leave the station; afterward, they marched on to the manager's house, to wreak revenge. When they did not find him they returned to Monimbó chanting "the people will make justice."[38]

The movement then fizzled only to reignite in May 1922, when the railroad decided to build a barrier around the station in Masaya. The construction of this wall, a more solid version of the one destroyed in 1919, directly blocked out the *vivanderas* (market women, including many Monimboseños) who sold their products at the station. The wall couldn't have come at a more inopportune moment, as the country was in the throes of severe recession: exports declined from 11 million to 8 million dollars, government expenditures had dropped from 4 million to 2.5 million, and the U.S.-controlled banks refused to grant loans, allowing moneylenders to charge rates up to 10 percent a month. In response to the crisis, the railroad had raised their freight rates from the coffee-growing Pueblos region, largely hurting the small producers and merchants. Similarly, the Conservative regime was suffering a crisis of legitimacy and Liberal and Conservative factions launched insurrectionary movements in May 1922.

Once again, the cacique of Monimbó, Vital Noriongue, led his people from the barrio toward the station. The U.S. ambassador filed the following report:

> One thousand people surrounded and tore down the high fence surrounding it . . . The riot was the result of increasing popular antagonism against the railroad management, enhanced by the recent erection of a large barrier around the station to keep out the merchants.[39]

Other sources suggested as many as 3,000 people, armed with clubs and machetes, rioted for two hours.[40]

In the context of the preceding social calm in urban Nicaragua, the Masaya and Nindirí riots, together with a stevedore strike in Corinto and criollo protests in Bluefields, seemed to forebode a social explosion, akin to contem- porary revolutionary movements in the rest of the world. One editorialist commented after the first Masaya riot: "[There is] a decomposition in the national organism. . . . Something abnormal is happening in the country and the authorities must establish order."[41]

Significantly, in the Masaya movements nonindigenous Nicaraguans recognized (at least informally) the leadership role of the Indians at a key moment in the struggle against U.S. intervention (in 1978 the Sutiabas and Monimboseños would play similar, if far more important, roles in the insurrections). These struggles in 1919 and 1922 condensed a variety of aspirations, resentments, and concrete demands of the three indigenous communities. Yet in Nindirí and Monimbó the 1919 and 1922 struggles did not appear to outsiders to have an indigenous content, for the protagonists framed their actions as aggrieved Nicaraguan citizens.[42]

The movement in Monimbó resembled a classic social protest involving artisans, vivanderas, and small landholders. Yet the movement emerged directly from the terrain of ethnic conflict and employed specifically indigenous forms of organization.

Vital Noriongue played an integral role in maintaining communal cohesion, despite major political and lineage splits. A colorful figure, to several generations of barrio folk he symbolized Monimboseño ethnicity. The ladino priest-poet Jacobo Ortegaray mocked him but nonetheless revealed something of his stature among his people:

> Era Vital un caudillo
> del Barrio de Monimbó
> indio lampiño y gritón.
>
> De guayacán escogido
> era el nudoso bastón,
> el que con gracia portaba
> dándose aires de señor.
>
> Descendiente de caciques,
> la indiada oía su voz,
> político era a su modo
> y militar y mandón.

En los tiempos de elecciones
con el hombre del tambor
alborotaba en el Barrio
llamando a la votación.

Fue zelayista sincero
y también conservador
sincero, no cabe duda,
pues lo era con los dos.

Era modelo perfecto
de caudillo vividor,
atronaba con sus vivas
al jefe de la nación.

Para bienes personales
nunca su influencia la usó
mas era paño de lágrimas
del que caía de prisión.

Era modelo perfecto
de caudillo vividor
y su recuerdo es consejo
del pueblo de Monimbó.[43]

Despite the derision of the caudillo's opportunism, the priest's poem evokes a nostalgic admiration for Noriongue's traditional style of authoritarian rule with such images as "el nudoso bastón," "descendencia de caciques," and "el tambor." What Ortegaray missed, of course, were events that revealed the cacique's capacity for autonomous action, such as the mass demonstrations against the key symbol of the U.S.-Conservative alliance.

Previously, Noriongue had guided his people through tense negotiations with the Conservative governments, to whom he had pledged allegiance and had helped to win more than 45 percent of the vote in a traditionally Liberal area. In return, the Conservatives offered some concessions to the Monimboseños, including the legalization of their communal land—21,000 hectares for the 6,000 inhabitants of the barrio. Unlike the Indians of the highlands, the Monimboseños were not interested in keeping much communal land per se, but rather in dividing it equitably among the families of the barrio. A threatened tradition of small agricultural plots in an area without sufficient space for cattle may account for the unique Monimboseño perspective on communal land. In the early 1930s, small landholders on the remaining communal land would lose it to a hacendado from Granado.

In 1918, relations became tense when the jefe político failed to confirm the directorate of the Comunidad.[44] During the same year, the Monimboseños pressured the government on two issues: to build a public road from their barrio to Lake Masaya (their source of water) and to survey and distribute communal land plots.[45] Chamorro responded by offering $200 for the road, and he promised to legalize the division of communal land.

Noriongue's traditional form of rule conformed, I would argue, to the ideal Indian leader discussed in the previous section and only superficially resembled that of other Central American caudillos.[46] The Indian cacique's period in office, which apparently stretched from the Zelaya era until the late 1920s, symbolized in Monimboseño memory the apex before the decline of indigenous society. The words of a Monimboseño elder and former alcalde de vara capture a key aspect of that social memory:

> At the time there was an abundance of food. . . . It was the time of Don Vital Norionte [*sic*]. . . . He went around with a *cotono maduro* [long-sleeved, collarless cotton shirt] and a palm sombrero, that's how he went around just like the other indígenas. One day everything turned a bit expensive. . . . The people said we have to do something, so let's go to see the alcalde. Such a thing had never been seen, so many people like that. They told him, "You are like a second president, so why did everything become so expensive?" The alcalde responded, "It's good that you have come, I can't solve the problem today, but tomorrow I'm going to Managua."[47]

In Managua, Noriongue headed for the presidential palace and once there announced: "I am Vital Norionte [*sic*], el alcalde del pueblo." Chamorro received him immediately and then asked what was going on. After listening to the cacique's report, Chamorro explained that a shortage of beans had caused the price increase but that Noriongue could go back and tell "el pueblo that it's all taken care of—the beans are being delivered."[48]

The tale paints a harmonious relation between "el pueblo," the cacique, and

Chamorro. Given the astronomical inflation of the Sandinista years and the fairly constant governmental corruption since the 1930s, the present surely affected the rendition of the past. That nostalgia relates to an idealized past when strong male leaders defended the community's moral economy. The story also probably drew from a political reality—the political relations between people, cacique, and Chamorro depended on a degree of organization and the threat of coercion from the bottom up. In that sense, the riots against the railroad, despite their negative implications for Chamorro, were nonetheless congruent with Noriongue's style of rule.

Noriongue was intensely suspicious of ladinos and ladino ways, but he was not opposed to their conception of progress. In this regard, Dr. D. M. Molloy, director of the "Relief and Control of Hookworm Disease in Nicaragua" project from 1915 to 1920, made some relevant observations. After describing the Spanish origins and growth of Masaya, one-half mile north of Monimbó, Molloy commented that the Indian inhabitants

> live today as they lived in the days before the Spanish invasion. While work was being conducted in Masaya proper, Monimbó was left untouched. The natives of Masaya prophesied that nothing could ever be done toward changing conditions in Monimbó, and many of them thought that the field men of the Department of Uncinariasis would take their lives in their hands if they visited the barrio for the purpose of interesting the people in the hookworm campaign. An Indian from Monimbó would occasionally visit one of the laboratories, where he would sit, absolutely non-committal, for a while—and go away. Little by little the field director gained the confidence and good-will of one or two of the chiefs, from which he finally secured permission to give some lectures to a selected group of people in the house of the chief.[49]

This ethnographic saga ended on a triumphant note: the hookworm campaign functioned successfully in Monimbó. For our purposes, the tale reveals a stark, fearful social and cultural distance between ladino and Monimboseño. The mutual fear derived in part from the need to police the boundaries of ethnic endogamy. As in Sutiaba, those fears played themselves out in street scuffles between male youths up until the 1970s. But the idea that the health workers would risk their lives, although an exaggeration, reflected deeper levels of paranoia and daily violence than existed in other Indian-ladino settings.

Two decades later, Gratus Haftmeyer, a writer who spent some time in the indigenous barrio, wrote a novel entitled *Monimbó* in which he commented:

> They never hold a conversation with anyone that is not of their casta, they never say anything about even the most trivial things, limiting themselves simply to the monosyllable: no, sí, quién sabe, no sé, tal vez, etc. Suspicious and scared, they think that the one that talks to them or asks them questions, does so with intent to harm them.[50]

Based on oral accounts of Indian-ladino relations, we can assume that the failure to communicate was a reasonable response to ladino forms of domination. That Monimboseños usually substituted the epithet "mulato" for ladino, regardless of skin color, further suggests a unique and historically conditioned level of hostility and bitterness that blocked much communication across ethnic lines. Haftmeyer's own vision suffered from a heavy dose of essentialism. Note, for example, his remark on Indians in the capital who go from the train station to the market,

> without looking to either side. They don't care much about the reinforced concrete building, with three or four floors. . . . They don't take pains even to lift their eyes to contemplate the engineering wonders, they don't want to know anything about progress.[51]

Despite Haftmeyer's sympathy for the Indians he failed to elucidate much about Monimboseño attitudes toward progress or politics. As Molloy's narrative indicates, Monimboseños were not at all opposed to progress, but rather to impositions that they could not control or which would create burdens on their fragile economy. Thus, Noriongue pressured Chamorro's administration, during an antihookworm campaign, not only to provide the wood for latrines but to pay barrio residents to dig the holes.[52] In similar fashion, they demonstrated against the Conservative monopoly water company when it failed to fulfill its promise of providing free water at the communal spout on Sundays.

This brief description of Monimboseño-ladino relations poses a question of interpretation. If those relations were so problematic, how could the Monimboseños play such a crucial role in a multiethnic movement? Although the Monimboseño movements shared communal organizational forms, they had neither the same demands nor the same styles of action as those of Boaco,

Camoapa, or Jinotega. The other indigenous groups eschewed direct confrontation and, rather, engaged in fence cutting, petition, or passive resistance (with the exception of the highlands Indians' participation in the anti-Zelayista movement of 1909 to 1910, which they understood as a war for emancipation). Although semiurban Monimbó did have communal lands, as a whole the community had become somewhat less dependent on agriculture and was much more dependent on artisanal production, field labor, and commerce than were the other Comunidades.

Monopolies threatened not only Monimbó's economic base but also its moral economy. The companies did not respond to what the people thought was a just price for their products or their demand for water during the sweltering days of the dry season. These problems affected nonindigenous communities as well, but due to the virtual nonexistence of unions or community organizations they were unable to provide much resistance against the electric and water monopolies. The Monimboseños, on the contrary, had a highly effective community organization and had experience in pushing the government to resolve their infrastructural problems.

Monimbó, therefore, was a privileged site of resistance in the nascent popular movement against U.S. intervention and monopolies. These struggles included ethnic-communal demands and resentments, but they were also about political and economic issues vital to many Nicaraguans. Although the ethnic dimension of these struggles was unclear to outsiders, the indigenous identity of the protagonists was obvious. This opacity ensued because the demonstrators framed their demands within the moral economy of an aggrieved Nicaraguan citizenry rather than as Indians.

The Indians' role in these nationalistic, but communally rooted, struggles might well have facilitated their ideological incorporation into the emerging mestizo nation by stretching the meaning of "Indo Hispanic." The inclusion of these indigenous groups would strengthen "nuestra raza" as an antagonistic pole against the United States and its oligarchic allies. Ironically, the integration of Indians as citizens at the same time marginalized them as ethnic groups—they were incorporated as equal citizens without special rights to cultural or political autonomy.[53]

This promise of integration and practice of exclusion had even more profound consequences for the rural indigenous population of the Central Highlands, whose contemporary struggles received virtually no support nor recognition from the nationalist movement. On the contrary, as we have seen, the nationalists viewed the highlands Indians as servile followers of antidemocratic and antipatriotic forces embodied in the Conservative party.

### Sandino and the Making of the Indo Hispanic Race

Urban indigenous participation in the popular, nationalistic struggles set the stage for a major linguistic and conceptual shift. During Augusto Sandino's war of national liberation, the Indo Hispanic race was discursively enshrined and the categories of ladino and Indian suppressed. Indeed, Sandino himself played an important role in that process, as he placed the Indo Hispanic race as the core symbol of popular nationalism.

Sandino's 1927 to 1933 war of resistance against U.S. intervention coincided with and provoked a variety of forms of rural class conflict. Although the majority of the highlands Indian population did not actively participate in Sandino's army, most indigenous groups *did* attempt to use the changing wartime political conjuncture to their advantage. In particular, they took advantage of the breakdown in the normal repressive operations of the state as the U.S. marines and the Guardia Nacional (National Guard) devoted most of their resources to the war effort.

Thus, some indigenous leaders in Matagalpa apparently operated as bandits with no clear political agenda or affiliation.[54] Others pursued specific collective goals. Consider the example of indigenous resistance against the English cafetalero Fred Fley. He was the owner of a relatively small plantation (valued at U.S. $2,500) situated near the village of San Marcos in the western part of the territory of the Comunidad Indígena of Matagalpa.[55] Since 1924, he had been involved in a land conflict with his neighbors. In 1927, after U.S. intervention ended the civil war, the Conservative government named Pedro López and Benacio Méndez as capitán de cañada and juez de mesta of San Marcos respectively. Much to Fley's chagrin, they were his principal antagonists in the land dispute. The cafetalero thus complained to the marines:

> They have shown me their enmity by robbing my cattle, by cutting my cows' tails and by inciting the other Indians against me and my family. . . . Now that they are representatives of law and order they are the only people who are armed with government rifles. Their duty is to

disarm everybody but they only disarm Liberals. . . . Here there are brutish, armed Indians (usually more drunk than sober) and the foreign element has nothing to defend themselves.[56]

At several points over the next six months Fley attempted to gain the support of the marines in his battle with his indigenous neighbors. Colonel Berry sympathized with Fley, but, as he explained, given the growing conflict with Sandino he needed to keep the capitanes de cañada armed until he was able to obtain more recruits for the Guardia Nacional. Fley responded that the situation was

> going very badly outside of the city Matagalpa. Armed Indians have occupied my land as squatters . . . they use my plantation as pasture. I have no legal protection. I ask the Marines for the protection that they promised—the intervention was to protect the property of foreigners— and *I want to know when are they going to keep their promise. . . .* I am rapidly losing the little cattle that I held onto following the revolution and I am sure that the thieves are these Indians who have squatted on my land, armed with government-issued Springfields. We are unarmed.[57]

A reading of Fley's racist complaint reveals something about how Sandino's resistance caused a shift in the local balance of power. Although Sandino did not gain significant indigenous support in the region, his presence in the nearby Segovias created conditions that also aided indigenous struggles against other cafetaleros. To cite another example, the indigenous inhabitants of Uluse, Matagalpa (near Pancasán), were able to claim and work 350 hectares of La Escocia plantation.[58]

Thanks to Sandino's battle with the marines, the Matagalpino Indians were also able to press their labor demands. Thus, indigenous coffee pickers thwarted cafetaleros' efforts to enforce debt obligations and pressured the planters to increase their wages.[59] Their multifaceted resistance during Sandino's rebellion bore fruit when in 1934 the Nicaraguan legislature enacted measures that effectively ended the seasonal debt peonage system (illegal since 1923).[60]

Although Sandino did not receive direct support from the Matagalpino Indians, they gave none to the marines or the Guardia, at least during the first three years of the struggle. In 1930, when a Matagalpino Indian helped the marines to capture a Sandinista who had kidnapped his wife, Major Cruse reported: "This incident is very important since it is virtually the first time during the three years of the campaign that the Marines or the Guardia Nacional have received any effective aid from these inhabitants."[61] Thus, despite the militarization of their local leaders (the capitanes), the Matagalpino Indians, in general, did not collaborate with the marines or the Guardia Nacional. It is indeed possible that the lack of collaboration reflected their awareness of Sandino's role in shifting the balance of power in favor of their land and labor demands.

There were also highlands Indians who *did* join Sandino and his army, particularly from the Comunidades Indígenas of Jinotega and San Lucas. Ramón Martínez, a Jinotegano ladino peasant who spent part of his adolescence working in the store of the Indian village of San Esteban, recalled: "There were a lot of Indians that went with Sandino. . . . All the Indians from there . . . were with him because Sandino fought against the Yanqui."[62] The Jinoteganos, according to Martínez, resented the U.S. presence specifically because U.S. officials had evacuated an area that included many indigenous villages in order to carry out a scorched-earth policy. Although the policy was suspended after one month, it probably earned the enmity of the indigenous inhabitants.[63] Ramón Martínez claimed that agrarian issues had little to do with indigenous support, and Sandino himself also discounted an "agrarian problem" in the zone. Yet, the political framework of the agrarian battles that flared up in the Jinotegano countryside from 1915 to 1921 (Conservative Indians versus Liberal *terratenientes* [landlords]) might provide a clue to how Sandino garnered Jinotegano Indian support. For example, in the electoral campaign of 1928 six Liberal leaders were assassinated near the Indian village of Mancotal, and according to one report: "a patrol of 40 to 50 men was responsible."[64] Furthermore, large groups of armed men had their base of operations in the Indian villages of El Roble and Paso Real.[65] It seems likely that during the 1928 campaign the partisan warfare created political opportunities for Sandino in the zone, in that his enemies were the class/ethnic antagonists of the Indians.

Despite such indigenous participation in Sandino's ranks—their numerically significant presence in the highlands and the pervasiveness of collective resistance against the ladino elites—Sandino's writings are *silent* on the

Comunidades Indígenas. He made his most notable statement about Indians in an interview with a Basque journalist in 1933:

> There is a saying that goes: "God will speak for the Indian of the Segovias." And he certainly has spoken! They are the ones who have done a great part of all this. The Indian here is timid, but cordial, sentimental and intelligent.[66]

Sandino then called over two Indians to introduce to the journalist. In order to show off their intelligence, he had them converse in Miskito, Spanish, and then English. Sandino continued,

> Well now you see that they are intelligent. But they have been entirely abandoned. There are some hundred thousand of them without education, without schools, without anything of government. This is what I want to do with the colony, to lift them up and make true men out of them.[67]

It is indeed striking that Sandino uttered the phrase about the "Segoviano Indians" and then, as it were, illustrated it with Miskito Indians, for the large majority of that group lived east of the Segovias. This confusion is remarkable, given the significant differences between the two groups, including language and dress and the Segoviano Indians' roots in the Segoviano mountains, a fact of much military importance to Sandino. In other words, in his use of the phrase "Indians of the Segovia," he apparently did not mean to include those of the Comunidades of Jinotega, Mozonte, San Lucas, or Telpaneca (who surely made up over 80 percent of the Segoviano Indians).

How are we to understand the apparent ignorance about the people of the Segovias on the part of the hero of the Segovias?[68] The interview also included a statement that denied the seriousness of the agrarian question in the Segovias despite recent expropriations of indigenous communal land, betraying a similar distortion in his view of the local social landscape. And yet in other parts of the interview, he describes with a great degree of complexity different aspects of Nicaraguan reality. Thus the textual evidence suggests that Sandino either knew relatively little about the local cultures of the Segovias or simply found such matters unimportant.

Sandino's silence with respect to the Comunidades derived, I would argue, from his nationalist project. As suggested by other scholars, Sandino was crafting a popular-nationalistic discourse; in effect, reinventing a nation that had become the "patrimony of oligarchs and traitors."[69] Sandino's nationalism was in turn rooted in a Central Americanist liberalism that was deeply enmeshed in Western notions of progress and civilization.[70] However sincere his commitment to aiding the Miskitos and Sumos, Sandino could not break free from the discourse of assimilation, which sought to "make true men out of them." Sandino's few statements about Nicaraguan Indians did not waver from this civilizing mission, "to do whatever necessary to civilize these Indians who are the marrow of our race."[71] That civilizing process, it is worth emphasizing, included Sandino's suppression of the role and practices of *suquias,* charismatic shamans, vital to the reproduction of Miskito culture.[72]

Sandino's nationalism and Liberalism impeded his understanding of the Comunidades Indígenas of the Segovias or Matagalpa on a more practical level as well. Creating a nation out of the divided and dominated political cultures of Nicaragua was a daunting task. Sandino thus stressed that which unified people: language and a shared colonial heritage. The fact that Segoviano and Matagalpino Indians spoke Spanish and in some cases were willing to support his army confirmed his belief that Nicaraguans in fact formed one Indo Hispanic race. In fairness to Sandino, it should also be stressed that a strong recognition of ethnic identity might well have damaged the cause of national liberation.

Since 1927, Sandino repeatedly called for the defense of the Indo Hispanic race.[73] Thus, for example, in 1933 following the departure of the U.S. marines he returned to the theme of Central American unity and issued a proclamation, which he signed: "the Indo-Hispanic citizen General Augusto C. Sandino: The spiritual vibration of la Raza Indo-Hispana at this time revolves around the Autonomist Army of Central America in order to save its racial dignity."[74]

Alejandro Bendaña has argued in his recent study *La mística de Sandino* that Sandino's indohispanismo "originated with the recognition of the fraternity and solidarity imposed by history, and by the ravages of colonialism past and present; it is a call to human fraternity. . . . It was part of the cultural sustenance of his political struggle."[75] Against my perception of Sandino's incomprehension of the Comunidades Indígenas, Bendaña further argues in defense of indohispanismo that "Sandino's commitment to communal self-management and the social character of property . . . embraces values and organizational forms that are compatible with the affirmation and defense of ethnic identity."[76] It is important not to confuse Sandino's heroic efforts on behalf of national liberation with the putative emancipatory nature of Sandino's indohispanismo. Sandino's indohispanismo was elastic enough to include Spaniards and Indians; it was so by necessity, and any questioning of the primordial value of mestizaje threatened that racial unity in the face of Anglo Saxon imperialism. Moreover, this discourse helped erase some of the racist opprobrium against darker-skinned Central American artisans and peasants. Also the blurring of ethnic boundaries among Sandino's social bases of support undoubtedly prevented, in 1934, the kind of anti-indigenous repression that had scorched the El Salvadoran countryside two years earlier.

Nevertheless, one should recognize the political and cultural cost of his project. Part of the cost surely was unintended—the political disenfranchisement of the Comunidades that accompanied the decline of the Conservative party. Although Sandino's struggle against U.S. intervention momentarily dealt a powerful blow against the bipolar world of Nicaraguan politics, it mainly undermined the Conservative party. In so doing, he helped to produce the political eclipse of the Conservative caudillo Emiliano Chamorro, who by 1934 would lose a senatorial election in Matagalpa, the Conservative's heretofore impenetrable bastion. We have already seen the degree to which the Indians had identified with Chamorro, an identification keyed to manipulation of the political system in defense of indigenous communal objectives.[77] Along with Chamorro's defeat those indios emilianistas lost their position as a vital fixture of the Nicaraguan political landscape, consequently losing their only available means of defense. Although Sandino was not directly responsible for that outcome, he made no effort to recast the disintegrating Indian-Chamorro alliance.

Sandino's lack of interest in the Comunidades derived in part from their traditional identification with Emiliano Chamorro, a classic traitor in his eyes. Regardless of the political context, Sandino did not recognize the independent existence and rights of the Comunidades Indígenas in the very mountains where he battled against the marines. Moreover, his failure to support the Comunidades was particularly grievous in light of its timing: that unique conjuncture where indigenous groups were in a position to rebound from decades of political, cultural, and economic losses.

Sandino provided a brilliant, dramatic symbol of anti-imperialist valor to the Central American Left and to the people it strove to represent. Yet his refusal to engage the indigenous communities also formed part of Sandino's legacy, and failing to recognize that silence in his discourse only covers up yet another land mine on the road to emancipatory politics in Central America.

## Gender and Mestizaje

Sandino's indohispanismo represented, in part, the culmination of the Central Americanist search for an anti-imperial symbol. Intellectuals, as we saw earlier, contributed to the evolving discourse of the raza indohispana. Thus, for example, in response to European scientific racism, the Unionist leader Salvador Mendieta developed a method for "constructive miscegenation" that effectively excluded indigenous males.[78]

Mendieta prescribed to "Central American parents" the proper physical characteristics for a prospective "pure Indian" daughter-in-law: "[She] should have a straight and wide back, prominent breasts and well formed hips as a vital receptacle for future healthy and strong men and women, full of intense vitality."[79] Less radical strands of Liberalism shared Mendieta's concern with the biological aspects of the Indo Hispanic race. For example, in 1943 a Liberal Somocista senator argued against Chinese immigration on the grounds that "Nicaraguan women by procreating children with the Chinese will degenerate the indolatino race of which we Nicaraguans are very, very proud."[80]

Mendieta's focus on constructive miscegenation was significant in that the discourse of mestizaje was built directly upon contradictory gendered images of Indians. Within the anti-imperialist resistance, the Indo Hispanic race was painted in virile images of pre-Hispanic Indian warriors. Yet simultaneously, the new race evolved out of the "feminization" of indigenous males. As we saw earlier in this chapter, the violent subjection of the Indians during the first decades of the century had solidified an effeminate image that contrasted with the masculine mestizos, inheritors of virile pre-Columbian indigenous blood, genetically apt for a democratic society. Poets and intellectuals expressed such an image frequently during the 1930s and 1940s.[81] For instance, in 1937 Albino Román issued the following patriotic appeal in the context of a border conflict with Honduras:

We are united by the bond of resolute and valiant blood, [that of] the Spanish; obstinate, unsubmissive, and prepared to sacrifice all for the

Patria, that is Indian blood. Compañeros, the race with nothing to shield themselves but their chests did not cede one handful of dirt without a Spanish grave; a heroic blood runs through our veins.[82]

In this vision, indigenous women transmitted the heroic, pre-Columbian blood into the Indo Hispanic race. Indigenous women in Nicaragua, as elsewhere, were also bearers of ethnic emblems, and endogamy was key to ethnic reproduction.[83] Strict patriarchal limitations on indigenous female sexuality, though, would to some degree thwart the biological mestizaje that Mendieta advocated as the foundation for Central American nationhood.[84]

Mendieta's plan for constructive miscegenation went to the heart of the problem of how to create the ethnic homogeneity that would unify a Central America and render it capable of withstanding North American imperialism: the Indian communities would have to be merged into the nation through an attack on indigenous patriarchy (an attack involving the feminization of indigenous males) and the appropriation of indigenous female sexuality by the makers of the new Central American race.

The success of Mendieta's program would involve overcoming indigenous endogamy. In Matagalpa, in particular, that would be quite difficult, given the existence of arranged, endogomous marriages until the 1950s. A male elder recalled the practice from his youth:

> The four parents met together and said, let's marry your daughter to our son. If they didn't like it, they were obedient. . . . My grandma got married young and they didn't talk until the day of the ceremony [when] they met who they were going to marry. And the daughter-in-law became like a domestic servant to the mother-in-law.[85]

Unfortunately, the lack of ethnographic interest in Matagalpa before 1990 impedes our efforts to understand the ideology and practice of arranged marriages. Three pages of notes by the ethnographer Doris Stone, the only such document available, confirm our oral testimony. She observed in the early 1950s that girls of eleven or twelve were subject to arranged marriages. "The girl moves to the boy's house," she wrote. "This is done with the idea that the young people 'grow up together' and that 'the boy will not leave home.' "[86] The few elderly people I interviewed who had "arranged marriages" did not have much to say against the practice; its memory was permeated with nostalgia for that era of deep respect for patriarchal authority that was sorely lacking today. Younger people, not surprisingly, found the practice somewhat laughable. The elderly folks did mention that some resisted the practice through elopement (which they called el rapto, "kidnapping"). In Matagalpa, the elders responded to that challenge with whippings and jailings.

In Monimbó the youthful "kidnapping" response to arranged marriages was often tinged with violence. Enrique Peña Hernández, a Masaya folklorist, observed in 1957:

> They are friends of harshness and violence. Many still procure a female in a primitive, even savage, practice. . . . The indio with implausible dexterity, hauls away his "morena." . . . Feeling conquered and dominated by the man, after all is said and done, appears to please the india.[87]

It is not clear how the folklorist brought into focus indigenous sexual relations. Notwithstanding, oral and secondary sources tend to support the notion that "el rapto" was (and still is) a typical marriage practice.[88] At the same time, however, throughout the essay, it is in the area of sexuality that the Monimboseños register their greatest distance from Peña.

The wall of patriarchy extended beyond arranged marriages. As we mentioned earlier in this chapter, indigenous youths literally patrolled the ethnic boundaries between Indian and ladino quarters and between the parcialidades. To cite one example among many, a Sutiaba recalled,

> Well the Calle Real separated Jiquilapa from Pueblo Grande and in those days it was sandy. Kids used to hide their *cutachas* [long, thin knives] in the sand. And when someone from the other barrio crossed over they often didn't make it back. Kids from León would hardly ever risk it.[89]

These walls of indigenous patriarchy not only contributed to internal tensions between the parcialidades but also blocked the vision of sympathetic outsiders—it was the most powerful form of "otherness." For example, a peasant leader from western Honduras claimed that her Lenca Indian neighbors in the 1940s practiced incest with the father, who exercised "his patriarchal right by deflowering his daughters." Similarly, a progressive Nicaraguan journalist visiting Sandino's camp in the Miskito zone of Bocay claimed that the practice of incest among the local Indians was "very common."

Ladino concerns about indigenous sexuality at times struck very close to home. Passed on to an elderly Matagalpino school teacher, a local ladino tale about the 1881 rebellion provides a graphic example:

> In that uprising the Indians surrounded the city. . . . There on the banks of the river are some very tall trees, and an aunt of mine that lived nearby heard them shouting and saying, "Ladinazos, sinvergüenzas, tomorrow at this time we will be sleeping between white legs." As it was nighttime, they thought that same night they were going to break in and take away the women from there.[90]

Strikingly similar tales emerged during the 1932 rebellion in the Indian areas of western El Salvador, where ladinos feared a *noche de bodas,* in which the Indian rebels would "seize all the pretty young girls of town . . . and parcel them out among the revolutionary forces."[91] It is tempting to speculate— while awaiting further research—about the role that such sexual roots had on the peculiar Central American construction of the mestizo nation in the 1930s and 1940s. At the very least the examples just given suggest two points: first, the drama of civilization versus barbarism played itself out vividly in the minds of nonindigenous actors (including those of the Left) and the images of barbarity were deeply sexual. Second, the examples suggest that the structures of indigenous patriarchy presented an extraordinarily powerful symbol to even sympathetic outsiders.[92]

Some evidence implies that indigenous groups were not immune to the sexual ideology that formed part of the discourse of mestizaje. In the 1850s, according to Wilhelm Mahr (a German scholar and a founder of anti-Semitic philosophy), in the Indian town of Masaya, local indigenous families "rented" their daughters for ten pesos to "whites," but specifically not to people of African descent, on the condition that the offspring be returned to the communities to participate in the family labor force.[93] The racial connotations in Mahr's account are striking: some Indians apparently were committed to a policy of whitening their population.

There is some circumstantial evidence to support Mahr's narrative. First, there are evident ambivalences in Monimboseño racial attitudes. Until recently barrio residents referred scornfully and ironically to ladinos of all complexions as "mulattos." That usage suggests at the least a legacy of scorn for Nicaraguans of African descent, laced with a harsh antagonism against ladinos as an ethnic group (calling whites "mulattoes" as verbal ammunition). Second, several informants expressed negative views of indigenous pheno- types typical of other Nicaraguans.[94] This is not to suggest that the Monim- boseños equated phenotype with ethnicity or that they internalized the color coding as a form of self-hatred. Nevertheless, as Lancaster pointed out, these color codes are by no means trivial. Writing of children in a Managua barrio, he notes:

> Niños blancos are more likely to be encouraged to finish their course of study on time, to go on to study in the university. . . . Given the connota- tions of color, it is also a temptation for families to apportion love in the same manner as economic activity. . . . Therein lies the imperialism of the sign: that so long after colonialism ceased to exist . . . color continues to order the entire range of social relations in Nicaragua.[95]

Indigenous Monimbó does not seem to have escaped from this particular legacy of colonialism.

The practice of renting daughters that fascinated Mahr fits within the general contours of twentieth-century practices whereby impoverished rural Nicaraguans gave away, lent, or even sold their children to wealthier families.[96] According to Agustín Gamboa, a local intellectual in Monimbó, this practice had a special, degrading twist among the indigenous families of Masaya dur- ing the depression years. José María Moncada, president from 1928 to 1932, built a mansion near Lake Masaya, to which some Monimboseños out of desperation sent their daughters:

> Monimbó started to feel hunger. . . . The winters were dry and the ground was arid. . . . Some heads of families sold the little they had to sell, others had nothing to sell except the virginity of their daughters, and many little girls with delicate bodies were carressed by the disgusting hands of the immoral President of Nicaragua, José María Moncada.[97]

Other Monimboseños affirm Gamboa's denunciation of Moncada for buying young, virgin Indian girls.[98] Moreover, in both Gamboa's narrative and the interviews with other Monimboseños, the image of the coerced, deflowered virgins directly involves the (repetition of) conquest relations that symbolized the emergence of mestizaje in the indigenous barrio. Although it is difficult to evaluate either how widespread the practice of prostituting daughters was or the degree of Moncada's involvement, there is no doubt that the discussion of biological mestizaje does touch a communal nerve in Monimbó.

The reproduction of the discourse of the Indo Hispanic race in an indigenous community like Monimbó has posed thorny questions. We have Mahr's report that the Indians actually sought to whiten their race. Similarly, elements of contemporary scholarly and political discourse suggest that the forging of the Indo Hispanic race has been a natural, voluntary process. Thus the anthropologist Claudio Esteva Fabregat wrote of the colonial period,

> Due to a facile sexual relation, it was not strange that these indias would often prefer those who had been victors in these battles; apart from pure sexual satisfaction, they had the symbolic reward of uniting with a conqueror.[99]

Esteva Fabregat's analysis, at the least, does reveal how felicitous the notion of mestizaje is for reading indigenous males, coercion, violence, and resistance out of the historical record.

The local intellectual Gamboa also makes reference to this particular form of racial ideological domination. He recalls how a beautiful woman during his youth spurned all Monimboseño suitors. Indeed, she made it clear that she sought to better her "race." With great vulgarity she turned away the Indian suitors: "this *cusuco* [literally, an armadillo] isn't for any Indian." She actively sought liaisons with light-skinned ladinos ("mulatos" in Monimboseño parlance). The tale, however, has a moralistic ending: the woman, rejected by her lovers, returned to the barrio. When she attempted to find a relationship, the Monimboseños scorned her, throwing back in her face her original, vulgar declaration.

This story, substantiated in interviews, reflects the relative success of the discourse of mestizaje.[100] Earlier we saw how the violence exercised against indigenous males helped create a portrait of their feminization. In a sense, these tales from Monimbó form a counterpart of that emasculation in that they make female sexuality a principal site of anxiety and contention. Whether or not the anecdote is an accurate reflection of historical reality, its plausibility for a Monimboseño audience signals the depths of male anxiety about miscegenation and the pervasiveness of the kind of internalization of dominant racial norms that Mahr reported in the 1850s. While awaiting further research, we can tentatively conclude that the construction of the Indo Hispanic race had some gnarled sexual roots and that it was far from a harmonious affair.

### Conclusion: Mestizaje after Sandino

A discourse of mestizaje became widely accepted in Central America shortly after it had become the official ideology of postrevolutionary Mexico. Alan Knight's analysis of indigenismo and mestizaje reveals the degree to which that discourse valorized the indigenous contribution to "lo indígena" in Mexican culture and recognized the existence and legitimacy of indigenous cultures. Knight outlines its fundamentally racist assumptions, but at the same time underscores how indigenismo has helped to break down preexisting castelike barriers. During the immediate postrevolutionary period, contemporary indigenous peoples were thus celebrated at an ideological level, despite the persistence of prejudice and social inequality. Knight cogently summarized the paradox in the following terms: "Official ideology proclaims their worth, even their superiority . . . but sociopolitical circumstances repeatedly display the reality of prejudice."[101]

Although formally similar to the Mexican discourse in its praise of the historic contribution of Indians to the nation, the middle isthmus version of mestizaje effaced indigenous communities from modern history with the violent bursts and silent fumes of ethnocide. In contrast to the Mexican case, by 1940 official and popular discourse in El Salvador, Honduras, and Nicaragua not only described their societies as mestizo, they posited that Indians had ceased to exist at some forgotten time in the deepest recesses of historical memory. To cite one example from the 1950s,

> The Nicaraguan people, formed during colonial times, was a product of mestizaje. In reality, there is no other Central American country where this process has been realized to the same degree. Practically speaking, the Indian element has ceased to exist.[102]

This reactionary texture of mestizaje derived, in large part, from the defeats suffered by Central American popular movements. The Guatemalan popular uprising, 1920–1921; Sandino, 1927–1934; El Salvador, 1932; and the Honduran labor movement of the 1920s (and a 1925 Lenca uprising) all went down in bitter defeat.

I would posit, however, that the radically distinct development of the discourses of mestizaje in Central America and in Mexico also had much to do with their different political cultures and not only the difference that a successful revolution could make. In particular Florencia Mallon and Peter Guardino's work on Mexico points to a vibrant nineteenth-century political tradition of popular Liberalism whose relative strength and geographical diversity marked it off dramatically from an analogous current in Central American Liberalism.[103] Moreover, Mexican popular Liberalism blurred the lines between municipal and indigenous lands and political autonomy in ways that at times favored the Indians. In Central America the lack of a rural variant of popular Liberalism allowed the state to drive a wedge between notions of citizenship and local, indigenous rights. These broad ideological and political contours, in turn, affected the way political actors understood the local cultures within which they operated. In this sense, a comparison between the levels of local knowledge of Farabundo Martí, Sandino, and Zapata would be interesting; for Zapata worked and fought with the peasants of his native Morelos, whereas Martí and Sandino had to organize and fight on unfamiliar ground.

Sandino left an important legacy in Nicaragua: the struggle to extend equal citizenship to all. As we shall see in the next chapter, progressives carried on this fight but without recognizing how problematic that concept had become for the indigenous communities of the isthmus. Even the most authoritarian regimes that arose following the defeat of the region's popular movements would have to address the workers and peasants in the language of citizenship and equal rights. At the same time, however, the progressives who survived the years of reaction or those who emerged in subsequent generations could not resolve a fundamental dilemma of Latin American Liberalism: the democratic demand for equal rights of citizens versus the recognition of special rights and autonomy for indigenous peoples.[104]

## Notes

1 Jeffrey Gould, "Vana Ilusión: The Highlands Indians and the Myth of Nicaragua Mestiza, 1880–1925," *Hispanic American Historical Review* 73, no. 3 (August 1993): 393–429.
2 See Gould, "Vana Ilusión."

3 Les Field provides a very able discussion of such trends in "Who are the Indians? Reconceptualizing Indigenous Identity, Resistance, and the Role of Social Science in Latin America," *Latin American Research Review* 29, no. 3 (1994): 237–248. The political discourse of mestizaje was particularly apparent in the May 1995 "Encuentro Interdisciplinario Sobre la Identidad y la Nación" in Managua, in which the majority of the talks glorified mestizaje as the core of the Nicaraguan nation. For the conference proceedings, see Frances Kinloch Tigerino, ed., *Nicaragua en busca de su identidad* (Managua: Editorial de la Universidad Centroamericana, 1996).

4 J. Jorge Klor de Alva, "The Postcolonization of the (Latin) American Experience: A Reconsideration of 'Colonialism,' 'Postcolonialism,' and 'Mestizaje,'" in Gyan Prakash, ed., *After Colonialism: Imperial Histories and Postcolonial Displacements* (Princeton: Princeton University Press, 1995), 257.

5 At a national level, without at all discarding its late colonial mixed-race meaning, ladino continued to mean non-Indian, very broadly defined. Under the impact of coffee and Liberalism, the use of ladino in opposition to Indian became a dominant meaning in coffee zones of Salvador, Nicaragua, and western Honduras. This usage sharpened the locally salient meaning of ladino implicitly referred to in the existence of a "ladino race."

6 Lomnitz-Adler, Claudio, *Exits from the Labyrinth: Culture and Ideology in the Mexican National Space* (Berkeley: University of California Press, 1992), 276.

7 For an excellent discussion of colonial racial categories, see Christopher Lutz, *Historia sociodemográfica de Santiago de Guatemala, 1541–1773* (Guatemala: CIRMA, 1984), 433–434.

8 Another meaning, albeit minor and subsidiary, also emerged during the mid eighteenth century, when "ladino" at times was used interchangeably with "mulatto," which in turn ceased to refer exclusively to the offspring of blacks and whites. Although the conflation of criollo, ladino, and mulatto might have been congruent with peninsular Spanish prejudices that viewed the criollos as people of dubious origin, it is also possible that this subsidiary meaning of ladino—especially its interchangeability with mulatto—emerged and circulated among the indigenous population as when the Indians of Monimbó referred to the mayor of Masaya as the "alcalde mulato."

9 Thus, for example, the census instructions for Honduras in 1887 suggested the exclusive use of ladino, "a fin de evitar confusión está dividida en ladinos, bajo cuya denominación se comprende a todos los individuos de cualquier raza y en indígenas del país." Special thanks to Darío Euraque for this reference.

10 Based on a revision of the municipal records of Boaco and Camoapa in the department of Boaco for the 1890s.

11 Salvador Mendieta, *La enfermedad de Centroamérica*, 3 vols. (Barcelona: Tipografía Maucci, 1919), 2:56.

12  Juan M. Mendoza, *Historia de Diriamba* (Guatemala City: Staebler, 1920), 78.

13  H. Falcinelli Graziozi, *Guía ilustrada del Estado de Nicaragua* (Rome, 1898), 210. Although the work was written by an Italian, there is little doubt that President Zelaya or at least his immediate subordinates approved its contents. The author wrote in a note to the reader: "Este libro está puesto bajo la protección del Exmo Señor General Don J. Santos Zelaya, Presidente del Estado de Nicaragua."

14  *Redención* (León), 2, no. 5 (January 1909): 73. On Armijo's acquisition of cultural capital as an Indian expert, see my "Y el buitre respondió: la cuestión indígena en Nicaragua occidental, 1920–1954," *Mesoamérica* (December 30, 1995): 327–354.

15  Mendoza, *Diriamba*, 78.

16  See Nancy Leys Stepan, *"The Hour of Eugenics": Race, Gender and Nation in Latin America* (Ithaca: Cornell University Press, 1991).

17  Manuel Quintana, "Nuestra Raza," *Paz y Bien* (León), July 29, 1923.

18  Beaulac to the secretary of state, March 18, 1932, U.S. National Archives, U.S. State Department, RG 57, 817.00/7373.

19  In the 1928 elections, won by the Liberals with 57.4 percent of the national vote, more than 80 percent of the indigenous vote in Matagalpa went Conservative. Electoral percentages calculated based on returns published by the Consejo Nacional de Elecciones, Managua 1929, and by the American Electoral Mission, U.S. National Archives, U.S. State Department, RG 57, 817.00/6298. The Conservatives received 65 percent of the Matagalpa departmental vote. They also received 59.3 percent of their total votes from the six departments with significant indigenous populations, which accounted for only 43 percent of the registered voters.

20  Letter to Ceferino Aguilar (author unknown), Matagalpa, Nicaragua, February 1922, Private Archives of Aurora Martínez (PAAM).

21  Macedonio Aguilar to Bartolomé Martínez, Jinotega, August 29, 1916, PAAM.

22  Gregorio Cedeño, cited in *La Noticia,* July 11, 1920.

23  "A nuestros correligionarios indígenas de Boaco, Jinotega, Matagalpa y Subtiava, 1920," El Comité Conservador Indígena, Legajo 573, Archivo del Instituto de Historia Centroamericano, Universidad Centroamericano, Managua.

24  *Cultura Setentrional,* 3, no. 43 (October 1924): 11.

25  Bartolomé Martínez to Emiliano Chamorro, February 23, 1912, in *Correspondencia privada escrita y recebida por el General Emiliano Chamorro, 1904–1929,* Biblioteca del Banco Central, Managua. Thanks go to Miguel Gobat for these letters.

26  *La coalición ante el Congreso: recurso de nulidad contra las elecciones de autoridades supremas de 1920* (Managua: Tipografía Alemán, 1920), 48–49.

27  Report on anti-Chamorrista repression in 1916 (no author, no date), PAAM.

28  Letter to Ceferino Aguilar, February 1922, PAAM.

29  Tío Perales to Bartolomé Martínez, September 2, 1923, PAAM.

30  Perales to Martínez, PAAM. From the context of the undated letter, it was probably written in 1922.

31  Even the term used to denounce oppression—"hartando a los indios"—can be understood either as pushing the Indians physically to their limit or as filling them up, presumably with food and liquor. For a fascinating discussion of the term "cochón," the feminine partner in a male homosexual encounter, see Roger N. Lancaster, *Life Is Hard: Machismo, Danger and the Intimacy of Power in Nicaragua* (Berkeley: University of California Press, 1994), 237–245.

32  Sebastián González and sixty-seven others to Bartolomé Martínez, January 1922, PAAM.

33  Interview with Emilio Sobalvarro, Boaco, January 1992.

34  There were a few, usually opportunistic, exceptions to the publicly expressed idea that Indians and particularly their Comunidades were antithetical to democracy. For example, Modesto Armijo, as a leader of the Liberal party, justified the electoral defeat of Emiliano Chamorro in 1934 by claiming that the Matagalpino Indians could never be coerced into voting against their will.

35  *El Comercio*, April 9, 1919; interview with Panflio Narváez, Nindirí, 1990.

36  Two other protests were against a non-Sutiaban priest running a school and against the church's removal of a sacred image. For a more detailed discussion, see Jeffrey L. Gould, " 'La raza rebelde': las luchas de la comunidad indígena de Subtiava," *Revista de Historia* (Costa Rica), 21–22 (January–December 1990): 69–117.

37  Charles Curtis to the secretary of state, January 28, 1919, U.S. National Archives, RG 57, 817.00/78.

38  *El Comercio*, April 9, 1919, and May 9, 1922; *La República*, January 26, 1919; *El Eco Nacional*, January 29, 1919; *El Fígaro*, January 22, 1919; Charles Curtis to the secretary of state, January 28, 1919, U.S. National Archives, RG 57, 817.00/78.

39  Ramer to the secretary of state, May 15, 1922, U.S. National Archives, State Department, RG 817.00/2872.

40  *El Comercio*, May 9, 1922, and *Eco Nacional*, May 9, 1922.

41  *El Comercio*, April 11, 1919.

42  For a detailed account of these struggles, see Jeffrey Gould, *El mito de Nicaragua mestiza y la resistencia indígena* (San José: Editorial de la Universidad de Costa Rica, 1997), 124–137.

43  Vital was a caudillo / from the Barrio of Monimbó / beardless, loudmouth Indio.
    Chosen from Guayacán / the gnarled rod, / he gracefully carried / giving himself the airs of a Señor.
    Descendant of caciques, / the Indians heard his voice, / he had a political style, / militarylike and authoritarian.
    In times of elections / with the drum beating / he stirred the Barrio / calling people to vote.
    He was a sincere Zelayista / and then a conservative / sincere, there's no doubt, / he was so with both of them.
    He was the perfect model / of an opportunist caudillo, / with his "Vivas!" thundered / to the current chief of the nation.

For personal gain / he never used his influence, / but he was a shoulder to cry on / for those who fell into prison.

He was a perfect model / of an opportunist caudillo / and his memory is counsel / to the people of Monimbó.

For the complete poem, see Jacobo Ortegaray Pbro., *Nicaraguanerías* (Masatepe: Editorial Arturo Cuadra, 1963), 45–48. He did employ the term *vividor,* which has a double meaning: crafty, wily, and opportunistic on the one hand, and a procurer on the other. Given his religious inclinations it is difficult to believe that Ortegaray intended the second meaning.

44  *El Comercio,* December 4, 1918.

45  *El Comercio,* December 12, 1918.

46  See Michael Schroeder, "Horse Thieves to Rebels to Dogs: Political Gang Violence and the State in the Western Segovias, Nicaragua, in the Time of Sandino, 1926–1934," *Journal of Latin American Studies* 28 (1996): 383–434.

47  Interview with Humberto Ortiz, Monimbó, 1995.

48  Ibid.

49  D. M. Molloy, "Relief and Control of Hookworm Disease in Nicaragua, Sept 22, 1915–December 31, 1920," Rockefeller Archive Center, RG 5, series 2, box 34, folder 202. Thanks to Steve Palmer for this report.

50  Gratus Haftmeyer, *Monimbó* (León: Editorial Hospicio, 1945), 46. Similarly, he explained how hard it was for him to find out anything about indigenous history: "He querido preguntarles algo que satisfaga mis inquietudes por la historiografía de mi patria, y me han contestado vagamente, con aires de idiotez, o desconfianza, como si al comunicarme algo, pudiesen perder su tesoro" (20).

51  Ibid., 31.

52  *El Eco Nacional,* April 6, 1919.

53  Curiously, from this period onward Monimbó is identified as the "cuna del folklor nacional," a key symbol of national mestizaje. Some Monimboseños today identify themselves as "mestizos" in contradistinction to other Nicaraguans.

54  See, for example, the U.S. Marine Corps (usmc) report "Informe de 24 de junio 1928, Jinotega": "Unverified information that the Captain Pablo Muñoz has organized a group of bandits in the Valley of Samulalí, jurisdiction of Matagalpa. He has four officers and about 12 men and they have a total of about 30 rifles." U.S. National Archives, RG 127, E209, box 2.

55  See the list of foreign coffee plantation owners in U.S. National Archives, usmc, RG 127, E198, box 7. The plantations were considered to be worth an average of $9,000.

56  Letter from Fred Fley to Major Erskine, September 6, 1927, U.S. National Archives, usmc, RG 127, E220, box 6.

57  Letter from Fred Fley to the British Consul, May 16, 1928, U.S. National Archives, usmc, RG 127, E220, box 6.

58  *Proceso legal* (Judicial dossier), "Neil Hawkins demanda a Catarino López y otros

por desocupación de terreno de 'La Escocia,' 1925–1935." Juzgado Civil, Matagalpa. The protest of the Muy Muy Comunidad leaders was published in *El Eco Nacional*, June 20, 1929. Neil Hawkins, a U.S. citizen, attempted to evict twenty-nine families who belonged to the Comunidad Indígena of Muy Muy. He sued the "squatters," who all received the legal backing of the Comunidad Indígena. For four years Hawkins attempted unsuccessfully to evict the indigenous families. It is probable that the combination of Sandinista incursions and the public protest of the Comunidad in 1929 convinced Hawkins to accept a tactical defeat. In 1935 Hawkins would emerge victorious thanks to the weakness of the Conservative Comunidad operating in a conjuncture in which Liberals dominated, with no balance provided by a Sandino.

59  See Gould, *El mito de Nicaragua mestiza*, chap. 5, 139–156.

60  See June 28, 1934, issues of *La Nueva Prensa* and *La Noticia*.

61  Report by Major Fred Cruse, July 1, 1930, U.S. National Archives, U.S. State Department, 817.00/6736.

62  Interview with Ramón Martínez, Matagalpa, February 1990.

63  Mathew Hanna to the secretary of state, Managua, June 6, 1930, U.S. National Archives, U.S. State Department, 817.00/6673.

64  Report from Rigoberto Reyes to the president of the Republic, September 30, 1928, National Archives, RG 127, E220, caja 7. The armed groups attempted to thwart the elections. It is unclear whether they were pro-Sandinista groups or dissident Conservatives.

65  Commanding officer of the Fifth Regiment to the brigade commander, February 23, 1928, U.S. National Archives, USMC, RG 127, E220, box 2. On the numerous military contacts in the indigenous zone, see Michael Schroeder, " 'To Defend Our Nation's Honor': Toward a Social and Cultural History of the Sandino Rebellion in Nicaragua, 1927–1934" (Ph.D. diss., University of Michigan, 1993).

66  Interview with Sandino, 1933, in Ramón de Belausteguigoitia, *Con Sandino en Nicaragua* (Managua: Editorial Nueva Nicaragua, 1985), 192.

67  Ibid., 193.

68  Perhaps Sandino merely wanted to simplify the defintion of "Indian" for a foreign journalist. But Belausteguigoitia did recognize that the two Indians were from the Atlantic Coast. It is also possible that Sandino was thinking of the Miskito Indians of Bocay (in the Segovias) as *the* Indians of the Segovias.

69  Sergio Ramírez, ed., *Augusto C. Sandino: el pensamiento vivo*, 2 vols. (Managua: Editorial Nueva Nicaragua, 1981), 1:151, 168. See, especially, the important work of Schroeder, "To Defend Our Nation's Honor." Also see Volker Wunderich's work, for example, *Sandino en la Costa* (Managua: Editorial Nueva Nicaragua, 1989).

70  Haya de la Torre's Indo American vision as translated through Esteban Pavletich arguably influenced Sandino's thought more than did the Unionists.

71  José Román, *Maldito país* (Managua: Ediciones la Pez y la Serpiente, 1983), 104.

72  Román, *Maldito país*, 102.

73 Letter to Froylán Turcios, September 20, 1927, in Ramírez, *Augusto C. Sandino*, 1:151.

74 "Suprema proclama de Unión Centroamericana," August 16, 1933, in ibid., 1:349.

75 Alejandro Bendaña, *La mística de Sandino* (Managua: Centro de Estudios Internacionales, 1994), 98–99.

76 Ibid., 99. Bendaña also defends Sandino from my charge of silence on the indigenous question and attacks the arguments with which I contextualized Sandino's position in my paper entitled "Nicaragua: la nación indohispana," presented at the "Semanario Balance Histórico del Estado-Nación en Centroamérica," FLACSO, San Salvador, November 22–24, 1993.

77 Thus, for example, the Portillo group attempted to spread the notion that Chamorro and Bartolomé Martínez "son los principales vendeterreno y todavía quieren volver a la presidencia." Although some Matagalpino indigenous land had been lost to lawyers during the administrations of Emiliano and Diego Chamorro (1917–1923), the government also granted 3,600 hectares of land to the Comunidad. Thus the observably false propaganda about land was less than successful in swaying indigenous support from Chamorro.

78 Leys Stepan, *The Hour of Eugenics*, 137, writes: "Especially damaging to Latin American self-images was the scientific view of racial hybridization, universally condemned by biologists abroad as a cause of Latin American degeneration. . . . They [intellectuals] asked whether racial mixture was always a sign of inferiority . . . whether hybridization could not have more positive biological-social meanings, whether it should be encouraged as a biological process of nation formation, allowing the emergence of a national homogeneous type through a process of racial fusion."

79 Salvador Mendieta, *La enfermedad de Centroamérica*, vol. 3.

80 *La Prensa*, August 26, 1943. On Mexico, see Alan Knight, "Racism, Revolution and Indigenismo: Mexico, 1910–1940," in Richard Graham, ed., *The Idea of Race in Latin America* (Austin: University of Texas Press, 1990), 96–98. On El Salvadoran Sinophobia in 1931 see Héctor Pérez-Brignoli, "Indians, Communists, and Peasants: The 1932 Rebellion in El Salvador," in William Roseberry et al., eds., *Coffee, Society and Power in Latin America* (Baltimore: Johns Hopkins University Press, 1995), 261.

81 According to Anthony Pagden in "Identity Formation in Spanish America," in Nicholas Canny and Anthony Pagden, eds., *Colonial Identity in the Atlantic World, 1500–1800* (Princeton: Princeton University Press, 1989), this elite use of the pre-Columbian past was even common during the colonial period. He explains, however, that such a rendition of the past did not aid the indigenous peoples: "Their culture destroyed by the conquerors, both lay and ecclesiastical and their identity all but erased by Spanish efforts to 'civilize' them, the living Indians were ill-suited to play the role of the heirs to the Aztec Empire" (75).

82 Albino Román, "Arenga a la juventud de Nicaragua," in *Academia de sociología e historia de San Pedro Canisio* (Granada: Colegio Centro-América, 1938), 44. In the

same publication, D. René Vivas wrote, "los descendientes de Nicarao y Dirangen que llevan en su venas la sangre . . . indómita del nativo" (46).

83 See Marisol de la Cadena, "Women are More Indian: Gender and Ethnicity in Cuzco," in *Ethnicity, Markets, and Migration in the Andes: At the Crossroads of History and Anthropology,* Brooke Larson, Olivia Harris, and Enrique Tandeter (Durham, N.C.: Duke University Press, 1995), 319–328.

84 It is probable that arranged marriages developed in order to maintain endogamy within the parcialidades. Without arranged marriages, endogamy would have been extremely difficult to achieve, given that the four lineages coexisted in the same villages.

85 Interview with Tiburcio Hernández, Samulalí, Matagalpa, 1992.

86 Doris Stone, "Brief Notes on the Matagalpa Indians of Nicaragua," in Richard N. Adams, ed., *Cultural Surveys of Panama, Nicaragua, Guatemala, El Salvador, and Honduras* (Washington: Pan-American Sanitary Bureau, 1957), 259. Unfortunately Adams's otherwise unique and invaluable survey is weak on Matagalpa. Adams relied on a ladino informant. He supplemented this information with an appendix by Doris Stone, which though interesting is quite thin.

87 Enrique Peña Hernández, *Panorama masayense: ensayo folklórico* (Managua: Talla Tipográfica San José, 1957), 30–31.

88 Javier García Bresó, *Monimbó: una comunidad india de Nicaragua* (Managua: Editorial Multiformas, 1992). This ethnographer writes: "En Monimbó es muy usual, más incluso que el matrimonio tradicional, el rapto de la novia" (179). He cites economic reasons and the opposition of the parents as the cause of this practice. Although this study is thorough and interesting, it has an extremely weak historical base.

89 Interview with Julián Bárcenas, León, 1988.

90 Interview with Josefina Arnesto, Matagalpa, 1995, by Victoria González.

91 Thomas Anderson, *Matanza,* 2d ed. (Willimantic, Conn.: Curbstone, 1992), 138.

92 On mestizaje and sexuality, see Carol Smith's pioneering article "The Symbolics of Blood," unpublished manuscript, and Vera Kutzinski's *Sugar's Secrets: Race and the Erotics of Cuban Nationalism* (Charlottesville: University of Virginia Press, 1993). Kutzinski writes that mestizaje at once "celebrates racial diversity while disavowing troubling social realities. . . . This evasiveness [about race] which implicitly extends to issues of gender and sexuality . . . is constitutive of what I term the discourse of mestizaje that nourishes Cuban nationalism." In analyzing a poem by Nicolás Guillén, she remarks that "mestizaje is a trope for racial mixing without female participation" (172).

93 Wilhelm Mahr, *Reise Nach Central-Amerika* (Hamburg: Otto Meisner), 264.

94 For an extremely stimulating discussion of color coding, see Roger N. Lancaster, "Skin Color, Race, and Racism in Nicaragua," *Ethnology* (1992): 339–353. Particularly interesting, but not atypical, was an interview with Isabela Nurinda in Monimbó, 1995, in which she discussed how "children with white blood looked so much better than the Indians."

95  Lancaster, "Skin Color, Race, and Racism," 350.

96  See, for example, Elizabeth Dore, "Property, Household, and Public Resolution of Domestic Life, in Diriomo, Nicaragua 1840–1900," *Journal of Latin American Studies* (forthcoming).

97  Agustín Gamboa, "Monimbó," unedited manuscript graciously provided by his son Flavio Gamboa. The manuscript was written during the 1980s, although based on notes recorded earlier. The Gamboa family was one of the wealthier families of Monimbó.

98  Interviews with Humberto Ortiz, Doña Adelaida, and Isabela Nurinda, Monimbó, 1995.

99  Claudio Esteva Fabregat, *El mestizaje en Iberoamérica* (Barcelona: Alhambra, 1988), 185. He also wrote, "las indias que no se les resistían y que se ofrecían libremente y con gusto a sus requerimientos" (129).

100 Interviews with Isabela Pérez, Pedro Namendi, and Humberto Ortiz, Monimbó, Masaya, April–May 1995.

101 Alan Knight, "Racism, Revolution and *Indigenismo,*" 101.

102 Editorial, *Revista Conservadora del Pensamiento Centramericano* 98 (November 1968), 1. Carlos Pereyra in 1940 wrote about El Salvador: "Su composición étnica se basa en un mestizaje muy avanzado de elementos indígenas y españoles." In the prologue to Rodolfo Barón Castro, *La población de el Salvador* (Madrid: Editorial Oviedo, 1940), 10. On Honduras, see the fascinating paper by Darío Euraque, "Labor Recruitment and Class Formation on the Banana Plantations of the United Fruit Co. and the Standard Fruit Co. in Honduras, 1910s–1930s," presented at American Historical Association, San Francisco, January 1994, in which he suggests that discourse of mestizaje evolved in opposition to the Caribbean and Garífuna presence on the North coast in the context of U.S. intervention.

103 See Peter Guardino, *Peasants, Politics, and the Formation of Mexico's National State: Guerrero 1800–1857* (Stanford: Stanford University Press, 1996) and Florencia Mallon, *Peasant and Nation: The Making of Postcolonial Mexico and Peru* (Berkeley: University of California Press, 1995).

104 The dilemma is not limited to Latin American Liberalism. On the roots of the problem in liberal thought and its relation to contemporary issues of multiculturalism, see Charles Taylor, *Multiculturalism and the Politics of Recognition* (Princeton: Princeton University Press, 1992).

Early twentieth-century view of the town of Matagalpa.

Artisanal cord manufacturing in Monimbó during the 1950s. (Photo by
Enrique Peña Hernández in his *Panorama masayense*, Managua, 1957)

Woman weaving a sombrero in Monimbó.
(Photo by Peña Ortiz, *Panorama masayense*)

Manuel Jiménez, alcade de vara of Monimbó, and his family during the 1950s. (Photo by Peña Ortiz, *Panorama masayense*)

Manuel Jiménez; note the vara in his right hand and the atabal. (Photo by Peña Hernández, *Panorama masayense*)

Doña Adelaida Aguilera (right) and her children, Monimbó, 1992.
(Photo by author)

Council of Elders, Monimbó, 1992. (Photo by author)

Communal Center that houses a school and weaving project in El Chile,
Matagalpa, 1992. (Photo by author)

Vidal Rivera (back right) and Santos Sánchez (to Rivera's left),
president and vice-president of the Comunidad Indígena of
Matagalpa, and their children, Susulí, 1992.(Photo by author)

Meeting of the Comunidad Indígena of Sutiaba, in the Biblioteca Fray Bartolomé de las Casas, 1993. (Photo by Holger Cisneros)

Survivors of the Comunidad Indígena of Camoapa, Las Trincheras, Camoapa, 1992.
(Photo by author)

# 5

# "En Pleno Siglo XX": Indigenous Resistance, Indigenismo, and Citizenship, 1930–1940

The black night of abandon and disorder had invaded this population [Alta Gracia, Ometepe] such that ruins dominated the scene. But Mayor Marín is showing us that Alta Gracia still lives. He has installed lighting in the streets, he has cleaned the streets, and he has whitewashed the municipal building.
—*La Prensa,* January 20, 1937

It is the pure race spiritually and physically. . . . He lives as if he were indifferent to the rest of the country. Neither patriotism nor religion can awaken his enthusiasm. . . . He continues to believe that he is nothing more than a dominated person, because the Nicaraguan ladino continues with the conquest legacy of cruelty: he robs the Indian, he insults him, he steals his daughter, he steals his daily wage, he drags him off to jail. . . . His destiny is to walk, to work, to live for the day. He has no roots in the land.
—Carlos Bravo, "La raza olvidada," 1956

Symbolic violence to put it as tersely and simply as possible is the *violence which is exercised upon a social agent with his or her complicity.* To say it more rigorously: social agents are knowing agents who, even if they are subjected to determinisms, contribute to producing the efficacy of that which determines them insofar as they structure what determines them. And it is almost always in the "fit" between determinants and the categories of perception that constitute them as such that the effect of domination arises. . . . I call *misrecognition* the fact of recognizing a violence which is wielded precisely inasmuch as one does not perceive it as such.
—Pierre Bourdieu, *An Invitation to Reflexive Sociology*

Following the assassination of Sandino on February 21, 1934, the Guardia Nacional administered a heavy dose of repression against his followers especially in the Segovias. Notwithstanding this wave of repression, over the next three years isolated indigenous groups throughout the highlands and Pacific regions resisted state, ladino, and church efforts to infringe upon their increasingly tenuous political, economic, and cultural autonomy. Although traditional Nicaraguan historiography has viewed this period as one of abysmal defeat for the popular classes, indigenous groups took advantage of intra-elite conflicts to press their largely defensive claims. Indigenous efforts to defend their cultural autonomy and their rights as workers were more successful than efforts to defend their communal land.

Indigenous protests during the 1930s lacked any thematic or organizational unity. Despite their disparate nature, we can understand most of the protests as defenses of moral economy, with the obvious proviso that their level of material needs was critical. These moral economic struggles ranged from the sacred to the nearly profane: from Sutiaba's effort to prevent the cutting down of a tree that provided shade for mourners to the Jinoteganos' attempt to prevent the building of a church on their lands. In every protest, however, the question of identity emerged in one form or another: as a direct challenge to indigenous identity in Matagalpa; as the calling up of an intermediate form of identity in San Lucas; or in the case of Uluse, as a commentary on the futility of indigenous organization in a society dominated by the power of expanding landlords. All of the examples reveal a sense of pervasive anxiety about the future of the Comunidades in the new post-Sandino Liberal order. That anxiety, in turn, was rooted in decades-old land conflicts in Camoapa, Boaco, Ometepe, and Sutiaba. In short, the Comunidades had sound historical reasons to be anxious.

This chapter also takes a longer look at the theme introduced in previous chapters of the role of both local and national intellectuals. Enriching Gramsci's original concepts of organic and traditional intellectuals, the anthropologist Steven Feierman fruitfully elaborates a concept of "peasant intellectuals": "Intellectuals are defined by their place in the unfolding social process: they engage in socially recognized organizational, directive, educative, or expressive activities."[1] Within this category of intellectuals, Feierman includes "teachers, artists, political leaders, healers, and bureaucrats."[2] His methodology aims to

explore the history of divergent groups of intellectuals within peasant society, or closely attached to peasant society and also to study streams of discourse and practice within their social contexts. It becomes possible to place discourse and intellectuals within the framework of larger historical processes, to ask which group authorizes a particular stream of discourse at a particular time.[3]

Although inspired by Gramsci's formulation, Feierman critiques him on several scores. Primarily, he argues against the Italian Marxist on political grounds, namely that the peasant intellectuals were capable of creating a counterdiscourse without the intervention of a revolutionary party. In my study of Chinandegano peasants I arrived at precisely the same conclusion.[4] Indeed one of the questions that has at once animated and frustrated this current study has been understanding why the indigenous peoples of the Central Highlands were seemingly unable to create such a counterdiscourse or produce noticeable effects on national discourse and politics, analogous to those produced by the Chinandeganos.

Building directly on Feierman's work, Florencia Mallon recently analyzed local intellectuals in Mexico and Peru. She makes an intriguing argument about their function in the articulation of local and national discourses. Discussing the historical work of a retired schoolteacher in the Puebla highlands, Mallon writes,

> Local intellectuals like Donna Rivera Moreno are thus the archivists of local counterhegemonic discourse. . . . If they choose to articulate local history as counterhegemony to a hegemonic discourse they can choose neither the form it will ultimately take nor the reciprocal effect this process will have at the local level. By choosing to mediate between their locales and the national political culture, local intellectuals also choose to enforce at least some of its tenets within their villages. In this sense, the more effective they are as mediators, the more they must also take on the role of enforcers.[5]

Mallon's discussion of local intellectuals in Mexico casts a new light on the question of the lack of an indigenous counterdiscourse in Nicaragua. Although Emilio Sobalvarro, Juan B. Morales, Samuel Meza, and Modesto Armijo had at some point played the role of local intellectuals in Mallon's sense of the term, these ladinos certainly did not forge any counterhegemonic notions. Yet by focusing on the problem of articulation between the local and the national and by emphasizing the broader national forces at work, Mallon provides us with insight into the Nicaraguan case.[6]

In Nicaragua, minimal forms of national integration developed far later than in Mexico. The simultaneous process of physical and discursive national integration conditioned the different quality of local intellectuals in the Nicaraguan highlands. For it was the "second conquest" of the highlands and its conversion into the fulcrum of a national coffee and cattle-based economy that provided the material basis for nationhood. The local ladino intellectuals who emerged in the highlands were thus well positioned to take part in a national intellectual community, that although still minuscule (600 university students during the 1940s) had grown significantly since the turn of the century.

Moreover, their emergence as part of the "second conquest" ensured that local intellectuals would represent only the ladino fraction of their local constituencies. Here, other differences with Mexican historical development are important. As Peter Guardino's work demonstrates, universal manhood suffrage in the mid nineteenth century was not only a battle cry of some rural Mexicans but also became an effective reality in some locales for crucial periods of time.[7] The discourse of popular federalism and universal suffrage had two effects on Mexican municipal politics that were absent in the Nicaraguan case. First, as Guardino and Mallon show, indigenous groups sometimes had the political strength to break off from nonindigenous controlled *cabeceras* (municipal seats) and create their own municipalities. Second, the indigenous groups could sometimes use their political strength and alliances to hold onto municipal governments despite the presence of nonindigenous elite groups.

In Nicaragua, as we saw earlier, those indigenous intellectuals, in Boaco for example, who attempted to resist the onslaught of ladino power fought that battle on the adverse discursive terrain of equal rights and citizenship. Others, in Matagalpa until the 1920s, relied on manipulating their clientelistic ties with the Conservative party. They thus had a significant impact on national politics and culture, but nonetheless failed to develop a counterhegemonic discourse that would have opposed the myth of mestizaje or Liberal anticommunitarianism.

During the 1930s and 1940s, the gulf continued to grow between the representations of indigenous life propagated by local and national ladino intellectuals on the one side and by the localized indigenous struggles against ladino cultural, political, and economic abuses on the other. Although the indigenous groups registered some victories during the 1930s, their failure to create the discursive and political elements of unity or to align themselves with other forces in society created the conditions for disastrous defeats during the 1940s and early 1950s.

## Indigenous Resistance after Sandino

When Juan B. Sacasa became president in January 1933, he inherited a ruined economy and a political and social fabric in tatters. The value of coffee exports, the crucial product, declined dramatically from $5.9 million to $2.4 million despite an increase in the quantity of exports.[8] Planters responded by slashing wages by as much as 50 percent, and coffee mill owners lowered the price they paid small growers. They also attempted to increase the quality of coffee by pushing for legislation that obliged growers to only harvest mature coffee, a measure that harmed both smaller producers and workers.[9]

Under the Sacasa and Somoza governments, efforts to defuse the social dynamite laid throughout the body politic over the previous years were not limited to military repression. That process of defusion ranged from the enactment of progressive legislation on behalf of the rural poor, to the issuing of identity cards to control crime and vagrancy. The Sacasa and especially the Somoza administrations were committed to reinserting the Nicaraguan economy into the world market. As part of that effort they attempted to repair and expand the skeletal infrastructure that had survived the seven years of war.

Such efforts to modernize the economy and moralize the citizenry consolidated Liberal alliances among regional economic elites. But, at the same time, the Liberals also sought to expand their own political bases among subaltern groups through coercion and progressive legislation, hoping to break the political alliance between the Chamorrista Conservatives and the highlands indigenous groups. This effort bore fruit, when Emiliano Chamorro lost his senatorial bid in Matagalpa in 1934.

During the mid-1930s, two indigenous communities allied with the ruling Liberal party engaged in militant actions in defense of both their religious and cultural traditions. In Sutiaba, according to a journalistic account substantiated in its details by oral testimonies, the protest movement began when construction was started on an airstrip near the barrio's cemetery. As the work crew was about to chop down a large guanacaste tree, indigenous leaders sent a note advising them not to proceed, because it provided shade for the mourners. The work crew did not pay any attention and then

> the tambores sounded and a short while later 500 men, armed with picks, shovels, machetes, and stones appeared at the cemetery and threatened the work crew. The crew leader immediately contacted the local National Guard commander and soon truckloads of National Guardsmen arrived on the scene.[10]

Only the mediation of General Modesto Valle, whose mother was a Sutiaba, prevented a massacre. The general intervened by sending a message to President Sacasa, asking him to finance the construction of a building that would provide shade for the entrance of the cemetery. Only when the Sutiabas saw construction begin on the cemetery building did they allow the crew to cut down the Guanacaste. Within a year the Sutiabas would organize themselves along barrio lines into a Junta Comunal, whose principal responsibility would be to care for the cemeteries. Although the Comunidad Indígena of Sutiaba had lost its official recognition during the civil war, these Juntas Comunales that grew out of the conflict over shade in the cemetery did receive such recognition and contributed to limited forms of communal solidarity. Thus, in the early 1940s, the tambores called out the community to physically impede church representatives from removing their "Santo Sepulcro." As the reader will recall, the church had attempted unsuccessfully to "expropriate" that same image in 1924.

An extraordinary coincidence exists between periods of Liberal rule and church moves to take over indigenous religious symbols during the 1890s, again in 1924, and during the late 1930s and 1940s. Some of the reasons for church efforts to purify its ranks seem clear. First, throughout Latin America, the church's primary response to Liberalism was to tighten ties with the Vatican, a move that led to greater theological and liturgical rigidity and the strengthening of its material and spiritual foundations.[11] Second, there was an undoubted economic motive because control over the image translated into alms and into payments for special masses. Third, control over the images also implied spiritual purification for the church and its flock. In the early 1940s

Acción Católica, which spearheaded these efforts, was part of an international movement and it is very doubtful that it responded to the conjunctural needs of the Nicaraguan church.

The church's timing was certainly off in El Viejo, Chinandega, where it could have used some help from the government. As in Sutiaba, the Comunidad Indígena of El Viejo had been engaged in an intermittent conflict with the church over its sacred images since the 1890s. In November 1937, in response to church efforts to gain control of the Virgen del Hato, members of the Comunidad Indígena armed with "iron bars, sticks, and stones" marched in protest and then staged a "violent occupation of the church." Significantly, the local Guardia Nacional lieutenant did not intervene, claiming that he could not "machine gun the people." Somoza also offered his support, arguing that "the Indians are the legitimate owners of everything." After five more years of hostility the church backed down and agreed to respect Comunidad control over the Virgen del Hato.[12]

In Jinotega, an indigenous protest merged cultural and economic concerns. Throughout 1934 and 1935, the Comunidad Indígena of Jinotega resisted the construction of a chapel in the village of El Roble. In a petition to ministro de gobernación Julián Irías, 400 members of the community, after professing their Catholicism, claimed that they were close enough to an established church (presumably in the city of Jinotega, over ten kilometers away) "to meet their religious needs." They then explained that the building of the chapel "is hurting us in every sense." Not only were they being coerced into making contributions of money and labor, they also feared ladino intentions: "after building the chapel, people say that they are going to found a town and give them ejidal land, although the land as it is well known belongs to the Comunidad Indígena."[13]

The leaders of the Comunidad Indígena of Jinotega did not resist the church for spiritual reasons but rather as an institution that was coercing their labor and infringing on the most fundamental aspect of their autonomy: their right to decide what to do with their land. Apparently the protests of the Comunidad managed to halt construction temporarily, but eventually the Catholic Church prevailed. This particular protest seemed to express the Jinotegano's anxiety about the consequences of the chapel for their communal land. We can speculate that such anxiety about the immediate future and the Comunidad's preemptive response demonstrated a desire to defend the communal structures against market and political forces that continually undermined them. Whatever the causes, the apprehension about future losses of land and autonomy was a constant source of interethnic tension during the 1930s.

Rather than participate in cultural conflicts, indigenous groups on the island of Ometepe and in Muy Muy (in Matagalpa), Masaya, and Camoapa battled to reverse the decades-long process of communal land loss. Let us focus on the island of Ometepe in the southeastern part of Lake Nicaragua. Since 1908 Manuel Flores, his family, and his allies fought to appropriate the 2,690 manzanas of the Comunidad Indígena of Urbaite and las Pilas. Using his putative status as a comunero, he successfully engineered the dissolution of the Comunidad in 1919, a verdict upheld by the court of appeals in 1921.[14] Although legally the Comunidad had ceased to exist, its lands were not surveyed until 1934. Members of the Comunidad refused to accept that verdict, and their passive or active resistance probably played a role in delaying the privatization of the land. When it began to be divided in 1936, the Flores family and others who had pushed for privatization attempted to obtain large chunks of the communal land. In protest against "the robbery of communal lands," 750 residents of Ometepe signed a petition to President Somoza that read in part: "[They are] taking advantage of the fertile land of simple people. . . . They have pushed us off the land and out of our homes where we were born. . . . The judges only see profit."[15] Although the initial response of the government was to halt the evictions, the indigenous resistance was unable to stop the legal privatization process that had been set in motion twenty years earlier. "The robbery of communal lands" took place under the administration of Mayor Ramón Marín, who himself was rapidly becoming a major landholder on the island. A Conservative who could play on the Indians' Chamorrista sympathies, Marín was astute enough to ingratiate himself with the new Liberal regime of Somoza. Indeed, it was probably through Marín's influence that Somoza was able to acquire important coffee plantations during the late 1930s on the southern end of the island. Although their communal organization had long before lost its official recognition, over the next few years the indigenous inhabitants of Ometepe resisted this new wave of privatization and expropriation.

On March 19, 1942, William Cochran, a U.S. Embassy official, reported that the land conflict had reached dramatic proportions:

There was a riot on Ometepe Island on Sunday March 15, 1942. According to the information reaching the Legation twenty Indians and three members of the Guardia Nacional were killed. It is reported that the trouble was caused by an attempt of the Guardia to drive the Indians from the land which they had been occupying as squatters.[16]

Although survivors of this period vividly recall the Guardia violently forcing people from their fields and homes, no one recalls that anyone died in those encounters. There is no sure way of accounting for the discrepancy between the memory of people actively involved in that land struggle and this State Department report. It is possible that this is a case of historical amnesia brought about by the trauma of the violent confrontation. Yet the island is so small (less than twenty-five miles long and ten miles wide), it is doubtful that deaths might have taken place without the awareness of noninvolved people. We can see this discrepancy between memory and report as symptomatic of the absence of community intellectuals who would have served as repositories of such memories and concomitantly have access to national information. Moreover, the identity of interest between the regime and the local landowners, combined with a sorely weakened and "illegitimate" community, created conditions in which either scenario was possible. In addition, two other points are clear: anti-Indian repression was indeed violent, and it furthered the ladino advance on indigenous land. In 1943, the new mayor of Alta Gracia (one of the island's two municipalities) denounced Marín for the continual sale of ejidal land against the interests of the Indians.[17]

In the cañada of Uluse, Matagalpa, a long-term conflict flared up, again (see chapter 4, note 58) pitting the members of the Comunidad Indígena of Muy Muy against the American cafetalero and cattle rancher Neil Hawkins. In 1925, twenty-nine families had taken over some 350 hectares of land that Hawkins claimed for his hacienda La Escocia. In 1935, arguing that the squatters were planning to seize more land, Hawkins moved again to have them evicted. According to one newspaper report, "Sr. Hocking [sic] . . . has ordered all of his peons . . . to work in that land without respecting the properties of the indígenas, cutting down cane, plantains, and burying cafetales."[18] The presence in the surrounding area of Sandino's forces during the late 1920s and early 1930s had prevented Hawkins from moving against the indígenas. But once that threat had been quelled, the cafetalero could obtain the support of the Guardia Nacional. The Comunidad Indígena, already weakened by large-scale privatization of the mejoras and by military conflicts, had declined to fewer than 1,000 people. Worse, in an era of Liberal party rule its residents were strongly identified with Chamorrismo. According to several informants whose parents participated in the struggle against Hawkins, the leadership of the Comunidad did not serve its members well. Víctor Guillén recalled, as recounted in the introduction:

> The people of Uluse collected funds so that the President of the Comunidad Indígena of Muy Muy could travel to Managua to meet with President Sacasa. But he didn't make it to Managua because he spent all the money partying. . . . Then the Yanqui had the support of Somoza. . . . The indigenous leaders were all Chamorristas.[19]

This tale of the failure of the leadership of the Comunidad Indígena of Muy Muy to defend communal interests encapsulates a key moment in its demise. During Guillén's adult life, he would have little to do with the remaining skeletal framework of the Comunidad. That lack of interest did not at all reflect a lack of political commitment. On the contrary, Guillén became a local peasant leader and a guerrilla fighter in the 1960s. As mentioned at the beginning of this book he became a hero in the Frente Sandinista's first major battle with the Guardia Nacional in nearby Pancasán in 1967. Yet, for Guillén, who never forgot the image of his father's burnt hut and prison stay, the irresponsibility of the Comunidad leadership was so shameful that the organization and the ethnic identity bound up in it were simply irrelevant.

A protest by the Comunidad Indígena of San Lucas, a former Sandinista bastion, also revealed something of the ambiguity of indigenous identity during the post-Sandino years. In 1935, 600 members of the San Lucas community protested the annexation of Santa Isabel, their settlement, to the municipality of Somoto, the departmental capital. The residents of Santa Isabel, a part of the municipality of San Lucas, recognized that their annexation to Somoto would imply the conversion of communal to municipal lands. In addition, due to the distance from Santa Isabel to Somoto, any official business conducted there would incur more time and resources. The protest concluded: "They treat us like ignorant indígenas, and the ladinos will try to take over our lands. . . . How can more than 1000 vecinos of Santa Isabel obey strangers and how much violence will occur?"[20] Violence did break out between the San Lucas group (including Santa Isabel) and state authorities. According to the jefe político of Madriz, "the indios of San Lucas got violent . . . and the public force had to repress these acts of violence . . . they [the Indians] would assault and retreat to Honduras."[21] The details of these guerrilla-like skirmishes are unclear, but the Comunidad of San Lucas, and especially their boundary disputes and elections, continued to pose problems for the Ministerio de Gobernación (Ministry of Government) for the next twenty years.[22]

Although "the indios of San Lucas" were engaged in an ethnically rooted conflict, the language of the petition suggests a more amorphous, perhaps transitional form of identity. Referring to when they partook in the formation of the municipality of San Lucas in 1913, the community leaders wrote earlier in the letter of protest that "We were a numerous indigenous caste (about 8,000)." The Spanish, "Eramos una casta indígena," is an ambiguous statement, but surely one of its references is to the numerical decline in the local indigenous population from some 8,000 in 1913 to 1,000 in 1935. Yet, the "éramos" could also go beyond the demographic meaning and refer to the ethnic characteristics or identity of the community. This interpretation is plausible in particular because there is no other use of "indígena" in the present tense as a form of self-identification. Such a reading gains further credence if we look at the only other use of the term "indígena": "They treat us like 'indígenas.'" The term "indio" was available as a typical label of denigration as opposed to the more neutral "indígena." That choice also suggests an ambiguous identity for the San Lucas folk, despite a vivid sense of their antagonism toward "ladinos."

As we saw in our discussion of Boaco, ladino power at times fragmented identities by directly pressuring indigenous organization. Such a direct attack took place in Matagalpa in 1937. The process of privatization of the "improvements" of the Matagalpino communal land had steadily advanced since the turn of the century. The process led not only to effective loss of communal land but also to greater internal social differentiation. The distribution of communal land began to depend more on the market and less on the Comunidad. One of the chief functions of the communal leadership began to erode precisely as that leadership began to differentiate itself along socioeconomic lines. Finally, the indigenous leadership long identified with Chamorrismo had failed to deliver the Indian vote to Emiliano Chamorro in numbers sufficient for him to win the senatorial election in 1934. In short, the indigenous leadership of the Comunidad was in a potentially vulnerable political position, even more so with the Liberal regime in power. It was at this moment that the jefe político challenged that leadership.

In December 1937, the jefe político imposed a non-Indian slate of candidates for the directorate of the Comunidad Indígena. In the words of Ciriaco Salgado, the president of the Comunidad, the nominees were non-Indians "because the jefe político did not take us into account."[23]

In the first round of the elections, on December 12, the Indians gathered in their communal house in the city but not a single member voted. The jefe político then ordered new elections for the following Sunday; the Indians once again met but refused to vote. On Sunday December 26 Carlos Vargas, the jefe político's secretary, intervened directly in the elections. In the words of Lucas Ochoa, the indigenous representative on the electoral board, "Vargas did as he pleased with the election."[24] He managed to persuade six indígenas and one inebriated ladino passerby to cast ballots. The indigenous representatives objected to Vargas's actions, in particular, his permitting a non-Indian to vote. Vargas replied, "he is a citizen . . . and everyone has a right to vote."[25] This argument was perfectly congruent with the jefe político's attempt to have non-Indians govern the Comunidad. But the action of recruiting a drunken ladino to vote reveals such a degree of arrogance that one suspects a conscious move to profane an electoral process that, however dependent on ladino authority, formed a fundamental aspect of indigenous identity, organization, and custom.

The indigenous leaders did attempt to vote for an unsanctioned slate of candidates, but Vargas nullified those ballots. As Lucas Ochoa stated, "There were more voters, but they decided not to vote when they saw the imposition of Vargas."[26] According to Ochoa, the indigenous leaders present at the election did not directly oppose Vargas, because "he [was] the secretary of the jefe político." However, they did persuade the Guardia Nacional commander to intervene. On January 6 Hermógenes Prado, the departmental commander, ordered the arrest of Vargas, accusing him not only of obstructing the election but also of "violating the will of the indígenas." The commandant's action echoed the role of the Guardia in El Viejo, and although it would be erroneous to deduce a coherent Somocista strategy toward the indigenous populations, the Guardia's actions in response to tactical exigencies did reflect the Somocista faction's struggle for dominance in the Liberal party.

Court testimony offers several clues about the situation of the Comunidad of Matagalpa during this period. First, we see a high degree of deference to and dependence on the jefe político. However, once again recourse to the work of James Scott suggests a reading of the testimony that reveals the seemingly excessive dependence on the ladino authorities as a form of passive resistance.[27] Consider their appearance per order of the jefe político, only to boycott the elections. The very unanimity of the boycott also points to a strong degree of communal identity despite the economic and political set-backs cited earlier. It is, of course, possible that fear and apathy played a role in the boycott. Yet there is no doubt that the boycott was a form of passive resistance that at the same time answered the jefe político's order to hold elections "each Sunday until people vote."

Finally, the question of identity was paramount both in the indigenous defense and in the ladino offense. The separate testimonies of three indigenous leaders are nearly identical in asserting that the reason no one voted for the slate is that it was headed by Felipe Sequira, "who does not belong to the body of the Comunidad Indígena." Similarly, the jefe político's rationale that all citizens had equal rights, including the right to vote and to govern the Comunidad Indígena, sharply challenged the identity or what Salgado called "the integrity" of the organization. As in Camoapa and Boaco, this seemingly democratic formula, framed within the discourse of citizenship, was used to give municipalities control over Indian lands. The logic was that because Indians are citizens and elected ladino authorities represent them, their communal land should be municipal land, open to ladinos. Although resisted by a momentarily unified Comunidad, the discourse of citizenship rights was gathering strength within the emerging Somocista elite and among progressive intellectuals.

### "Civilizing the State": Political Response to Sandinismo and to Indigenous Resistance

The combined impact of Sandinismo and indigenous resistance helped convert "citizenship rights" into a *mot d'ordre* of Liberalism. Chamorrista Conservatives, anxious to hold on to their shrinking political base, also adopted an equal rights perspective. Indeed, they joined with progressive Liberals in backing three important pieces of legislation that directly benefited the highlands communities: a 1934 law that fined any official involved in enforcing debt peonage, a 1935 prohibition against the sale of ejidal or communal land, and a 1937 tax in favor of indigenous education that affected uncultivated hacienda land and ladino renters of indigenous land. Although these laws did not amount to a dramatic reversal of the second conquest of the Comunidades, they did momentarily stall the pace of dispossession.

For a brief moment in the 1930s, rightist Chamorristas and Liberal progressives joined forces on behalf of Indian workers. The legacy of decades of Chamorrista political dependence on highlands Indians coincided with the political push toward the countryside that Sandinismo had given to the urban-based Liberal party, for the Sandinista struggle had illuminated aspects of the highlands social landscape and converted its inhabitants into a potential political base for a nascent social democratic Left inside the Liberal party.

Inspired by the abolition of debt peonage in Guatemala, Ernesto Salazar, a Chamorrista deputy from Matagalpa, worked with progressive Liberal party deputy General Andrés Murillo to push for a law that would "end the slavery of the Nicaraguan Indian."[28] Salazar explained the necessity of such a law in the following terms:

> There are at least 70,000 indígenas who live, together with their wives and children, in true slavery. . . . The police chiefs receive payments from the hacendados, especially the foreigners so that they are always willing to order the captures and the searches of Indians' homes whom they then carry off, tied up, to the hacienda, where they have to work for an indefinite period of time. . . . When I bought my hacienda the former owner gave me many contracts . . . which transferred dozens of slaves and their family [to my ownership].[29]

The antipeonage law, approved unanimously by the legislature, fined and fired all members of the police force who ordered or carried out arrests of indebted workers. The joint declaration that introduced the law reads:

> Our constitution prohibits imprisonment for debts and offers guarantees against unlawful searches. Yet these constitutional rights are a dead letter for the poor laborers of Matagalpa, who are as much citizens as we are and who for the same reason have as much a right to be respected in their ranch hut as does the potentate in his opulent mansion.[30]

The introduction further develops the theme of extending citizenship toward the indigenous highlands: "We propose this law so that individual rights are respected . . . and so that the iniquities that we have signaled are no longer repeated in this twentieth century in a civilized country."[31] Here we can glimpse the transformation of the discourse of civilization that had excluded "barbaric" Indians. Prompted, in part, by the Sandinista and indigenous struggles, this new permutation aimed to "civilize" the state so that the Indians could become citizens. In calling for schools and "nationalistic propaganda" for the Indians, a Matagalpino newspaper underscored the social change that permitted the transformation of the civilization-barbarism dichotomy. The editorial claims that the cañadas "before were a nest of revolutionaries and crimes" but that the Indian "was becoming civilized and had ceased to be a savage."[32]

Anastasio Somoza's seizure of power in 1936 had no immediate effect on this push to civilize the state by granting citizenship rights to the Indians. On the contrary, in the 1937 debate on legislation to benefit the indigenous groups of Boaco and Matagalpa, Arturo Cerna (whom we briefly encountered in chapter 4), a Somocista Liberal deputy, stated:

> It's terrible, the situation that the casta indígena is passing through. It's sad to see sixty or seventy thousand people who don't know how to read. . . . Sixty or seventy thousand men and women that have never received a ray of light. Those people are born, vegetate and die like beasts of burden. How nice it would be to see sixty or seventy thousand individuals fit and equipped for life; with that Nicaragua could count an army without rifles, that would rescue the country through progress and light.[33]

Most significant, Senator Espinoza (a Conservative) used Cerna's initiative to directly support the indígenas in their decades-long conflict with the Liberal municipality of Boaco:

> Due to the fact that there are ongoing civil trials, the judges resolved that the Municipios should not collect taxes for this land. But the Municipio de Boaco has been collecting for some time a tax of three centavos, such that it does not directly benefit the Indians; the Junta de la Casta Indígena has been annulled.[34]

Espinoza argued that the tax should directly benefit indigenous education and that the casta indígena leadership should be recognized.

Espinoza stands out as perhaps the only public figure who supported the demands of a Comunidad qua Comunidad. The senator's brief remarks also indicate that he grasped the importance of the municipal government's failure to recognize the indigenous organization. "The junta of the Casta Indígena has been annulled" referred to the municipal government's refusal to legalize its existence. Although the congressional proposal to tax uncultivated hacienda lands was eventually cut back from three to two centavos per hectare, the legislation represented an implicit recognition, however belated, of the asymmetrical relationship between the haciendas and the indigenous communities. That the restitution would come in the form of education was, of course, far more congruent with the discourse of citizenship than would have been an ethnically based agrarian reform.

The labor law, the prohibition against the sale of Comunidad or ejidal land, and the tax in favor of Indian education all responded to a vague indigenista influence emanating from postrevolutionary Mexico. Likewise, Sandino's discourse in favor of the exploited surely pushed the boundaries of acceptable political positions, especially within the Liberal party, giving force to the desire to extend effective citizenship rights into the countryside.

## Mestizaje, Citizenship, and Indigenista Intellectuals

On December 19, 1941, the Nicaraguan government ratified the Pátzcuaro Convention on the creation of the Instituto Indigenista Interamericano. The treaty obliged the government to create an Instituto Indigenista Nacional (IIN), an autonomous institution and member of the continental organization. The signing of the treaty, less than two weeks after the Pearl Harbor attack, had far more to do with Somoza's strategic alliance with the United States than with any particular program in favor of the country's Indians.

Notwithstanding the opportunism involved in the creation of the IIN, to some extent its agenda represented a continuation of the pro-Indian legislative program of the 1930s. At least Leonardo Argüello, Somoza's ministro de gobernación and a Liberal party statesman, took the indigenista commitment seriously. Moreover, Argüello attempted to support what he called *núcleos indígenas*. In 1942, in explaining how he wished to reform the law of the Comunidades Indígenas, he wrote,

> As a survival of colonial life, the Comunidades Indígenas have engendered serious problems in the modern life of the country, and the government intends definitively to resolve the rights of the indigenous nuclei that make up the Comunidades, considering the incorporation of the Indian into active life and society to be one of its most important aspirations; it is a . . . vital problem throughout the Continent.[35]

Although Argüello, unlike his predecessors, did not propose abolition of the Comunidades Indígenas and spoke instead of defending indigenous rights, he did not propose a solution to the "problem" of the Comunidades, which for him meant ladino domination and manipulation. Argüello attempted to carry out the founding task of the IIN, "to study the indigenous problem in Nicaragua . . . with the aim of bettering the conditions of life of the Nicaraguan Indian," but his failure to "definitively guarantee [their] rights" derived in part from his lack of knowledge about local cultures and conflicts.[36] The ministro de gobernación did appoint people to the IIN board of directors who were serious intellectuals, rather than political hacks. For example, the original board included Alfonso Valle (who intervened in the 1935 Sutiaba conflict), Ramón Romero (the former Sandinista supporter), and Emilio Alvarez Lejarza (a legal scholar). These intellectuals were the Nicaraguan equivalent of the Mexican or Peruvian indigenistas of the 1920s.

A disjuncture existed, however, between the acquired knowledge of these intellectuals with an interest in things "indígena" and the daily realities of local communities. Indeed, their intellectual and political interest in Indians did little to inspire them to question the evolving national discourse of ethnic homogeneity, nor did it lead to direct contact with the indigenous communities. Although the Nicaraguan indigenista intellectuals were most concerned with linking pre-Columbian greatness to a national discourse of mestizaje, they usually had only a passing acquaintance with indigenous village life.[37] On the other hand, the local intellectuals of the highlands were invariably ladinos and far too close to the ethnic conflicts to take the indigenous side seriously.

Modesto Armijo's approach straddled these two intellectual styles. One of Nicaragua's most outstanding intellectuals and for decades a Central American unionist, Armijo, as we mentioned earlier, was a product of highlands ladino culture. Specifically, he had worked as a lawyer defending elite interests against the Matagalpino Indians. That intimate knowledge allowed him to become an "Indian expert." The reader will recall that in 1919, he headed a national commission to study the indigenous question. During the 1950s he served on the executive board of the IIN. As the congressional leader of the Liberal party in the 1930s, he called upon his early memories of Matagalpino Indian politics to combat Conservative charges about intimidation in the 1934 election:

> [The charge is false] that the Conservative citizens were threatened so that they voted for liberalism; I say that it would be a utopia to think that the Indians of the Matagalpa casta are susceptible to being intimidated as was seen in the year 1916 in which the party of the government's friends having all the elements for triumph at their disposal were defeated in Matagalpa [by Chamorrismo].[38]

Despite Armijo's former sympathies for Sandino, Somoza appointed him as minister of education in 1937. In the mid-1940s, Armijo would emerge as a key anti-Somoza figure. In the following statement Armijo fused an expanded notion of citizenship with the growing acceptance of a vision of a mestizo Nicaragua. As minister of education, he wrote:

> The coexistence of Indians and the other ethnic elements of the population suggests that the state should not create special programs that would only serve to weaken the spiritual unity of the Nation. On the contrary the school should fully incorporate the Indian into Nicaraguan society.[39]

Armijo's equal rights argument called for the treatment of Indians as normal citizens, while preventing them from developing any repressed notions of ethnicity that might challenge the construction of the nation-state. These enunciations are congruent, for he claimed that the Matagalpino Indians already acted as citizens by voting without succumbing to intimidation. Yet his description of ethnic "coexistence" and his goal of "spiritual" national (or ethnic) unity omitted the numerous indigenous conflicts throughout the country. Because those conflicts all remained isolated and localized, his argument was plausible to an urban audience.

Indigenista defenders of the indigenous communities tended to view them paternalistically and from some distance. Consider the case of Ramón Romero, a pro-Sandinista intellectual who served as chief magistrate in the city of Matagalpa following the withdrawal of the U.S. marines. In 1934, he penned a blistering attack against the expropriation of indigenous lands, with special reference to Matagalpa. Romero was an outsider who nonetheless claimed knowledge of the Indians he was defending. In the same article in which he cited Peruvian Marxist Mariátegui's defense of the Andean peoples, Romero wrote the following about the Matagalpino Indians:

> The strange part is that he is a citizen without any rights. . . . The Indian is the natural product of the mountains. . . . They give him everything . . . when he becomes a man, he is the same child whiling away hours in the communal hut.[40]

Romero, along with most other progressive actors, could not move beyond some form of the civilization-barbarism dichotomy. But the progressives of the 1930s, as we saw, inverted the terms of the problem. Rather than conquer the barbarians, it was necessary to civilize the state. The juxtaposition between Armijo and Romero allows us to make a preliminary argument: public figures and intellectuals operating within the general discourse of citizenship rights can be understood at least in part according to their proximity to local indigenous and ladino cultures. For it was the disjunction between national myths and local realities that made the re-creation of the Nicaraguan indigenous communities after 1900 at once so violent and yet so invisible. That disjunction allowed national experts to emerge from local environments where ladinos and Indians still confronted one another. But, at the same time, the gulf cut off more committed defenders of indigenous rights from local arenas of struggle.

Let us examine the writings of Ernesto Barahona López, an author who had previously specialized in editing tourist and investment guides to Nicaragua. In 1943, Barahona wrote a serious book, entitled *Realidades de la vida nicaragüense.* These essays were linked thematically by a commitment to the eradication of illiteracy (an estimated 70 percent of the population) and to the world struggle against fascism. Barahona's essays combined intense moralizing against ignorance, backwardness, licentiousness, and laziness with social democratic politics in favor of the "universal proletariat." He based his attack on "archaic" mutualist societies as much on the members' lack of culture and education as on their failure to evolve into trade unions that "have made workers respectable and happy in other climes."[41]

Barahona's indigenismo was at once strongly influenced by the Mexican revolution and closely tied to his goal of eradicating illiteracy. He described Mexico as "that Great Republic where the Indian, the dominant element of the population, has been socially reincorporated through education."[42] In particular, he admired Mexico's experimental rural schools, which he believed were especially sensitive to indigenous culture, and he urged the Nicaraguan government to devise similar ones. In other respects, Barahona's indigenismo seemed particularly remote from concrete historical or political reality. For example, he argued:

> Our Indian degrades himself with the vice of alcoholism that makes him more imbecilic. Let us awaken in him the vivacity of ingenuity that characterized his ancestors. . . . Let us incorporate the Nicaraguan Indian into the vital circulation of the civilized Nation, so that he ceases to be a cipher without value and becomes an active factor of culture, awakening in him the dormant attributes of the glorious race of the Maya from which our Indian is descended.[43]

The notion that Nicaraguan Indians were descended from the Maya formed part of the arsenal of indigenismo (in Honduras as well), a product of recent archaeological discoveries in the Yucatán. The Maya connection, however, had little basis in the available historical documentation of the era. Yet the antiracist use of this ersatz Maya past was obvious. For if modern Indians of Boaco or Masaya descended from the great Maya civilizations, nothing genetically stopped them from contributing some of their greatness to the nation:

> This race that created such beauty . . . today remains in fragmentary groups: timid, fearful . . . in the shadow that projects its legendary past; lost in the obscurity of their inertia. . . . The Indian has been despoiled of everything. Nothing do they possess except for sadness, desolation, misery. . . . In Matagalpa alone there are more than 20,000 Indians disseminated throughout the mountains, half-naked, on the margin of civilization, devoted to hunting and a little rudimentary agriculture. Let us redeem the Indian; give him love, hope . . . and piety; so that he feels like a citizen and not a pariah.[44]

Barahona's program for indigenous redemption was far more mundane: establish rural schools that would have some degree of sympathy for indigenous culture. Despite the simplicity of the program and his failure to address the agrarian problem, Barahona's indigenista sympathies are significant in that he forcefully attempted to link a past, however fanciful, with a concrete present in order to combat the prevalent racism in Nicaraguan society. Notwithstanding his effort to wage battle against it, Barahona could not break loose himself from biological racism. In arguing for European immigration, he reinvented Mendieta's eugenic dreams when he wrote: "They enlarge and better our demography through the coupling that will be consumed between the autochthonous sexes and those of the vigorous race that will come to us."[45]

Dr. Emilio Alvarez Lejarza achieved a far greater degree of intellectual and political clarity than did the other indigenistas. One of Nicaragua's outstanding legal scholars, Alvarez wrote a study in 1943 that he submitted to the Instituto Indigenista Interamericano. Alvarez shared with Barahona a desire to contrast the current degradation of the Nicaraguan Indians with the glories of their pre-Columbian forebears. Although he avoided making claims of Maya origins, he did conflate the preconquest groups with the contemporary Comunidades by arguing for the existence of "eight races of Indians." Although the confusion between "race" and communal group betrayed something of Alvarez's distance from the communities, he nonetheless made astute observations based on his understanding of ladino culture. Thus, he argued that a campaign in the press, radio, and movies should be launched to "wipe out that deeply-rooted prejudice against the Indian, against whom people feel the strongest disdain."[46] Alvarez then recounted numerous popular expressions of prejudice, such as "No hay que poner al indio a repartir chicha" (Don't ask an Indian to pass out the chicha), and of hatred, such as "Indio, guanaco, y zanate, manda la ley que se mate" (Indian, buzzard, the law orders then execution), or "un indio menos, un plátano más" (one Indian less, one plantain more). Although these expressions by no means always referred to concrete Indians, their frequent use, variety, and harshness could not fail to influence the formation of racist mentalities.[47]

Despite Alvarez's insightful remarks on Nicaraguan racism, his own program "for the definitive incorporation of the Indian" betrayed, at best, a lack of originality. Along with Barahona and every other person who had discussed Indians since 1881, Alvarez argued for the creation of rural schools. His only modification to the usual recipe was that they should not be coeducational, to avoid scandals that would ensue "in these torpid climes."[48] Also unoriginal was his suggestion that the key to civilizing the Indians would be to found separate "Indian" towns alongside the roads then being built in the Segovias, Matagalpa, and Boaco. In these mid twentieth century "reducciones" the Indian would be provided with "milk, corn, bananas, fish, salt and honey while he produces his own food and clothes to cover himself; in this way, he will learn to better appreciate this [urban] life."[49]

Yet in addition to this melange of colonialist and progressive ideas, Alvarez registered a stinging protest against the ladino robbery of indigenous land:

> The Indio of Matagalpa, Boaco, Ometepe and of Jinotega must be defended from the trickery of the ladinos. . . . They live in constant anxiety with the ladinos so close and tempted by greed for the land, which miraculously the indios have yet managed to conserve. . . . The national government must pursue these swindlers . . . yet no one dares go against them. They call themselves defenders of the current regime; the most faithful friends. . . . What a dark future awaits these natives. . . . The poor ignorant Indian, even illiterate, is elevated in sarcasm to the status of *citizen*, with rights equal to those of the academics in the University. As such, it is natural that no public official exists to defend the indio. . . . And the indio returns to his *choza* [hut] to tell that his farm had been taken away, and the father, mother and son wander around as members of a conquered race paying for a sin that they never committed.[50]

Alvarez's eloquent attack on the use of "citizenship" to undercut indigenous rights represents a uniquely penetrating analysis of the contradiction engulfing the Comunidades: the need for equal rights in matters of politics and labor and the need to defend themselves against the grotesque application of the same doctrine (e.g., the Matagalpino Comunidad elections of 1937). Furthermore, he grasped the role of both ladino and indigenous "caudillos populares," who emerged under Somoza with a different kind of cultural capital. Thus, in this brief essay prompted by the creation of the IIN, the writer formulated an attack that highlighted the dilemma of Liberalism's doctrine of equal rights for the Indians and the specific practices of Somocista Liberalism on a local level. Alvarez's Conservative political formation undoubtedly helped him achieve the necessary political and ideological distance from the Somoza regime and from Liberalism to make such a critique.

Yet Alvarez's distance from Liberalism and the regime and his obvious sympathy for the indigenous population did not provide him with any more access to local knowledge than that possessed by Barahona or Ramón Romero. To reiterate our previous suggestion: these indigenista intellectuals *conformed* to the rule that sympathetic national intellectuals were cut off from the local realities of ethnic conflict and that the local intellectuals invariably viewed those realities from ladino perspectives, distorting their representations of indigenous reality.

That distance not only blurred Sandino's vision in the Segovias, it created difficulties for those progressives who, inspired by Sandino's popular nationalism, continued to struggle on behalf of the rural poor. Although progressives succeeded during the mid-1930s in passing legislation that benefited the highlands Indians, no intellectuals emerged as defenders of indigenous rights. On the contrary, those who defended the Indians did so at a distance and remained firmly within a discourse of equal citizenship and integration-civilization.

That gulf, as we shall see in the next chapter, proved to be devastatingly wide. Although the indigenistas Barahona and Alvarez authenticated their writings with "concrete" references to the Indians of Ometepe and Matagalpa, they omitted any reference to the violent confrontation in Ometepe or to an equally decisive struggle that took place in Matagalpa. Those violent attacks on indigenous people and culture occurred in 1942, the year before Alvarez and Barahona published their indigenista writings.

## Notes

1 Steven Feierman, *Peasant Intellectuals: Anthropology and History in Tanzania* (Madison: University of Wisconsin, 1990), 17–18.

2 Ibid., 20.

3 Ibid., 33.

4 Jeffrey Gould, *To Lead as Equals: Rural Protest and Political Consciousness in Chinandega, Nicaragua, 1912–1979* (Chapel Hill: University of North Carolina Press, 1990). See especially chap. 7 and the conclusion.

5 Florencia Mallon, *Peasant and Nation: The Making of Postcolonial Mexico and Peru* (Berkeley: University of California Press, 1995), 285.

6  She argues that Peruvian local intellectuals failed to articulate their discourses onto a master narrative, due primarily to the inability of Peruvian elites to construct "a structure of mediation." Ibid., 308. Also see Joanne Rappaport's superb work on indigenous intellectuals in *Cumbé Reborn: An Andean Ethnography of History* (Chicago: University of Chicago Press, 1994).

7  See Peter Guardino, *Peasants, Politics, and the Formation of Mexico's National State* (Stanford: Stanford University Press, 1996).

8  See Knut Walter, *The Regime of Anastasio Somoza, 1936–1956* (Chapel Hill: University of North Carolina Press, 1994), 36–37, for a solid analysis of government response to the crisis.

9  See *La Gaceta*, July 27, 1935, and October 1, 1937, on the debate over the law prohibiting the picking of *corte sobado* (green coffee). See letter to the ministro de gobernación from Luis Eduardo Moncada, mayor of San Marcos, October 21, 1936, in the Archivo Nacional de Nicaragua, caja 7, in which the mayor argues that the *beneficio* (processing plant) owners are "the *pequeños agricultores.*"

10 Ramiro Ortiz Núñez, *Dirangén: padre de la Patria Nicaragüense* (Managua: Tipografía Brenes, 1953), 8–9.

11 For a discussion of the church response to Liberalism, see José Oscar Beozzo, "The Church and the Liberal States," in Enrique Dussel, ed., *The Church in Latin America: 1492–1992* (Kent: Burns and Oates, 1992), 130–131. Unfortunately the only published scholarly articles that deal with the church under the Zelaya regime just touch on the response of the ecclesiastical hierarchy toward the regime and do not focus on the relationship between the church and the popular classes. For example, see Jorge Eduardo Arellano, "La reorganización de la Iglesia ante el estado liberal: Nicaragua," in Enrique Dussel, ed., *Historia general de la Iglesia en América Latina* (Salamanca: Ediciones Sígueme), 6:324–331.

12 Padre Luis Castillo to the secretario del vicariato, November 23, 1937 and February 28, 1938, Archivo de la Diócesis de León (ADL), caja 390/1. Somoza cited by Castillo in letter to Mons. Tigerino y Loásiga, October 24, 1940, ADL.

13 Letter from Ciro Estrada (and 400 others) to Julián Irías, 1935, Archivo Nacional de Nicaragua, Fondo de Gobernación, no. 6.

14 "Manuel Flores contra la Comunidad de Urbaite y Juzgado Civil de Rivas," September 1, 1919. Also see the Appeal in the court of appeals of Masaya, October 28, 1921.

15 Petition signed by Cipriano Aguirre and 750 others to Anastasio Somoza García, January 30, 1937, Archivo General de Nicaragua, Fondo de Gobernación, no. 5.

16 William Cochran, chargé d'affaires ad interim, to secretary of state, March 19, 1942, U.S. National Archives, U.S. State Department, 817.00/8909.

17 It is also unlikely that the embassy official was misinformed purposefully by an anti-Somocista, because Cochran also reported that Somoza, himself, was annoyed with the Guardia for the violence. It is more probable that the reports of the violent incident were exaggerated en route from the island to Managua. On further land

problems, see the letter to the Ministerio de Gobernación from the alcalde Tomás Martínez of Alta Gracia, Ometepe, March 3, 1943, Archivo Nacional de Nicaragua, Fondo de Gobernación, no. 57.

18 *Diario Latino* (Managua), April 10, 1935.

19 Interview with Víctor Guillén, Pancasán, Matagalpa, 1990.

20 Some 600 members of the *carta de los vecinos* (petition) of Santa Isabel to the ministro de gobernación, March 12, 1935. Archivo Nacional de Nicaragua, Fondo de Gobernación.

21 Juan Cabrera to the ministro de gobernación, September 11, 1935, Archivo General de Nicaragua, Fondo de Gobernación, 5.

22 Ibid. Also see Juan Padilla to ministro de gobernación, Archivo Nacional de Nicaragua, Somoto, September 23, 1943.

23 "Capitán Hermógenes Prado al juez del distrito, Matagalpa, 6 enero 1938." Legal document found in a closet of the Juzgado Civil, Matagalpa.

24 Ibid.

25 Ibid.

26 Ibid.

27 James Scott, *Domination and the Arts of Resistance: Hidden Transcripts* (New Haven: Yale University Press, 1990).

28 *La Noticia,* June 27, 1934.

29 Ibid.

30 *La Nueva Prensa,* June 15, 1934. The exposition continues: "Las autoridades rurales . . . allanan a cualquier hora de día o de noches los ranchos de aquellos infelices. . . . La cantidad adeudada se vuelve una deuda caribe. . . . Conociendo la ignorancia de ellos, celebran contratos por los cuales comprometen no sólo su persona, sino también la de su mujer y de sus hijos, para ir a desquitar con su trabajo personal, por el precio y en las condiciones establecidas por el patrón en su hacienda."

31 Ibid.

32 *El Nuevo Debate,* March 12, 1933.

33 *La Gaceta,* January 23, 1937, pp. 2249–2250.

34 *La Gaceta,* November 10, 1937, p. 2378. In another speech, November 18, 1937, p. 2434, Espinoza argued "Respecto a los de Boaco, creo muy justo que se le excluya la parte que corresponda a los arrendamientos, porque esos terrenos son de indígenas."

35 "Exposición del ministro," in *Memorias del Ministerio de Gobernación, 1941–1942* (Managua: Talleres Nacionales, 1942), xvi.

36 *La Gaceta,* December 1, 1943.

37 For example, from 1945 to 1963 in *Nicaragua Indígena,* the official journal of the INN, not a single article appeared about the still sizable Indian community of Matagalpa.

38 *La Gaceta,* March 18, 1935, reporting the senatorial session of January 10, 1935. On the 1916 intimidation of Chamorristas, see chapter 2.

39  "Informe del Ministerio de Instrucción Pública, 1937" (Managua: Talleres Nacionales, 1937), 46–47.

40  Reproduced in *La Prensa*, August 3, 1943.

41  Ernesto Barahona López, *Realidades de la vida nicaragüense: comentarios de problemas nacionales que necesitan solución* (Managua: Tipografía Excelsior, 1943), 43.

42  Ibid., 15.

43  Ibid., 20. On Mayanism in Honduras, see Darío Euraque, *Estado, Poder, Nacionalidad y Raza en la Historia de Honduras* (Tegucigalpa: Ediciones Subirana, 1996).

44  Ibid., 21.

45  Ibid., 72.

46  Emilio Alvarez Lejarza, "El problema del indio en Nicaragua," *Nicaragua Indígena* 3, no. 47 (1969): 43. Originally published in pamphlet form (Managua: Editorial Nuevo Horizontes, 1943).

47  Ibid. They were probably often employed in similar ways to the 1950s childhood expression "Eeny, meany, miney, mo / catch a nigger by a toe" or the common phrase "to jew someone down." In neither case were people thinking of blacks or Jews, but undoubtedly frequent use of the expressions served to reinforce stereotypes through an acceptable language of denigration.

48  Ibid., 44.

49  Ibid., 47.

50  Emilio Alvarez Lejarza, *El problema del indio en Nicaragua*, pamphlet (Managua: Editorial Nuevo Horizontes, 1943), 8.

# 6

## Crimes in the Countryside: Burning Bushes, Stolen Saints, and Murder, 1940–1954

Hegemony is beyond direct argument; ideology is more likely to be perceived as a matter of inimical opinion and interest and hence is more open to contestation. Hegemony, at its most effective is mute; ideology invites argument.

Hegemony, then, is that part of a dominant ideology that has been naturalized and, having contrived a tangible world in its image, does not appear to be ideological at all. Conversely, the ideologies of the subordinate may express hitherto voiceless experience, often sparked by contradictions that a prevailing culture no longer hides. The manner in which a sectarian worldview actually comes to naturalize structures of inequality—or, conversely the commonplace come to be questioned—is always a historically specific issue.
—John and Jean Comaroff, *Ethnography and the Historical Imagination*

As long as the framework for forming Indian identities and the criteria by which Indian identities are judged are continually reshaped by the violence of the larger society, then to be an Indian is to have one's own social identity formed and judged both within and against that violence.
—Gerald Sider, *Lumbee Indian Histories*

Cándida Salgado, a member of the Comunidad Indígena of Matagalpa, recently recalled a critical event that took place probably late in 1942.

> When my eldest son was little, the Guardia prohibited us from growing cotton and from weaving clothes. They said that this business of going around with a manta was an Indian thing. The patrols came here and burned down the houses and farms of many families because they had cotton growing.[1]

According to other Comunidad members, the Guardia Nacional marched into the villages and uprooted every cotton bush they found, beating and arresting those who protested.[2] Remarkably, at a time when the indigenista intellectuals were thinking and writing about Indians past and present, there are no written documents about this crucial event in Matagalpa's history.

The terrain for the Guardia's actions was prepared unintentionally by a strategic economic treaty with the United States about which the Indians were unaware. The Nicaraguan government agreed in 1942 to restrict its cotton acreage to 6,000 acres. This treaty in part responded to a conjunctural economic problem caused by the war: Japan had been a principal cotton importer. Following the 1941 to 1942 harvest, 1,400 tons of cotton remained in Nicaraguan warehouses without a buyer. The United States promised to purchase that cotton on condition that Nicaragua agree to transform the cotton plants into basic grains, "necessary in the western hemisphere for food and for strategic purposes."[3] As soon as representatives of the two countries signed the treaty, the Nicaraguan government assigned every cotton-growing department a proportion of the 6,000 acres corresponding to its previous production and then ordered the jefe políticos to restrict the output accordingly.

The jefe político of Matagalpa, Francisco Navarro, interpreted the decree to include *algodón silvestre* (nonindustrial cotton bushes)—on half-acre to one-acre plots—used by the highlands Indians exclusively for clothing and blankets. In the municipality of Matagalpa, where Indians formed the majority of the rural population, only 270 manzanas of cotton had been cultivated out of a national total of 11,000 manzanas.[4] Regardless of whether this figure included the "silvestre," it is obvious that the indigenous production represented an insignificant part of the amount that needed to be cut back.

The Indians produced their clothes using only community resources. Women wove brightly colored mantas that were wrapped around their waists and descended to their ankles; above their waists they wore a short-sleeve *güipil*. The men's clothing also served as ethnic markers; they wore pants made out of the same cloth woven from the algodón silvestre.[5]

Although we do not know why Navarro would have moved in such a way against the indigenous economy and culture, surely some of his rationale derived from his own roots in the highlands coffee culture. A leading coffee producer in Matagalpa, in 1930 his plantation was worth $10,000, had 140,000 coffee trees, and employed 40 permanent workers and 100 mostly indigenous seasonal workers.[6] In 1934 a long-time resident and the U.S. consul in Matagalpa wrote the following description:

Don Francisco Navarro, candidate for suplente Senator . . . was of great assistance to the Liberal ticket. He has never held a public office and has assisted . . . every Liberal election campaign with considerable funds. He is a young fellow, a good spender, and very popular. Born in Matagalpa.[7]

We can assume Navarro's interpretation of the cotton decree was the result of a conscious decision and that he was fully cognizant of the impact his measures would have on the indigenous community. Because we have no written sources and those city folk who might have access to the details do not remember anything about the event, we are forced into the realm of speculation. Probably Navarro moved from a combination of two motives. First, banning indigenous cotton cultivation would force people into a greater commitment to wage labor. Second, it would eradicate an ethnic marker that could have otherwise helped Indians to claim special privileges (such as to land) in the new, more favorable climate that the founding of the Instituto Indigenista Nacional (IIN) might have signified to Navarro.

Regardless of Navarro's motives, it is fairly certain that the Indians understood the ban against cotton growing as a prohibition against the manufacture of their clothing.[8] For Cándida Salgado, there was a clear connection between the Guardia's torching of huts and fields and the wearing of traditional clothes. For others as well, the prohibition of cotton growing was a decisive moment of forced assimilation, synthesized in the phrase of a soldier of the Guardia: "eso de andar mantiada es cosa de indios" (going around with a manta is an Indian thing).

Most Indian men and women stopped making the traditional clothes, although some indigenous women managed to hide some cotton bushes, and far more continued for years to make clothes with store-bought cotton or cotton cloth. With pride one weaver recalled, "You die before the fabric would tear."[9] But within several years, most women practicing that form of resistance desisted for a variety of reasons. In particular, the cost of the cotton and the time invested in weaving made store-bought clothes appear attractive.

Yet there was probably another cause for the end of indigenous dress. A sympathetic priest, unaware of the events of 1942, wrote in 1950 that the Indians stopped wearing their colorful clothes because the ladinos "made fun of them." Undoubtedly over the years ladinos did mock indigenous dress just as they mocked all visible manifestations of indigenous culture.[10] One informant's memory of shame was so powerful that he denied that the Guardia was responsible and rather attributed the demise of native dress to the aesthetic qualities of the clothes: "my Mama made me old and ugly shirts, because of that people didn't like how [the indios] looked when they were in Matagalpa."[11] Surely such scorn played an important role in weakening resistance to the perceived ban on indigenous dress.

Regardless of the proportion of fear and mockery involved in its suppression, the elimination of native dress as an ethnic emblem was a significant defeat for it gave yet another weapon to the Indians' adversaries. The similarity of the Indians' appearance with other peasants now made it easier for coffee growers or politicians to dismiss any demands made on behalf of the indigenous community, scorning its identity as fictitious.

It was primarily the political and social isolation of the Comunidad that impeded its members at the time from understanding the legal basis of the ban. No indigenista intellectual was aware of the local implications of the treaty, nor were any local intellectuals interested in defending the indigenous community from Navarro's malicious interpretation or from the Guardia's wrath. Indeed, retrospectively, Ernesto Barahona's description of the Matagalpino Indians as "half-naked" (cited in the last chapter) seems to symbolically replicate the prohibition of their native dress. Most likely he saw the native mantas as a state of undress and was simply unaware of the tragic events in the highlands villages in 1942 because he was not there.

Although lack of access to information about the treaty conditioned their defeat, those who experienced its effects have struggled to interpret their memory of the Guardia's action. Many cited Somoza's involvement in the textile industry as the principal cause. Patrocinio López, who was in his twenties at the time, explained:

> Cotton was outlawed because Somoza had started a business and he didn't want the indígenas to cultivate cotton so that they would have to buy from him the clothes they were going to wear. . . . So they would go after someone if he was going around wearing woven cotton clothes and threw him in jail. During that time, the indígena didn't have to work for anybody because he had no need to buy corn or beans. . . . Then the rich wanted to force the indígena to work more, and since they had to buy clothes, so all the women and men had to work for the rich folk.[12]

Nicaragua's first textile factory did in fact get started during the early 1940s, although Somoza's foray into the textile business did not come until the end of the decade. Whether the nascent textile industry influenced the jefe político's decision is impossible to determine. Thirty or forty thousand new consumers of textiles would have had some impact in a country with fewer than one million inhabitants. Moreover, it was certainly an excellent assumption that the decision involved Somoza on the one hand and an assault on indigenous economic practices on the other. Since colonial times, all market relations (including consumption) between Indians and ladinos had exhibited strongly coercive elements. Similarly, Somoza's drive to accumulate capital often involved practices directly reminiscent of what Marx described as primitive accumulation. Finally, whatever the conjunctural intentions, the burning of the cotton bushes formed part of a long process of violent dispossession of the means of production and the extraeconomic coercion of indigenous labor.

Additional evidence supports the indigenous economic explanation; a significant shortage of coffee labor in the highlands existed during this period. A serious and well-publicized study of the coffee economy published but three years earlier underscored the easy availability of indigenous labor in Matagalpa and the lack of any shortage. Yet, high-paying salaries on the Pan-American highway drained off some indigenous labor from the plantations. In 1942, cafetaleros claimed that they only had one-fifth of the coffee pickers they needed. Even allowing for some exaggeration, there is no doubt that there was a critical labor shortage.[13] A serious blow against the subsistence economy would have probably forced more people into wage labor.

Indeed, the indigenous memory of this epoch emphasizes the violent repression of the indigenous economy: "then all of the women and men had to work for the rich." Rather than address the suppression of a crucial ethnic emblem of identity, the testimonies emphasize the loss of self-sufficiency and the increased dependence on the ladinos. The repression of 1942 stands out as symbolic of the destruction of the indigenous economy, in part because it occurred during a period of retreat and isolation, in which forced labor had finally ceased to exist (1934) and in which the rate of land expropriation had subsided. In recent interviews, the history of forced labor and major ladino expropriations of land such as the Vita takeover of Yúcul have been pushed into the distant past and the period preceding 1942 resembles a "golden age."

The march of the Guardia into the cañadas stands out in bold relief, condensing new forms of dependence brought on by a modern version of the colonial practice of "forced" consumption.

Those events also came to symbolize the impotence of indigenous leadership and the creation of enormous wealth differentials within the community; beyond the lack of outside political support, the continual leadership crisis of the Comunidad also impeded its defensive efforts. Ciriaco Salgado, the president of the Comunidad who led the boycott of the 1937 elections in opposition to the jefe político, had by 1942 established himself as the virtual dictator of the Comunidad Indígena. In the electoral conflict, he had established an alliance with the commander of the Guardia Nacional that probably led to his appointment as an lieutenant in the Guardia. Salgado surely was not in favor of the Guardia's actions in 1942; he would have had no interest in precipitating the rapid political and cultural disintegration of his own political base. But neither was he interested in jeopardizing his Guardia position in order to defend the Comunidad. Until his overthrow in 1965 Salgado, who often wore his uniform, used that position against all dissidents within the community and as a method to enrich himself by accumulating thousands of manzanas of land. A union report from 1962 sheds some light on Salgado's methods of exploitation:

> This señor has gotten himself named President of the Comunidad, he charges the peasants rent to work the lands that belong to the Comunidad; when due to bad winters they don't pay him, he ties them up, making them spend entire nights in the patio of his house which serves as the base of the Reserva Civil, making the indígenas sign whatever he felt like putting before them.[14]

Dissidents and survivors of the epoch claimed that he practiced this method of enrichment over the previous decades and that the end result was the campesinos would have to cede their land to pay the debt. He would also arrest inebriated people and then offer to release them on bail, which they posted with their land titles as collateral.

Salgado was also unwilling to stand up to Acción Católica when it moved to suppress the religious practices of the indigenous people. Founded in Nicaragua in the early 1940s, Acción Católica's principal aim was to purify religious practices, and its secondary goal was to engage in works of Christian charity.[15] Toward the latter part of the decade, Acción Católica grew in importance throughout Central America as it became the principal arm of the Catholic Church in the holy war against communism.

As anthropologists Ricardo Falla and Kay Warren have demonstrated, Acción Católica registered its greatest successes in its battles with the *costumbristas* (practitioners of traditional religion) of Guatemala, rather than against the communists.[16] Although there have been no analogous studies in Nicaragua, it appears that the church-sponsored group also systematically set out to radically reform traditional religious practices in indigenous communities, in particular to eliminate the "profane" from the festivities. In Matagalpa, between 1948 and 1952 Acción Católica waged a campaign to remove from communal control the sacred images that belonged to the four parcialidades. Their success dealt a serious blow to the religious structures of the Comunidad, especially the alcaldes de vara.[17] A small minority of people at the time and many more in subsequent years justified Acción Católica. For example, one informant argued: "They seized [the images] since many Indians were killed because of the chicha. . . . [The fiestas] went on for four days of food and chicha, and many drunks were killed by machete blows."[18] From another informant's testimony, however, we can glimpse something of the joy in the ceremonies and the personification of the saints:

> It was a tradition for the images to come visit the homes. They arrived close to the house where they were going to spend the night and the people in the house received them with a fiesta and balloons and music and everything. . . . They formed a procession and when it got to the house, they made a vigil in Zapote, El Chile, Samulali. The saints were the Santísimo, el Corazón de Jesús, and San Antonio. Acción Católica and the priests of the church were opposed because they worried about where the alms were going that were collected [during the vigils] since they never saw them. . . . [They also didn't like that] a lot of chicha was served in the vigils.[19]

As with the prohibition of cotton cultivation, the Matagalpinos' collective memory emphasizes economic motives for the church's actions, in particular the need to collect the money spent on alms given in the presence of the images. The elders of the Comunidad deeply resented both repressive actions, but the loss of the saints was felt more deeply. In the case of the cotton, it was the repressive actions of the Guardia rather than the loss of the mantas that provokes anger among the elders. Yet the removal of the saints is still deeply resented, even more than the repressive and arbitrary manner in which they were "expropriated." For the festivals and the elaborate religious structures associated with the saints provided both a sense of solidarity within the communities and moments of joy in otherwise painful and precarious lives.

Although there is no reason to doubt the indigenous claim that the church resented the waste of revenues, there were other motives as well. Since the 1890s, the church had consistently acted to suppress indigenous religious practices throughout Nicaragua. In the 1930s and 1940s, the church struck with greater success but still provoked popular opposition, particularly in Sutiaba, in Diriomo, and in El Viejo.[20] The Matagalpino Indians also resisted the church's imposition. One witness recalled:

> They took away from my father the image of the Señor de Veracruz and then he went to the church and stole the old stone that's in the high altar of the church, and he told them that if they didn't give [the image] back, he wasn't going to give back the stone, so that's how he managed to get them to give back his image.[21]

Acción Católica went beyond taking away the saints; it attempted to disarticulate the indigenous religious organization. One informant recalled how they blocked the election of the prioste:

> During the time of Acción Católica, the church didn't want us to do that [elect the priostes]. I remember when they took away some of the saints of the Comunidad. You can't imagine how hard we have struggled so that we could go on electing priostes, because who is going to be in charge of the cemetery if not someone from the community? That's what the prioste is for. . . . My papa was a prioste and he guarded that image there in the altar, he couldn't separate himself from the image he had. . . . When you are prioste, the elders give you the opportunity to get to do something for the Comunidad. By just participating in these things, we are going to be able to raise up this Comunidad Indígena again, going back to doing the things that our ancestors used to do.[22]

Indigenous resistance to the church enjoyed limited success, as they continued to elect the prioste and venerate the saints clandestinely. But with no allies, the small groups of Indians were unable to reappropriate most of their saints, and the community began to lose control over their most important religious practices.

Thus, two attacks in less than a decade struck hard against emblems of ethnic identity, the economy, and the religious organizational structure of the Comunidad Indígena of Matagalpa. These acts of aggression occurred in silence; no wonder, with the indigenista intellectuals out of touch, a Conservative party eclipsed and impotent, and the reins of the Comunidad in the hands of Lieutenant Ciriaco Salgado.

As we saw in chapter 5, throughout the 1930s and 1940s Romero, Barahona, and other national intellectuals who defended the indigenous population were not in touch with the communities. On the other hand, the local intelligentsia with firsthand expertise—who consistently claimed friendship and loyalty—did not come to the defense of the institutions of the Comunidad Indígena. We have briefly touched on the locally rooted careers of Emilio Sobalvarro in Boaco and Samuel Meza the lawyer-poet and Modesto Armijo the intellectual-politician in Matagalpa. Let us listen to Ramón Gutiérrez Castro, a Matagalpino intellectual, who in the 1950s became a formative influence on Carlos Fonseca, the founder of the Frente Sandinista de Liberación Nacional. In 1954, Gutiérrez wrote a brief history of the Indian rebellion of 1881, a story that acquired authenticity through his own lived experience. He wrote:

> I have had my experience with the indios in this departamento. They are surly, gloomy, indifferent, jealous, suspicious, and not much given to work. The indio seems to transform himself when he leaves the city. . . . He's not the tame indio, but the primitive beast, resentful, holder of grudges. He's a dangerous man who waits by the side of the road making sparks with his machete against a boulder.[23]

This passage, authenticating a putatively objective history, at the same time reveals an unconscious racial fantasy that most likely was shared to varying degrees by other members of the local intelligentsia. We can at least intuit, then, how emotional layers of distrust and fear created a social environment in which assaults against indigenous culture and indeed massacres could occur without much thought or comment.

These asymmetrical sources of knowledge seem to reflect the same national-local gulf whereby nationally Indians did not exist and locally were despised. In provincial towns such as Camoapa and Matagalpa, the proximity of the Indian populations and the salience of ethnic conflict and prejudice in the lives of the townsfolk made it unlikely that local ladino intellectuals would devote their efforts to defending the casta indígena. This division between local and national culture helps to explain why the Indians and their defenders could do little to question the increasingly powerful myth of Nicaragua mestiza.

Whereas in Mexico local intellectuals mediated between the state and the communities, in Nicaragua they could neither block nor record those acts of vandalism committed against indigenous culture. The armed repression, the uprooting of the cotton trees, and the expropriation of religious symbols all seem to have been the result of objective, naturalized processes. Thus, a writer in 1946 placed the loss of indigenous dress in "aquellos felices tiempones" (those grand old days) and creates an equivalence in his prose between the loss of native dress and the deforestation around the city of Matagalpa. Similarly, only twelve years after the uprooting of the cotton bushes, Gutiérrez Castro bemoaned the fact that "One no longer sees those Indian women of 50 years ago, draped in their mantas that they wove themselves."[24]

Similar forms of probably unconscious distortion occurred in the religious field. But two years after the forcible expropriation of the Matagalpino Indians' sacred images, a locally based writer informed national opinion that "The Indian still conserves in the most pure form his customs and beliefs that he has held for ages."[25] Moreover, Monseñor García, who probably orchestrated the expropriations, seemed not to understand the impact of his actions, when he exclaimed a couple of years later:

> The indios so good and with a soul so fragrant like that of Juan Diego. . . . What beautiful faith, that of those hearts . . . like the zenzontles, that look to the quetzales and pray to the Ave María: You were conceived with no stain.[26]

Such declarations unwittingly transformed direct attacks by the state or the church into long-term objective processes. Following the Comaroffs, I suggest that this naturalization forms integral pieces of the architecture of hegemony.[27] By studying the manner in which local events (and ideas and outlooks) are communicated nationally, we can see how expert testimony, rooted in the terrain of local facts, became the basis for creating national policy or rewriting a national history.

Chagüitillo: The Socialist Exception

One small group did attempt to bridge the gulf that separated local sites of resistance and repression from national politics. The involvement of the intensely persecuted Partido Socialista Nicaragüense (PSN) was essentially limited to defending the Comunidad Indígena of Sébaco, Matagalpa. In 1918, as we saw in chapter 1, the poet and lawyer Samuel Meza appropriated some 1,500 hectares from that Comunidad, thus initiating a period of rapid loss of land and autonomy. This process accelerated in 1936, when former marine Guy Rourk manipulated the Comunidad leader Eliseo Miranda into ceding him a large chunk of land and in the process booted between 150 and 200 families from their holdings. A PSN militant recalled this event a few years later:

> The victims tell the story that they couldn't even take their fences with them; they lost everything, and that there were cases where heads of families, miserable and humiliated, finding themselves robbed of their land . . . they ran away to the mountains.[28]

Although the Socialists denounced the expropriations in Sébaco and other highlands communities, they could not successfully develop any organizational base. After barely surviving the intense repressive waves of 1947 and 1948, the Socialists began to reorganize themselves in 1950 principally in the unions and in a united front called the Unión Nacional de Acción Popular (UNAP).[29] Once again they took up the cause of Sébaco and at the same time tried to organize peasant unions among the highlands peoples of Matagalpa. Evidence of limited success came toward the end of 1950, when the unions organized a demonstration in which some indigenous peasants participated.[30]

Domingo Sánchez Sánchez was the key Socialist organizer in Sébaco and throughout the highlands. As a child Sánchez witnessed the Guardia kick his family off of their land in the village of Chagüitillo, part of the Comunidad of Sébaco. Sánchez (known throughout the country as "Chagüitillo") bridged the divide between local and national political cultures. Although he hadn't lived among the Sébaco group since his family had been pushed off their land, he worked for several years during the early 1940s as a farm laborer alongside the Matagalpino Indians. Regardless of his intimate knowledge, in the following declaration Sánchez established his own authenticity without mentioning his family past:

> [We must not] leave them abandoned so that this race does not continue to slowly extinguish itself for lack of social services. The UNAP is the party that comes before the people of Nicaragua with its program. . . . We are aware of the problems of those dense masses of indígenas, their trials and fatalism [because] we have lived very close to them, we have eaten with them in the palenques of the Mosquitos . . . and in the cañadas of Apante and Samulalí [Matagalpa]. UNAP FOR THE REDEMPTION OF THE INDIO![31]

Despite the passion and intelligence of this remarkable militant of indigenous origin, he could not break free from the civilizing, integrationist discourse of mestizaje. Nevertheless, Sánchez and the PSN were prepared to suffer jail and torture on behalf of the Comunidades Indígenas. The Socialists attempted to unify and to support "the legitimate representatives of the Comunidad Indígena that had not been expropriated and, even more justifiably, the representatives of the Comunidades Indígenas that had been expropriated."[32]

Domingo Sánchez had a unique perspective on the problem of indigenous identity in Sébaco during the period following their defeats. In his analysis of the slow death of communal life in Sébaco, the militant wrote:

> Because . . . the greater part of the legitimate heirs, in absurd mimicry, even feel shame for being descendants of the indígena race so that the Comunidad authorities named by the members don't belong to the race: rather they are "advenizos" [opportunists] that have absconded with the little wealth left in the community.[33]

The harsh tone of the criticism should not obscure its insight: the intimate relationship among the loss of the battles over communal land, the loss of political autonomy, and the increased acceptance of nonindigenous identities. Although it would be hard to prove Sánchez's thesis that a sense of shame led the Comunidad members to vote for non-Indians, from the 1930s the leadership did serve the interests of ladino terratenientes.

The case of Sébaco was not unique, for during the 1940s and 1950s other

Comunidades fell into the hands of ladinos or corrupt Indians like Ciricaco Salgado. Such forms of governance became immediate and powerful ideological arms in the hands of Comunidad enemies, who never tired of demanding their abolition. Of course, the idea of a democratic Comunidad government under an authoritarian regime was perhaps a chimera, but the Socialists were exceptional in their pluralistic belief that the democratization of the Comunidades was part and parcel of the democratization of the country.

Sánchez continued fighting to democratize and defend the Comunidad Indígena of Sébaco right up through the 1960s, when he helped found a union that sought successfully to rectify the absurdly unequal distribution of the communal lands. Comunidad members in Sébaco were compelled to pay more than double the rate that terratenientes paid for 2,000-manzana blocks of communal land. Sánchez managed to help Sébaco campesinos at least momentarily win back control over their Comunidad and put a stop to the blatant allocation of favors to the terratenientes.

In a country where accusations of corruption are as much a daily part of life as rice and beans, "Chagüitillo's" reputation has remained unsullied (the length of his speeches, however, became such a butt of people's jokes that the word "chagüite" came to mean a long-winded speech). Moreover, Sánchez's lifetime commitment to campesinos and rural labor has been unmatched in the country. Yet there is something about the language he employed in the early 1950s that revealed the social cost of his militant education and commitment.

Sánchez's use of the term "descendants" suggests a sense of alienation not only of the rural folk who belonged to the Comunidad of Sébaco, but also of Sánchez himself. In the UNAP message he did not identify himself as an indígena but only as one who had spent much time with them. Moreover, in another article he pointed out that the Sébaco folk did not speak like other indígenas. He wrote: "They don't have the same peculiar intonation of other Indians; they speak more or less correctly."[34] Though a militant who defended Indians and their Comunidades, he evaluated them on the basis of their fluency in standard Spanish instead of recognizing the legitimacy of the Spanish-based dialects. This prejudice was typical. Even among leaders of the Comunidades, "lo indígena" was defined as ignorance and ignorance was signified by poor Spanish. In the case of Sánchez, such a conception of Indianness probably had something to do with his education as a militant. At the cost of huge sacrifices, he had converted himself into an organic intellectual.

The discourse of civilization versus barbarism, synthesized in the phrase "for the redemption of the Indian," thus framed the thought of this mid-twentieth-century Marxist. At the same time, however, it is important to recognize that Sánchez's vision reflected the changing social world of the Indians (particularly those of Sébaco). The Socialist, through his own experience, was able to capture intellectually that transformation of identity. That sensitivity probably aided the struggle for indigenous rights. Yet during the early 1950s Sánchez and his comrades faced a reign of extreme repression that caused the virtual collapse of Nicaragua's labor movement.[35] So, outside of Sébaco, the Socialists did not have the organizational strength to offer support to indigenous struggles, such as the one that would erupt in Camoapa.

### Return to Camoapa

In 1905, President Zelaya sent José León Sandino to Boaco and Camoapa as a commissioner charged with the task of resolving the conflict between the municipal governments and the indigenous communities. Sandino's report revealed both a sympathy for the plight of the Indians and a strong dose of racist ideology. Most significant, he favored the side of the municipalities in the land dispute. Sandino nevertheless stayed in contact with area Indians, serving as their notary during the 1910s; he became their legal representative in the 1930s and held that position until at least 1943. His transformation from "adversary" to "representative" was similar to those of Eudoro Baca, Samuel Meza, and Modesto Armijo, but his serious efforts to defend indigenous land made Sandino an exception to the local and national intellectual currents painted earlier.

Sandino occupied a unique position with respect to the other lawyers, intellectuals, and politicians we have discussed: he really cannot be categorized as either a local intellectual with national pretensions or a national figure with indigenous interests. Rather, he lived and worked in Granada, although he traveled to Boaco and Camoapa as a notary. Through Zelaya's assignment and his notarial work, he acquired knowledge and later friendship with the Camoapan indigenous population.

In 1935, with the inauguration of the latifundista Juan B. Morales as the jefe político of the newly created department of Boaco, the municipal government picked up the standard that they had dropped in the mid-1920s. Led by Hildebrando Flores, once again the municipality tried to collect land taxes from the indigenous peoples. J. L. Sandino worked closely with Paulino Pérez, the president of the Comunidad Indígena of Camoapa (a name that Sandino probably persuaded them to adopt for at least official purposes), to protest the imposition of municipal taxes on land that they claimed as their own.

Unfortunately for the Comunidad, the discourse of equal rights and municipal representative democracy that Sandino had helped to create in 1905 was becoming hegemonic at a national level by the mid-1930s. After studying the indigenous position the ministro de gobernación, León de Bayle (Anastasio Somoza García's brother-in-law), wrote: "I don't find any local tax that obliges the members of the aforementioned Comunidad to pay the *canon* [land tax] to which you refer. There only appears on the books a tax on the leasing of municipal lands."[36] De Bayle did not recognize the essential point of the indigenous protest, namely that their own claim to the land should exonerate them from paying any municipal tax to use what they considered to be theirs. Perhaps the ministro de gobernación was being purposefully obtuse. More likely, he simply could not visualize an indigenous claim to land ownership expressed as a refusal to pay taxes that all citizens who rented land had to pay. Once again, De Bayle saw the Indians as citizens like all others with neither special claims nor penalties.

Over the next seven years, the Comunidad Indígena of Camoapa continued to protest in the fields and courts against the payment of rent to the municipality and against evictions for nonpayment. Yet following the creation of the IIN and the appointment of Leonard Argüello as ministro de gobierno, the balance of power seemed to be shifting slightly. In 1943, Sandino wrote Argüello asking the national government to compel the municipality to eliminate the land tax and other taxes on the members of the Comunidad Indígena:

> Due to the lack of the instruction of the indígenas, another race of people have taken away their lands. . . . The Municipalidad of Camoapa which is not the owner of one handful of dirt demands that the indígenas pay rent to it. . . . All members of the Comunidad . . . belong to the Liberal Democratic creed and they gave their vote to our current President. . . . I

ask you to do justice to them, relieving them from these municipal duties, whose only purpose is to create a bad atmosphere for the government. . . . There are many abuses that the indígenas, the fundamental blood of our race, suffer.[37]

Sandino covered his own tracks here, consciously or not. The Indians had not lost their land because ladinos outwitted them. Rather than dredge up that history from forty years before, Sandino painted an ahistorical portrait and draped it in the discourse of mestizaje, Liberalism, and patronage, which he hoped the national government would understand. To make a convincing argument about the land issue itself, he would have had to present an examination of the agenda he had helped frame for the Zelaya regime. Instead, he offered up the same phrase that the municipal government had used against the community in 1922: the municipality does not own "un palmo de tierra" (a handful of dirt). He astutely emphasized the Indians' Liberal political affiliation. Whatever his role in their conversion—and he was a lifelong Liberal—by the late 1930s they had wisely shed their Chamorrismo.

Minister Argüello responded immediately and wrote to the mayor of Camoapa, warning him that the government was interested in "defending the interests of the indigenous groups."[38] Hildebrando Flores, still mayor of Camoapa, answered Argüello by excavating the political discourse of the early 1920s (see chapter 2):

> [In Camoapa] there are ejidal lands, private lands purchased from the government and national lands. The Indian Comunidad doesn't have their own land. This Comunidad during the time that I have been at the head of this Alacaldía has done nothing, much less present a land deed that upholds its ownership of the land.[39]

It should not come as a surprise to the reader that the indigenous leaders of Camoapa saw no point in presenting petitions to Mayor Flores. Flores, however, used against them their failure to protest. Because, unlike other modern organizations within civil society, they failed to petition within the established bureaucratic procedure, Flores could cast doubt (once again) on their legitimacy. In addition, the mayor of Camoapa cited the 1936 ruling of Argüello's predecessor on the tax issue.

Mayor Flores used the same arrogant, uncompromising arguments to superiors with nearly the same words as his predecessor's in 1922—no land, no community, stay out of our business. The repetition of 1920s discourse on both sides of the divide is striking. But Flores's banal repetition oozed common sense, whereas Sandino's argument repeated a suppressed narrative of community that no national group recognized, a narrative that, ironically enough, he had contributed to suppressing.

In Camoapa, then, during the 1940s the ladino and indigenous dialogue seemed frozen in time. Since 1930, the Camoapan Indians had lost their representation in the municipal government and whatever capacity they had to project their claims nationally. The ladinos, in contrast, had grown in numerical and political strength. Although the ladinos' discourse of municipal rights had not changed, the national myth of mestizaje now made those repetitive words far more convincing than they had been thirty years earlier. Up against the self-righteousness of local ladino power, with barely any representation and no native intellectual voice, indigenous resistance in Camoapa became increasingly perilous.

### "They Let out All Their Hatred on Us"

The smoldering ethnic conflict in Camoapa flared up when Hugo Cerna Baca became mayor in the early 1950s. Cerna came from a prosperous ladino family that had lived in the area for several generations. The family possessed large cattle ranches, and Cerna's brother (later a congressional deputy) owned the most powerful trucking company in the area. During his administration, Cerna worked indefatigably to stimulate the area's economic growth, building a slaughterhouse and roads, as well as improving the town's infrastructure and appearance. Camoapa would soon become a strategic location in a cattle boom that would see beef exports rise from zero to 10 million dollars between 1957 and 1966 and then to 40 million dollars by 1972.

To successfully launch Camoapa on the road to cattle export progress, the mayor first had to open up indigenous lands for cattle ranchers. According to one witness, Cerna had boasted at his inauguration that "these damn Indians have played around with all the mayors up till now, but not with me they won't." That threat was even more ominous in the context of previous mayoral declarations and actions. And Cerna followed through: rather than merely compel the members of the casta indígena to pay taxes on the municipal land, the mayor and his cattlemen allies were more interested in extending their own domains. They claimed what they needed as "national land," and then Cerna provided the muscle to push people out. One witness recalled: "Cerna was cruel with the *pobretería* [poor people]—to take over land they would throw everything from the house. . . . Even though they had planted *chagüites* [a type of plantain], cafetales, milpas . . . they had to leave."[40] Ranchers also used the time-honored method of letting their cattle trample the peasants' corn.[41] When those tactics did not work, Cerna called out the obliging Guardia Nacional to drive Indian families off their land.

Several survivors from that era remember how early in his term Hugo Cerna rode out with a posse to Salinas, where the Indians still had access to communal lands, and refused to pay rental fees to the municipality. Salinas in 1950 was a small village (381 inhabitants) that had grown up over the previous few decades; most of its residents had migrated from other Camoapan indigenous villages, where they had lost their land. The village thus had symbolic importance: it was the last place Indians could go and still maintain some cohesiveness as a community. Beyond Salinas, the only escape lay in the mountainous jungles to the east.

In Salinas, Cerna and his group located and seized the casta indígena's colonial land title, which had been "written in letters of gold." That robbery of the title dealt a crushing blow to the morale of the indigenous leadership, who believed that the "original" title was their key legal weapon in the defense of their land.

Some of Cerna's other unsavory activities aroused hostility among the town elite. Upon leaving office in 1953, he was denounced first for receiving "kickbacks on municipal contracts." The next administration also forced him to allow a road to pass through one of his properties on the edge of town.[42] Rather than climbing the political ladder, Cerna had to retire to private life. In 1954, he began to invest his time and resources in his cattle ranch.

That year was not a good one for popular resistance in the country in general, but it was particularly nasty in the department of Boaco. First, in April 1954 a group of anti-Somocista exiles, including some former officers in the Guardia, staged an invasion in Olama, a short distance from Camoapa. The landing was supposed to ignite an insurrection, but the Guardia was waiting for the group and immediately killed or captured all the participants and in the process discovered some Conservative supporters in Camoapa.

Second, although the PSN had no links to the movement, it was under constant pressure from the regime since 1948 and therefore had no way of expanding beyond its original bases of support, for example, into Boaco. Finally, the Comunidades Indígenas remained completely isolated from one another. For decades the Camoapan Indians had maintained a strong degree of internal solidarity and put up solid resistance, but under Cerna there was no doubt that they had lost major battles, and they believed that they were on the verge of extinction as a community.

Late in the afternoon of July 30, 1954, Cerna was riding back into town when suddenly Elevorio Borges stepped out from behind a clump of trees. After exchanging insults, Borges shot Cerna with a .22-caliber rifle. According to one account Cerna, on his hospital bed, was asked who the assassin was. The last words he uttered were that he couldn't imagine who because he didn't have any enemies.[43]

"The event has produced a great deal of indignation . . . for the cold-blooded way in which the murder was committed," exclaimed one reporter.[44] The Guardia investigators claimed that the assassin had shot him in the back and that the outraged citizens of Camoapa knew who was responsible: the casta indígena. The Guardia proved them right. Within days they claimed to have discovered the murder weapon in the house of Regalado López, and identified its owner as his uncle Paulino Pérez, president of the Comunidad Indígena. But they never found the assassin.

Thirty-seven years after the assassination, some surviving Indian elders, believing that Elevorio Borges is still alive, and still suspicious of the ladino authorities, refused to identify Borges to me as the mayor's executioner. But others believed that he had died in Costa Rica some years back and were willing to discuss the case. According to their account, Borges had some education that he had acquired away from Camoapa and his family was well off by local standards. But Cerna destroyed the family by having them evicted from their land. Court records substantiate that claim: in 1952, his family lost a court case involving their 100-manzana farm.[45] According to oral testimony, shortly after the legal battle "the [local authorities] destroyed their cacao plants, their cafetal, their chagüites. And then they burned their house and everything in it."[46]

Upon his return to Camoapa, some believe, Borges found his once-prosperous family destitute and the casta organization in a state of acute demoralization. His response was to begin to plot the assassination. One informant recalled a moment from his youth: "Borges spent a few days spying on Cerna. I remember seeing him behind a tree alongside the road, right by the point called 'El Guayabito.' He had a pile of cigarette butts beside him."[47] Although the informants state that Borges prepared a trap, they refute the charge that he shot Cerna in the back.[48] That story, they claim, was just invented to justify the ferocity of the repression. And repression there was: the president along with fifteen other members of the Comunidad were thrown in jail and tortured as a prelude to generalized anti-indigenous jailings. As one witness expressed it, "when the Guardia found an Indian, bam, into the hole."[49] One elderly woman with pain in her voice and a reflection of horror on her face explained, "it was against the law to be an Indian in Camoapa. . . . The ladinos let out all their hatred on us."[50]

During the wave of violent repression that followed the assassination, Borges went to the center of town to personally deliver a letter to Cerna's widow in which he took full responsibility for the crime and pleaded with her to ask the Guardia Nacional to stop the torture of innocent Indians. Despite Borges's bold proclamation of his own guilt, the repression continued unabated, unreported even in the anti-Somocista press. Yet a wanted poster with Borges's portrait circulated as far away as Matagalpa.[51]

According to one informant, Borges did not leave the area for some time: "he had real military discipline. . . . You'd see him and then he'd disappear. . . . The Indians took care of him, giving him food and hiding him."[52] There was nothing that Borges could do, however, to halt the repression, and the possibilities of collective resistance were nil. After a few months he left the area, without any words of advice for the other members of the casta.

A year passed, and the repression ceased; the Indian leaders were released. Paulino Pérez, the president of the Comunidad, vowed to drive out the *buitres jodidos* (damn buzzards) from the communal land. But the repression had weakened the community; scores of families had fled to the mountainous jungle to the east. The small group willing to continue the struggle had even lost their communal house in Camoapa, for they had to sell it to raise funds for legal fees.[53]

Today the ten-kilometer road to Salinas is as miserable as it was forty years ago; on foot or on horseback, one climbs and descends on large slabs of rock, only to trip along foot-deep ruts formed by cattle. The isolation makes the lives of the folk even worse. Their main products—ceramics and oranges—can be sold only in bulk through intermediaries who can afford to send in pack animals and then intercept the caravan with jeeps in Aguacate, halfway to Camoapa. In 1995, when I was last in Salinas, the producers were selling 1,000 oranges to the intermediaries for the equivalent of four dollars. Worse still, most of the indigenous families lack any land at all; they work on ladino-owned farms and ranches for a dollar a day. Five families control most of the land in the Salinas area, and ladinos dominate the entire Camoapan countryside. Only in Salinas do some thirty Indian families still make up one-half of the population. And even in that village, the children know nothing of Borges's action or its consequences for the community. Fear, shame, and flight have disintegrated the bonds of the Indian community, so today in the highland fields of Camoapa no one under forty years old easily accepts an Indian identity. In the words of an Indian elder: "the youth do not want to know our history; they do not care about our history."[54]

## Conclusion

The silencing of the narrative of community and of the indigenous voices that sustained it had devastating consequences for popular consciousness, both Indian and mestizo. The dialectic of symbolic and real violence has left a trail of destruction throughout Nicaragua and indeed throughout Central America. In Matagalpa and Camoapa, the relationship between these two dimensions of ladino power is clear. In 1940s Matagalpa, there existed an indigenous community that defined itself and was defined through its religious organization (tied to the Comunidad) and recognized through its native dress. As if by a miracle, Indian dress and religion by the early 1950s seemed like a replica of those of other Nicaraguans. In Camoapa, in 1954, there existed an indigenous community that despite being squeezed by agrarian capitalism still maintained strong internal cohesion based on centuries of communal defense. Today, that community only remains in the memories of its elders. The theft of land that prompted the mayor's assassination and the racist repression that followed prepared the terrain for another kind of violence—the silencing of indigenous history. And the ladino version either omits the repression or (in its Sandinista variant) treats the struggle for indigenous rights as indistinguishable from that of other peasants and regards la casta indígena as a relic of the distant past.[55] With the Indians' loss of communal land and institutions, the ladino version of history predominates in Camoapa as it does throughout Nicaragua. To repeat the words of the elder, "the youth do not wish to know about our history, they do not care." As they were unable to drive the "buitre jodido" from their fields, today as lord of those lands and of social memory, the buzzard agrees: "There are no Indians here."

## Notes

1   Cándida Salgado, interviewed by Alexis White, cited in "La cuestión indígena en Nicaragua: el caso de Matagalpa" (master's thesis, Escuela de Sociología, Universidad Centroamericana, 1993), 69.

2   *La Gaceta*, August 19, 1942. In fact, the order stipulated that any cotton beyond the 3,600-manzana limit had to be destroyed. Interviews with Gregorio Aráuz, Francisco Arceda, Pablo García, Patrocinio López, Valerio Mercado, Santos Pérez, and César Salgado, Matagalpa, 1990 and 1992.

3   See June 30, 1942 entry, U.S. National Archives, U.S. State Department, RG 57, 817.61321/17.

4   Matagalpa previously cultivated only about 400 acres of cotton. Dirección General de Estadístico y Censo, *Anuario estadístico* (Managua: Tallerés Nacionales, 1938).

5   Josefina Arnesto, "Breves apuntes de la historia de Matagalpa," pamphlet, Colegio San Luis, Matagalpa, 1962.

6   D. A. Stafford, "Data re: Coffee Plantations in Matagalpa District," Matagalpa, December 18, 1930, Marine Corps Historical Center, Private Papers Collection, J. C. Smith/7. I want to thank Michael Schroeder for passing on this document to me.

7   Willey to Allen Dawson, interim chargé d'affaires, October 18, 1934. U.S. National Archives, U.S. State Department, 817.00/8160, October 26, 1934.

8   By the early 1950s, according to Stone, "The Matagalpa wear the same cheap clothing as the ordinary laborer. Little trace of their ancient weaving remains. However, occasionally one sees a crude imitation of a spinning wheel itself of cedar." Doris Stone, "Brief Notes on the Matagalpa Indians of Nicaragua," in Richard N. Adams, ed., *Cultural Surveys of Panama, Nicaragua, Guatemala, El Salvador, and Honduras* (Washington: Pan-American Sanitary Bureau, 1957), 258.

9   Interview with Cristina Hernández, Matagalpa, 1995, by Victoria González.

10  Arnesto, "Breves apuntes de la historia de Matagalpa," 5–6. Arnesto describes how ladino boys would disrupt and mock the Indians' ceremony on the Día de los Difuntos by stealing their candles to make wax balls.

11  Interview with Silvanio Cruz, El Zapote, 1995, by Victoria González.

12  Interview with Patrocinio López, Matagalpa, March 1990. Other interviews with La Reforma in January and July 1992 gave virtually the same explanations.

13  See *La Prensa,* December 3, 1942, December 25, 1942, and November 28, 1942. This argument admittedly is as imprecise as our date for the Guardia march into the cañadas. It is possible that the low turnout for coffee picking derived in part from the fear that permeated the villages following that action.

14  "Informe presentado por el Comité Ejecutivo de la Confederación General del Trabajo al VIII Congreso 'Regino Escobar' correspondiente al período del 15 de setiembre 1960 al 24 de mayo de 1964."

15  *La Prensa* (Managua), June 25, 1942; Jorge Eduardo Arellano, "El laicado y la cuestión social: Nicaragua," in Enrique Dussel, ed., *Historia general de la Iglesia en América Latina* (Salamanca: Ediciones Sígueme, 1985), 6:403.

16  Kay Warren, *Symbolism of Subordination* (Austin: University of Texas Press, 1978); Ricardo Falla, *Quiché rebelde* (Guatemala City: Editorial Universitaria, 1980). Ann Chapman, in *Hijos de copal y candela* (Mexico City: Universidad Autónoma Nacional de México) has documented a similar conflict in the Lenca region of Honduras.

17  Although I have not been able to specify the exact date of the removal of the saints, based on a reading of the *actas* (minutes) of the alcalde de vara of the parcialidad of Laborío and the testimony that Estanislao García was priest at the time, we can be fairly certain that the events took place between 1948 and 1952. *Actas de la Alcaldía de la vara Alta de Laborío, 1945–1947,* in possession of the Comunidad Indígena of Matagalpa.

18  Ibid.

19  Interview with Santos Pérez, Matagalpa, July 1992.

20  Ramiro Ortiz Núñez, *Dirangén: padre de la Patria Nicaragüense* (Managua: Editorial Brenes, 1953), 81.

21  Interview with Tiburcio Hernández, Susulí, Matagalpa, January 1992.

22  Interview with Pedro González, Los Limones, Matagalpa, 1992, by Alexis White. Cited in White, "La cuestión indígena," 78.

23  J. R. Gutiérrez Castro, *La guerra de los indios* (Matagalpa, 1954), 11.

24  Ibid., 8.

25  Victor Mixter, cited in *La Noticia,* August 31, 1954. Similarly the degree of alienation of the national intellectuals from their subjects is revealed in the following report on the extinction of the Matagalpino language by Jaime Incer, noted geographer and government minister (1990–1996). "This language [Matagalpino] persisted through the first few decades of this century among the ladinos of Matagalpa and San Ramón." Jaime Incer, *Toponimias indígenas de Nicaragua* (San José: Libro Libre, 1985), 265.

26  Cited in *La Flecha,* November 25, 1954.

27  Jean and John Comaroff, *Of Revelation and Revolution: Christianity, Colonialism, and Consciousness in South Africa* (Chicago: University of Chicago Press, 1991), 25.

28  *Ahora* (Managua), October 27, 1946.

29  See Jeffrey L. Gould, "Nicaragua," in Ian Roxborough and Leslie Bethell, eds., *Latin*

*America between the Second World War and the Cold War* (Cambridge: Cambridge University Press, 1993).

30  *La Voz Sindical,* December 30, 1950.

31  *Adentro,* April 22, 1950.

32  *Orientación,* June 15, 1952.

33  *La Voz Sindical,* October 7, 1950. Although the article was not signed, according to Sánchez he was the only union activist to write about Sébaco. Interview with Domingo Sánchez, Managua, 1989.

34  *La Voz Sindical,* November 4, 1950. It was probably Domingo Sánchez who wrote this given that he wrote several articles in *La Voz Sindical* during that period. In an interview he recalls doing so. Interview with Domingo Sánchez, Managua, July 1989.

35  In 1951, to cite one of numerous examples, Sánchez was jailed in Matagalpa. See U.S. National Archives, U.S. State Department Reports, RG 59, 717.00, April 21, 1951.

36  "Carta del Ministro de Gobernación, León de Bayle a José León Sandino," April 2, 1936, Archivo Nacional de Nicaragua, Fondo de Gobernación, sección "Alcaldía."

37  J. L. Sandino to Leonardo Argüello, March 12, 1943, Granada, Archivo Nacional de Nicaragua, Fondo de Gobernación, sección "Alcaldía" 6:0, folder 3 (1942–1944), box 21.

38  Leonardo Argüello to the mayor of Camoapa, March 15, 1943, Archivo Nacional de Nicaragua, Fondo de Gobernación, sección "Alcaldía," Camoapa.

39  H. Flores to the ministro de gobernación, April 2, 1943, Archivo Nacional de Nicaragua, Fondo de Gobernación, sección "Alcaldía," Camoapa.

40  Interview with Mercedes López, Salinas, 1992.

41  Interviews with Juan García López, Camoapa, 1992, and Santos Suazo, Las Trincheras, 1992.

42  January 1, 1954, *Libro de actas de la Municipalidad de Camoapa,* municipal office of Camoapa.

43  *La Prensa,* August 14, 1954. Other newspaper accounts state that he was dead on arrival at the hospital.

44  *La Noticia,* July 31, 1954.

45  "José Dolores López Borge v. Zenón Marín," June 1952, in *Libro de Sentencias Civiles, Boaco, 1951–52.*

46  Interview with Carmela López, Salinas, Camoapa, 1992.

47  Interview with Juan García López, Camoapa, 1992.

48  Interview with Santos Suazo, Las Trincheras, Camoapa, 1992.

49  Interview with Mercedes Pérez, Salinas, Camoapa, 1992.

50  Interview with Carmela López, Salinas, Camoapa, 1992.

51  "Charla del compañero Carlos Fonseca Amador," Archive of the Ejército Popular Sandinista, box 6, 00292, September 10–11, 1973, pp. 15–16. I thank Matilde Zimmerman for providing me with this document.

52  Interview with Juan García López, Camoapa, 1992.

53  Interview with Santos Suazo, Las Trincheras, Camoapa, 1992.

54  Ibid.

55  See Carlos Fonseca's statement, "Charla del compañero Carlos Fonseca," Archive of the Ejército Popular Sandinista, box 6, 00292, September 10–11, 1973: "We remember that around 1953 . . . that some campesinos in Boaco, one of the most backward zones in the country, had their lands taken away from them and there still existed the tradition of the comunidad indígena. The lands had been lost collectively and thus the campesinos considered that they had been hurt not as individuals, they thus decided to assassinate the chief thieving latifundista of the area. In effect the campesino who was chosen to carry out this mission was chosen collectively and he disappeared protected by the campesino population. . . . I cite this example so that we can better appreciate spontaneous struggles among our people. We have to be aware of this compañeros, where there are exploited people there is class struggle." Matilde Zimmerman suggested to me that this document shows that Fonseca had a more sensitive view of the ethnic question. Perhaps he did, especially in comparison with other Sandinista leaders. Notwithstanding, I would suggest that the preceding quote does not challenge our general interpretation for the following reasons: (1) Fonseca did not consider the event important enough to find out the correct date. (2) The phrase "aún existía tradición de comunidad indígena" juxtaposed with "una de las zonas más atrasadas del país" in the context of the entire statement suggests that the role of the Comunidad Indígenas was of little consequence or importance to Fonseca's analysis. (3) This is the only recorded reference of the Sandinistas to the events at Camoapa, and it is worth underscoring that it occurred as part of internal talk.

# 7

## Memories of Mestizaje, Memories of Accumulation:
## The Indigenous Dimension in the Peasant Movements, 1954–1965

And we started to project Sandino in Subtiava. They had a cacique who was their most representative historical figure: Adiac. We projected Sandino as a follower of Adiac. . . . Then from house to house, from Indian to Indian, the idea began to circulate . . . Adiac . . . Sandino . . . class struggle . . . vanguard . . . FSLN.
—Omar Cabezas, *La montaña es algo más que una inmensa estepa verde*

This primitive accumulation plays approximately the same role in political economy as original sin does in theology. Adam bit the apple, and thereupon sin fell on the human race. Its origin is supposed to be explained when it is told as an anecdote about the past. Long, long ago there were two sorts of people; one the diligent, intelligent and above all frugal elite; the other the lazy rascals, spending their substance and more in riotous living. The legend of theological original sin tells us certainly how man came to be condemned to earn his bread in the sweat of his brow; but the history of economic original sin reveals to us there are people to whom this is by no means essential. . . . In actual history it is a notorious fact that conquest, enslavement, robbery, murder, in short, force, play the greatest part. . . . As a matter of fact, the methods of primitive accumulation are anything but idyllic.
—Karl Marx, *Capital*, v. 1

The individual is gradually torn loose from the old personal security networks and eventually many come to see themselves alone and to think of his fate as most comprehensive in terms of his own acts. . . . Proletarian class membership carries with it a consciousness of individuality within the class, as well as the consciousness of the class itself.
—Sidney Mintz, "The Rural Proletariat and the Problem of Rural Proletarian Consciousness"

Memory has recorded the repercussions: the suffering due to inequalities, frustrations endured or witnessed. But not only that. For memory speaks from today. It speaks from the point of view of a constructed identity, a political identity in the old sense of the term: a citizenship conferred; a shared identity, participation in the creation of one's own life and in the invention of culture.

It is this identity that tries to create for itself a memory and that must re-interpret the past.—Luisa Passerini, *Autobiography of a Generation: Italy 1968*

The repression of the Indians of Camoapa in 1954 appears as the logical outcome of the history of Indian-ladino relations in the Boaco area, charac-terized by the racism, violence, and cultural conflict analyzed in previous chapters. What does not seem at all inevitable, however, is that politicians, scholars, and revolutionaries have failed to mention, let alone take seriously, the events of Camoapa, which remain enveloped in a pervasive silence.[1]

The inability of the Frente Sandinista, in particular, to incorporate the events of Camoapa into its nationalistic, emancipatory narrative had to do in part with its lack of familiarity with the region. More significant, the indige-nous memory of the events is precarious and fragmented, because the assault on indigenous lands and the postassassination repression tore asunder the physical and cultural bonds of community. Many families fled or were pushed out of the area; others apparently wanted to forget about the memories of struggle against the victorious townsfolk. Following suit, the ladinos in their version highlighted the tragedy of the mayor's assassination and omitted mention of the ethnically specific repression.

This chapter will explore the ways in which other narratives of repression, expropriation, and resistance are incorporated or suppressed in revolution-ary nationalist discourse, most specifically that of the Frente Sandinista de Liberación Nacional. Rather than constituting an entirely unique event, the Camoapa repression can be placed within the context of two analytically separable, but intimately connected, movements: the agrarian protest strug-gles that erupted throughout Nicaragua in the 1950s and 1960s, and the elite thrusts against the remaining resources and institutions of the Comunidades Indígenas—and the corresponding communal responses. These movements were often overlapping, and the indigenous component of the campesino movements of the 1950s and 1960s, though largely ignored, was indeed of considerable importance. Sutiaba was the best-known point of intersection between indigenous and agrarian protest. The key role played by indigenous intellectuals distinguished Sutiaba from the other sites of protest. In the preface to the analysis of the Sutiaban case we will briefly look at Ernesto Cardenal's poetry, which inspired the indigenous intellectuals. Moreover, Cardenal's work represents the most significant attempt by the Sandinistas to appropriate Indianness. He created a revolutionary aesthetic that attuned Sandinista sensibilities to the importance of the Indian and the rural poor in the forging of a national identity.

The thrust of this chapter is to understand how nationalist discourse absorbs local history; we will focus on some points of intersection between the indigenous and peasant movements by examining the different forms of collective memory and identity that emerged.

One avenue toward understanding the local silences within nationalist discourse is explored in the work of Ann Norton. In her discussion of the historiography and memory of postcolonial Africa and Asia, she points out that the nationalists continued to employ metropolitan narrative forms. When they expelled colonialism from their memory, they suppressed their own history. She writes, "Thus the histories of the nationalists had their lacunae, their deceptions and their silences. The distance between the historical and the remembered nation was as great in independence as it was under colonization."[2]

The Nicaraguan cases reveal a similar contradiction between the creation of a national historical memory and the multiple local memories from which it draws its sustenance. Local memories of the demise of indigenous dress or the Boaqueño land conflict blend into a national narrative of harmonious mestizaje. Yet, the radically distinct and largely suppressed memories of the repression in the Matagalpino cañadas or in the fields of Camoapa pose a challenge to that national discourse, in all of its political inflections.

Norton makes the argument that shame must be absent from local memory for the memory to be absorbed into a national narrative.[3] Yet each subaltern memory that we will examine contains an element of shame or at least of complicity with its own oppressors. The subaltern memories of Sébaco, Camoapa, and the Matagalpino cañadas exhibit different kinds of shame, of complicity with oppression, or of violent repression in response to a bold act of resistance (that may leave as a legacy a sense of guilt).

Norton's notion of shame and complicity also provides us with a way to address the question of why revolutionary nationalism had such difficulty in accepting indigenous identities, yet has been so politically successful among those immediate descendants of indigenous communities that had recently disappeared. Collective memories of social struggles during the 1950s and 1960s in other communities were successfully integrated into the emerging narrative of revolutionary nationalism during the 1970s and 1980s. One of the differences between the two types of communities—one represented by the Comunidad Indígena of Matagalpa, the other by Yúcul and Uluse—that we will explore is that in those "formerly" indigenous areas (Yúcul and Uluse) the strands of shame and complicity are separable from a more heroic narrative that may be assimilated into the nationalist vision, whereas in the other memories of complicity block such a transformation.

The other methodological proposition I am putting forth is that memories of "primitive accumulation," at historical moments of repetition, are particularly susceptible to incorporation into nationalist narratives. Moreover, they may closely interact with memories of mestizaje. By employing the notion of a memory of "primitive accumulation" I am aligning myself with those who suggest that social memories are only comprehensible with reference, however indirect and provisional, to material, historical reality. I am also referring to Karl Marx, who interrogated and then appropriated the concept of "so-called primitive accumulation." Whereas bourgeois economists used the term to separate the process from the history of capitalism, Marx used "primitive accumulation" in the following terms:

> [It] is nothing else than the historical process of divorcing the producer from the means of production . . . the historical movement which changes the producers into wage-laborers appears, on the one hand, as their emancipation from serfdom and from the fetters of the guilds, and it is this aspect of the movement which alone exists for our bourgeois historians. But, on the other hand, these newly freed men became sellers of themselves only after they had been robbed of all their means of production. . . . And this history, the history of their expropriation, is written in the annals of mankind in letters of blood and fire.[4]

In his discussion of the centuries-long process in England and Europe, Marx emphasized not only the role of land expropriation but also other forms of extraeconomic coercion, especially vagrancy laws and forced labor. In our

attempt to understand something of memory, identity, and political consciousness, the notion of primitive accumulation is particularly useful. Our
working assumption is that the study of how a memory of accumulation was
produced or how it continues to be transmitted will shed much light on the
evolution and transformation of a particular subaltern group. In particular,
the historical process analyzed by Marx is typically punctuated by decisive,
memorable events of "blood and fire." Moreover, because the process can
cover an entire historical epoch it is rarely terminated with those first blows of
accumulation. Thus, certain moments of accumulation may be experienced as
a repetition of earlier experiences. It is those moments that seem like repeti-
tions that may trigger memories either from childhood or those that have been
transmitted communally. Finally, the appeal to a memory of a key moment in
that process may contribute dramatically to communal mobilization.

It is worth underscoring the somewhat obvious point that the struggle for
control over these memories will determine the level of the memories' incorporation into the nationalist narrative. At the same time, the struggle to
maintain a unitary version of the memory is always a social and political
struggle. To illustrate the interconnection between mestizaje, accumulation,
and forms of subaltern resistance, let us return to the highland fields of Yúcul,
where, as we saw in chapter 1, José Vita had swallowed up huge chunks of
indigenous land.

## Yúcul

John Comaroff ended an article on ethnicity with the following challenge:
"Much more vexing . . . is the question of when and why ethnic ideologies
break down and class consciousness rises to replace it—if indeed this ever
happens in straightforward terms."[5] The Yúcul case suggests that the agrarian
bourgeois conquest of indigenous villages may create conditions for such a
breakdown of ethnic ideology and its replacement by something resembling a
rural proletarian consciousness. Yet we must state two caveats. First, Yúcul
and the nearby village of Uluse were anomalous cases. As we have seen earlier
in this book, withdrawal into relatively closed communities and migration
were far more common indigenous responses to elite aggression against their
land and labor. In the Matagalpino case, the retreat to marginal communities
undoubtedly sustained a form of ethnic consciousness. Where the Indians lost

their ethnic identity, rarely was it replaced by a class-rooted view of the world; family migrations led to the breakup of communities from Boaco to the Segovias and to the erosion of their ethnic identity without the emergence of class consciousness. Second, although the Yúcul experience seems to support the perspective that links proletarianization and ladinoization, Yúcul is far from an open-and-shut case, for the Yuculeños did maintain a separate identity and a sense of their own history. Their autochthonous form of identity, rooted in a memory of primitive accumulation, played a crucial role in their contemporary struggles.

As we saw in chapter 1, during the 1910s José Vita, a large coffee grower of Italian origin, came into possession of the indigenous cañada of Yúcul. For five years Bibiano Díaz, an elected leader of the Comunidad Indígena of Matagalpa, led the resistance to Vita in the courtroom and in the fields. But by 1916, Díaz had lost the battle and left Yúcul while some thirty families remained and became Vita's colonos. Soon, the victorious Vita confiscated their *fincas* (small farms), leaving them with but one manzana per male adult. The landlord forbade them to have livestock or to plant coffee on their parcel; their corn was purchased at below market rates. In return for limited control of their parcel, all family members were obliged to pick Vita's coffee and weed 8,000 coffee trees a year, at far less than the going wage. During the period of 1916 to 1963, if a Yuculeño did not show up to work one day, Vita (and then his son) sent his own "civilian police" to drag the recalcitrant worker off to the plantation jail. As one veteran explained:

> If you were sick one day and couldn't go to work they came and hauled you down to hacienda's jail. They'd keep you there three or four days and then put you to work with a "machete" that wasn't a machete, it was made of wood.[6]

Not surprisingly, Vita carried along a fair amount of racist baggage. His daughter-in-law recalls that once during the 1930s when she was strolling with him through his plantation, La Laguna, they happened upon the area where Indian coffee pickers from the cañadas were housed. She questioned Vita about why the Indians had to sleep on the dirt floor. He replied, "Los inditos don't like to sleep on bunks, they get too hot."[7]

Vita's proletarianization of the Yuculeños was accompanied by a process of de-Indianization so thorough that the grandchildren of Bibiano Díaz do not recall that he was a leader of the Comunidad Indígena. Between 1916 and 1950 the Yuculeños lost contact with Indian villages only ten miles away. Gradually, prodded by ladino migrants to Yúcul, they began to look upon the Indian families who came to pick Vita's coffee in the 1930s and 1940s as people of a different ethnic group. The Yuculeños, both the descendants of the indigenous community and the migrants, called them the *mantiadas* for their dress, and those of *lenguaje enredado* (garbled language) for their Spanish-based dialect: "They talked all garbled. They couldn't talk with ladinos, they were embarrassed. . . . They couldn't talk about a lot of things, they were embarrassed. It was beyond their grasp."[8] The relationships among the original Yuculeños, the ladino migrants, and the indigenous coffee pickers were far more complex than we can possibly reconstruct. For example, at least until the 1950s the indigenous families did not allow ladinos to visit their homes or go to their fiestas. Doña Macaria, who arrived with her family to the area during the 1930s, recalled how the migrants came to interact with those original Yuculeño families who were still considered to be Indian.

> I met the López when I was little. . . . Those "inditos" were poor. My mama knew how to pray. . . . When an "indito" died, they would come and say, Doña Pascuala, I want you to go pray for my father. . . . We got along really well.[9]

When asked by Doña Macaria why they did not lead the prayers, the Indians responded to her that they did not know how. Doña Macaria then replied in a friendly tone, "learn . . . it's good."

Whatever her good intentions, that condescension from a poor ladino migrant surely whittled away at the remaining bonds of indigenous pride, already shattered by Vita's conquest of their land and community. Over the course of a generation the daily contact of the Indians of Yúcul with the migrant settlers combined with memories of shame to obliterate their sense of a specifically indigenous identity. Doña Macaria's recollection, assuming a reasonable degree of accuracy, is stunning precisely because of the indigenous acceptance of ladino superiority in the religious arena, where indigenous peoples had always maintained culturally specific rites and practices and a sense of religious superiority over ladinos.

Her story can be connected to another Yuculeño narrative of defeated Indians admitting cultural inferiority to the ladino world. A direct descendant of the expropriated group recounted a collective memory of primitive accumulation:

> Before Vita took over, the land was free for all the indígenas. . . . Vita arrived with old shoes. . . . The indios were rich. . . . That's how they celebrated their victories. . . . They were drunk when Vita took away the title. . . . Vita had the mark of the devil.[10]

The idealization of Yúcul before the Vita takeover allows us to get a glimpse at an aspect of collective memory that included a positive, if romantic, notion of indigenous life. Yet, that valorization was accompanied by a view of a poor and humble Vita who outfoxed the stupid, drunken Indians. The social memory of drunkenness as the cause of land loss meshed well with typical ladino stereotypes of Indians and in particular with Acción Católica's critique of indigenous religious practices. Similarly, the emphasis on ladino superiority undoubtedly offered a message that would help to distance the community from any notion of solidarity with those "mantiados" of "lenguaje enredado."

Nevertheless, the loss of an indigenous identity did not signify the adoption of some homogenous national one. Rather, the descendants of the expropriated Indians maintained a unique local identity, something akin to an autochthonous consciousness, as descendants of indigenous people who had "always" inhabited Yúcul. If the last indigenous generation of Yúcul ceded decisive cultural terrain to their ladino neighbors, those neighbors also assimilated into the Yuculeño community by appropriating existing collective memories of accumulation and identity. Thus, both migrant and indigenous people shared a belief that Vita's body had the "mark of the devil." Both groups also recognized that although they made up a small minority of Vita's workforce, the Yuculeños were highly overrepresented in his jail.[11]

The migrants became so integrated into the community that they began to share a common social language with the local folk. By the 1950s, they both referred to outsiders as "ladinos" and to themselves as simply "Yuculeños," and they ascribed a particular set of character traits to each group.[12] Moreover, they continued to practice aspects of Matagalpino Indian traditions that maintained a degree of communal unity. For example, a local Reforma played a prominent role in religious practices in the area. Furthermore, the two groups shared pride in their pre-Columbian ancestry and the role of Yúcul in the rebellion of 1881. The Yuculeños have internalized the dominant discourse and so regard "indios" as uncivilized, but their contradictory consciousness suggests a more problematic relation between proletarianization and ladino-ization. Although they did not consider themselves to be "indios," as Delfina Díaz, a granddaughter of Bibiano Díaz put it: "we were indígenas before Vita took the land, the land was free."[13] Indeed a memory of indigenous life and primitive accumulation informed the organization of a labor union in 1963 to battle against Vita's heir.

Early in 1963, a few Yuculeños heard about a union-organizing drive in rural Matagalpa. Rural labor and peasant organizing had been on the rise throughout Nicaragua since 1960, spurred on by a minimum wage law in 1962 and agrarian reform legislation signed in April 1963.[14] Beginning in 1957, the leftist Partido Socialista Nicaragüense had begun to rebuild the Matagalpino labor movement that had been destroyed in the nationwide crackdown in 1948. In October 1960, PSN militants had led a relatively successful general strike in the coffee beneficios of Matagalpa. Since 1962, they had begun to organize the nuclei of several unions in the eastern Matagalpino countryside. By 1964, militants had helped to organize seven village-based unions, made up mostly of colonos or squatters who worked seasonally on coffee plantations.

After informing themselves about the union, the Yuculeños sought out its principal rural labor organizer, Santos Sánchez. He listened to their multitude of complaints. They sorely resented the historic abuses of their community— the annual contracts that obliged them to work for the ridiculous sum of seven córdobas (one dollar) for cleaning approximately 2,000 coffee trees, a task that usually took eight or nine days. They detested Vita's practice of imprisoning workers for failing to fulfill that contract or for missing a day's work in the harvest or for (women workers') failing to make their quota of coffee baskets. But they were also outraged by more conjunctural matters during the coffee-picking season such as irregular scales for weighing coffee, cockroaches in the luncheon beans, and the most outrageous insult on a coffee plantation—the serving of a coffee substitute made from millet.[15]

Under Santos Sánchez's guidance, within several months 127 Yuculeños had organized a union, the Sindicato Agrícola de Yúcul, affiliated regionally with the leftist-led Sindicato de Trabajadores Agrícolas de Matagalpa. In July, the Yuculeños joined other workers and campesinos from Matagalpa at a *mitín obrero-campesino*. At the demonstration, the Yuculeños presented their de-mands that included a raise from seven to sixty córdobas a week, better work conditions, paid vacations, an end to being treated like "colonos of Vita's fief" and the end of hacienda police-repression.[16]

The demand for an eightfold increase in wages and paid vacations signified a desire to abolish the colono system the Vitas had managed since 1916. For even a raise of 100 percent would have made the system unprofitable for Vita, as the raise would have brought the wages in line with free labor. Although at the time they did not demand land, the colonos believed they had the right to their parcels both because the land had been robbed by Vita, the father, and because of the extreme and coerced forms of exploitation: "the land belonged to us for the stolen labor."[17] At the same time, the leftist labor militants informed them of their rights under the new agrarian reform law of 1963.

The social memory of primitive accumulation weighed heavily on both sides of the conflict. Vita's son recognized the determination of his colonos to redress their generations of grievances, and he also surely recognized that the political conjuncture, in particular the agrarian reform law, was decidedly unfavorable to his particular form of land tenure and labor relations. Moreover, he probably feared that the labor union contagion would pass on to the main core of his La Laguna coffee plantation. Whatever the particular mix of motives, within weeks of the July demonstration, Vita, in anticipation of the agrarian reform, offered to cede ownership of the land parcels to the colonos and to end their labor obligations.

Vita, however, was playing a game with them. Rather than distributing the land as promised, Vita sold most of his hacienda to Pedro Buitrago, who attempted to evict the union members–colonos. Doña Macaria recalls: "Florentino, Urbano, Dionisio—there were about twelve working. . . . The Guardia kicked them off the land, beating them with their rifle butts."[18]

The children and grandchildren of Bibiano Díaz and the others expropriated in 1916 experienced a brutal expropriation on the exact same land. The sense of repetition of an outrage served to consolidate the solidarity of the core group of colonos—some thirty families in 1963—whereas those who worked at La Laguna and others who initially sympathized with the union were frightened off. One union militant recalled: "the struggle was hard because many folks were on the boss's side out of fear. . . . The ones who lived in the hacienda were on his side."[19] Probably 150 union members either quit the organization or fled the area.[20]

The two years following Vita's promise in 1963 were punctuated by arrests, beatings, bribery, betrayals, and marches in Managua. Those efforts culminated in 1965, when thirty-six families were able to gain possession of 360 manzanas.[21] The Yuculeños persevered, in large part motivated by that shared memory of land robbery. One union activist expressed an acute sense of that history when he stated in 1963 that "52 years of exploitation have passed since the expropriation of our ancestors by the father of José Vita."[22]

The social memory of primitive accumulation played a pivotal role in the successful mobilization by providing a strong common group identity, despite its heterogenous origins. Similarly, the memory provided a clear sense of injustice. Moreover, the Yuculeños' depiction of a process of primitive accumulation that was reproduced in their contemporary daily lives created an instant bridge of communication to a wide range of progressive actors.

There seems to have existed a strong connection in the Yuculeños' memory between what the elder Vita did to the Indians and what his son did to their community. Despite the temporal distance the oppressors were at times interchangeable in their memories. One could say that he or she had "spent my life ruining my back for Vita . . . with calluses on my neck," without distinguishing between father and son. Similarly, the dawn of the union struggle resuscitated the historical memory of the father's actions that were added to the family list of wrongs. For example, the veterans remembered how the elder "kicked you if he found you standing around or if you were eating an orange." Such violent reactions to Yuculeño behavior surely fertilized the terrain for more overt and collective forms of struggle.

But at the same time, the memory of the indigenous identity of the original subjects of the expropriation was severed from the present and placed in a time when "all the land was free and all the people were indios." Thus the ambiguity of the Yuculeño identity—people with rebellious, indigenous blood but "the same" as other Nicaraguans—favored the Yuculeños' incorporation into the union and radical movements.

Comaroff's challenge remains unanswered, but the descendants of the highlands Indians have provided some clues for further research. Ethnic identities that died out under decades of ideological, political, and economic harassment generally became atomized into kin-based identities. In Yúcul, on the contrary, the violent takeover of the Indian village eradicated its ties to the Comunidad Indígena and dissipated its sense of ethnic identity. But in response to a knowable and visible history of oppression, the villagers developed a rural proletarian perspective that hinged to a large extent on an "autochthonous" sense of identity.[23] That ambiguous but distinctive local identity, however muted and removed from "Indianness," was deeply rooted in a particular memory of accumulation.

## Uluse

During the early 1960s, some twenty kilometers from Yúcul in the village of Uluse Ignacio ("Nacho") Aráuz, a wealthy peasant of indigenous descent, purchased the hacienda "El Jobo" from the Sullivan family. The coffee plantation and cattle ranch bordered on La Escocia, where, the reader will recall, Neil Hawkins battled the Comunidad Indígena of Muy Muy from 1925 to 1935. The recent sale of the land had prompted a change in the economic arrangement between El Jobo and his colonos, largely made up of families who had been expropriated by Hawkins. Before 1963, the hacienda had ceded two manzanas of land to the peasants in return for a commitment to work two months in the coffee harvest. As in Yúcul, those who did not work in the harvest were expelled from the hacienda (though usually not arrested). Unlike in Yúcul, the work of cleaning around the coffee bushes of El Jobo was voluntary and remunerated at the minimum rather than the coerced, subminimum wage.

In response to a rapidly rising demand for beef exports, Aráuz decided to convert the peasant basic grain area of the hacienda into pastureland and thus prohibited the colonos from preparing the land for planting. José Esteban Peña, a nonindigenous *curandero* (healer) affiliated with Acción Católica, suggested to his fellow colonos that they seek help from the Sindicato de Trabajadores Agrícolas de Matagalpa, which had already organized unions in Yúcul and other Matagalpino villages.

In August 1964, most of the colonos—some of whom, like Peña, possessed sizable farms of up to fifty manzanas—had formed a local union under Peña's leadership, affiliated with the departmental labor federation. Sixty union members along with thirteen from Yúcul joined other peasants organized by the psn's labor federation (the cgt Independiente) and journeyed to Managua, where they each presented their petitions.[24] Rather than make exclusively wage demands, the Uluse union directly demanded the land that had been expropriated in the past from the Comunidad Indígena. Moreover, they claimed, as "indígenas" they were being dispossessed by terratenientes.

The use of the term "indígenas," however, was neither consistent nor particularly common among the union militants and usually referred to their historical claim to the land.[25] Indeed, two of the key leaders, Victor Guillén and Pascual Granados, were sons of members of the Comunidad Indígena who had battled Hawkins in the 1920s and 1930s.[26] Guillén, for example, had vivid memories of hacienda thugs burning their rancho following the defeat of the Comunidad. Yet, this sense of historical identification with the Comunidad did not play a determinant role in the contemporary collective identity of most Uluse campesinos. First, most union members usually did not refer to themselves as members of the Comunidad Indígena, an organization that had barely functioned over the previous decades. Second, Peña, the key leader of the union, was a ladino migrant to Uluse, as were many other members of the community.

Although the Uluse union fought for land, its members also participated in a departmentwide movement (including the Yúcul union) that made a series of demands on coffee planters including higher wages, better working and living conditions, and an end to profiteering by the plantation commissary. By September 1964, the Matagalpino labor movement felt strong enough to threaten a general strike in support of its demands.

By supporting the coffee workers' movement, the Uluse union antagonized all of the plantation owners in the area. Through the local juez de mesta and the national media, the local coffee elite unleashed a wave of anticommunist propaganda directed against the Uluse peasants. In a widely publicized accusation, the juez de mesta denounced Tomás Pravia, the Matagalpino labor head, and Peña, the Uluse union leader, for "propagating Communism in Uluse" and calling for the "abolition of private property."[27] Peña was arrested and brought handcuffed to Managua.[28] A high level of combative rhetoric on both sides continued until November, with the union staging demonstrations and threatening a general strike of the coffee industry and the cafetaleros denouncing the "illegal" unions and the communist agitation among the peasants, particularly in the Uluse region, which, they contended, urged "the peasants to occupy private property."[29]

Amidst the rising tension in the Matagalpino countryside, a lawyer for the coffee elite was murdered.[30] The manhunt for the murderer of Dr. León Lara Manning provided the pretext for repression against the growing rural union movement. First National Security agents arrested Pravia and Peña (who had only recently been released).[31] Then they brought in another Uluse leader, Rufino Aráuz. Most likely under torture, he turned on his fellow militants, accusing Peña and others from Uluse of plotting three murders: the coffee planter "Nacho" Aráuz, the local juez de mesta, and another coffee planter.[32] A total of thirty peasants, mostly from Uluse, were arrested and brought into Matagalpa.[33] Most rank-and-file militants were released after a week, when two lawyers were arrested for Lara's murder. Nevertheless, the repression had succeeded in thwarting the coffee workers' movement.[34]

In any case, the land protests continued. In February 1965, the Uluse campesinos boldly denounced repression: "We are determined not to cowardly leave our land."[35] In March of 1965, they joined campesinos from Yúcul and from other villages in Matagalpa and Jinotega in an occupation of the Instituto Agraria Nicaragüense (IAN) in Managua in protest against repression by the Guardia Nacional and in support of their demand for land. With the active participation of Domingo Sánchez, the PSN leader, the campesinos held the institute to its promise of a prompt resolution of their land conflicts so that they could begin preparing their land for planting. Within a week, the IAN guaranteed the distribution of land to the campesinos of Yúcul and Uluse.

Notwithstanding the IAN's agreement, by the end of May the local Guardia Nacional once again began to arrest union militants in Uluse. In response, the campesinos returned to Managua, this time demanding a meeting with the president of the Republic, René Schick. Following demonstrations with other peasants organized by the PSN, the secretary of the president promised to investigate and to put an end to arbitrary acts of repression.[36]

Late in August, a small Guardia Nacional patrol arrested some union militants in Uluse as they prepared to attend a labor congress in Managua. With their prisoners tied up, the patrol started back across the river that separated El Jobo from the peasant-occupied lands. Before they got to the other side, hundreds of peasants emerged from behind trees and bushes. Surrounded by the machete-wielding peasants, the Guardia released their prisoners and retreated back to Aráuz's hacienda.

This dramatic encounter convinced Aráuz to cede 500 manzanas of land with supposedly no strings attached. Although the peasants would not be evicted again, they did not receive title to the land and they would continue to endure harassment from the local elite. The Uluse campesinos then raised the stakes and began to actively work with the guerrillas of the Frente Sandinista de Liberación Nacional. Several peasant militants from Uluse lost their lives in 1967 in the battle at nearby Pancasán, an event celebrated in the annals of Sandinista history. The survivors would go on to actively support the guerrilla movement in the late 1970s.

The radicalization process in Uluse resembles that of other sites of rebellion in Nicaragua and other parts of the world: the peasant march through state institutions emboldened their tactics as their goals became legitimated and then frustrated. But what set apart the Uluse and Yúcul activist groups from others were their particular histories as villages within Comunidades Indígenas that were devoured by latifundistas during the early part of the twentieth century. Their collective memories of that process—of primitive accumulation and mestizaje—played critical roles in the creation of a common discursive framework with working-class leftist militants.

The memory of primitive accumulation and of the demise of the Indian community in Uluse was symbolized by a trope remarkably similar to that of Yúcul: a drunken fiesta. In Yúcul, Vita arrived in *zapatos viejos* (old shoes) to a drunken celebration, and in Uluse the president of the Comunidad Indígena spent all of the money on liquor and "never made it to Managua" for a scheduled meeting with Juan B. Sacasa, the Nicaraguan president in the early 1930s. The drunkenness did not by any means excuse or minimize the crime of Vita or Hawkins. Rather, it symbolized both the backwardness of their Indian grandparents and the decisive moment in the process of primitive accumulation. The fiesta trope also reflected dominant stereotypes of lazy, drunken Indians and the Acción Católica critique (1940s to 1960s) of indigenous religious practices. Yet the memories of Indianness were not all negative, but rather distant and separated by the divide of land robbery.

For instance, one descendant of the indigenous group in Yúcul remembered the social relationships between Indians and ladinos as a set of opposed, essential characteristics. The Indians were humble and respectful in their verbal and nonverbal communication, whereas ladinos were aggressive, arrogant, and disrespectful. In Uluse, Victor Guillén, who scoffed at the Indian leader who got lost on the way to Managua, nonetheless spoke with reverence about the origins of his people who fled from the Masaya region (when Mexican groups migrated to the region, presumably before the conquest).

In attempting to ascertain the connection in collective memory and in historical reality between the ladino expropriation of land and the development of "mestizo" identities, it is important to remember that this second "conquest" implied a loss of total control over residence in the community and that face-to-face relations above all else contributed to the relatively rapid fragmentation of indigenous identities. Thus, nonindigenous migrants moved into the communities. These people—displaced by the Sandino's rebellion against U.S. intervention of the 1920s, the depression, or the agroexport development of the 1940s and 1950s—moved to the more or less new communities that sprung up around coffee plantations and cattle ranches in eastern Matagalpa. Although, as we pointed out earlier, it is difficult to probe the evolving texture of relations between Indians and poor ladinos in Yúcul and Uluse, we can approximate its reality in a few areas. As we saw in Yúcul, at least until the 1940s, indigenous families still maintained separate if nonexclusive identities, cultural practices such as La Reforma, and linguistic codes. Moreover, the contact between indigenous and ladino in Yúcul was far from harmonious. Notwithstanding, they had to live and work in close proximity and in very similar situations, for Vita and Hawkins were not capable or interested in attempting to develop an ethnic division of labor among their colonos (though they did employ exclusively Indian cuadrillas from the cañadas in the coffee harvest). Second, both had to face severe everyday hardships exacerbated by the arbitrary uses of authority imposed by the cafetaleros and their Guardia Nacional allies.

In these circumstances, the boundaries between the two impoverished groups broke down over two generations. The indigenous families, without shedding an important degree of respect for their indigenous forebears and a memory of expropriation, nonetheless began to permit marriages with ladinos and moreover to open up to ladino customs and attitudes, including negative attitudes toward "uncivilized" Indians. Similarly, when the hacendados attempted to expropriate the campesinos in the 1960s, the colonos of nonindigenous origin had acquired the same collective memory of the original theft of land so that they also felt the new aggression as a repetition of a past injustice. The emerging collective identity in Yúcul and Uluse, then, hinged on a shared and in part borrowed memory of primitive accumulation and indigenous ancestry. This partially borrowed version of the communal past facilitated identification of the original victims as Indians, while attributing a qualitatively different non-Indian, but local, identity to the community inhabitants in the present.

Curiously, the forging of a peasant community memory coincided with the perspective of social scientists in the 1970s and 1980s who posited a decisive transformation of indigenous communities into a nonindigenous rural proletariat, at the end of the nineteenth century.[37] That coincidence between the theoretical position of revolutionary intellectuals and the collective identity of the local groups allowed the FSLN to incorporate, albeit in partial form, the local histories into the nationalist narrative, a capacity that in turn allows us to glimpse something of their mutual affinity.

That mutual affinity derived to some extent from the existence of people whom we earlier defined as local intellectuals. These people, usually with some degree of literacy, were capable of understanding the broad contours of national politics and discourse as interpreted (in this case) by leftist militants and, in turn, were capable of transmitting back to the militants a sufficient understanding of local history and reality. Local intellectuals like José Esteban Peña, Victor Guillén, and Pascual Granados in Uluse and Urbano Pérez, Florentino Rodríguez (killed by the Guardia), and Eusebio García in Yúcul, differed from those discussed by Mallon and Feierman. First, excepting Peña of Acción Católica, they played no unique structural role in the community, such as a healer or teacher. Second, very quickly in their development as militants–social intellectuals they had to submit to what amounted to military discipline due to the repression. They also had to display remarkable courage as they became the obvious targets of repression. Yet at the same time, life on the run had its price in terms of intellectual development. Such a precarious existence sharply circumscribed their capacity for mediation between national and local discourses and tended to allow much greater weight to the former.

Returning to Norton's thesis about silences within the nationalist discourse, the histories of Uluse and Yúcul were told only with broad strokes as heroic examples of mestizaje and resistance to the terratenientes. They embodied and reinforced the story of how agrarian capitalism destroyed the Indian communities through violence and expropriation and created new groups of Nicaraguan peasant-proletarians disposed to struggle to redress the historic wrong done to their noble grandparents.

The words of the union leader on the state farm created on the former Vita plantation are evocative: "Yúcul has always been revolutionary. During the indigenous rebellion of 1881, Yúcul played an extremely important role, the bastion of the rebellion. Here the FSLN always had great support."[38] This broad vision omits the complex process of rejection of their parents' indigenous identity and the decades of complicity with their own oppression. The suppressed stories that included what Norton called shame could be excised from the community narratives without distorting the narrative's coherence. Indeed, to some degree, the shaping of a local narrative of community cohesion in the face of elite adversaries depended upon such suppression. Moreover, the narrative of the loss of Indian institutions and customs was softened by the perspective that made mestizaje a function of land expropriation. As a story of an inevitable process, something automatic and involuntary, it suppressed the trauma of rejecting the ways of people's parents and accepting the view that described those practices as primitive and uncivilized. Freed from the shame and ambiguity that characterized the peasants' history from the first to the second stage of land expropriation, the memory of the Indian past could be reactivated and mobilized in the struggle for land and decent labor conditions. Indeed, it was the elite move to push the peasant-colonos off the land that, to paraphrase Benjamin, threw up an image of the destroyed indigenous past that inflamed the consciousness of present injustice.[39]

### Sutiaba: Local Intellectuals and Agrarian Protest under the Somoza Regime

Ernesto Cardenal's poetry inspired a generation of progressive students and intellectuals, sensitizing them to the indigenous roots of the rural poor. Cardenal's indigenista poetry in the 1960s and 1970s posited a fundamental link between pre-Columbian society—the font of artistic creativity and social egalitarianism—and a contemporary social and political project. His Indian poems used pre-Columbian themes both to ennoble the indigenous roots of contemporary Latin American society and to adumbrate a more egalitarian and less materialistic society: "and because there was no money there was neither prostitution nor plunder."[40] The Indian poems also made allusions to the Somoza regime as they recounted ancient tales of indigenous greatness.

In the 1970s, he began to incorporate into his "documentary" poems far more specific natural and social images from contemporary Nicaragua. For example, in "Nicaraguan Canto" he paints an exuberant portrait of the natural beauty of the Tuma region of Matagalpa:

> The Tuma! Oh to see the Tuma
> country once again . . . Coffee in bloom, and corn.
> In March the cobs are tender.
> Mist over the coffee plantations and, in the mist,
> the whitish scent of coffee flowers (like the orange blossom) with
>      chichitotes
> singing
> and the "whistler."
> Campesino campesino
> what lovely fields you have! It's a shame the capitalists own them.[41]

In the "Campesinas de Cuá" Cardenal entered more directly into the lives of the peasant women:

> Voy a hablarles de los gritos del Cuá
> gritos de mujeres como de parto
> María Venancia de 90 años, sorda, casi cadáver
> grita a los guardias no he visto muchachos
> la Amanda Aguilar de 50 años
> con sus hijitas Petrona y Erlinda
> no he visto muchachos
> como de parto.
> Esta es la historia de los gritos del Cuá
> triste como el canto de los cocorocas
> la historia que cuentan las campesinas del Cuá
> que cuentan llorando
> como entrevienedo tras la neblina de las lágrimas
> una cárcel
> y sobre ella un helicóptero.[42]

The striking natural imagery of "Canto" and the peasant portraits in "Campesinas" demonstrate Cardenal's capacity to observe and powerfully evoke rural life in Nicaragua. It is therefore all the more remarkable that despite his fascination for and commitment to indigenous culture, his poetry lacks concrete references to contemporary indigenous communities in western Nicaragua. When he did write of indigenous areas such as Tuma, a coffee-growing region in Matagalpa, or Nindirí, the imagery was entirely about the natural world and lacked social references. This lack of specificity contrasted sharply with his poetry about non-Nicaraguan contemporary Indians, such as the Kuna of Panama, which exhibited a plethora of details about indigenous politics, society, and culture. Cardenal does write of the Nicaraguan Miskitos in the "Canto" and "the Mosquito Kingdom." Yet in these poems, he imputes an anti-imperialist consciousness to the Miskitos that does not correspond to the historical record (as do his other "Indian poems"). For example, in "Nicaraguan Canto" he writes:

The Canadian said to the Miskito: communism is bad
it takes all that we own. And the Miskito (who listens to Radio Havana in
Miskito) answered: bad for you, got everything, good for Miskito he not got
anything.[43]

His distance from the concrete everyday reality of contemporary Nicaraguan Indians was similar to that of the national intellectuals of the 1940s that we discussed in chapter 5. Yet, his overwhelmingly powerful vision of indigenous greatness and goodness had far more profound effects than the words and actions of the indigenista intellectuals. The cumulative effect of Cardenal's poetry offered to the revolutionary generation a radical vision of mestizaje, communicating a deep admiration for indigenous civilization and values coupled with sensitive respect (even love) for rural folk. This revolutionary aesthetic opened the minds of revolutionaries to the indigenous roots in the memories of mestizaje in Yúcul and Uluse. If Cardenal did not ennoble the indigenous identity of Samulalí, his writing did inspire indigenous youths in Sutiaba whose poetry would play crucial roles in re-creating indigenous identity in their community and beyond.

Elsewhere, I have discussed the origins and development of the Sutiaban agrarian protest movement in the 1950s and 1960s.[44] Rather than recount that critical episode in Nicaraguan social history, I will focus here on the re-creation of local memories of ethnic identity and mestizaje and their impact on communal consciousness in the 1950s and 1960s.

As the reader will recall, the city of León annexed the indigenous municipality of Sutiaba in 1902 along with its ejidos. That event, learned by every Sutiaban child, symbolized the determinant moment of primitive accumulation. The condensation of political, ethnic, and economic oppression distinguishes that memory of primitive accumulation from those in Yúcul and Uluse.

As we saw earlier, following a period of erosion of political and economic autonomy, the Sutiabas recast their ethnic identity during the protests of 1920 to 1924. Yet the partisan strife of the mid-1920s terminated the period of ethnic-communal resurgence. Moreover, the organization of the Comunidad Indígena that the Sutiaba militants had created in 1915 in order to legitimize their claim to land collapsed into a prolonged period of dormancy. Even the library, a source of communal pride and organization, lost its municipal support in the 1930s because it had failed to elect a governing board.[45]

Sutiaban community identity, weakened by the demise of the Comunidad, was recuperated primarily through religious practices during the 1930s and 1940s. Twice a year, Sutiaban drums would call the residents to clean up the cemeteries of the barrios and to bring food and drink to their ancestors. Funeral processions and the cemetery were and still are particularly essential sites for the reaffirmation of ethnic identity.[46] The Sutiabas also violently opposed two different attempts to take away their sacred symbols. As we saw earlier, they protested the cutting of a tree in the cemetery in the 1930s and in the early 1940s impeded church attempts to take away their "Santo Sepulcro," as they had done in 1924.[47]

At the same time, between 1930 and 1950 many social and economic forces conspired against the perpetuation of ethnic identity in Sutiaba. In particular, horizontal social contacts within the Leonés working class grew during the 1940s, reinforcing a tendency toward class solidarity that had started in the 1920s. The high point of this tendency was the election of an obrerista mayor in 1929 with massive Sutiaban support. As a result of the economic growth of the 1940s, an increasing number of Sutiabas, especially women, worked in newly established León factories and artisanal workshops. In addition, Sutiaban participation in the León labor movement indicates a significant level of interethnic harmony. During the 1940s, as in the 1920s, at least four Sutiaban workers came to hold positions of trade union leadership. In 1945 several female match factory workers from the barrio participated in the largest strike of the decade in León.[48]

It is quite possible that the participation of Sutiabas in the labor movement diminished Leonés prejudice against the Indians. Racially motivated physical attacks certainly declined, if not disappeared, during this period as La Ronda (the market dividing line between the barrio and the rest of the city) lost its symbolic quality of danger. Nevertheless, verbal insults were common. For example, a Leonés might exclaim in the heat of discussion, "What do you know? Aren't you from Sutiaba? Aren't you an Indian?"[49]

A new advance of agrarian capitalism threatened once again to undermine the remnants of the community's social bases. Between 1935 and 1950, hacendados began to increase their cattle holdings and to plant sesame on the lands appropriated during the Zelaya years. During this period those Sutiabas who did not hold land titles—at least half of the campesinos—lost access to land. This intensified the process of proletarianization begun at the end of the previous century. Agro-export development in the 1940s thus prepared the terrain for the dramatic social and economic transformation in the Sutiaban countryside wrought by the cotton boom.[50]

By 1954, when the Sutiaban protest movement first broke out, the organizational bonds of community were at their weakest point, and ethnic markers were so unimportant that the first anthropologist to study Sutiaba wrote with ample empirical justification:

> The fact that they are called *indios* seems to the writer to be a case of the survival of a traditional term for the group even though in most respects the group has at present lost almost all characteristics which would warrant the use of the term. . . . [They] must be considered a segment of the general lower class which has tended to be kept somewhat distinct in the minds of the Leonese through the use of the traditional term indio.[51]

Regardless of Sutiaba's lack of ethnic markers, however, when shortly after the ethnographic survey Salvador Marín began to fence off part of "San Silvestre," a former Sutiaban cofradía, the size and vigor of the Sutiaban protest were astounding—far stronger than any communal response elsewhere in the country over the previous three decades. Moreover, the fencing affected only a small minority of the community, blocking the access to a river for the cattle of fifteen Sutiaban campesinos. The new fences also made it difficult for another relatively small group of Sutiabas to harvest shellfish in the coastal estuary. Moreover, women used it for washing.[52]

Marín's fences symbolically violated the lands of the entire community, igniting a collective memory of primitive accumulation and ethnically rooted resistance. San Silvestre had been a cofradía of the Sutiabas until its expropriation by the Zelaya regime in 1899; the Marín family acquired it a few years later when a family member was mayor of León. Not only did the fences rub against raw historical nerves, but they also provided the first collective target of resistance after two decades of individualized land loss and increasing immiseration. Ernestina Roque explained that "The people rose up with San Silvestre because they couldn't take any more."[53]

Roque played a key role in this struggle, as her family had entrusted her with the community land titles, which she kept hidden in a box that had once contained Griffen All-White shoe polish (vintage 1941).[54] Perhaps the family had decided on that hiding place for tactical reasons, but more likely it reflected the general apathy regarding communal institutions that permeated the ranks of even the principal indigenous families before the fencing of San Silvestre.

Within days of the fencing "that set off an alarm in Sutiaba," a general assembly met to elect a new governing board of the Comunidad Indígena that had not functioned for over two decades.[55] Not surprisingly, the same arguments used against the legitimacy of the Comunidad in the 1920s resurfaced again: that it had never been a "Comunidad" but rather a "pueblo de indios" that had long been just another barrio of León. But the depth of support for the movement—among women, who formed their own support organizations, artisans, laborers, students, peasants, and seasonal laborers—demonstrated that even if the Comunidad's origins were not pristine, there existed a very real community of people among those people called indios by the Leonese.

An opposition editorial underscored the movement's unusual mass quality as well as its support from Leonés progressive circles: "[It] attracts considerable attention in all the university circles, since it marks the first time that the indigenous people of that region posed as a united front together with the different intellectual groups from León."[56] This new insurgency in Sutiaba thus received support from progressive students and intellectuals who were themselves slowly regrouping after the collapse of the labor and anti-Somocista movements that resulted from the fierce repression of the late 1940s. As I've mentioned elsewhere,

> Unlike in the politically insulated Chinandegan countryside, since the 1940s, progressive students and labor leaders had maintained at least informal contact with some Sutiaban artisans and students. . . . The regime then set out to plug such a dangerous leak in the ideological dam between the popular movements and the opposition.[57]

Despite constant efforts by the regime to contain the movement, this early political support by intellectuals for the Sutiaban struggle would provide a crucial link between the emerging discourse of revolutionary nationalism and the language of ethnicity in Sutiaba. The affinity between Leonés intellectuals and Sutiabas derived, among other factors, from the relatively large number of local intellectuals in the indigenous barrio and from a shared (moderate) leftist political culture rooted in the decades-old labor movement. The existence of indigenous intellectuals set Sutiaba apart dramatically from the indigenous communities of the central highlands and played a key role in the reproduction of ethnically rooted discourses.

A Sutiaban intellectual tradition had existed for at least 150 years. It had always been stimulated by community elders and more recently had been promoted by a vigorous adult education program and the availability of secondary schooling for the leading students from the barrio. The relatively large number of local intellectuals, I would argue, played a vital role in the reshaping of the collective memory and ethnic identity as this second stage of primitive accumulation disrupted the interrelated everyday processes of communal disintegration (mestizaje) and proletarianization.

Sutiaban intellectuals acted as major organizers of the agrarian protest movement that commenced in 1954 and which eventually spilled over into the revolutionary insurrectionary movement of 1978 to 1979. Part of their usefulness to the movement lay in their function as repositories of oral tradition. The land titles themselves could be recounted—the sixty-three caballerías, *medida antigua* (ancient measure), purchased from King Ferdinand VII, that extend from El Tamarindo along the Pacific to El Realejo; the land could not be sold, but passed on from generation to generation—such that it formed the central piece of the community narrative.[58] Within that story a key moment took place during the repression that followed the annexation of Sutiaba in 1902. The Zelaya regime tortured Sutiaban leaders in order to recover the title; one Indian was tortured to death without revealing its location.[59] Other tales of resistance include the story of how Indians during colonial times would hide in the (still visible) large holes in the patios of Sutiaban homes. That the holes were used to hide goods from tax authorities does not diminish the importance of militant resistance as the key trope in Sutiaban discourse.

Beyond their role in the transmission of community tales of resistance, some local intellectuals through their poetry reestablished symbols that served as powerful internal ethnic markers. It is interesting to note that the four most renowned Sutiaban poets of the past fifty years all resided for most of their adult lives outside Sutiaba. That distance, I would argue, allowed them to become particularly articulate in the language of national intellectuals and, moreover, to understand how Sutiabas were imagined by different outside social and political groups. The distance also created an overwhelming sense of nostalgia for an idyllic, heroic epoch and for a passing era evoked in their childhood memories.

In a country that has produced several poets of international fame, literary critics consider Antenor Sandino Hernández to be a primary one. Although several elderly Sutiabas I spoke with were certain that Sandino Hernández was born and raised in that barrio, there is no evidence, literary or otherwise, to support the contention. Assuming that he was Sutiaban, and I have no reason to doubt the informants, it is striking how concrete symbols of Sutiaban life are absent from his poetry, which specifically deals with "indigenista" themes.[60]

Sandino's poem "El tiangüe" is typical of indigenista poetry in that it recreates the lost epoch of pre-Columbian greatness, freely appropriating indigenous cultural symbols from Mexico, the Mayas, and the Incas. It also glorifies the specifically Nicaraguan heroes such as Tenderí and Diriangén, important Nicaraguan Indian caciques at the time of the conquest, the latter immortalized for his leadership of a rebellion against the Spanish.[61]

What strikes me as unique about the poem is that its vivid illustration of the market at "la Ronda" makes no reference to Sutiaba (except the use of the general pre-Columbian ethnic designation *nagrandano*). The use of the concrete symbolism of the market—indeed informants were moved by its evocation of that time and place—nonetheless strips La Ronda and its people of their lived experience. Similarly, Sandino Hernández always referred to himself as an Indian, although he did so in the abstract. None of his poetry dealt with the pain and confusion that characterized those who attempted to maintain an indigenous identity.

Fernando Centeno Zapata also lacked a strong identity as a Sutiaba; his father and mother moved to the Calle Reale of Sutiaba before he was born. His mother, who may have been of Sutiaban origin, died when he was less than two years old. In the mid-1940s he attended the University in León, a privilege shared by only 600 other students in the country. Yet in 1945, when he published his book of poems, his militancy in the Partido Socialista threatened to abort his aspirations to become a lawyer; he was indeed thrown in jail by the regime that year. In short, we can assume that those poems were written in a moment of crisis.

No doubt his childhood memories informed his political militancy, and in turn, his poetry at once mourned the passing of the "greatness of your imperial race" and essentialized the rebellious nature of the Sutiabas. That juxtaposition of imagery can be discerned in the following stanzas taken from Centeno's "Poema al viejo tamarindo de Subtiava," his ode to the tamarind tree where the colonial authorities hung the cacique Adiact in 1610.

> Viejo Tamarindo abuelo de mi raza, ronco y arrugado
> en tus ramas hay llanto y hay plegaria y amor,
> y hay un arrepentimiento quizás para el pasado
> y un perdón para Cehuatli Misquetli (el traidor)
>
> Y tu carne y tu sangre y tu eterna rebeldía
> Y tu músculo de acero y tu frente levantada
> Y tu herencia y tu leyenda y tu historia
> tomó sabor de tiempo y señal de lejanía.[62]

The poem contrasts an epic, tragic past with the contemporary "race kicked into the winds and waves." Centeno's poem differs from "El tiangüe" in that "Tamarindo" places concrete symbols of Sutiaban history in stark opposition to "the imbecilic babble of *hispanidad.*" Yet, Centeno's identification with this indigenous tradition is vague and tentative: "Old Tamarindo, I want to be like you: Dismantled heart that the wind swept away."[63] Centeno's tamarindo is a symbol of a defeated, great race, but at the same time its eternal essence permits an existential escape, a manner in which identities may emerge to cope with a sense of alienation and individual fate (to paraphrase Sidney Mintz's description of rural proletarian consciousness).[64] Centeno, plagued with doubts about his new and dangerous political world, saw the tree as a symbol of rootedness both in a mythical history and in his own sense of self. But he also saw it as something that could consume his entire alienated being and therefore give it meaning beyond his contradictory pursuit of a law career and political militancy.

Within a decade, as the Sutiaban protests gathered strength another poet would transform the symbol of the *tamarindón* (large *tamarindo*). Adolfo Isaac Sánchez, a small-time merchant with some education, dedicated a great deal of effort to reviving the Sutiaban language, which had all but been extinguished. Although his effort failed, he did compile and circulate a short Spanish-Sutiaba dictionary. From the 1950s through the 1980s Sánchez combined what he called "poesía indigenista," a militant call to arms, with the study and local teaching of pre-Columbian Sutiaban culture. One stanza of his "Oda al tamarindón" reads,

> Milenario tamarindón que vuestros brazos cargan a nuestro padre el
> Cacique.
> Pues te jugastes la suerte en este gran coliseo donde Adiact halló la
> muerte . . .
> Velás el eterno sueño del Cacique gran soldado. Que hordas
> conquistadores un
> día dejaron ahorcado en tus ramas tamarindón—quien duerme al
> compás del atabal.[65]

Here the tamarindón once again incarnates the essence of Sutiaba, "father of our race," but it also makes a sharp contemporary reference—the *atabal* or *tambor* is another vital aspect of Sutiaban ethnic imagery. For the drum calls the community to meetings, to the *faenas* (the biannual collective cleaning of the cemeteries), and to battle against the terratenientes. The tamarindón, symbol of "la raza," rests only to the rhythm of the drum of resistance. Such a symbol, rooted in the daily life of Sutiabas, then becomes meaningful for poets and militants who wish to renew a collective memory: "there's the tamarindón" reminds people of the risks of betraying the community. Similarly, one of the most common myths of Sutiaba, "el punche de oro," has a direct anticolonialist moral:

> Aquí en Sutiaba hay un inmenso tesoro enterrado y el espíritu de ese tesoro sale por las noches. Es un inmenso Punche de Oro. . . . El punche es el espíritu de un tesoro de la comunidad indígena. Sale por las noches después de la muerte del último cacique a manos del Español.[66]

The poetic interpretation of Sutiaba as a site of eternal rebellion has its source in the clear condensation of primitive accumulation that occurred with the 1902 loss of political autonomy, which in turn echoed the hanging of Adiact on the Tamarindón. That loss of land is very much connected in the collective memory and the poetic imagination with the loss of the Sutiaban way of life and its ethnic signs. Another Sánchez poem, "Sutiaba mía," makes that connection:

> Herido está mi pueblo
> por la ignominia.
> Exterminado le legan:
> ya no se caza venado
> Ni se mangla
> Ni se pesca
> Ya no se oye el cla -a-a-a-
> de la concha.
> Sólo el tropel de las hordas
> atisbando de los indios
> el manejo del machete.[67]

The poem fuses an image of proletarianization "spying on the machete work of the Indians" with the loss of traditional resources tied to the communal lands. Such imagery finds an echo in the collective memory of the barrio: the oldest generation of Sutiabas in the 1980s remembered how the community leaders of the 1920s fostered a fierce attitude of ethnic pride and defense of communal traditions in their struggle to revitalize the indigenous municipality. Yet, according to the informants, the leaders appeared to oppose what most of the rank-and-file Sutiabas considered to be progress: roads, schools (run by outsiders), and electricity.

The traditional discourse, recaptured by poets themselves alienated from the community, equated indigenous ethnicity with traditional and therefore primitive customs. The traditional leaders and poets created an image of Sutiaba that in effect invited questions about the authenticity of the community, because of the discrepancy between the image they created and the way the community was actually living and given the high degree of intellectual and labor interaction between Sutiabas and the non-Indian world. And as we have seen earlier, since the 1920s Leonés liberals did in fact delegitimize Sutiaban indigenous credentials.

Leonés intellectuals, traditionalist militants (before the 1950s), and indigenista poets thus shared a discursive framework in which indigenous authenticity was predicated on a communal essence—a more or less "natural" way of life that was rapidly disappearing. Not surprisingly, many Sutiabas operating within the same discursive framework tended to distance themselves from such a notion of indigenous identity.

Yet at the same time, the discursive framework allowed for the relatively easy admission of Sutiabas into the revolutionary nationalist narrative as a group demonstrating "authentic values" of the nation, and even as an exemplary model of mestizaje. Here the term "Indian" could be used without representing an unknown "other." As we have discussed elsewhere, the Sutiaban agrarian struggles prepared the terrain for its critical role in the Sandinista revolution. The revolutionary militancy of so many people within the community was both the product and the reproducer of an essentialized vision of Sutiabas as a rebellious people, a version of ethnicity that was perfectly congruent with the emerging national narrative of the Sandinistas. As in Mexico, this revolutionary mestizo nation's character and valor would be derived from its Indian blood.[68]

Although Sutiaban militants gladly accepted their lofty place in the new revolutionary narrative, two types of tensions remained within the communal identities. The first tension derived from the impossible standard set by a collective identity as eternal rebels, the greatest of revolutionaries. Obviously, many people either could not or would not live up to such a community identity and indeed resented it as an outside imposition. The other tension was more complex, involving something akin to the shame and complicity discussed earlier. Most Sutiabas accepted the dominant discursive framework and concretely the notion of Sutiabas as "civilized" and therefore roughly the same as other Nicaraguans. Yet at the same time, those aspects of communal life and identity that distinguished them from others—the memories of the land titles and the symbols that people used as cognitive tools to organize their struggles—involved a degree of veneration for ancestors and what people imagined they represented. In other words, if Sutiabas were "the same" as other Nicaraguans, then how could they base their struggle against the terratenientes on their uniqueness? Within post-1950 Sutiaban identity, I would argue, there exists a tension between the Sutiabas' acceptance as equals in daily life and in national discourse on the one side, and on the other, their own recognition of fundamental differences, rooted in a memory that venerates ancestors and communal symbols.

Some of that tension is revealed by Enrique de la Concepción Fonseca. Like the other poets, Fonseca also left the community. He worked many years in the San Antonio sugar mill in Chichigalpa, thirty miles northwest of León. At the mill, he became active in the union. He participated in grassroots efforts to democratize the union and to organize the fieldworkers, supporting their militant strike in 1964. When he returned to Sutiaba in the early 1970s (then in his early forties), he supported the new wave of agrarian protest and actively campaigned to supplant the Somocista leadership of the Comunidad Indígena with an independent group, sympathetic to the FSLN. In 1973, at the height of both conflicts, he wrote "El sutiaba":

> El Sutiaba ha de ser siempre lo mismo
> siempre lo mismo sin llegar a igual,
> mañana como ayer, lo mismo siempre,
> no puede ser igual quien no ha cambiado
> quien sigue siendo sin dejar de ser.[69]

In the following verses he repeatedly evokes the traditional Sutiaba who acts in accordance with natural laws. The poem concludes by interspersing images of naturalized and cultural identities:

> El indio es ahijado de la luna.
> Todavía hay sutiabas en Sutiaba
> que no hacen el amor con su mujer
> en luna tierna,
> ni bañan a sus niños,

hasta después de los tres días, de recorrer el cielo,
para que el hijo nazca, crezca y viva saludable.
Por tanto, los invito,
a buscar en los sutiabas en Sutiaba
a ése que no ven porque no quieren,
y esto es para que no les digan
lo que una vez Jesús de Nazareno
le dijo a los gentiles:
—Que teniendo ojos para ver no miran
y oídos para oír no oyen—[70]

The poem lucidly and elegantly poses the question of contemporary versus traditional identity. The poet successfully bridged the gulf between the essentialized notion of an authentic Indian and a vision of a contemporary Indian that becomes "modern" without losing a Sutiaban identity. Moreover, it suggests that the beauty of traditional Sutiaban culture notwithstanding, the contemporary Indians can and must transform their culture and the ladino "other" must recognize that transformation and respect their cultural difference.

Social and geographic distance from Sutiaba was a common denominator in the lives of the four poets. Arguably, it provided a vantage point with which to examine those aspects of Sutiaban culture that seemed significant from the outside yet which would also have resonance within the community. Fonseca, through his poetry, was able to do something unique within the context of Nicaraguan local intellectuals. He stimulated external recognition for the indigenous identity of modern Sutiabas, regardless of their congruence with traditional images of authentic Indians. The poet (in fact known in the barrio as "El Poeta") thus aided the Sutiaban insurgent cause by underscoring the identification of current barrio residents with their land and also the identification between generations of Sutiabas. Those who do not see those identities, Fonseca argues, "do not wish to see." The cultural difference that Fonseca rediscovered would help unite Sutiabas in a struggle that would allow revolutionary nationalists to incorporate them into their heroic narrative. Nevertheless, the revolutionaries would also confuse the appearance of similarity with the denial of a meaningful and politically consequential indigenous identity.

An account of primitive accumulation was sharply etched in the collective memories of Yúcul, Uluse, and Sutiaba. Similarly, primitive accumulation also called forth a memory of mestizaje; the story of land loss pointed to the difference between the authentic indigenous past and the mestizo present. In Sutiaba, unlike in the Matagalpino cases, relatively high levels of education produced a group of local intellectuals, ranging from poets to labor activists. They were able to interpret to the outside and ennoble to the Sutiabas salient, internal ethnic markers: the tamarindón, faenas, and the communal land that survived the first wave of agrarian capitalism. Despite this unique ethnic dimension, revolutionary nationalists were able to appropriate the tale of Sutiaba much as they did those of Yúcul and Uluse as stories of the heroic construction of the mestizo nation.

### Caciques, Cotton, and Saints: Memory and Identity in the Cañadas

Despite the close geographic proximity of the Comunidad Indígena of Matagalpa to Uluse and Yúcul, the memories of accumulation and mestizaje of the former are dramatically different from those of the latter two. Moreover, the Frente Sandinista could never successfully incorporate the Comunidad's memories into its nationalist narrative. We have already seen how the process of accumulation in the highlands was very protracted and incomplete. Between one-quarter and one-third of communal lands were expropriated by coffee growers at the end of the nineteenth and the beginning of the twentieth century, and most Indians suffered a form of seasonal debt peonage. By the 1930s, however, the process of primitive accumulation slowed down and labor became voluntary. The ensuing period of "social peace" blurred the sharp edges of a memory of primitive accumulation.

In the 1950s the rates of coffee production, land accumulation, and dispossession accelerated. Coffee exports jumped from $5 million to $25 million.[71] The northern region of the country was the focal point of the new expansion of the industry. One key difference between the two historical cycles of coffee expansion was the greater participation during the second cycle of what we might call an Indian bourgeoisie and petit bourgeoisie, whose own roots in the coffee industry often extended back to the first cycle. Much of the land loss and labor recruitment during this period (late 1940s and 1950s) occurred through traditional paternalistic means, ranging from the offering of a steer for a fiesta to *compadrazgo* (fictive kinship) based loans.

More significant, the presence of officers of the Guardia Nacional like Ciriaco Salgado (discussed in the previous chapter) and Rafael Torres made it difficult to stop the increasing land inequality within the Comunidad. When the Sandinista revolution triumphed, an estimated 70 percent of the indigenous population of Matagalpa possessed under six manzanas of land each and 30 percent had none.[72]

As the Matagalpino indigenous people once again had to confront their growing loss of land, the dominant community memories concerned the destruction of cotton bushes that had led to the demise of traditional dress and the elimination of their religious images. Unlike the Yuculeño memory of accumulation the destruction of the cotton bushes offered an ambiguous, rather than a clear-cut, moral. The Guardia's action pushed the Indians further into the clutches of the cash economy and away from the subsistence bases (however tenuous and partial) of their previous economic existence. Yet concomitantly, another message was captured in the words of a Guardia officer who made the statement "going around with a manta is an Indian thing," as if they must move beyond Indianness. Although the Guardia forced them further into the cash economy it also "helped" to push them into a potentially "non-Indian" category because they would "look" less Indian. In other words, the key memory of primitive accumulation, at the same time a memory of mestizaje, had both negative and vaguely positive consequences for the survivors.

Surely an element of shame persists in the local memory, whether about wearing the garments, about the lack of resistance to their prohibition, or about the lack of a clear interpretation of the events. A similar ambiguity and ambivalence laced the memories of mestizaje that revolved around the Acción Católica's elimination of the indigenous sacred images, thereby removing the raison d'être of the religious organizational structure of the Comunidad.

This period of coffee expansion in the 1950s also occurred at the same time that ladinos first came to reside in indigenous villages. Ladino residence in those villages coincided with a serious breakdown of indigenous patriarchy as well. As was pointed out in chapter 4, marriages were arranged by parents. Fathers often had unwanted suitors sent to prison, and that was only an extreme expression of daily forms of patriarchal rule. Any adult, for example, had the authority to whip any child for any perceived infraction of community behavioral norms, including talking back to an elder. Arranged marriages, dependent on harsh patriarchal control, also provided an effective means of keeping ladinos out of the cañadas. Indeed, the testimony of our informants is unanimous in this regard: no ladinos lived in their villages during their youth or young adulthood (roughly before 1950).

The memory of ladino migration, a significant cause of mestizaje, is even more ambivalent and nuanced than those of cotton and the saints. That ambivalence probably has much to do with the tight historical tie between extreme forms of indigenous patriarchy and the ethnically exclusive nature of village life. The story of the arrival of the ladinos in the 1950s is told in quite neutral tones, as for example this version related by a thirty-five-year-old:

> My grandma said that my aunt got mixed up with a man from Darío that bought and sold pigs and that's how they got involved and she washed his clothes for him in the house and they gave him food and that's how they settled down and he stayed there to live.[73]

Another informant, who was an adolescent in the 1950s, explained, "In Darío it didn't rain and here it rained, so some of them came and some from here left and that's how the race got mixed." Yet other memories were not so benign. One elderly man recalled, "the race was lost when they mixed so much" and, after a pause he added, "they stole a lot of land." An elderly woman noted: "Before we didn't see any *cheles* [whites], here we were pure indios. . . . Today we don't pay any attention to the difference."[74]

The indigenous informants' ambivalent memories of ladino migration lead to varying depictions: On the one hand, the arrival of ladino families coincided with the loss of land and with indigenous migration to the east. The marriage of Indians and ladinos also signaled the end of absolute indigenous endogamy, and with it the correspondingly high degree of communal solidarity. But it also coincided with an end to the iron hand of patriarchy.

In broad strokes, then, the Comunidad's memories of primitive accumulation and mestizaje are poorly focused and open to multiple interpretations, including those that justify ladino migration and the actions against the cotton and the saints. Both the themes and ambivalence around the dominant memories in the cañadas made them very difficult to assimilate for nationalist discourse. Such ambivalence derived in part from the unique history alluded to earlier, in which the more typical moments of primitive accumulation were pushed into the recesses of collective memory by a lengthy period of relative "social peace" and by the foregrounding of the memories of the cotton plants and the saints. Moreover, the relative lack of (educated) local intellectuals until the 1970s made it virtually impossible to develop a written narrative of the events that would aid in organizing and controlling the local memory.

The relative paucity of local intellectuals was in part the consequence of the marginalization of the communities; those indigenous people who were able to achieve more than the most basic level of education almost invariably moved to cities of Matagalpa or Managua, severing ties with the Comunidad (Sutiabas, on the contrary, could be educated in León without leaving home). Familial patriarchal authority also militated against the creation of local intellectuals—indeed children's queries were frowned upon as a questioning of the authority of the elders. The very political structure of the Comunidad Indígena also made life difficult for a young indigenous intellectual.

In chapter 1 we discussed the existence of an informal political pact between the state and the Comunidad, whereby the latter would enjoy an important degree of economic and political autonomy in return for loyalty to the ruling party.[75] Conservatives tended to honor this arrangement far more than did the Liberals. Notwithstanding, in the 1930s the Comunidad still commanded a great deal of loyalty from its rank and file. This loyalty combined with the religious hierarchy that coexisted within the Comunidad and thus allowed for the reproduction of communal ethnic identities. Under Somoza García, the state chopped away at the Comunidad's autonomy, and as we saw in the previous chapter, Ciriaco Salgado created something akin to a microcosmic model of the regime. Playing on his dual role as officer in the Guardia Reserve and president of the Comunidad, he amassed thousands of manzanas of land and exploited large numbers of indigenous workers. Under his rule, the minimal conditions for the functioning of local intellectuals were wanting. According to one informant, "When people wanted to meet together to discuss any community problem, the word would come down that Ciriaco prohibited the meeting. . . . He'd say, 'Here no one gets involved in any of that.' "[76] Moreover, the ominous shadow that his forty years of power cast on the Comunidad Indígena diminished people's pride in their main institutional site of ethnic identity.

Salgado's rule was, however, challenged from within the Comunidad in the 1960s. A group of Indians from the village of El Chile denounced the expropriations by Salgado, by another Indian, and by a ladino in the Guardia and called for an end to his rule and for agrarian reform.[77] Salgado was able to withstand this initial questioning of his authority, and he was able to thwart a union-organizing effort on his coffee plantations in 1962.

Despite his acute political skills, Salgado committed a considerable mistake in 1963. With prompting by the jefe político of Matagalpa (who also served as treasurer of the Comunidad Indígena), Salgado decided to sell the communal house of the parcialidad, or barrio, of Solingalpa in the city of Matagalpa. The house had enormous symbolic value for the Comunidad as it embodied one of its four parcialidades (lineages). An elderly man commented, "Ciriaco sold Solingalpa,"[78] identifying the residence with the parcialidad. It also had a practical value, as members of the barrio of Solingalpa would stay in the house during their visits to Matagalpa when they came to sell their products.[79]

Eleven members of La Reforma publicly protested against Salgado's action, thus pitting the traditional collective authority against the president. They enlisted the support of the *comandante departamental* of the Guardia, Juan José Rodríguez Somoza, who denounced the role of the jefe político (who apparently profited from the transaction).[80] Although the group of elders had an interview with the apparently sympathetic Nicaraguan president René Schick, it was deemed too late to stop the sale.

Two years later, in the midst of a measles epidemic that killed twenty-one children in three weeks in Salgado's home village of Susulí, several members of La Reforma started an electoral movement aimed at deposing Salgado. The group of dissidents managed to obtain the backing of a congressional deputy who stated that "Salgado is completely repudiated by the comunidad."[81] Following the electoral defeat of Salgado, a group from El Chile demanded that the Instituto Agrario Nicaragüense expropriate Salgado's land.[82] The level of tension became so high in the cañadas that a journalist suggested that only their religiosity prevented "a social explosion of thousands of Indians."[83]

Despite the success of the dissident movement, the Somoza regime managed to co-opt the new leadership. Neither agrarian nor political reform came to the Indian villages until 1979. Yet the promise of the Sandinista revolution was never realized in the indigenous cañadas. That failure derived in large part, I would argue, from the difficulty of assimilating the indigenous memories of accumulation and cultural transformation (and their related identities) into the narrative of revolutionary nationalism.

## Conclusion

The preceding discussion of collective memory, social struggles, and revolutionary discourse should provide some insight into the Central American Left's failure to resolve the dilemmas of Liberalism and in particular its tragic inability to come to terms with ethnic identities.

This chapter also has offered the methodological proposition that the memory of primitive accumulation lends itself to a mobilization narrative precisely because an entire historical process can be condensed into one event with far more facility than a memory of other forms of economic domination; for example, low wages or unequal exchange in the market. Memories of land expropriation in Sutiaba, Yúcul, and Uluse provided not only a dramatic reference point but also a diaphanous vision of good and evil, so powerful that whoever shared the memory had to recognize the justice of the cause.

In Sutiaba, Yúcul, and Uluse sharp memories of primitive accumulation flared up during the 1950s and 1960s, when the process appeared to repeat itself. Those memories had specific effects on local identities and social practice. The temporal distance between the two historical moments coincided with a certain form of mestizaje, that is a growing sense of ambiguity in local identities. That growing ambiguity derived directly from the disintegrative impact the first stage of primitive accumulation exerted on the indigenous communities.

Yet the relighting of the memory of accumulation also provoked or at least coincided with a transformation of social consciousness. Nationalistic revolutionaries fomented this new militancy and that ambiguous sense of autochthonous, rather than Indian, identity. Indeed the revolutionaries' language of mestizaje favored the incorporation of the campesinos into union and insurrectionary movements, presenting them simultaneously as rebels of indigenous ancestry but Nicaraguans like everyone else.

In Yúcul, then, the ambiguous identity that emerged from the narrative of primitive accumulation and mestizaje could be easily assimilated into the discourse of revolutionary nationalism. The memory of accumulation in Yúcul and Uluse has been interwoven with a memory of mestizaje that refers directly to indigenous ancestors but which recognizes a fundamental cultural transformation that occurred between the distant past and the present.

Yuculeños could recognize the indigenous character of their grandparents' generation, while attributing to themselves a distinct identity.

We suggested that in Sutiaba the existence of local, powerful symbols and the intellectuals capable of interpreting them inside and outside of the community marked the crucial difference between this local identity and those in Yúcul and Uluse. The local intellectuals were able to re-create roughly the same sort of memories—a sharp separation between a traditional, primordial past of Indians roaming in free, open spaces and the modern, "civilized" peasant fighting for the right to land—and maintain a strong sense of continuity despite the fragmentation of identities after the earlier stage of expropriations. Thus, the Sutiabas could be incorporated into the revolutionary narrative with the label "Indian," which looked honorific on the outside but was a badge of pride and honor to the intellectuals and those who were listening the closest to their tales.

We have glimpsed the Matagalpino Indians' principal memory of primitive accumulation: the Guardia Nacional's march into the cañadas to uproot the Indians' cotton bushes, an event that triggered the demise of indigenous weaving. The destruction of a subsistence economy was the strongest social memory in Matagalpa in part because the elite expropriation of communal land, such as its loss of Yúcul, had been partial and largely terminated by the late 1920s. Moreover, the Indian caciques such as Salgado were largely responsible for the continued loss of land through the privatization of the mejoras.

Taken together with similar assaults on the Indians' culture during the same period, the memory of these events also demonstrated the bankruptcy of the indigenous leadership. The memories of the loss of *mantiado* dress, the impotent leadership, and the endless moments of humility before ladinos incorporated a strong element of shame into the self-image. To recall Norton's assessment, shame—a sense of complicity with one's own oppressors—must be absent from local memory for it to be absorbed into a nationalist narrative.[84] In Matagalpa, such memories have been conditioned by those political compromises necessary for the limited reproduction of cultural autonomy and indigenous identity. And it has been that element of complicity and shame interwoven into the narrative of indigenous resistance that has proved incompatible with the discourse of mestizaje and revolutionary nationalism.

To the nationalists, the stench of colonial complicity relegates that indigenous memory to a recycling bin marked "artifacts of the past."

This tension between national narrative and local memory has a direct relationship with the cultural gulf between revolutionary militants and indigenous peasants.[85] The militants' lack of access to local, ethnically salient memories of complicity with oppression thwarted Sandinista efforts to bring revolutionary change to the indigenous cañadas. Yet the revolution of 1979 did bring about a radical change in peasant consciousness in Matagalpa. For example, an indigenous leader who had been an anti-Sandinista since he had learned of the group's existence commented: "In 1979 we woke up and never again will we be tricked by any *rico!*"[86] Remarkably, he did not attribute any significant role to the Frente Sandinista in the awakening of the indigenous peasantry in 1979. He could marginalize the Frente from the revolutionary process because the militants had themselves been blind to indigenous identity in Matagalpa. At the same time the revolutionary vanguard could not imagine a radical change in peasant consciousness without being able to assume responsibility and represent the subjects of that transformation. The Frente Sandinista was thus incapable of understanding both the limitations and extent of their great achievement: the creation of conditions for radical change in the countryside through the destruction of the Somoza regime. The short statement by the rightist indigenous leader reveals the tension between nationalist discourse and local memory. At the national level July 19, 1979, represented liberation from a dictatorial regime and from U.S. imperialism, the victory enjoyed by all who supported the Frente Sandinista. Yet in a dirt-poor indigenous village, people could experience a sense of liberation without any of its national references. The historic antagonists of both the Indians of Matagalpa and of the Frente Sandinista have artfully exploited that deep misunderstanding with tragic consequences for all Nicaraguans.

## Notes

1  See chapter 6, note 55 for an exception.

2  Ann Norton, "Ruling Memory," *Political Theory* 21, no. 3 (August 1993): 458–459.

3  Ibid.

4  Karl Marx, *Capital,* 3 vols. (Middlesex: Penguin, 1976), 1:875. Although "proletarianization" might be used synonymously with "accumulation," we prefer the

latter term because it refers directly to a process in which agents of change are crucial.

5 John Comaroff, "Of Totemism and Ethnicity," *Ethnos* 52, nos. 3–4 (1987): 319.

6 Interview with Urbano Pérez corroborated by interviews with Delfina Díaz (1990), Blas García (January 1992), Macaria Hernández (1990–1992), Juan Polanco (1990), and Eusebio Pérez (1990, 1992), all in Yúcul, Matagalpa.

7 Interview with Doña Adelaida de Vita, Matagalpa, 1990.

8 Interview with Doña Macaria Hernández, Yúcul, 1992.

9 Ibid.

10 Interview with Urbano Pérez, Yúcul, February 1990.

11 Interview with Urbano Pérez, Yúcul, March 1990.

12 Interviews with Blas García and Eusebio Urbina, Yúcul, Matagalpa, January 1992. These informants stated that they believed that ladinos were always *altivos* (haughty) and the indígenas were *humildes* and *respetuosos.*

13 Interview with Delfina Díaz, Yúcul, March 1990.

14 See Gould, *To Lead as Equals: Rural Protest and Political Consciousness in Chinandega, Nicaragua, 1912–1979* (Chapel Hill: University of North Carolina Press, 1990), 245–269.

15 Interviews with Delfina Díaz, Urbano Pérez, Ignacia Polanco, Juan Polanco, Eusebio García, and Macaria Hernández, Yúcul, 1990.

16 *Orientación Popular* (Managua), July 21, 1963.

17 Interview with Eusebio García, Yúcul, January 1992.

18 Interview with Macaria Hernández, Yúcul, December 1992.

19 Interview with Juan Polanco, Yúcul, November 1990.

20 Interview with Eusebio García, Yúcul, January 1992.

21 *La Prensa,* April 1, 1965.

22 *Orientación Popular,* March 14, 1964.

23 In the 1990 elections, for example, the Sandinistas won more than 60 percent of the vote in the Yúcul area while losing in the areas of the Comunidades Indígenas of Matagalpa and Jinotega by margins of 4 to 1 and 5 to 1.

24 *La Nación,* August 2, 1964.

25 In purely tactical terms, however, the use of "indígena" was not necessary for a successful mobilization given that the Uluse campesinos qualified to receive the land under the agrarian reform law of 1963, as colonos or as squatters.

26 In *El Movimiento de Colaboradores de la Guerrilla Sandinista* (Managua: CIERA, 1985), 48. Pascual Granados is cited as *dirigente histórico* (historical leader) of the "comunidad indígena." Although Granados recognized a degree of cooperation from the Comunidad Indígena of Muy Muy, he did not conflate that organization with the Uluse union. He never belonged to the Comunidad Indígena. Interview with Pascual Granados, Pancasán, 1990.

27 *La Prensa,* August 22, 1964.

28  *La Nación* (Managua), August 19, 1964.

29  *La Prensa,* September 3, 1964 and September 24, 1964.

30  *La Prensa,* October 29, 1964.

31  *La Prensa,* November 4, 1964, and *La Noticia,* November 17, 1964.

32  *La Prensa,* November 16, 1964.

33  *La Prensa,* November 13, 1964.

34  *La Prensa,* November 14, 1964.

35  *La Noticia,* February 3, 1965.

36  *La Noticia,* May 29 and 30, 1965.

37  For example, see Jaime Wheelock, *Las raíces indígenas de la lucha anticolonialista* (Managua: Editorial Nueva Nicaragua, 1981).

38  Interview with union leader (anonymous), "La Laguna," San Ramón, Matagalpa, 1990.

39  Walter Benjamin, *Illuminations* (New York: Schocken Books, 1988), 255.

40  "The Economy of Tahuantinsuyu" in Russell Salmon, ed., *Los Ovnis del Oro/ Golden UFOs* (Bloomington: Indiana University Press), 374–387.

41  Ernesto Cardenal, "Nicaraguan Canto," in Donald Walsh, ed., *Zero Hour and Other Documentary Poems* (New York: New Directions, 1980), 26.

42              I am going to speak to you about the screams of Cuá.
              Screams of women as if they were in labor
              María Venancia, 90 years old, deaf, almost a corpse
              shouts at the Guardias that she has not seen the muchachos
              Armanda Aguilar, 50 years old
              with her daughters Petrona and Erlinda
              I have not seen the muchachos
              like in labor.
              This is the story of the screams of Cuá
              sad as the song of the cocoroca birds
              the story told by the campesinas of Cuá
              that is told crying
              like glimpsing behind the fog of tears
              a jail
              and above it a heliocopter.

    Ernesto Cardenal, "Las campesinas del Cuá," in *Nueva antología poética,* 3d ed. (Mexico: Siglo XXI, 1980), 237–240.

43  Cardenal, *Zero Hour,* Nicaraguan Canto, 30.

44  Jeffrey Gould, *To Lead as Equals* and "La raza rebelde," *Revista de Historia* 21–22 (January–December 1991): 69–117.

45  In *Libro de actas de la Biblioteca Bartolomé de las Casas,* intermittent 1927–1968. The entry for September 8, 1953, states, "la junta fue desintegrada en su totalidad y por cuya razón le fue suspendida la subvención municipal."

46  For an excellent ethnographic account of Sutiaba during the first few years of the

1950s, consult Richard N. Adams, *Cultural Surveys of Panama, Nicaragua, Guatemala, El Salvador, and Honduras* (Washington: Pan-American Sanitary Bureau, 1957), 249.

47 Interviews with Esteban Bárcenas, Sutiaba, 1988, 1990, 1992. Interview with Julián Bárcenas, León, 1988.

48 See Jeffrey L. Gould, "For an Organized Nicaragua," *Journal of Latin American Studies* 19 (November 2, 1987): 353–387. The Sutiabas had a significant presence in both the Somocista and the leftist faction with the León labor movement, yet both groups within Sutiaba worked closely together.

49 Interviews with Esteban Bárcenas, Marcos Amaya, and Tomás Pérez, 1988.

50 *Anuario estadístico* (Managua: Talleres Nacionales, 1947). On the cotton boom, see Robert Williams, *Export Agriculture and the Crisis in Central America* (Chapel Hill: University of North Carolina Press, 1986) and Gould, *To Lead as Equals* and "La raza rebelde," 99–109.

51 Adams, *Cultural Surveys*, 238.

52 According to Silvia Torres's recent research, the fences also obstructed the work of Sutiaban women who used the river for washing. Moreover, Torres adduces evidence of a stronger role for women in the agrarian protests than I had suggested in previous writings. See Silvia Torres, "Identity, Ethnic Resistance, and Tradition in Sutiaba, Nicaragua," paper presented at the 1997 Meeting of the Latin American Studies Association, Guadalajara, Mexico.

53 Interview with Ernestina Roque, Sutiaba, 1988.

54 Ibid.; *La Prensa*, March 25, 1958.

55 *El Cronista* (León), December 3 and 5, 1954.

56 *El Gran Diario*, December 12, 1954.

57 Gould, *To Lead as Equals*, 265.

58 A paraphrase of Félix Pedro Antón as quoted in *La Prensa*, March 25, 1958. Very similar declarations were made by militants active in the 1950s—Esteban Bárcenas, Julián Bárcenas, Tomás Pérez, and Marcos Amaya—in interviews in 1988 and 1990.

59 *Impacto* (Managua), May 3, 1960; interviews with Ernestina Roque, Ernestina and Julián Bárcenas, and Marcos Amaya, 1988–1990.

60 In its reference to obscure origin, the following stanza about his mother from his 1939 poem "A mi madre" perhaps suggests a less than clear maternal identification with the barrio of Sutiaba despite a recognition of indigenous origin:

> Madre humilde, madre de obscuro origen
> como el barro nativo con que hiciste mi ser;
> madre mía del pueblo, con el sabor de aborigen
> madre del poeta eres . . . madre del padecer!

(Humble mother, mother of obscure origin / like the native clay from which you bore me; / my mother with the people, with aboriginal flavor / mother of a poet . . . mother of suffering!)

Antenor Sandino Hernández, *Alma y los vientos* (León: Editorial Vicente Ibarra, 1945), 10.

61 Es un Mercado Indio: hay mariscos y flores
y ubérrimas frutas pringadas de arrebol;
petates nagrandanos tejidos con primores
para alfombrar el paso de Netezahualcoyotl
Del barro chorotega tinajas de colores
con pintores de pájaros que de oro llena el sol,
que han de evocar, al verse repletas de fulgores,
los faustos del Cacique, bajo el quitasol.
Hay conchas del Pacífico, que saben del oleaje
como el hombre del beso de pérfida mujer
en canastas autóctonas del nativo boscaje;
punches de grandes manos velludas que, correr
aún parece mirarse, bajo el ancho paisaje
de las costas, doradas por el amanecer,
abriendo hoyos, huyendo de algún indio salvaje
mientras sus arabescos el mar se pone a leer.

Antenor Sandino Hernández, *Tiangüe o mercado indio y otros poemas* (León: Editorial los Hechos, 1956), 8–9

62 Old tamarind tree, father of my race, hoarse and wrinkled / In your branches there is weeping and prayer and love / And there is repentance perhaps of the past / And a pardon for Cehuatli Misquetli (the traitor).

 And your flesh and your blood and your eternal rebellious spirit / And your muscle of steel and your lifted head / And your heritage and your legend and your history / Acquired the flavor of time and the sign of far away.

 Fernando Centeno Zapata, *Voces de tierra adentro* (León: Tipografía Hernández, 1945), 59–61.

63 Zapata, *Voces de tierra adentro*, 59–61.

64 Sidney Mintz, "Rural Proletarians and the Problem of Rural Proletarian Consciousness," *Journal of Peasant Studies* 1, no. 3 (April 1974): 310.

65 Millenarian tamarind tree, your arms bear our father the Cacique. / Because you fought the odds in the great coliseum where Adiact found death . . . / You watch over the eternal sleep of the great soldier Cacique. One day the hordes of conquistadors / left him hung in your branches, Tamarindón—who sleeps to the beat of the / drum.

66 Here in Sutiaba there is an immense buried treasure and the spirit of that treasure comes out during the night. It is an immense golden "crab." The crab is the spirit of the indigenous community's treasure. It comes out at night ever since the death of the last Cacique at the hands of the Spanish.

 Anonymous interview cited by Milagros Palma in *Por los senderos míticos de Nicaragua* (Managua: Editorial Nueva Nicaragua, 1984), 178.

67  Wounded are my people / by ignominy. / Extermination has been their legacy / now they do not hunt deer / nor work in the mangrove swamp / nor fish. / Now they do not hear the cla -a-a-a- / of the shell. / Only the throng of the hordes / spying on the Indians / how they use the machete.

  Adolfo Isaac Sánchez Hernández, *Flechas y espigas de Sutiaba* (León, 1986), 28.

68  Alan Knight, "Racism, Revolution and Indigenismo: Mexico, 1910–1940," in Richard Grahm, ed., *The Idea of Race in America* (Austin: University of Texas Press, 1990), 96–98.

69  The Sutiaba must always be the same / always the same without ever being identical, / tomorrow like yesterday, the same always, / He cannot be the same, he who has not changed / who continues being without ceasing to be.

  *La Prensa Literaria*, October 7, 1989, reprinted. (Originally published in 1973.)

70  The Indian is godson of the moon. / There are still Sutiabas in Sutiaba / that do not make love with their woman / in the new moon, / nor do they bathe their children / until the moon has waxed for three days / so that the son is born, grows and lives healthy. / Therefore, I invite you, / to look in the Sutiabas in Sutiaba / those who do not see do not want to / and this is so that they do not tell you / that which Jesus of Nazarus once / told the gentiles: / "Those who have eyes to see, do not see / and ears to hear, do not hear."

  Ibid.

71  Victor Bulmer-Thomas, *The Political Economy of Central America* (Cambridge: Cambridge University Press, 1987), 110–111.

72  Alexis White, "La cuestión indígena en Nicaragua: el caso de Matagalpa" (master's thesis, Escuela de Sociología, Universidad Centroamericana, 1993), 62. The data is valid for the indigenous lands within the municipality of San Dionisio.

73  Interview with María Natividad López Hernández, Matagalpa, 1995, by Victoria González.

74  Interview with Santos Pérez, Susulí, 1990.

75  According to David McCreery, in Guatemala there existed in the late nineteenth century something akin to a "colonial compact" that legitimated the state's right to land and labor in return for leaving indigenous groups "space" within which to survive. See David McCreery, *Rural Guatemala, 1760–1940* (Stanford: Stanford University Press, 1994), 333–334.

76  Interview with Santos Marcelino, El Chile, 1992.

77  *La Prensa*, March 12, 1960, and March 31, 1961. Interviews with Patrocinio López and Francisco Arceda, Matagalpa, 1990.

78  Interview with Patricinio López, Matagalpa, February 1990.

79  *La Prensa*, August 19, 1964.

80  Interview with Tomás Pravia, Matagalpa, January 1990. Pravia, leader of the departmental labor federation, claims that Rodríguez Somoza jailed the jefe político.

81  *La Gaceta*, June 2, 1965, and *La Prensa*, April 28, 1965.

82  *La Prensa*, April 30, 1965.

83  *La Prensa,* June 9, 1965.

84  On shame in memory, see Ann Norton, "Ruling Memory," *Political Theory* 21, no. 3 (August 1993): 458–459.

85  I discuss this gulf at some length in connection with the struggles of mestizo peasants in Chinandega in *To Lead as Equals.* See, in particular, chaps. 8 and 9.

86  Interview with Santos Pérez, Susulí, Matagalpa, 1990.

# Epilogue

The ladinos always called us *pata rajada* ["cut-up feet," i.e., not owning shoes] and *caitudo* [dumb] . . . and we had to call the señoras *niñas* [virgins] even if they had five children. We had to take it, you know, but I said to myself someday this will end and they'll have to treat us as equals . . . then we'll come out better because of all our work and sufferings. Some people used to feel insulted but I always felt proud to be an Indian.

—Doña Adelaida Aguilera, Monimbó, 1992

There are no real Indians in Matagalpa.

—FSLN Political secretary of Matagalpa, 1990

"We woke up in 1979!" Santos Pérez's understanding of the Nicaraguan revolution—a transformation of social relations that had little to do with the Frente Sandinista—was an extreme formulation of a vision shared by many indigenous people. The revolution indeed raised expectations of land reform and political autonomy that it could not meet.

It is not so remarkable that the FSLN refused to grant the fundamental demands of the Comunidades Indígenas. Following the worker and peasant mobilizations during the first two years of the revolution, the government restrained most forms of autonomous struggles. Thus, indigenous efforts to gain political and economic space from the revolutionary state should be viewed within the framework of the Sandinistas' attempt to mute class and gender contradictions that threatened their own vanguard role and their strategic multiclass coalition.

There was, however, something unique about Sandinista policy toward the Comunidades Indígenas that reflected the revolutionary organization's deep immersion in the myth of Nicaragua mestiza. Shortly before the 1990 elections I interviewed the regional political secretary of the FSLN in Matagalpa. After briefly summarizing some of my research interests in the cañadas, I asked how the FSLN was responding to the demands of the Comunidad

Indígena for land and political autonomy. He replied, "There are no 'real Indians' in Matagalpa . . . and so their demands aren't valid."[1] This Sandinista leader was a native of Matagalpa and also had extensive political experience on the Atlantic Coast in the 1980s. Surely he counterposed the indígenas of Matagalpa with the Miskitos of the coast, who spoke different languages and exhibited distinct cultural characteristics. Yet his personal experience and observation reflected an important aspect of a larger cultural construct: as ladinos and the state undermined indigenous communities, Indians often escaped to the east, where in the collective imagination of Nicaragua mestiza "real Indians" lived.[2] Moreover, he had assimilated what had become the Frente Sandinistas' political line on the Comunidades.

We can see that line begin to emerge in Rafael Córdova Rivas's speech in 1980. One of three members of the Junta de Reconstrucción Nacional, Córdova delivered a speech to the "Primer encuentro de Comunidades Indígenas," in which he offered a brief historical description of the Comunidades. The description emphasized their colonial origins and anomalous character.[3] He then explained that the expropriation and return of land to the Comunidades were difficult because of the indigenous origins of many terratenientes. Although there might be some confiscation and devolution, he argued that "the People's Property was difficult to distinguish from the property of the Comunidad." Notwithstanding such fluidity between revolutionary and Comunidad boundaries he declared:

> The government will undoubtedly respect the comunidades indígenas: they are part of our cultural heritage, part of our nationality, and we want them to survive; but we want them to survive in congruence with the principles of the Revolution; we will give all of our support to the comunidades indígenas as long as . . . they operate within the revolutionary reality.[4]

Despite his strong gesture in favor of granting the demands of the Comunidades, Córdova Rivas simply did not recognize the negative resonance of his discourse of limited autonomy that endeavored to mold the communities to fit within the revolutionary state's project. Since at least the 1880s, the Comunidades had survived organizationally only through the careful, often treacherous negotiation of their political autonomy. The constant elite and state intromission in their organizations had produced numerous corrupt leaders who undermined the legitimacy of the organizations. After a century of such problems what the Comunidad membership needed and demanded was unrestricted freedom of thought and action. Whether out of fear or principle, the FSLN was not about to make an exception in its Leninist policy on extraparty organizations in order to grant the Comunidades that organizational space.

The FSLN sought to place its militants or sympathizers in leadership positions of the Comunidades. At the same meeting, the speeches from indigenous leaders made it clear that its sympathizers were in key roles and were speaking the language of revolutionary nationalism. They did, however, make concrete demands. The Matagalpino indigenous representative, after denouncing the murder of six Salvadoran leftist leaders, requested that the government oblige terratenientes to pay market-value rent to the Comunidad. Moreover, he called for the organization of a Federación de Comunidades Indígenas and for the inclusion of indigenous representatives in the Consejo de Estado (the equivalent of a parliament until 1984).[5]

Although Córdova Rivas did present the promise of rental payments, the revolutionary government did not respond to the call for a national federation nor for seats on the Consejo de Estado. On the contrary, according to Mario Rizo, who elaborated a study of indigenous laws: "In the new juridical-political order established by the Revolution the indigenous communities of the Pacific, Center, and North occupied no space."[6] The decision to block off the possibilities for organizational growth probably derived in part from a fear that the Comunidades would become controlled by anti-Sandinista forces. In this sense, the experience in Jinotega was instructive.

In April 1981, Macario Ponce defeated a Sandinista supporter 1052 to 513 in elections for the presidency of the Comunidad Indígena of Jinotega.[7] According to Ponce and other members of the Comunidad, as a direct result of that election the local Sandinista municipal government refused to formally recognize the Comunidad. Given the historic legitimizing role of the municipal government toward the Comunidad—every year the mayor would swear in the Junta Directiva—that act, carrying an implicit threat of repression, was a decisive blow against the indigenous organization. As one disaffected Comunidad member explained, "They took away our autonomy."[8]

Although the first revolutionary leaders in Matagalpa were Sandinistas, they faced problems similar to those that plagued the Comunidad leaders of Jinotega. Very early on, the Matagalpino leaders recognized that they had to subordinate the immediate and strategic needs of the Comunidad to those of the government. In the words of the first revolutionary-era president of the Comunidad: "It was hard for the authorities to accept the fact that we had our own laws. . . . They tried to manipulate us, saying that the laws were against the ideology of the Frente Sandinista, but we did not accept that."[9]

Agrarian conflicts emerged first. The expropriation of coffee and cattle haciendas might well have met the needs of land-poor Comunidad members (recall that 30 percent possessed no land). The revolutionary state could have simply distributed those lands to the landless members of the Comunidad, even in the form of cooperatives where necessary for reasons of scale. Instead, neither national nor regional Sandinista leaders saw the need to organize cooperatives or to distribute land according to Comunidad-based criteria. Thus, despite the fact that a substantial minority of indigenous people gained access to land, most viewed the agrarian reform as a political tool or as a measure to benefit ladinos, many of whom came to the Matagalpino cañadas driven either by war or poverty. So for many indígenas in Jinotega and Mata-galpa, the agrarian reform did not mean the expropriation of their expropria-tors but rather simple "confiscations." One of the post–Sandinista era leaders explained the process in the following terms:

> [Our government] requested that the Indians provide them with their property titles and they answered that the land belonged to the Comuni-dad, but that wasn't enough for them, so they gave the land to people from Santa Rosa, Estelí, or León.[10]

Vidal Rivera, the 1992 to 1994 president of the Comunidad, summarized many indígenas' view of the reform: "Jaime Wheelock [minister of agrarian reform] came here to distribute lands but they weren't his to distribute."[11] According to Rivera, the failure of the agrarian reform meant that nearly 3,000 of the 7,000 indigenous families did not have enough land for subsistence.[12]

Despite the will of the Sandinista indigenous leaders (and Córdova Rivas's speech), the revolutionary government refused to back the leaders' efforts to collect canon from the remaining large-scale landholders. As one Sandinista recalled, "We spoke with Comandante Daniel Ortega about this situation and about the presence of state lands inside the communal ones since this meant that the government was not recognizing the existence of the Comunidad. . . . Nothing changed."[13]

The indigenous Sandinistas faced a thorny dilemma. They wished to serve their communities and to contribute to the revolutionary process. Although they saw no insoluble contradiction between those goals, their revolutionary allies viewed the Comunidades as organizations of minor importance. To the rank and file of the Comunidad and to La Reforma that they had revived the leadership group seemed incapable of making their alliance with government pay any dividends. For them, that alliance only seemed to bring trouble to the Comunidad, particularly in the form of the military draft. Finally, because the government would not back the indigenous Sandinista leaders in their efforts to collect rent from the ladino landholders or from the state farms, the Comunidad lacked the resources to advance on its own.

After decades of subordination to the jefes políticos, the Comunidades Indígenas of Matagalpa and Jinotega needed a high degree of political autonomy in order to rediscover their own communal forms of organization and to redefine their own communal identity. The triumph of 1979 set the stage for such a historic achievement, but the revolutionary leadership drew the curtain in the first act out of ignorance about local history and culture and a touch of political paranoia.

The revolution, nevertheless, left some positive legacies in Matagalpa and elsewhere. First, as mentioned earlier, the agrarian reform, despite its limitations and its non-Comunidad focus, did aid many indigenous families. More important, those indígenas who worked as laborers on state or private coffee plantations often experienced something of the transformation of labor relations that occurred with uneven intensity throughout the country. Santos Pérez's remark about the awakening in the cañadas surely referred to the transformation of degraded, deferential peons into rural workers who demanded (and to a significant extent received) decent treatment. Those limited forms of material and spiritual empowerment were a fundamental consequence of the revolution.

The government also helped channel funds from Holland for the construction of a large house for the Comunidad Indígena in the city of Matagalpa, thereby providing a modern structure for a vital indigenous institution. In addition to serving as the administrative headquarters of the Comunidad, the house served as a place for many folks from outlying villages within the Comunidad to spend the night when in town to market or purchase goods.

But it was in the realm of cultural politics that the revolution made a concerted effort to contribute to the revitalization of the Comunidades. The poet-priest, Ernesto Cardenal, minister of culture from 1979 to 1987, strove to achieve through state policy what he had envisioned in his poetry. As minister of culture Cardenal endeavored to stimulate indigenous cultural production. The Ministry of Culture helped to found the Museo Adiact, for example, a small museum in Sutiaba that also served as the headquarters for the Comunidad Indígena. Cardenal also personally made important efforts to revive indigenous artisanry, in particular in the indigenous village of El Chile in Matagalpa and in Masaya.

Les Field, an anthropologist who studied the experience of potters in San Juan del Oriente (near Monimbó), analyzed Cardenal's cultural project in the following terms:

> Cardenal envisioned a theoretical and practical unity between the legacies of pre-Columbian civilizations and indigenous arts in Nicaragua and the construction of a revolutionary culture. . . . The Ministry of Culture's move to "rescue" folk arts and communities of artisans underscored Cardenal's view of artisans as the survivors of pre-Columbian cultures and indigenous populations, respectively.[14]

Field's analysis of the failure of the Ministry of Culture's work among the indigenous artisans of San Juan lays the blame both on bureaucratic ineptitude (a perennial problem in revolutionary Nicaragua) and on the failure of revolutionary indigenismo to relate in a meaningful way to local identities. Field argues convincingly that rather than accept the concrete local Indian identity, the ministry functionaries imposed their own imaginary construct of "Indianness" on the artisans.

Cardenal made a special commitment to reviving indigenous weaving in the cañada of Matagalpa. He made an explicit point of highlighting the revolutionary resurrection of weaving following its death during Somocismo (research on the actual historical event was not a priority for the ministry). This project unfortunately also ended in relative failure. The weaving cooperative's greatest problem derived from its inevitable immersion in the local political terrain. That terrain was marked by intense political factionalism that erupted during the ten years of revolution. In that context, the weaving project became yet another site of polarization. Nevertheless, despite the lack of significant success in stimulating indigenous artisanry, Cardenal and the Ministry of Culture recognized the validity of indigenous identity in western Nicaragua with a depth never equaled by any Nicaraguan government.

The revolutionary legacy for the Sutiabas was less negative than for the other Comunidades. The Sutiabas, like the Monimboseños, launched an important insurrection in early 1978, before the rest of Nicaragua erupted in September. The revolutionary government did relatively little to build upon the massive support it enjoyed in Sutiaba in 1979, and as elsewhere much of it eroded over the next ten years due to the war, the draft, and the strangled economy. In addition, many Sutiabas, including revolutionary sympathizers, found the sectarianism of the local leadership intolerable. As with the other Comunidades, there were no elections during the revolutionary years, guaranteeing at least the perception of a corrupt political leadership. Nevertheless, the FSLN won a majority of the vote in the 1990 elections in the barrio, and moreover Sutiaban Sandinistas won the Comunidad Indígena elections in 1991, 1993, and 1995. The relative success of Sutiaban Sandinismo derives in large part from the unconventional brand of Sandinismo practiced. Traditions of resistance provided militants with the experience and resources to pursue a semiautonomous political path that involved significant challenges to the Frente Sandinista.

The revolutionary government thus did not always look kindly on its supporters in this barrio of some 20,000 inhabitants. According to several informants, some national Sandinista leaders in the early years wanted to close down the Comunidad because "it was going to radicalize the revolution."[15] Specifically, the Sutiabas and the government did not agree about either the form or the extent of the agrarian reform. Although there were some expropriations of major haciendas, the government converted them into state farms rather than distributing them directly to indigenous families or to cooperatives. Similarly, many haciendas were not touched by the agrarian reform, because their owners were considered to be "patriotic bourgeois."

In 1988, the Sutiaban Sandinista leadership unleashed an offensive that included the takeover of state and private hacienda land. Despite the bitter opposition of the minister of agrarian reform, the Sutiabas eventually regained some 3,000 manzanas. That the local leadership was willing to confront the revolutionary government contrasted dramatically with the political behavior of Sandinistas in other Comunidades. The Sutiabas recognized that their own ability to maintain a base of support hinged on their commitment to local demands.

The election of Violeta Barrios de Chamorro in 1990 provoked political turmoil in Sutiaba. The local revolutionary leadership, strengthened by demobilized soldiers, occupied state farms demanding their distribution to indigenous cooperatives. At the same time, the anti-Sandinista leadership, including some older veterans of the 1950s agrarian movement, allied themselves with a few expropriated landlords who sought to reclaim their land. Although the rightist group brought in former contra soldiers, government intervention impeded serious violence. The local peace accords included the scheduling of 1991 elections, which were won by the traditional Sandinista leadership with 55 percent of the votes.

Over the next three years the leadership of the Comunidad pursued a militant agenda that aimed to recuperate those communal lands lost in the past. The most significant mobilization aimed to win back land from the Ingenio (sugar mill) San Antonio; the Comunidad leadership took up where the Sutiabas had left off in 1959, when the Guardia Nacional crushed their movement.[16] As if to show bipartisanship, the Sutiabas also launched an occupation of lands administered by a Sandinista deputy. It is difficult to evaluate the political and social impact of these mobilizations. Although they achieved only limited success, they certainly reaffirmed an internal and external image of the Sutiabas as a rebellious people. The 1995 Comunidad elections revealed once again to what extent the Sutiabas marched to a different, more militant drummer than the rest of Nicaragua. Three tendencies disputed the leadership: the traditional Sandinista group, the anti-Sandinista group, and a Sandinista group that renounced party affiliations and sectarianism. In a hotly contested election with massive voter turnout, the dissident Sandinista faction won an absolute majority of the votes, while the traditional Sandinista group finished second.

Sutiaba stands alone among the Comunidades as a site where the revolutionary process tended to stimulate rather than fragment community struggles. As suggested in chapter 7, the unique history of the barrio with its heavy concentration of indigenous intellectuals allowed for the reproduction of a community indigenous identity and memory that could be incorporated into the revolutionary nationalist narrative. Moreover, the recent history of militant struggle to reclaim the communal land created a group of indigenous revolutionaries who had a strong enough base to challenge the leadership of the Frente Sandinista when its national policy contradicted the local movement.

Other Comunidades such as Jinotega, Matagalpa, and Monimbó have become mired in paralyzing factional splits. Those splits impeded the successful development of a Federación of Comunidades at a time (1992) when the international political and economic climate favored such an organization. The Comunidades have failed, as well, to gain access to the relatively generous funds that international organizations distributed elsewhere to indigenous groups during this decade. It seems that yet another historical opportunity has been missed.

It is nonetheless remarkable that Comunidades have survived at all in the face of the unrelenting push of mestizaje depicted in this book. We should recall that the indigenous people of Nicaragua have been shamed and coerced into losing their dress and language. Those blows made it so much easier for the state and elites to disregard the people's minimal demands for survival. We should remember that at least six times from 1880 to 1925, the Comunidades were either abolished or threatened with legal extinction. We should recognize the intensity of local scorn and official neglect the indigenous folk have endured. Yet before the quincentenary celebrations commodified Indian identity, over 80 percent of the inhabitants of the Matagalpino cañadas and the barrios of Sutiaba and Monimbó acknowledged their indigenous identities.[17] The founding document of the Federación de Comunidades Indígenas stated:

> Here we are standing with much pride. . . . Many parties have come here and now we are more divided than ever. . . . We listened to them but they did not listen to us; they took advantage of our hopes, but they never opened up their intentions to us.[18]

We have seen that since 1880 no one has been listening. It is about time.

## Notes

1  Interview with José González, Matagalpa 1990.

2  Several people—including Edmund Gordon, Galio Gurdián, and William Rose-berry—have suggested that I examine the meaning of the frontier in the making of the myth of Nicaragua mestiza. Unfortunately, I can do little more than allude to its significance in the hope that other researchers will pursue this theme.

3  He cited the case of the Comunidad of Mozonte, which in 1914 donated workers to a Honduran latifundista (reminiscent of the colonial *repartimiento* [labor drafts]). The revolutionary statesman also suggested that there was a problem in finding and understanding land titles.

4  Rafael Córdova Rivas, *Contribución a la revolución* (Managua: Editorial CPASA, 1983), 59.

5  *Barricada,* December 1, 1980.

6  Mario Rizo Zeledón, "Etnicidad, legalidad, y demandas de las comunidades indígenas del norte, centro, y del pacífico de Nicaragua," Germán Romero Vargas, et al., eds., in *Persistencia indígena en Nicaragua* (Managua: CIDCA-UCA, 1992).

7  Entry for April 19, 1981, in *Libro de actas de la Municipalidad de Jinotega.* Located in the Municipal Building of Jinotega (no archive).

8  Interview with Adolfo Hernández, Los Robles, Jinotega, 1990.

9  Interview with Juan Ochoa, cited by Alexis White in "La cuestión indígena en Nicaragua: el casa de Matagalpa" (master's thesis, Escuela de Sociología, Universidad Centroamericana, 1993), 52.

10  Interview with Leonardo Figueroa, Matagalpa, February 1992.

11  Interview with Vidal Rivera, president of the Junta Directiva, Matagalpa, 1992.

12  Interview with Vidal Rivera and Santos Sánchez, Matagalpa, 1992.

13  Cited in White, "La cuestión indígena," 55.

14  Les Field, "Constructing Local Identities in a Revolutionary Nation: The Cultural Politics of the Artisan Class in Nicaragua, 1979–1990," *American Ethnologist* 22, no. 4 (1995): 789.

15  Interviews with Chilo Flores, Sutiaba, 1988; Roger Montoya, Sutiaba, 1990; and Enrique de la Concepción Fonseca, Sutiaba, 1992.

16  See *Barricada, La Prensa,* and *El Nuevo Diario* for June 1994.

17  See introduction.

18  "Documento constitutivo de la Federación de Comunidades Indígenas," Monimbó, March 27, 1992, 2–3.

# Conclusion

Mestizaje is what defines our being and our activities as Latin Americans. . . .
Our present and our future are constructed on the basis of mestizaje. To
deny that is to deny our own being.
—Carlos Tünnermann, *Nicaragua en busca de su identidad,* 1995

We know that mestizaje did not take place because the Spaniards were
thinking in terms of equality and of mutual respect. Many of our grand-
mothers were raped and the product of that rape we cannot compare with
the harmony of an encounter of two . . . cultures. Today our countries are
controlled by criollos or privileged mestizos. That speaks of the imposition
of one culture on another.—Rigoberta Menchú, 1992

The failure of the Sandinista revolution to seriously address their historic
claims was a major setback to the Comunidades Indígenas. The revolution,
pregnant with emancipatory possibilities in 1979, left division and demoralization as its principal legacy in the Comunidades. The massive disaffection of
the indigenous peoples certainly contributed to the strength of the counterrevolution and to the Sandinistas' electoral defeat of 1990.

This book has attempted to explain the historical conditions that contributed to the tragic incapacity of the Sandinistas to deal constructively with the
Comunidades. The processes described in this book are not, however, unique
to Nicaragua. A current research project I am conducting in collaboration
with Darío Euraque, Charles R. Hale, and Carol Smith strongly suggests
analogous processes of mestizaje in twentieth-century El Salvador and Honduras and in regionally and temporally specific moments in Guatemala. Recent work by Thomas Abercrombie in Bolivia, Marisol de la Cadena in Peru,
Alan Knight in Mexico, Florencia Mallon in Peru and Mexico, and Peter Wade
in Colombia makes it amply clear that mestizaje is a vitally important nationalist discourse throughout Latin America.[1] All those authors share a critical stance toward mestizaje as a form of domination, as a potential agent of

283

emancipation, and in Charles Hale's words "as a site for thinking through the construction of social inequality."[2] They all view mestizaje as a historiographical and ethnographic problem that demands further investigation and reflection. In an attempt to further stimulate that line of inquiry, I will briefly recapitulate those methodological aspects that might have relevance to further research.

The mode of transmission of local knowledge has provided a key to understanding this emergence of the discourse of mestizaje in which alternative versions of reality are so blatantly suppressed. The birth of mestizaje and the demise of the indigenous communities were closely interconnected. On a national level, we saw how images of the "historic" Indian became virile national symbols as contemporary Indians were viewed with disdain. Similarly, the twentieth-century tales of resistance that were most easily assimilable into revolutionary national discourse were those told with some distance from the indigenous community. Locally, the intellectuals' transmission of events and conflicts at once conditioned the national-level discourse of mestizaje and tilted the balance of power against the indigenous communities, eventually helping to erode the identification of indigenous people with their institutions. In Matagalpa and Boaco those intellectuals—principally lawyers—presented gendered versions of local history that not only represented a ladino perspective but did so with a blatant disregard for indigenous reality. Recall, for example, the poet-lawyer Samuel Meza who appropriated indigenous land while claiming to defend the Indians poetically and politically, or the journalist who sung praises of Indians' religiosity as Acción Católica swept up their sacred images. Those forms of disrespect and denial demand some kind of explanation, even if very tentative.

Let us start with two caveats. First, we have only been able to examine shreds of writing and fragments of biographical information. Second, we should assume that these intellectuals were not necessarily cynical liars. Rather, they were probably sensitive people who believed quite sincerely in their version of events. Despite what retrospectively seems to be the crudest of cynicism, we should view their declarations through another lens.

Those versions sharply contradict the alternative stories of ethnic and class strife we have uncovered from other archives and from oral testimonies. Their suppressions, whether conscious or not, formed vital markers on a field of symbolic and material power struggles at a historical moment when social identities were becoming more salient and more contested than at any time since the colonial era.[3]

Operating with this national field of power, local ladinos were able to mobilize a series of discursive and material attacks on the indigenous communities, presenting visions of cowed, effeminate indigenous males that could only be redeemed through mestizo progress. On a national level, as I argued in chapter 4, Liberal and progressive intellectuals and militants strove to create a virile Indo Hispanic national identity in opposition to U.S. imperialism. On a local level, ladino elites phrased their struggles against the Comunidades Indígenas in a language that would gain national support. They called upon democratic notions of citizenship and equal rights to question the legitimacy of the Comunidades and their claims to land. Their political success hinged to an important degree on their appropriation and creation of those key elements of the emerging national political discourse. Equally important was their questioning of the authenticity of the indigenous organizations that had become the "hard" border within which its members reproduced their identities.[4] In every significant legal battle with the Comunidades, the denigration of indigenous authenticity was the most powerful weapon in the ladino discursive arsenal, one that facilitated their use of state repression against their adversaries.

The simultaneity of this process was important. The creation of democratic liberal discourse not only coincided with but moreover animated attacks on the indigenous communities. Recall how the ladino seizure of the reins of municipal power created the political conditions for the expropriation of indigenous communal land in Boaco and Camoapa. Henceforth, ladino municipal authorities claimed that as the democratic representatives of all citizens, they had the duty to distribute the land to ladino and Indian alike. In other words, the battle for Indian land was fought and won under the banner of democracy. Those origins have contributed to the deep ruts that mark contemporary Nicaraguan political culture.

It is remarkable that these interwoven discourses of mestizaje and democracy were created in the same national space—that is, local intellectuals communicated with national figures—but that their success depended on a growing gulf between the two groups. In other words, in addition to economic power and the ability in key moments to call on the state's repressive apparatus, intellectuals needed to keep outsiders from acquiring other forms of local knowledge. The credibility of the local intellectuals depended on their successful delegitimization of indigenous identity. In this context, the ladino intellectual style of blatant denial is somewhat more comprehensible. Their struggle required very hard, nonporous boundaries; any weak points, any slippage, any recognition would put the whole discursive edifice in jeopardy, before its boundaries had solidified. At the same time, however, those national intellectuals who maintained an interest or even a commitment to the indigenous people remained cut off and ignorant of their everyday reality and struggles.

The impact the emergence of mestizaje had on the indigenous people may be better appreciated with recourse to the notion of "the unthinkable." Michel-Rolph Trouillot cites Pierre Bourdieu's remark that the unthinkable of an epoch is so not only for ethical and political inclinations but also because of a lack of conceptual instruments. Trouillot then adds, "The unthinkable is that which one cannot conceive within the range of possible alternatives, that which perverts all answers because it defies the terms under which the questions were phrased."[5]

The creation of the "unthinkable" poses a challenge for historians and anthropologists. The development of the conceptual field that allowed for the growth of mestizaje was not a linear process. Indeed, the inability to conceive of educated or autonomous Indians was a turn-of-the-century phenomenon (see chapters 2 and 3). Perhaps the suppression of what was once thinkable—even if with sharply different meanings—is as important a historiographical problem as the creation of those conceptual tools that allow people to think about the previously unthinkable.

What was the cost of that kind of discursive suppression? What difference did it make to an indigenous community what the local lawyers or literati were saying to the folks in the capital? What difference does it make in the long run that one version of reality was transmitted as history and the others remained dispersed memories? This book has offered evidence that suggests that these moves mattered a great deal.

The silencing of indigenous memories aided the construction of a hegemonic discourse in the two senses of the term discussed in the introduction. On the one hand following the Comaroffs, the suppression of the ethnic categories "ladino" and "indígena" simultaneously involved the transformation of ideological statements into naturalized, commonsense notions about

Nicaragua as an ethnically homogenous society.[6] Similarly, following Rose-berry, by removing notions of indigenous (as opposed to citizen) rights from discussion, the language of hegemonic struggle was radically transformed.[7] In this sense, Charles R. Hale's comments on the indígena-popular divide are particularly apposite: "Non-elite members of the dominant (Mestizo) culture find themselves forced to make political claims ... such that they win rights at the cost of reinforcing divisions between themselves and the culturally dis-tinct 'others.' "[8] Hale's comments are directed toward those societies sharply divided along ethnic lines, such as Guatemala or Peru. Yet they also under-score a particularly high cost of the silencing of indigenous history in societies such as western Nicaragua where ethnic divisions have been virtually sub-sumed within the dominant discourse of mestizaje.

Henceforth, popular victories were achieved in the form of claims that strengthened the national mestizo identity. Moreover, that dynamic tended to create a deep disconnectedness between popular militants and the indigenous histories that framed many local struggles. Recall the career of Domingo Sánchez, the child of dispossessed Indians, who framed his own story within Liberal and Marxist notions of acculturation and class struggle (chapter 6). Likewise, Víctor Guillén, with a similar biography, felt that his roots in the Comunidad Indígena were barely worth mentioning (see the introduction and chapter 7). Thus even the logical points of intersection between the popular and indigenous movements were disconnected.

One major consequence of this particular form of silencing was to block the possibility of serious understanding between any popular movement and the embattled Comunidades Indígenas. Given the division and isolation of those surviving communities and the disintegrative impact of mestizaje on identities, the lack of alliances with progressive forces made it extraordinarily difficult for an autonomous, indigenous movement to emerge as it has, for example, in Guatemala, Ecuador, and Bolivia. The impossibility of such al-liances sealed the fate of some of the Comunidades such as Boaco, Camoapa, and Ometepe. Without external defense, intense repression destroyed those Comunidades as institutions and as bonded networks of extended families.

The death of those communities and the crippling of others (Matagalpa, Jinotega, Sébaco) suggest the need for reconsidering the notion of "cultural loss." The constant negation of the authenticity of indigenous identity in the context of land dispossession, forced labor, and political violence severely constrained the way in which people could reconfigure their identities. Indeed, the gendered, violent language of ethnic factionalism on the one hand, and the sexual stories of ethnic self-denial on the other, emerged as a consequence of the growing power of mestizaje (chapter 4).

This does not mean that the indigenous people maintained one identity and that the other identities encroached upon them in a zero sum game. On the contrary, we have seen much evidence that an identification with a local Comunidad Indígena did not necessarily signify a broader pan-Indian identity nor did it contradict other political or national loyalties. Rather, in the Nicaraguan context—but I am sure that there are analogous situations throughout Latin America—massive repressive blows to the land and people of those communities eroded the organizational structure that allowed for the transmission of culturally salient stories and their linkage to particular indigenous identities. During those decades of disruption, migration, intimidation, and demoralization, to the extent that identities were negotiated, they were done so under terms that approximated surrender.

The postmodern ethnographic critique of traditional, essentialist notions of "cultural survival" represents an important methodological breakthrough in history and anthropology.[9] The analysis of an ensemble of ethnic markers and traits in terms of retention or loss, in contrast, does very little to aid our understanding of the history or reality of indigenous communities. But we should also listen to the cautionary tales from the Nicaraguan highlands. Communities were destroyed through forced or voluntary migration and their cultures along with them. We have also witnessed forms of cultural violence: the constant challenging, disparaging, and denying of the authenticity of indigenous identity transformed ethnic relations in a way that dulled creative expression and weakened cultural, economic, and political resistance.

The contemporary history of the Nicaraguan Comunidades is not only a grim tale of destruction. Certain indigenous groups in Matagalpa and Sutiaba combining multiple forms of resistance that respond to many layers of identity will survive with dignity into the next century. Rather than focus on the means of contemporary survival, however, this study has attempted to understand something of the collective memories of the survivors and how those memories have been ignored or misunderstood by those who have sought to aid them.

Finally, this study has some relevance to broader discussions of postcolonial nationalism. Despite the problem underscored by Klor de Alva of applying "postcolonial" to the nonindigenous peoples of Latin America, the possibility for cross-regional comparative analysis can enrich our understandings, as is demonstrated by the recent work of Florencia Mallon among others.[10] In the Nicaraguan case, both Sandino's resistance and the Sandinista movement bear sharp resemblances to anticolonial and postcolonial nationalist insurgencies. The FSLN, in particular, placed Somocismo within a neocolonial paradigm, portraying its clique as an illegitimate, antipatriotic comprador bourgeoisie. In this sense, our analysis of the Sandinistas' revolutionary nationalist narrative and local memories may well be useful beyond Nicaragua's borders.

Following the theoretical lead of Partha Chatterjee, Mallon urges historians, when considering nationalism, to ask

> What mobilizing effect does the universal promise of a national-democratic project have on different subaltern groups? . . . When and how do the colonial, patriarchal and hierarchical underpinnings of national development end up justifying the repression of the more radical forms of the national-popular? Finally, how are "the marks of disjuncture . . . suppressed" to create a unitary, rational, and linear account of historical development?[11]

We have already discussed the Nicaraguan case in the context of the latter two aspects of her agenda for a "historical archaeology." Indeed, the local intellectuals' blatant statements of denial exemplify how "sutures" healed historical wounds of disjuncture. By recapitulating some of the argument on collective memories from chapter 7, we can address the first question.

In Nicaragua, as elsewhere, the "universal promise" of justice and equality has appeared in nationalist political discourse at various moments throughout this century. In each period the meaning of that promise has been interpreted in distinct ways by different subaltern groups. Those changing interpretations, in turn, derived from the preexisting histories of those meanings embedded in particular memories. The promise of justice that animated the Yuculeños in the 1960s was significantly different from that experienced by their grandparents in the 1910s. The 1960s generation's collective memory of primitive accumulation—their loss of land and their conversion into peons—was a social reconstruction of their past. Two aspects of that memory greatly facilitated its appropriation by revolutionary nationalism. First, it condensed two founding myths of mestizaje: the revolutionary variant that stressed the violent loss of land and that which portrayed the harmonious, biological fusion of peoples. Second, the memory made a powerful, unambiguous moral statement about the goodness of the contemporary community of Yúcul and the evil that has oppressed its members for generations. As John Bodnar states,

> The grounding in relationships insures that collective memory is largely about moral values. . . . Collective memory is inscribed with discussions or relations that pervade group life in the past and assessments of qualities that appear to threaten those values in the present.[12]

Revolutionary nationalists could engage with those threatened values and claim to defend them. The emerging revolutionary nationalist narrative could thus incorporate such a local memory with relative ease precisely because it provided moral clarity and a powerful symbol of popular nationalism. Put differently, revolutionary militants could communicate in this particular dialect of mestizaje and were predisposed to deliver on the promise of justice.

Revolutionary nationalism could not, however, successfully incorporate those memories from nearby communities that maintained indigenous identities nor in those recently disintegrated communities such as Boaco or Camoapa. On one level, the problem was that these stories had far more complex moral judgments and values.

Recall the Indians' principal memory of primitive accumulation: the Guardia Nacional's burning of cotton bushes in Matagalpa, an event that within a few years eliminated a strong ethnic marker and thrust the Indians further into the clutches of the cash economy. Unlike the Yuculeño memory of accumulation, the destruction of the cotton bushes offered an ambiguous rather than a clear-cut moral. The Guardia's action weakened the subsistence bases (however tenuous and partial) of their previous economic existence. Yet at the same time another message was captured in the words of a Guardia officer who made the statement "this business of going around mantiado [an indigenous woman's garment] is something only Indians do," as if they must move beyond Indianness. The Guardia's move also helped to push them into a "non-Indian" category. In other words, the key memory of primitive accumulation, at the same time a memory of mestizaje, allowed for both negative and vaguely positive moral judgments by the Matagalpinos.

In *To Lead as Equals* I proposed that "the dialectical interplay between inherited dependency and discovered autonomy has been at the core of campesino action and consciousness."[13] Similarly, the subaltern school has also conceptualized peasant consciousness as "the contradictory unity" of dependence and autonomy.[14] I am now convinced that beyond the need to recognize the porosity of the terms "dependency" and "autonomy," we must realize that the question of autonomy is complicated by the degree of complexity and ambiguity of the collective memory of a given peasant community. That complexity, in turn, derives from the level of internal stratification and division and from the nature of those political compromises necessary for the limited reproduction of cultural autonomy and communal identity. In Matagalpa, a high level of internal stratification led to more consequential forms of collaboration between the indigenous elite and the ladino authorities. Resistance became more complex and difficult as it involved two distinct antagonists. To attack the indigenous elite undermined community solidarity, and the elite muted efforts to resist the authorities. Throughout the Nicaraguan highlands, those sharp symbols of complicity with ladino authority—even the identification of Indian with deference—broke up the narrative of indigenous resistance. Those deferential markers and detours rendered the narrative incompatible with the discourse of mestizaje and revolutionary nationalism.

Much of *To Lead as Equals* deals with how nonindigenous peasants, recently thrown together in makeshift communities, appropriated and transformed Liberal and Somocista political concepts. This present study, in part, aimed to grasp whether some kind of analogous process worked in indigenous communities with firmer roots and more autonomous political and cultural traditions. In the light of this work that problem seems inadequately conceptualized, for those memories of mestizaje and accumulation, though very distinct, were closely intertwined. Even in Sutiaba, where we found a strong sense of autonomous values and history, the local resonance of those tales of resistance depended upon external validation and reference points. In the indigenous highland communities, the degree of interpenetration of cultural repertoires and frames of reference has been even more intense. As a result, the meanings of one generation have been increasingly more difficult to transmit to members of the next generation, who are more inclined to understand the meanings through one version or another of the dominant discourse.

I will close by sharing a bit of my postmodern doubt. That doubt leads me to question whether it matters that the ethnic discourse of the Comunidades is weak, because thanks in large measure to the Sandinista revolution all subaltern Nicaraguans are now more conversant with a universal language of justice and human rights. Likewise, I ponder the meaning of a Monimboseño Sandinista's declaration that "We are the true mestizos."[15] Was this yet another example of the alienating power of the dominant discourse or rather its creative appropriation that aids the refashioning of an indigenous identity? He surely meant to emphasize the uniqueness of the Monimboseño identity, bound up with its contribution to the nation. Does the category "mestizo" matter in this context?

As I was riding back to town with the mayor of Camoapa after visiting the indigenous village of Salinas in 1992, we engaged in a jerky conversation. The mayor was in the midst of a severe, physically threatening attack from the local Right for his efforts to steer a moderate, pluralistic course. The Sandinistas were too weak in Camoapa to offer any meaningful support. Although his distant relatives had appropriated indigenous land, he had worked as an artisan and his family lived modestly. Earlier that day in Salinas I had noticed how an elderly survivor of the 1954 repression had moved the mayor when she recounted her memory of the events. Previously he had only heard the ladino version of the story and now the informant was demanding retribution and the recognition of Salinas as a "comunidad indígena." I asked him what he thought about the encounter and he replied, "very interesting." But what about her demand, what are you going to do? "Well," he replied, "it's too late now after all these years . . . you know those wounds could still bleed."[16]

## Notes

1  For the articles by Abercrombie, de la Cadena, and Hale and commentaries by Florencia Mallon and Carol A. Smith, see the special issue on mestizaje in the *Journal of Latin American Anthropology* 2, no. 1 (Fall 1996). Also see Darío Euraque, *Estado, Poder, Nacionalidad y Raza en la Historia de Honduras* (Tegucigalpa: Ediciones Subirana, 1996); Alan Knight, "Racism, Revolution and *Indigenismo:* Mexico, 1910–1940," in Richard Graham, ed., *The Idea of Race in Latin America* (Austin:

University of Texas Press, 1990); Florencia Mallon, *Peasant and Nation: The Making of Postcolonial Mexico and Peru* (Berkeley: University of California Press, 1995); and Peter Wade, *Blackness and Race Mixture: the Dynamics of Racial Identity in Colombia* (Baltimore: Johns Hopkins University Press, 1993).

2 Charles Hale, introduction to the special issue on Mestizaje, *Journal of Latin American Anthropology,* 2.

3 On the concept of "field of power" see William Roseberry's introduction to William Roseberry, Lowell Gudmundson, and Mario Samper Kutschbach, *Coffee, Society and Power in Latin America* (Baltimore: Johns Hopkins University Press, 1995), 8.

4 Presenjjit Duara has defined "soft boundaries" as those cultural practices—"rituals, language, dialect, music, kinship rules or culinary habits"—that can be shared by another group. Those boundaries become hard when one group "succeeds in imposing a historical narrative" that "transforms the perception of the boundaries of communities." See Duara, *Rescuing History From the Nation* (Chicago: University of Chicago Press, 1995), 65–66.

5 Michel-Rolph Trouillot, *Silencing the Past: Power and the Production of History* (Boston: Beacon, 1995), 82.

6 See the introduction. Jean and John Comaroff, *Of Revelation and Revolution: Christianity, Colonialism, and Consciousness in South Africa* (Chicago: University of Chicago Press, 1991), 25.

7 See the introduction. William Roseberry, "The Language of Contention" in Gilbert Joseph and Daniel Nugent, eds., *Everyday Forms of State Formation: Revolution and the Negotiation of Rule in Modern Mexico* (Durham, N.C.: Duke University Press, 1994), 360–361.

8 Charles R. Hale, "Between Ché Guevara and the Pachamama: Mestizos, Indians, and Identity Politics in the Anti-Quincentenary Campaign," *Critique of Anthropology,* 14, no. 9 (1994), 26.

9 See, in particular, Kay Warren, "Transforming Memories and Histories: The Meanings of Ethnic Resurgence for Mayan Indians," in Alfred Stepan, ed., *Americas: New Interpretive Essays* (New York: Oxford University Press, 1992), 189–219.

10 J. Jorge Klor de Alva, "The Postcolonialization of the (Latin) American Experience: A Reconsideration of 'Colonialism,' 'Postcolonialism,' and Mestizaje,'" in Gyan Prakash, ed., *After Colonialism: Imperial Histories and Postcolonial Displacements* (Princeton: Princeton University Press, 1995).

11 Florencia Mallon, *Peasant and Nation,* 14.

12 John Bodnar, "Moral Patriotism and Collective Memory in Whiting, Indiana, 1920–1992," in John Bodnar, ed., *Bonds of Affection: Americans Define Their Patriotism* (Princeton: Princeton University Press), 293.

13 Jeffrey L. Gould, *To Lead as Equals: Rural Protest and Political Consciousness in Chinandega, Nicaragua, 1912–1979* (Chapel Hill: University of North Carolina Press, 1990), 301.

14 See Partha Chatterjee's discussion of the subaltern school methodological approach to peasant consciousness in *The Nation and Its Fragments: Colonial and Postcolonial Histories* (Princeton: Princeton University Press, 1993), 158–172.

15 Interview with Miguel Gómez, Monimbó, 1992.

16 Interview with Jorge Duarte, Camoapa, 1992.

# Selected Bibliography

*Archival Sources*
Actas de la Biblioteca Bartolomé de las Cases, León
Archivo de la Corte de Apelaciones de Masaya
Archivo de la Diócesis de León (ADL), León, Nicaragua
Archivo del Instituto de Historia Centroamericana, Universidad Centroamericana
Archivo Municipal de León—Universidad Nacional Autónoma de Nicaragua (León Campus)
Archivo Nacional de Nicaragua, Fondo de Gobernación
Correspondencia Joaquín Zavala, Tulane University Library
Juzgado Civil—Boaco, Matagalpa, Rivas
Libros de Actas y Acuerdos de la Municipalidad de Boaco
Libros de Actas y Acuerdos de la Municipalidad de Camoapa
Libros de Actas y Acuerdos de la Municipalidad de Jinotega
Private Archive Aurora Martínez (Matagalpa)
Registro de Propiedades—Boaco, León, Rivas

*Government Documents*
Memorias del Ministerio de Gobernación
Memorias del Ministerio de Fomento
La Gaceta
Diario Oficial
U.S. National Archives, Washington, D.C. Record Group 59, Records of the Department of State Relating to the Internal Affairs of Nicaragua, 1910–1929

*Newspapers and Magazines*
Diario de Granada (Granada)
El Centroamericano (León)
El Comercio
El Cronista (León)
El Diario de Nicaragua
El Eco Nacional
El Heraldo
El Independiente
El Municipio (León)
La Nueva Prensa
El Porvenir (León)

La Prensa
La Semanal Nicaragüense
La Voz Sindical
Los Anales (Masaya)
Nicaragua Indígena
Orientación Popular

*Books and Journal Articles*

Abercrombie, Thomas. "To Be Indian, To Be Bolivian: Ethnic and National Discourses of Identity," in Joel Sherzer and Greg Urban, eds., *Indians and Nation-States in Latin America*, 95–130. Austin: University of Texas Press, 1991.

Adams, Richard N. *Cultural Surveys of Panama, Nicaragua, Guatemala, El Salvador, and Honduras.* Washington, D.C.: Pan American Sanitary Bureau, 1957.

———. "Ethnic Images and Strategies in 1944," in Carol A. Smith, ed., *Guatemalan Indians and the State, 1540–1988*, 141–162. Austin: University of Texas Press, 1990.

Alvarez Lejarza, Emilio. *El Problema del Indio en Nicaragua.* Managua: Editorial Nuevo Horizontes, 1943.

Barahona Lopez, Ernesto. *Realidades de la Vida Nicaragüense: Comentarios de Problemas Nacionales Que Necesitan Solución.* Managua: Tipografía Excelsior, 1943.

Baron Castro, Rodolfo. *La Población de El Salvador.* Madrid: Consejo Superior de Investigaciones Científicas, 1940.

Beverley, John, and Marc Zimmerman. *Literature and Politics in the Central American Revolutions.* Austin: University of Texas Press, 1990.

Bodnar, John. "Moral Patriotism and Collective Memory in Whiting, Indiana," in John Bodnar, ed., *Bonds of Affection: Americans Define Their Patriotism*, 290–304. Princeton: Princeton University Press, 1996.

Bourdieu, Pierre, and Loic J. D. Wacquant. *Invitation to Reflexive Sociology.* Chicago: University of Chicago Press, 1992.

Boyle, Frederick. *A Ride Across a Continent: A Personal Narrative of Wanderings Through Nicaragua and Costa Rica.* London: Bentley, 1868.

Burns, E. Bradford. *Patriarch and Folk: The Emergence of Nicaragua, 1798–1858.* Cambridge: Harvard University Press, 1991.

Cardenal, Ernesto. *Zero Hour and Other Documentary Poems,* edited by Donald Walsh. New York: New Directions, 1980.

———. *Nueva Antología Poética.* Third edition. Mexico: Siglo XXI, 1980.

Chatterjee, Partha. *The Nation and Its Fragments: Colonial and Postcolonial Histories.* Princeton: Princeton University Press, 1993.

Cuadra, Pablo Antonio. *La Aventura Literaria del Mestizaje.* San José: Editorial Libro Libre, 1988.

Comaroff, Jean, and John L. Comaroff. *Of Revelation and Revolution: Christianity, Colonialism, and Consciousness in South Africa.* Chicago: University of Chicago Press, 1991.

——. *Ethnography and the Historical Imagination.* Boulder: Westview Press, 1992.

Costa, Emília Viotti da. *The Brazilian Empire: Myths and Histories.* Chicago: University of Chicago Press, 1985.

de la Cadena, Marisol. "Women Are More Indian: Gender and Ethnicity in Cuzco," in Brooke Larson, Olivia Harris, and Enrique Tandeter, eds., *Ethnicity, Markets, and Migration in the Andes: At the Crossroads of History and Anthropology,* 319–328. Durham: Duke University Press, 1995.

Duara, Presenjit. *Rescuing History from the Nation.* Chicago: University of Chicago Press, 1995.

Euraque, Darío. *Estado, Poder, Nacionalidad y Raza en la Historia de Honduras.* Tegucigalpa: Ediciones Subirana, 1996.

Feierman, Steven. *Peasant Intellectuals: Anthropology and History in Tanzania.* Madison: University of Wisconsin Press, 1990.

Field, Les. "Constructing Local Identities in a Revolutionary Nation: The Cultural Politics of the Artisan Class in Nicaragua, 1979–1990." *American Ethnologist* 22:4 (1995): 786–806.

Gould, Jeffrey L. *To Lead as Equals: Rural Protest and Political Consciousness in Chinandega, Nicaragua, 1912–1979.* Chapel Hill: University of North Carolina Press, 1990.

——. *El Mito de Mestizaje y La Resistencia Indígena.* San José: Editorial de la Universidad de Costa Rica, 1997.

Guardino, Peter. *Peasants, Politics, and the Formation of Mexico's National State: Guerrero 1800–1857.* Stanford: Stanford University Press, 1996.

Guerrero, Julián. *Boaco.* Managua: Tipografía Alemana, 1957.

Hale, Charles. *Contradictory Consciousness: Miskitu Indians and the Nicaraguan State in the Era of United States Hegemony.* Stanford: Stanford University Press, 1994.

——. "Between Ché Guevara and the Pachamama: Mestizos, Indians, and Identity Politics in the Anti-Quincentenary Campaign." *Critique of Anthropology* 14:9 (1994): 9–39.

——. "Mestizaje, Hybridity, and the Cultural Politics of Difference in Post-revolutionary Central America." *Journal of Latin American Anthropology* 2:1 (1996): 34–61.

James, Daniel. "Tales Told Out on the Borderlands: Doña María's Story, Oral History, and Issues of Gender," in John French and Daniel James, eds., *The Gendered Worlds of Latin American Women Workers,* 31–52. Durham: Duke University Press, 1997.

Kinloch Tijerino, Frances, ed. *Nicaragua en Busca de su Identidad.* Managua: Editorial de la Universidad Centroamericana, 1996.

Klor de Alva, J. Jorge. "'The Postcolonization of the (Latin) American Experience: A Reconsideration of 'Colonialism,' 'Postcolonialism,' and 'Mestizaje,'" in Gyan Prakash, ed., *After Colonialism: Imperial Histories and Postcolonial Displacements,* 241–275. Princeton: Princeton University Press, 1995.

Knight, Alan. "Racism, Revolution, and Indigenismo: Mexico 1910–1940," in Richard

Graham, ed., *The Idea of Race in Latin America, 1870–1940*, 71–113. Austin: University of Texas Press, 1990.

Lancaster, Roger N. *Life is Hard: Machismo, Danger, and the Intimacy of Power in Nicaragua.* Berkeley: University of California Press, 1994.

Lomnitz-Adler, Claudio. *Exits From the Labyrinth: Culture and Ideology in the Mexican National Space.* Berkeley: University of California Press, 1993.

Mallon, Florencia. *Peasant and Nation: The Making of Postcolonial Mexico and Peru.* Berkeley: University of California Press, 1995.

McCreery, David. *Rural Guatemala, 1760–1940.* Stanford: Stanford University Press, 1994.

Membreño Idiaquez, Marcos. *La Estructura de las Comunidades Etnicas.* Managua: Editorial Envío, 1994.

Newson, Linda. *Indian Survival in Colonial Nicaragua.* Norman, Oklahoma: Oklahoma University Press, 1987.

Niederlein, Gustavo. *The State of Nicaragua in the Greater Republic of Central America.* Philadelphia: Philadelphia Commercial Museum, 1898.

Norton, Ann. "Ruling Memory." *Political Theory* 21:3 (1993): 453–464.

Ortega Arancibia, Francisco. *Cuarenta Años (1838–1878) de Historia de Nicaragua.* Third edition. Reprint, Managua: Banco de América, 1975.

Pérez, Rafael, S. J. *La Compañía de Jesus en Colombia y Centroamérica,* 4 vols. Valladolid: Imprenta Castellana, 1898.

Rappaport, Joanne. *Cumbé Reborn: An Andean Ethnography of History.* Chicago: University of Chicago Press, 1994.

Romero Vargas, Germán. *Las Estructuras Sociales de Nicaragua en el Siglo XVIII.* Managua: Editorial Vanguardia, 1988.

Roseberry, William. "The Language of Contention," in Gilbert Joseph and Daniel Nugent, eds., *Everyday Forms of State Formation: Revolution and the Negotiation of Rule in Modern Mexico,* 355–366. Durham: Duke University Press, 1994.

Roseberry, William, Lowell Gudmundson, and Mario Samper Kutschbach, eds., *Coffee, Society, and Power in Latin America.* Baltimore: Johns Hopkins University Press, 1995.

Scherzer, Carl. *Travels in the Free States of Central America: Nicaragua, Honduras, and El Salvador.* London: Longman, 1857.

Schroeder, Michael. "To Defend Our Nation's Honor: Toward a Social and Cultural History of the Sandino Rebellion in Nicaragua, 1927–1934." Ph.D. thesis, University of Michigan, 1993.

Scott, James. *Domination and the Arts of Resistance: The Hidden Transcripts.* New Haven: Yale University Press, 1990.

Sider, Gerald M. *Lumbee Indian Histories: Race, Ethnicity, and Indian Identity in the Southern United States.* New York: Cambridge University Press, 1994.

Smith, Carol A. "Local History in a Global Context: Social and Economic Transitions in Western Guatemala." *Comparative Studies in Society and History* 26:2 (1984): 193–228.

Stepan, Nancy Leys. *"The Hour of Eugenics": Race, Gender, and Nation in Latin America*. Ithaca: Cornell University Press, 1991.

Stone, Doris. "Brief Notes on the Matagalpa Indians of Nicaragua," in Richard N. Adams, *Cultural Surveys of Panama, Nicaragua, Guatemala, El Salvador, and Honduras*, 256–260. Washington, D.C.: Pan American Sanitary Bureau, 1957.

Taylor, Charles. *An Essay on Multiculturalism and the Politics of Recognition*. Princeton: Princeton University Press, 1992.

Trouillot, Michel-Rolph. *Silencing the Past: Power and the Production of History*. Boston: Beacon Press, 1995.

Urban, Greg. "The Semiotics of State-Indian Relationships: Peru, Paraguay, and Brazil," in Greg Urban and Carl Scherzer, eds. *Nation-States and Indians in Latin America*, 307–330. Austin: University of Texas Press, 1991.

Wade, Peter. *Blackness and Race Mixture: The Dynamics of Racial Identity in Colombia*. Baltimore: Johns Hopkins University Press, 1993.

Warren, Kay. "Transforming Memories and Histories: The Meanings of Ethnic Resurgence for Mayan Indians," in Alfred Stepan, ed., *Americas: New Interpretive Essays*, 189–219. New York: Oxford University Press, 1992.

Wheelock, Jaime. *Raíces Indígenas de las Luchas Anti Colonialistas*. Managua: Editorial Nueva Nicaragua, 1981.

Williams, Robert G. *States and Social Evolution: Coffee and the Rise of National Governments in Central America*. Chapel Hill: University of North Carolina Press, 1994.

# Index

Jeffrey L. Gould is Associate Professor of History and Director of the Center for Latin American and Caribbean Studies at Indiana University. He is the author of *To Lead as Equals: Rural Protest and Political Consciousness in Chinandega, Nicaragua, 1912–1979*.

*Library of Congress Cataloging-in-Publication Data*
Gould, Jeffrey L.
 To die in this way : Nicaraguan Indians and the myth of mestizaje, 1880–1965 / Jeffrey L. Gould.
  p.  cm.
 Includes index.
  ISBN 0-8223-2084-3 (cloth : alk. paper).—ISBN 0-8223-2098-3 (pbk. : alk. paper)
  1. Indians of Central America—Nicaragua—Cultural assimilation.  2. Mestizaje—Nicaragua.  3. Indians of Central America—Nicaragua—Ethnic identity.  4. Indians, Treatment of—Nicaragua—History.  I. Title.
 F1525.3.C84G68   1998
 305.897′07285—DC21                    97-39534